Community Service-Learning

SUNY Series, Democracy and Education
George H. Wood, Editor

Community Service-Learning

*A Guide to Including Service
in the Public School Curriculum*

Rahima C. Wade, Editor

State University of New York Press

Published by
State University of New York Press, Albany

For information, address State University of New York
Press, State University Plaza, Albany, N.Y., 12246

Production by E. Moore
Marketing by Fran Keneston

Library of Congress Cataloging-in-Publication Data

Community service-learning : a guide to including service in the
    public school curriculum / Rahima C. Wade, editor.
        p.   cm. — (SUNY series, democracy and education)
    Includes bibliographical references and index.
    ISBN 0-7914-3183-5 (hardcover : alk. paper). — ISBN 0-7914-3184-3
(pbk. : alk. paper)
    1. Student service—United States. 2. Student volunteers in
social service—United States. I. Wade, Rahima Carol. II. Series.
LC220.5.C65 1997
361.3'7—dc20   96-3226
                                                                     CIP

10 9 8 7 6 5 4 3

Contents

Part 2
Service-Learning in Schools

Part 3
Voices from the Field

Part 4
The Future of Service-Learning

Preface

In 1971, as a senior in high school, I was a member of Friends of the Earth, an extracurricular environmental service club. One of our projects was to develop plans for a recycling center in the coastal hamlet of Scituate, Massachusetts. I clearly remember the May evening we took our proposal before the town Board of Selectmen (no Selectwomen in those days). I'm not sure if our faculty supervisor had spoken with the Board before we delivered our speeches or if the financial climate was positive at the time. Whatever the reason, the selectmen approved our plan on the spot!

I will never forget the feeling of elation as I thought to myself, for the first time, "I have been a part of something that will make a difference in the world." Though I was an excellent student, involved in many extracurricular activities, everything else I had done in school was for me, to develop my skills and knowledge, to prepare myself for college, and so forth. Never before had I participated in a school-related project that was focused on helping others in the community. More than twenty-five years later, the Scituate recycling center is still in operation, a fact that gives me a good deal of pride and satisfaction.

My high school experience and many subsequent years of incorporating service in my teaching from kindergarten through college have contributed to my belief that service-learning holds tremendous promise for both student learning and community improvement. Yet, as I have worked with public school teachers on service-learning projects over the years, I have increasingly recognized the many challenges involved in developing projects that incorporate both meaningful service and valuable student learning, student empowerment and community collaboration, critical reflection and enthusiastic celebration of one's efforts. This book is one attempt to meet those challenges; its primary intent is to help service-learning practitioners develop quality service-learning experiences for public school students, schools, and communities.

Service-learning programs, can of course, be based in many settings, including those outside of the public school curriculum. Service activities are often included in extracurricular school clubs, community education programs, recreation programs such as Boy and Girl Scouts, and private schools, for example. While coordinators of these programs will find much in this book to inform their practice of service-learning, the focus here is on public school programs that integrate service in the curriculum. From the beginning, the mission of public schooling has been, in part, to develop an informed and active democratic citizenry. When service and learning goals are mutually supportive, service-learning can be justified as an effective teaching strategy in the public school curriculum.

The notion of service-learning as a means for developing active and informed citizens in our democratic society is a central thread woven through-out the book. As a strategy for civic education, service-learning can provide students with real reasons to learn their civics lessons and opportunities to put school knowledge into practice. In our diverse democratic society, service-learning has the potential to unite us in working together on shared goals, bridging the gaps in age, gender, race, ethnicity, class, and ability.

These principles have influenced not only the content, but the design of this book. Readers will not find separate chapters on multicultural service-learning or service projects for special education. Rather, diverse voices tell the stories of their service-learning work: a classroom teacher from a southwestern pueblo; students from rural Iowa to New York City. From coast to coast, "veterans" in the service-learning movement as well as inspired beginners share their experiences. Thus, the book attempts to model the ideal democratic society, honoring individual voices and integrating our efforts toward the common good.

Following this preface, readers will find an introduction focused on the link between civic education and service-learning. This discussion, both theoretical and practical in nature, addresses the current lack of participation in our democracy, the ineffectual nature of civic education as it currently exists in most schools, and the two main perspectives—liberalism and participatory republicanism—that inform various beliefs about citizenship and approaches to civic education. The introduction concludes with an assertion that service-learning should occupy a central position in public schools' civic education efforts. While the introduction does not deal with the specifics of service-learning practice, the discussion will prove useful for readers seeking a strong rationale for service-learning in our nation's schools.

The remainder of the book is divided into four parts, each with a different scope and purpose. While those new to service-learning will benefit most from reading chapters 1 through 7 in order, experienced service-learning practitioners can use this book in a "menu" format, seeking information about specific aspects of practice, program descriptions at different levels, and various roles in service-learning involvement. The scope of the book mixes theory and practice in an attempt to honor a variety of perspectives on service-learning and to meet the needs of readers with different interests.

Part 1 covers essential information on quality service-learning practice. Separate chapters address effective practices for preparation, collaboration, service, curriculum integration, reflection, and building support for service-learning programs. Designed in a workbook format, each chapter includes key questions that have been asked by practitioners, "spotlight" thinking exercises, and a challenge activity through which readers can apply the information in the chapter to a hypothetical situation. This part of the book has been designed for use in college service-learning classes, public school staff development programs, and informal groups of service-learning practitioners. Individual program leaders, service-learning teachers, and students will also be able to use the information in these chapters to plan effective service-learning activities in their schools.

Two terms used throughout Part 1 need definition. *Program leader* refers to whoever is in charge of a service-learning program; this could be an individual classroom teacher, a school program coordinator, or a student group. Similarly, the term *program planners* refers to those individuals who are responsible for planning and overseeing the program. In many cases, this may be a mixed group of students, teachers, and community members.

Part 2, Service-Learning in Schools, begins with a chapter addressing the essential elements of K–12 service-learning practice in a democratic society. The following three chapters provide concrete examples of service-learning at the elementary, middle, and high school levels. Each of the authors situates their descriptions of service-learning programs in both the developmental needs of students and the current structure of schooling at that level. They also present a series of challenges to effective practice in public elementary, middle, and high schools. A final chapter in part 2 examines the critical role of the classroom teacher in designing and implementing service-learning activities in the public school curriculum. Part 2 provides readers the opportunity to examine the practices outlined in Part 1 as they take shape in real schools within real service-learning programs.

Stories from the many and varied participants in the service-learning movement comprise Part 3, Voices from the Field. While the service-learning literature often highlights the importance of collaboration, rarely are many of these voices heard. From student to community agency member to administrator, the authors of these chapters tell their own stories of service-learning involvement, discuss issues for other individuals who share their roles, and highlight recommendations for effective action. Given that each person's experience with service-learning is unique, these chapters should be viewed as case studies of service-learning practitioners; they provide "windows" into the perspectives of those who experience this work from different positions and vantage points.

Throughout the book, the ideal is contrasted with the reality of service-learning practice. In Part 4, The Future of Service-Learning, I explore the many challenges to effective practice: in the structure of public schooling in the United States, in the practice of service-learning in school programs, and in the national service-learning movement. A critical aspect of ensuring service-learning's future in public education is relegated a chapter unto itself: the integration of service-learning in preservice teacher education. Finally, the conclusion addresses the steps educators will need to take if service-learning is to fulfill its role as an effective means for democratic civic education.

No single book can cover all aspects, issues, and perspectives on a given topic. Readers interested in stories of how service-learning contributes to changing school culture or how service-learning fits with other types of school reform efforts should seek out other publications. Our attempt has been to provide a comprehensive resource focused on the essential elements of quality service-learning practice for civic education in public schools and a description of different programs at the elementary, middle, and high school levels as well as in teacher education. Further, we have focused on modeling the importance of honoring diverse voices and views in a democratic society by including many of these perspectives and have organized the book in a format that can be used effectively by busy education professionals.

This book meets a timely need in the education field. Interest in adding service to the public school curriculum has surged in recent years. Supported by federal funding and educational organizations' endorsement, as well as national conference presentations and numerous publications devoted to its practice, service-learning is being implemented in every state in the nation, from kindergarten to college. This momentum may seem to have sprung from out of the blue to the uninformed; those who have worked tirelessly for service-learning at the local, state, and national levels know that these events have come about because of the hard work and commitment of many educators, policy makers, and legislators over the last twenty years. This book could not have been written without them; my hope is that it will serve as both a testimony to their efforts and an inspiration for the improvement and expansion of service-learning programs in public schools and teacher education programs nationwide.

In the next few years, many fledgling programs will be put to the test in their schools and local communities. Educators, community members, policy makers, and potential funders will be watching, waiting, and ultimately asking, "Well, does it work? Does service-learning really make a difference for students, schools, and communities? Is it worth the time, energy, and funds to coordinate and carry out collaborative service-learning projects?" While the future of the service-learning movement may ultimately depend on our responses, this book cannot answer to the quality of the nation's service-learning programs. What it can do is provide service-learning practitioners with creative and effective ideas which, if put into practice, will lead them to answer these questions about the worth and value of their service-learning programs with a resounding "*Yes!*"

Service-learning is a response to the many needs of our faltering democracy, a call to educators who still believe it may be possible to change the world, and an opportunity for students to realize a meaningful and valued role in their communities. Those who are involved with service-learning are aware that while the journey may be challenging and perplexing at times, there is tremendous growth, fulfillment, and excitement to be experienced along the way. Welcome to the journey!

RAHIMA C. WADE

Community Service-Learning in a Democracy: An Introduction

Rahima C. Wade

The premise of this book is that community service-learning should have a central place in our nation's public schools. Embodying the original mission of public schooling, to create active and informed citizens, community service-learning has the potential to assist in reviving an apathetic citizenry through the transformation of civic education. In this chapter, I begin with a discussion of our faltering democracy and ineffectual civic education practices. Along with many other scholars, I propose that a vision of society based solely on respect for individual rights is an inappropriate view to guide civic education in a democracy. Instead, an alternate view of civic education, guided by both individualistic and communal values, is presented. The chapter concludes with a discussion of service-learning and its central role in democratic citizenship education.

WHY IS OUR DEMOCRACY FALTERING?

For more than two hundred years, the American people have lived with democracy as their form of government, in Abraham Lincoln's words, "government of, by, and for the people." Democracy is characterized by both rights and responsibilities. At its core, democracy upholds respect for the dignity of the individual and the right of all citizens to participate in decision making (Engle and Ochoa, 1988). A democracy cannot function effectively without these basic tenets. A democracy in many ways should be an open society, where individuals have the right to dissent, where differences are accepted, and where efforts to change and improve the quality of life are commonplace.

While these ideals of democratic life have not varied much over more than two centuries, in practice our democracy has gone through numerous changes and transformations. In the early years of English settlements, democracy functioned primarily within local associations and town meetings. Political decision making was an extension of the communal participation so necessary for the health and well-being of each person. Citizens needed each other not only to decide on local laws and regulations, but to build homes, grow food, and provide a wide array of goods and services necessary for living.

The onset of industrialization is marked by some scholars as the beginning of a profound shift in the lives of communities and the livelihood of American democracy. Since the beginning of the exodus from farm life to the cities, Americans have increasingly valued independence and personal success over their commitment to a participatory egalitarian society. Alexis de Tocqueville (1840/1969) recognized that a healthy democracy was integrally connected to a lively moral civic culture engendered by local communities and associations. He was prescient in his fear that economic enterprise would turn citizens away from a vigorous civic life in the public sphere and toward individual concern for wealth and happiness in the private sphere.

As national markets and large scale enterprise gradually replaced small-town America, the survival of democracy depended on meeting the concentration of economic power with a concentration of political power. Some were positive about the possibility of the nationalization of political, economic, and social life resulting in "an essentially formative and enlightening political transformation" (Croly, 1965, p. 270). But the nationalization of politics and the centralization of government promoted in the appeal for the consolidation of the union and consummated in the New Deal failed to engender a strong sense of national unity. The scale proved too large across which to cultivate the shared values, ideals, and commitment necessary to community. "And so the gradual shift, in our practices and institutions, from a public philosophy of common purposes to one of fair procedures, from a politics of good to a politics of right, from the national republic to the procedural republic" (Sandel, 1984, p. 93).

As the scale of our social and political organization has grown, the sense of our collective identity as a people with common needs and purposes has become increasingly fragmented. As we have increasingly placed individual good ahead of the common good, we have forgotten our common roots as Americans. Bellah and his colleagues (1985) noted that many Americans feel isolated from their institutions—schools, governments, and churches. Institutional problems seem too large, too complex; the result is frustration, lack of trust, and ultimately withdrawal from active involvement in the decision making process. Numerous studies have confirmed young people's disengagement from political involvement in particular (Center for Civic Education, 1994). As just one example of this fact, the mean voter turnout for presidential elections in the United States since World War II has hovered around 50 percent, the lowest percentage for any noncompulsory democracy in the West. "In a country where voting is the primary expression of citizenship, the refusal to vote signals the bankruptcy of democracy" (Barber, 1984, p. xiv).

Further evidence of our fragmentation as a national community can be seen in citizens' views of the nation state. Many view the state as distant and alien, an overly intrusive and powerful presence that must be carefully watched lest we become its victims. At the same time, the state is seen as disempowered, unable to effectively control the nation's economy or respond capably to persistent social problems (Sandel, 1984).

While the vestiges of a more participatory democracy can still be found in some New England town meetings or in grassroots movements for social change, for many citizens, democratic life seems to be a thing of the past. A democracy lacking in participation by the majority of its constituents is a democracy at risk. Bellah and his colleagues (1985) conclude, "We have failed at every level; we have put our own good, as individuals, as groups, as a nation, ahead of the common good" (p. 285). For a thriving democracy, we need a majority of concerned citizens willing to participate in decisions from the local to the national level that effect their own lives and the common good.

Where do we turn then in our efforts to resuscitate a faltering democracy? Clearly, efforts must be mounted on many fronts if we are to develop a vibrant national life. The purpose of this book is to explore just one potential means: community service-learning in public education. Given the original mission of public schooling as civic education, we turn now to a discussion of the school's role in educating citizens. This discussion will illuminate the failure of education to foster a participatory public lifestyle for American citizens.

WHAT IS THE ROLE OF PUBLIC SCHOOLING
IN EDUCATING CITIZENS?

The founders of our democratic society and the formulators of public schooling believed that one of the central purposes of education was to develop informed and active citizens. Historically, public education was education for community, a means for making both plurality and difference honored in civic life. Aristotle noted that citizens are made, not born. Many years later, Jefferson, in his support for public schooling, hoped that education would enable citizens' moral and intellectual development so that they could create good government. Jefferson, Madison, Adams, and others realized that a free society depends on the knowledge, skills, and virtues of its citizens (Center for Civic Education, 1994). The theme of education for citizenship has continued throughout the history of education in the work of Horace Mann, Henry

Bernard, John Dewey, Arthur Bestor, Max Rafferty, and contemporary scholars such as Benjamin Barber who asserted, "There are certain things a democracy simply must teach, employing its full authority to do so: citizenship is first among them" (1992, p. 256).

Schools were (and still are) the sole institution available to society as a whole to train youth in the theory and practice of democratic citizenship. Many civic qualities cannot be learned in private spheres such as the family. They must, therefore, be taught and learned with public support and guidance. While family, church, the media, and the streets all play powerful roles in children's development, it is schools that provide the greatest opportunity for youth to experience community, to work toward common goals, and to uphold both individual rights and collective good. The communal nature of public school classrooms offers students an excellent opportunity to balance the development of individual character, autonomy, and confidence with the strengthening of a public self through dialogue, decision making, and cooperative learning.

HOW HAS CIVIC EDUCATION FAILED TO CREATE ACTIVE CITIZENS?

While most educators acknowledge the potential of public schooling for civic training, the results of traditional civic education have been far from promising. Despite a variety of curricular innovations over the last twenty-five years, most efforts at teaching citizenship in the schools fall on the shoulders of narrowly conceived social studies courses that in most cases have failed to engender student interest, involvement, or competence in political life (Ferguson, 1991). Research has shown that most high school government and civics courses have little impact on students' democratic political attitudes, in part because they fail to link cognitive information with the affective lessons of citizenship (Battistoni, 1985). Bellah and his colleagues (1992) observed that "On the whole Americans have done better in developing their educational resources for the transmission of specialized knowledge and skills than they have for citizenship" (p. 175).

Educators have offered other reasons for the ineffectual nature of the civics curriculum as well. First, students have little reason to become interested in simply reading about civics. "Give people some significant power and they will quickly appreciate the need for knowledge, but foist knowledge on them without giving them responsibility and they will display only indifference" (Barber, 1984, p. 234). Thus, traditional teaching strategies provide little incentive for students' taking to heart and acting on the lessons in their social studies textbooks.

This finding points to a second and related reason for the failure of traditional schooling to create active, informed citizens: the school's hierarchical social arrangements. Schools cannot teach democracy when they are not democratic places themselves. Civic education in our schools is much more than what goes on in social studies classes; civic education is influenced by the whole school environment. Dewey contended that any educational regimen consisting of "authorities at the upper end handing down to receivers at the lower end what they must accept" was an education "fit to subvert, pervert, and destroy the foundations of democratic society" (Dewey, 1916/1969: 133). Purpel (1989) similarly saw schooling as a powerful force for social, intellectual, and personal oppression. The reasons for this oppression are rooted in our history and represent the deeply held values of hierarchical power, materialism, and individualism.

Students learn powerful lessons from the "hidden curriculum," the school's structural elements and the sum total of human experience in schools (Purpel, 1989; Purpel and Giroux, 1987). In addition to the message of obeying authority without question, students are also taught that individual success is what matters. What else can students conclude when teachers tell them to "mind their own business" and "keep to yourself" as a matter of course in learning? Many of the structures of traditional schooling—individual seat work, competitive grading, discouragement of collaboration, training in docility—foster an ethic of individual success over collective learning and of obedience over empowerment.

Pratte (1988) maintained that we cannot bring about civic education for a truly democratic society "by isolating it as a subject, by teaching it through lecture or recitation, or by separating it from the social life of the school and community" (p. 17). Bellah and his colleagues (1992) concurred, stating that "learning is never the result of the efforts of isolated, competitive individuals alone" (p. 172).

A third reason, perhaps underlying both of the others presented here, is lack of a consensus opinion on the nature of a "good citizen." Purpel (1989) noted that social/cultural demands and limited economic resources have distracted us from a commitment to the values underlying our common heritage: love, justice, equality, and community. Bellah and his colleagues (1985) concluded their interviews of over 200 U.S. citizens with the following observation,

> It seemed particularly hard for those we interviewed to articulate a language of citizenship based neither on the metaphor of extended kinship nor on a conflict of interests. It was difficult for them to conceive of a common good or a public interest that recognizes economic, social, and cultural differences between people but sees them all as parts of a single society on which they all depend. (pp. 191–92)

Current civic education efforts in our nation's schools reflect this uncertainty about the nature of citizenship, although most civic educational practices support the individualistic values so prevalent in almost all American public schools. Bellah and his coauthors (1992) noted the inadequacy of this approach, even for individualistic goals.

> The idea of an education that simply gives individuals the methods and skills they need to get ahead in the world is almost certainly inadequate, even as "job preparation," in an advanced technical economy, which requires morally and socially sensitive people capable of responsible interaction. It is even more inadequate for preparing citizens for active participation in a complex world. (p. 170)

While we cannot ignore the need for individual freedom and rights in our society, neither can we dismiss the need for active public engagement in a healthy democracy. In order to create a more balanced view of citizenship and ultimately, civic education, I turn now to exploring in greater depth the nature of the predominant individualistic perspective. This view is informed by the political theory of liberalism (not to be confused with the liberal/conservative dichotomy). The ideas of liberalism will be contrasted with another political perspective with a long legacy in American history, that of participatory-republicanism.

In this discussion, I will highlight the benefits and shortcomings of both perspectives. It would be unproductive to promote one approach to the exclusion of the other. Walzer (1990) noted that political theory will always debate the advantages of individual choice versus communal bonds and Neal (1990) astutely pointed out that both perspectives have legitimate critiques of the other. Green (1990) advocated that rather than treating liberalism as "the enemy," we should respect the need to guarantee rights, but work toward bringing about a more connected society.

WHAT IS THE LIBERAL VIEW
OF THE DEMOCRATIC CITIZEN?

The term "liberal" is derived from the word "liberty." The ideas associated with liberalism originated during the Protestant Reformation and were further developed during the rise of market economies and free enterprise and eighteenth century Enlightenment. Thinkers such as John Locke argued that the primary purpose of government is the protection of individual rights and that the authority of the government, which should be limited to the protection of those rights, is based on the consent of the people (Center for Civic Education, 1994).

At the center of the liberal democratic view stands the individual. The goal in life is the peaceful enjoyment of private independence. Historically, liberals have taken as their foundation a theory of individualism and natural rights; their approach separates private and public life in an effort to guarantee the secure existence and free activity of the individual (Walzer, 1984). Many believe that the principal characteristic of a democratic society is that the government leaves its citizens free to pursue their own interests and ambitions (Battistoni, 1985).

What matters most from the liberal perspective is not the ends chosen but our capacity to choose that which is meaningful to us as individuals (Sandel, 1984). The common good in the liberal perspective is the protection of individual freedom and the practices of independence and pursuit of private interests. Smith (1989) argues that "a liberal polity should be united . . . by a shared political and social purpose: to promote ways of life that advance liberty for all" (p. 290).

In the liberal view, the "good citizen" is one who has adopted certain rules and standards of public behavior that are useful in providing for the orderly accommodation of private wishes in the public realm (Battistoni, 1985). Thus, "good citizens" will participate in politics to the extent necessary to ensure their private interests, for example, by voting for leaders who will represent them and by occasionally running for public office themselves.

From a liberal perspective, civic education should consist of the 3 Rs and certain rules and standards of public behavior. Liberalism envisions the function of education to facilitate individuals' coexistence as distinct persons, rather than giving students the knowledge, skills, and values to participate actively in public life. Most of the virtues to be learned in life are personal or social, not political. Thus, civic education involving practical democratic experience in the school or community would generally be viewed as undesirable or unnecessary from the liberal perspective.

WHAT ARE SOME PROBLEMS WITH LIBERALISM?

Walzer (1984) has labeled liberalism "a world of walls" (p. 315). Yet the goal set by liberalism, each person within his or her own circle, is literally unattainable. We live in a social world; the rights we enjoy exist within the framework of the many ongoing institutions of our lives. Walzer (1984) maintained that "We aim, or we should aim, not at the freedom of the solitary individual but at what can best be called institutional integrity. Individuals should be free, indeed, in all sorts of ways, but we don't set them free by separating them from their fellows" (p. 325).

A free state in a complex society such as ours is one that is in the hands of its citizens. Aristotle noted long ago that the civic bond is the one that orders and governs all the others. It is the bond that creates the public structure within which personal and private social relationships can flourish. Bellah and his colleagues (1985) interviewed hundreds of U.S. citizens about their private and public lives and came to the conclusion that a quest for purely private fulfillment is illusory and often ends up empty; private fulfillment and public involvement are likely intricately connected.

While the liberal citizen sees the private sphere of life as the source of fulfillment, others maintain that people have an inherent need for political life (Barber, 1984; Battistoni, 1985; Bellah et al., 1985; Lappe and DuBois, 1994; Sandel, 1984; Walzer, 1984). Personal relationships and accomplishments are not enough in their view. Mutual recognition and communion are necessary to the complete development of the self. It is in association with others—in relationships characterized by mutual respect, justice, fairness, benevolence, truthfulness, caring about others, and fellowship—that human nature most fully expresses itself (Pratte, 1988).

In sum, the liberal vision alone is unsuited to our modern democracy. It does not present an accurate view of the individual, separate from the institutions with which he or she is integrally connected. Nor does it recognize the individuals' need for public life or the positive aspirations of the individual as one who seeks to contribute to the lives of others rather than just to protect oneself from them. Finally, as Sandel (1984) argued, the liberal view is not morally or practically self-sufficient. In order to guarantee the individual rights so central to the liberal citizen's view, we need a majority who are active participants in democratic decision making. We turn now to an another view of citizenship, described as civic or participatory republicanism in the political science literature and recast in recent works as "strong democracy" (Barber, 1984) or "living democracy" (Lappe and DuBois, 1994).

WHAT IS THE PARTICIPATORY REPUBLICAN VIEW OF THE DEMOCRATIC CITIZEN?

The founders of American democracy were influenced by the republican ideas of both ancient Greece and Rome. Classical republicanism stressed two primary ideas: first, that the primary purpose of government is to promote the common good of the whole society and second, that civic virtue is a necessary characteristic of citizens. Civic virtue requires individuals to place the common good above private interest (Center for Civic Education, 1994).

The participatory-republican perspective (Battistoni, 1985) combines elements of the republican and participatory traditions in the history of political thought. Although these two traditions have their differences, there are points at which they have converged in history. Battistoni (1985) noted that modern participatory democrats have called upon aspects of the republican tradition, such as the concern for public virtue and the primacy of civic life, to inform their vision of politics and republican thinkers have at times promoted greater citizen participation in political decision making. These traditions are combined here, in part, because they may offer the theoretical foundation for solutions to contemporary problems in civic education (Battistoni, 1985).

In the participatory-republican perspective, the recognition of conflicting interests of the liberal tradition is just one element; the other is the belief that we also have common bonds and mutual interests as members of a political community. "A democratic community sees its members as equal partners who mutually contend and reciprocally persuade each other in the process of public deliberation, decision, and action" (Battistoni, 1985, p. 58). In the participatory-republican view one must be a good citizen to be a good person. The process of mutual dialogue and collective action develops individual character so that private interests are transformed into public issues and personalities expand to balance private with public concerns.

In recent years, a few scholars have reconceptualized and relabeled the participatory-republican perspective in an attempt to breathe new life into our faltering democracy. One of these scholars, Benjamin Barber (1984) at Rutgers University, has proposed the notion of "strong democracy." Strong democracy is defined by Barber (1984) as the resolution of conflict "through a participatory process of ongoing, proximate self-legislation and the creation of a political community capable of transforming dependent, private individuals into free citizens and partial and private interests, into public goods" (p. 132).

Transformation is at the heart of strong democracy. Barber does not ignore the presence of personal interest and ensuing conflict in public life. Instead, he argues that strong democracy aspires to transform conflict through inventiveness and discovery. Thus, human nature is envisioned as both benign and malevolent, both cooperative and antagonistic.

The hallmarks of strong democracy include activity, commitment, obligation, service, common deliberation, common decision, and common work. Strong democracy is self-government by citizens, not just representative government in the name of citizens. "In strong democratic politics, participation is a way of defining the self, just as citizenship is a way of living" (Barber, 1984: 4). Thus, the "good" citizen in a strong democracy participates directly in the democratic process, both locally and nationally, and is transformed in the process of doing so.

Lappe and DuBois (1994) proposed a similar type of participatory republicanism they labeled "living democracy." Their proposal for active citizenship involves reconceptualizing the notions of public life, self-interest, and power. Although many Americans view public life as an unnecessary and time consuming involvement, Lappe and DuBois assert that we each have a public life that often enhances our private lives. Every day, at work, school, in civic and social groups, our behavior shapes the public world. Like other proponents of the participatory-republican perspective, the authors believe that public life fulfills a deep human need, to know that one's life counts and makes a difference in the world. While in public life we often encounter conflict with others, Lappe and Dubois join Barber in the assertion that this conflict can be healthy and informative and can lead to new insights about ourselves and new solutions to community problems.

Rather than working in a self-sacrificial manner for the "common good," Lappe and DuBois propose that lasting solutions depend upon meeting the needs of others along with our own needs. They maintain that this "relational self-interest" expands possibilities for many people at once while trying to serve others alone may defeat the goal of healthy communities. To effectively work for common goals involves the exercise of power in the public sphere.

WHAT ARE SOME PROBLEMS WITH PARTICIPATORY REPUBLICANISM?

While these contemporary models of citizenship hold potential for revitalizing civic education, they cannot absolve participatory republicanism from its share of criticism. One of the most common critiques of this perspective is that its proponents are vague or unrealistic about what needs to happen to bring about a society informed by communal values (Burtt, 1993; Neal, 1990; Wolfe, 1986). Neal (1990) asserted that advocates of a participatory citizenry should be able to explain and justify an alternative vision of society that would guarantee individual freedom and rights.

One problem with this task is the large scale in which participatory decision-making would need to take place. While modern states can offer their citizens opportunities to engage citizens through referenda or reorganization of local government, the overwhelming cognitive complexity of modern government keeps them from subjecting the continuing exercise of state power to a truly democratic decision-making procedure (Dunn, 1986). Barber (1984) offered an ambitious agenda for local to national participation through technological means, local community meetings, national referenda and other "imaginative" ideas (Mansbridge, 1987). Yet to some critics, they seem implausible and idealistic (Burtt, 1993; Dunn, 1986; Wolfe, 1986), given the current state of society.

Burtt (1993) criticized Barber's proposal on yet another count, that purely public virtue asks too great an abstraction from the self. Burtt's views are more in line with Lappe and Dubois' (1994) "relational self-interest." Burtt argued that self-interest should not be seen as an obstacle to civic virtue, but rather as the source of individuals' contributions to the public good. Perhaps then citizens could be brought to civically virtuous activity through reflection on matters of importance to them. Indeed, it is likely that liberalism prevails over participatory republicanism because individuals' interests for their own gains and interests predominate over concern for others.

While these are not the only criticisms of participatory republicanism, they are frequently cited and legitimate concerns. It seems obvious then that the optimal approach to civic education will draw on both liberalism and participatory republicanism in a way that promotes their strengths and cautiously addresses their limitations. The vision of civic education presented here affirms both individual rights and communal vision. Some of the ideas presented here—notably those that deal with participatory skills and direct involvement in schools and communities—may seem more consistent with a participatory republican perspective. Others, such as basic knowledge of our governmental system and attitudes supportive of individual rights, may appear to be aligned with the liberal view.

Together these and other civic education practices have the potential to enhance the development of citizens who can both work for their own individual interests and promote the common good in society as a whole. While there will always be some conflict between these two pursuits, Lappe and DuBois (1994) and Burtt (1993) pointed out that these goals do not have to stand in opposition. Through expanding rather than subduing personal interest, citizens can engage each other in the public sphere and work toward both mutual goals and personal satisfaction.

Spotlight on Views of the Democratic Citizen
Summarize both the liberal and the participatory-republican views of the citizen in a paragraph on each. Which view do you personally feel is most important? Why? What experiences in your life thus far have led you to think as you do?

WHAT ARE THE ESSENTIAL COMPONENTS OF DEMOCRATIC CIVIC EDUCATION?

Plato believed that if people intellectually understood the good, they would be good. Aristotle, on the other hand, felt that people would become good only if they engaged in the practice of just and virtuous actions. Many advocates of civic education assert that we should heed both of these sages' advice, lest we risk action without conviction or reasoning that does not carry over into action (Lickona, 1991). The broad recommendations here for civic education focus on (1) intellectual understanding, (2) skills for participation, (3) civic attitudes, and (4) direct participation in schools and communities.

All democratic citizens should have a foundation of basic knowledge about civics. Pratte (1988) emphasized the importance of understanding our democratic processes and institutions. Battistoni (1985) maintained that approaching civic education through an integrated curriculum is vital; students should study the conflict and content in U.S. history, for example, as well as explore civic concepts in lessons on natural communities in science. Barber (1984) also recommended formal instruction in civics, history, and citizenship.

Yet all of these educators, and many others, assert that knowledge alone will not suffice in efforts to develop active citizens. A second essential component of civic education concerns the skills citizens need to participate effectively in public life. Battistoni (1985) recommended communication and rhetorical skills; critical thinking; verbal reasoning; skills in persuasion, bargaining, and compromise; and the ability to recognize common interests. This list is very similar to Barber's (1984) skills needed for strong democratic talk.

Yet even if we were to teach American young people all of these skills and the knowledge of our democratic institutions and history, there is still the matter of engendering the will to act in the public sphere. Thus, a third critical component of civic education is the development of civic attitudes. Civic attitudes taught in schools should affirm both individual rights and the common good. One of the goals of civic education should be to reduce ethnocentrism; citizens should develop tolerance if not appreciation for diversity and sincere empathy for others. Pratte (1988) described the development of a civic disposition as

> a willingness to act, in behalf of the public good while being attentive to and considerate of the feelings, needs, and attitudes of others. Civic virtue has an internal landscape reflected in the obligation or duty to be fair to others, to show kindness and tact, and above all to render agreeable service to the community. (p. 17)

He further asserted that the self-development of citizens in identity, self-esteem, and autonomy should be balanced with "the particular conditions of democracy via the ethical obligations of concern, care for others, tolerance, civility, humaneness, esteem, respect, compassion, benevolence, fairness, and integrity" (Pratte, 1988, p. 64). Lappe and DuBois (1994) maintained that while it is important to develop these qualities, citizens should not do so in a sacrificial manner. Rather, they should balance individual and public concerns through "relational self-interest."

The knowledge, skills, and attitudes discussed here comprise the "what" of civic education. The last critical dimension is concerned with the "how." As mentioned previously, the means through which civic education is presented to students is probably a more powerful teacher than any formally taught facts or principles. Thus, educating students for democratic participation must entail their active involvement in the life of the school and community.

Pratte (1988) asserted that students don't need isolated civics lessons, they need opportunities to practice civic behaviors. Dewey advocated building community in public schooling through students' participation in the planning process and their active contributions to doing good works for the school (Beninga, 1991). Citing research supporting participatory modes in the class-room, Battistoni (1985) recommended a student-centered pedagogy that stresses knowledge through self-discovery and the incitement of interest in one's learning along with the overall context of group learning.

While students can practice democracy within the school community, educators contend that involvement in the community can reap rich rewards for civic learning as well (Barber, 1984, 1992; Battistoni, 1985; Lappe and DuBois, 1994; Pratte, 1988). When students work on complex community problems, they have the potential to learn not only the skills and knowledge necessary for civic action, but also democratic attitudes—the will to participate and the ability to care for others.

Battistoni (1985) noted that educators who have initiated programs involving students in community projects, community research, social service organizations, and government agencies have observed a number of positive benefits. When students work on common goals and have others depend on their actions, they learn the cognitive and affective knowledge of democratic citizenship better than through classroom instruction alone. Classroom discussion about broad political and social issues is also enhanced by participation. Student participation in the community can also provide important benefits for the community: services provided, solutions found, and an improved image of the role of youth in society.

While youth can have many varied and positive experiences working in the community, civic education can be most effective when it includes experiential learning of the kind offered by community service (Barber, 1992). The remainder of this chapter focuses on the role of service-learning as a key component in civic education for a participatory democracy.

WHAT IS THE ROLE OF COMMUNITY SERVICE-LEARNING IN CIVIC EDUCATION?

Community service-learning integrates school or community-based service projects with academic skills and content and provides opportunities for structured reflection on the service experience (Cairn and Kielsmeier, 1991).

Service-learning projects address a diversity of environmental and social issues. For example, elementary students might design and build a bird sanctuary in conjunction with science units on birds and trees. As part of the social studies curriculum, older students might publish a history of their community, drawing on oral testimonies from senior citizens and documents from the local historical society. Other service-learning projects involve cross-age tutoring, environmental clean-up efforts, and meeting the needs of the homeless or hungry. Effective service-learning activities address a need or problem in the community or school and at the same time incorporate curriculum-based learning objectives for students. (See chapter 2 for a further description of the essential components of quality service-learning.)

Barber (1992) maintained that service is central to the civics curriculum in order for students to realize the obligations engendered in democratic citizenship. "Service is something we owe to ourselves or to that part of ourselves that is embedded in the civic community. It assumes that our rights and liberties are not acquired for free; that unless we assume the responsibilities of citizens, we will not be able to preserve the liberties they entail" (Barber, 1992, p. 246).

Both Barber (1992) and Lappe and DuBois (1994) cautioned that service should not be seen as a form of charity or be completed in a self-sacrificial manner. Instead, citizens should work alongside those in need, recognizing our common purpose, and enabling those being served to become more empowered in the process. Service is not a matter of sacrificing private interests to moral virtue. "The language of citizenship suggests that self-interests are always embedded in communities of action and that in serving neighbors one also serves oneself. Self and community, private interest and public good, are necessarily linked" (Barber, 1992, p. 249).

Community service-learning has the potential to reveal that personal fulfillment and public contribution are not antithetical. Through carefully structured service-learning experiences, students can come to realize that individualism alone will lead to a vacuous life (Pratte, 1988) and that helping others in the community results in a great deal of personal satisfaction (Lappe and DuBois, 1994). Through civic service, students fulfill an obligation to the community through the outward expression of civic virtue aimed at promoting the public good (Pratte, 1988).

Community service-learning can bring together all four essential components of civic education: intellectual understanding, participation skills, civic attitudes and direct participation in schools and communities. Through working alongside others to address common concerns and problems, students have a purpose for learning about the history of our democratic institutions and the legacy of citizens' social action efforts. Participation skills and civic attitudes become more than topics for class discussion or items on a test; students learn skills in collaboration and communication by practicing them in their service work. Service-learning provides students with a means for self-development as well as the development of civic attitudes such as concern, care for others, tolerance, respect, compassion, fairness, and integrity. Finally, community service-learning is one form of direct and active participation in the school and community. Clearly, service-learning has the potential to be an effective means for civic education in a democratic society.

Will we reach this potential in the practice of service-learning in our nation's schools? If we do, it will only be through working together—as educators, community members, parents, and students—with common purposes, open minds, enthusiastic energy, and caring hearts. In the early years of America's history, civic education was the province not only of the school but of the whole community. Perhaps through service-learning, we can return to the roots of our heritage, teaching our youth the ways of democratic citizenship, and, in the process, creating healthy communities and a vibrant national life.

Part 1

Community Service-Learning

Following an overview of service-learning, its history in the United States, and the existing research supporting the inclusion of service-learning in the curriculum the chapters in part 1 are devoted to the essential components of quality service-learning programs: preparation, collaboration, service, curriculum integration, and reflection. The final chapter in this section is devoted to building support for service-learning programs through documentation, fundraising, celebration, and public relations.

Reflection is an important aspect of service-learning.
Photo Credit: Craig Barrett

T-shirt sales raise needed funds for community agencies.
Photo Credit: Andy Scott

Chapter 1

Community Service-Learning: An Overview

Rahima C. Wade

The notion of involving young people in serving their communities is universally appealing. In response to the growing social and environmental problems in the communities of the United States as well as the tremendous potential for both youth and educational reform, service-learning programs are increasing at a rapid rate in the nation's schools. In this chapter, I present a definition, the essential components, and the potential outcomes of service-learning followed by a rationale for the inclusion of service in the public school curriculum. The rationale is based on the needs of youth and their communities, the legacy of service in our nation's history, the potential outcomes of service-learning activities, and tentative support from research and evaluation about the benefits of service-learning for youth, schools, and communities.

WHAT IS COMMUNITY SERVICE-LEARNING?

Service-learning programs can take a variety of shapes and forms, making the defining of service-learning a challenging task. In recognition of the need for a widely agreed-on definition of service-learning and a set of standards by which to judge programs, a diverse group of service-learning educators nationwide formed the Alliance for Service-Learning in Education Reform (ASLER). The definition established by the group reads as follows:

> Service-learning is a method by which young people learn and develop through active participation in thoughtfully-organized service experiences: that meet actual community needs, that are coordinated in collaboration with the school and community, that are integrated into each young person's academic curriculum, that provide structured time for a

young person to think, talk, and write about what he/she did and saw during the actual service activity, that provide young people with opportunities to use newly acquired academic skills and knowledge in real life situations in their own communities, that enhance what is taught in the school by extending student learning beyond the classroom, and that help to foster the development of a sense of caring for others. (ASLER, 1993, p. 1)

This definition is almost exactly the same as the definition presented in the National and Community Service Act of 1990. One small but significant difference exists: the 1990 version specified that service experiences could be integrated in the academic curriculum *or* that structured to time to think, talk, and write about the service experience (reflection) be included. The ASLER version includes both curriculum integration and reflection as important aspects of service-learning.

The components of curriculum integration and reflection are, in fact, what distinguishes service-learning from community service. Community service in schools tends to be extracurricular club activities, winter clothing and canned food collections, or one-time visits to a nursing home or soup kitchen. While schools have often included these types of activities through which students help others, most have not made service a part of the curriculum. Service-learning is not an extracurricular activity; it is a pedagogical method in which service projects form the basis of learning opportunities. Furthermore, service-learning is a means for students to develop real world skills and knowledge they can apply both inside and outside of the classroom. Kielsmeier (1992) noted that service-learning "challenges the superficial level of knowledge we measure in standardized tests and drives deeply to questions about application of knowledge and how we live what we know" (p. 5).

Service-learning is based on a vision of youth as capable, productive, and essential contributors to their communities. In quality service-learning programs, youth themselves are given significant decision-making opportunities. Service-learning program leaders should invest significant responsibility in youth participants so that young people come to believe that they can be depended on and that their contributions can make valuable differences in the lives of others.

WHAT ARE THE ESSENTIAL COMPONENTS OF QUALITY SERVICE-LEARNING?

The ASLER (1993) definition lists many of the essential components of quality service-learning; others are emphasized in a list of eleven standards in the publication *Standards of Quality for School-based Service-learning* (ASLER, 1993). Additional sources for the components listed below are *Principles of Good Practice for Combining Service and Learning* (Giles, Honnet, and Migliore, 1991), *Best Practices in Community Service* (Conrad and Hedin, 1981), *Maryland's Best Practices: An improvement guide for school-based service-learning* (Maryland Student Service Alliance, 1995) and *Service-Learning: Core Elements* (Langseth, 1990). While the wording and emphasis vary, these documents promote a common core of essential components for quality service-learning programs. Included with a brief description of each component below is reference to the chapter(s) in this book that further addresses each topic.

Preparation

Preparation is a critical aspect of quality service-learning programs. Preparation involves careful planning by all those involved in the program, the construction of a time line for the project, a list of responsibilities and outcomes, and details on who will complete which tasks by what dates. At the planning stage, program leaders should have an overview of the entire project including the steps needed to evaluate and celebrate the project. Clear service and learning goals should be articulated for everyone involved. Preparation also includes setting up trainings and orientations for the project participants, helping students brainstorm solutions to potential problems, and facilitating group building activities. Preparation in service-learning programs is the focus of chapter 2.

Collaboration

Collaboration in service-learning programs involves school district personnel, students, and community members working together to develop a program that is appropriate, flexible, and in the best interests of all the participants. Effective program leaders recognize that service providers and needs should be matched through a process that is based on the recognition of changing circumstances in schools and communities. There are many potential collaborators in any service-learning project; effective programs generate genuine, active, and sustained commitment from the organizations and individuals involved. Quality programs also include participation by and with diverse populations. While youth empowerment is a goal in any quality youth service program; adult guidance, supervision, monitoring, and support are essential. Collaboration is featured in chapter 3. See also chapters 15, 18, and 19 for ideas on collaborating with specific school and community members.

Service

Service is the cornerstone of a quality service-learning program. Service activities should engage young people in responsible and challenging actions for the common good. They should also offer those who are being served the opportunities to define their needs and to participate in the design and conduct of the project. True service is not the same as charity; service involves working *with* rather than just *for* others. Whether students are involved in indirect, direct, or advocacy projects, they should be working in partnership with those who will benefit from the service activities. The possibilities for service activities are endless; typically K–12 service-learning projects fall into one of the following categories: intergenerational, environmental, hunger and poverty, school community, or animals. An exploration of the concept of service and over 100 examples of service activities are presented in chapter 4.

Curriculum Integration

When service is integrated with the academic curriculum, students not only meet important community needs, they also have the opportunity to learn academic skills and content in concert with helping. Many program leaders have observed that the service activity brings meaning to academics; students' motivation to learn skills and content in school subjects increases when they realize that they will need to use their knowledge to help others or to improve the environment. Through applying academics to service activities, students readily learn that school knowledge is relevant in the real world. Because we retain more of what we learn through experience than what we just read or write about, academic achievement can be enhanced through adding a service component to the curriculum. Service-learning projects can enhance the learning objectives in any subject area. Many ideas for teaching academic skills and content through service-learning are discussed in chapter 5.

Reflection

In order for students to learn from their service experience, program leaders must provide structured opportunities for students to reflect critically on the service experience. Reflection exercises can take many shapes and forms; students can write, discuss, draw, dance, construct displays, or develop presentations about their service activities. When youth are involved in checking their perceptions and biases, developing an understanding of the social and environmental issues that influence their communities, and reflecting on their views of the role of service in the life of a democratic citizen they can learn valuable lessons about themselves, others, and the act of serving. Reflection is covered in chapter 6.

Celebration

Given service-learning's goal of youth empowerment, celebration and recognition by others in the school and the community is an important means for rewarding student competence. When students learn new skills, engage in risk-taking, take on new responsibilities, and offer their hearts and hands to others, it is appropriate to honor and recognize their efforts. Celebration events serve not only to show students that their contributions are appreciated; they also provide opportunities to publicize the program, gain new supporters and participants, and motivate youth to want to continue to serve. Celebration is one of the topics addressed in chapter 7 on Building Support for Service-Learning Programs.

While these six components are essential for service-learning programs, other elements also contribute to effectiveness. For example, Cairn (1993) identifies adequate training, meaningful service, and structured reflection as three core components yet adds these additional keys to effectiveness: young people as leaders, clear roles, clear goals, adequate supervision, cultural sensitivity, strong community spirit, teacher as facilitator, and organizational commitment.

The ASLER standards also highlight two aspects of quality service-learning programs not mentioned in the other documents cited above: evaluation and teacher education. Effective evaluation is essential for assessing the outcomes of service-learning programs, for making decisions about improving the program, and for strengthening support for the program in the school district and community. The best evaluation efforts are woven into the fabric of the program from its inception; initial questions focus on information that is needed and desired, identification of those who will use the evaluation information, and determination of the appropriate methods for collecting the needed information. Evaluation in service-learning programs is discussed further in chapter 2.

If service-learning is to become a central part of the nation's schools, effective in-service and preservice training is essential. Teachers must be trained in how to conduct effective service-learning projects that promote all of the aspects of quality service-learning discussed in this chapter. Issues relevant to staff development and preservice teacher education are discussed in a number of the chapters in this book, including chapters 12, 17, and 22.

WHAT IS THE HISTORY OF COMMUNITY SERVICE AND SERVICE-LEARNING IN THE UNITED STATES?

Community service has a long history in the United States. The roots of community service can be found in the early history of Native peoples as well as in the pioneers' ethic to help one's neighbor with harvesting crops or raising a barn. The notion of caring for others in the community and helping out when needed as a natural matter of course were not just the embodiment of an ideal, they were a necessity for survival. While Americans are often characterized as individualists, our communal ethic continues to this day and can be seen throughout history in grassroots movements such as the abolition of slavery, women's suffrage, and the civil rights movement as well as in children's organizations such as the Girl Scouts, the Boy Scouts, and 4-H.

The idea of national service through government-sponsored programs can be traced back to 1910, when William James, an American philosopher, envisioned nonmilitary national service in his essay, "The Moral Equivalent of War" (Landrum, 1992). Since then, numerous national service programs have been proposed in Congress; some of those promoted by presidents in office have been successful. In 1933, Franklin Delano Roosevelt established the Civilian Conservation Corps through which over 3 million unemployed young men served their country before it ended in 1942. Citizens in 1961 saw John F. Kennedy establish the Peace Corps. In 1964, Lyndon Baines Johnson's "War on Poverty" led to Volunteers in Service to America (VISTA), a National Teacher Corps, the Job Corps, and the University Year of Action, though some of these programs faded as the Vietnam War dominated the national agenda.

In the years between 1969 and 1989, numerous proposals at the federal level to create other national service programs were unsuccessful, although states and grassroots movements established the following promising ventures. In 1970, the Youth Conservation Corps provided 38,000 young people ages fourteen through eighteen with the opportunity to help in summer environmental programs. In 1976, Governor Jerry Brown established the first statewide youth corps, the California Conservation Corps. In 1978, the Young Adult Conservation Corps created small corps in many states.

As these initiatives were launched, private corporations, such as Ford and Mott, were instrumental in providing funding and support for building the service movement. In 1984, networking among the various service "streams" began to increase dramatically and service-learning programs began spreading in K–12 schools and higher education (Minnesota Office on Volunteer Services, 1993). Through the founding of the Campus Outreach Opportunity League in 1984, Campus Compact in 1985, the National Association of Service and Conservation Corps in 1985, and Youth Service America, also in 1985, the youth service movement was building momentum. By the late 1980s, governors of twenty states had started initiatives for statewide youth service programs (Conrad and Hedin, 1989).

Then, in 1989, President George Bush established an Office of National Service in the White House and the much publicized Points of Light Foundation to promote volunteerism. W. K. Kellogg and DeWitt Wallace-Reader's Digest Foundations joined the growing list of private corporations supporting service initiatives. In 1990, Congress passed the National and Community Service Act that created the Commission on National and Community Service to provide program funds, training, and technical assistance to states and communities to develop and expand service opportunities for citizens of all ages. President Bush and Congress approved seventy-three million dollars for program activities in 1992 and a similar amount in 1993. Over 25 percent of these funds went to K–12 and higher-education service programs.

In 1993, with strong bipartisan support, President Clinton and Congress passed the National and Community Service Trust Act. The Act established the Americorps program to provide opportunities for college-age young people to serve their communities and garner postservice educational benefits in the process. The Act also greatly increased funds allotted to states for K–12 service-learning programs, further developed the program for higher education service-learning, and subsumed related programs such as VISTA and the Older American Volunteer Programs, all under the administration of the newly established Corporation for National Service. Almost all states, with support from the Corporation, have set up state commissions on community service to oversee the various programs and fund allotments within the state.

While the term "service-learning" is a relative newcomer on the educational scene (experiential educators trace it back to the early 1970s), the notion of service in the public school curriculum was promoted by earlier scholars such as John Dewey, Hilda Taba, and Ralph Tyler (Kinsley, 1990). In concert with the youth service movement at the state and national levels, interest in the educational field for adding service-learning to the public school agenda has surged in recent years. National reports such as *Turning Points: Preparing American Youth for the Twenty-first Century* (Carnegie Council on Adolescent Development, 1989), *The Next Stage of Reform* (Education Commission of the States, 1985), and *The Forgotten Half: Pathways to Success for America's Youth and Young Families* (William T. Grant Foundation, 1988) all call for youth service initiatives. Noted contemporary educators such as Ted Sizer, Ernest Boyer, and John Goodlad have added their voices to the call; and prominent education organizations—the Association for Supervision and Curriculum Development, the Council of Chief State School Officers, and the National Association of Secondary School Principals—to name just a few—have also endorsed the idea of youth involvement in service-learning. As a result, thousands of schools, from kindergarten through high school, are infusing service in the curriculum.

WHAT ARE THE THEORETICAL RATIONALES SUPPORTING SERVICE-LEARNING IN PUBLIC SCHOOLING?

The rationales for service-learning are rooted in a concern for the development of young people socially, psychologically, and intellectually as well as in an interest in the transformation of schools and learning. Conrad (1991) posited a variety of social and cultural conditions supporting the inclusion of service-learning programs in schools. Since the mid-1960s, there has been growing concern about young people's involvement (or lack of it) in the social and political lives of their communities. "Charges of increased privatism, hedonism, and aimlessness among adolescents have become commonplace among findings that they feel powerless in relation to the larger society and have no sense of fulfilling a significant role in it" (Conrad, 1991, p. 541).

The rationale for service-learning described above is advocated by service-learning supporters labeled by Conrad and Hedin (1989) as "youth reformers." Proponents of this view offer statistics on teen pregnancy, violent crime, drug abuse, high school dropouts, and other social ills directly relevant to youth. Service-learning is seen as an effective and needed means for improving young people's values and behavior and for empowering them to develop self-confidence and self-esteem as well as to participate as valued contributors to their communities. Caskey (1991), providing an example of the "youth reformer's" views on the new vision of youth promoted through service-learning, noted that service-learning is

> a movement that calls for a shift in society's view of the nature of young people. It requires educators to recognize that young people's capacities for curiosity, playfulness, open-mindedness, flexibility, humor, sincerity, creativity, enthusiasm, and compassion uniquely qualifies them to address many critical unmet needs in society. Instead of viewing young people as passive recipients of education, as clients or consumers, service-learning suggests that we view young people as competent, capable producers and willing contributors. (pp. 18–19)

A related yet different view is taken by service-learning advocates termed "education reformers" (Conrad and Hedin, 1989). Education reformers view service-learning as an effective tool for helping young people learn more and retain more of what they learn. Educators taking this perspective are also concerned with transforming school culture and creating school communities that empower students to be lifelong learners.

While education reformers look to contemporary educators' work to support their position, theoretically their views are grounded in the legacy surrounding experiential education. Cognitive theorists beginning with Aristotle and Rousseau, and continuing from Piaget and Dewey to Coleman and Kolb have asserted that direct experience and reflection are essential to effective learning. The essential argument for the role of experience in learning is that "real learning and intellectual development occur as the individual interacts with the environment, with experience serving variously as a source and test of knowledge, a stimulus for thought, and a guard against meaningless abstraction" (Conrad, 1991, p. 544). Kolb's (1984) work, in particular, has elaborated on a sequence of events that takes place in experiential education. First, students observe or experience events, then they reflect on their experiences. Third, they develop concepts that explain the events and allow them to generalize from their experiences. Finally, they test these concepts in varied situations.

In reality, most service-learning advocates cannot be divided into just one of the two camps described here. Most supporters of service-learning believe that it is a method that supports youth development and contributes to educational reform, as well as meets important community needs.

WHAT ARE THE POTENTIAL OUTCOMES OF SERVICE-LEARNING FOR STUDENTS, SCHOOLS, AND COMMUNITIES?

Service-learning advocates maintain that there are numerous benefits for students, schools, and communities when they work together on service-learning projects. When the resources and collaborative efforts of all three are combined, the sum is more than its parts. When program leaders are aware of these potential outcomes for students, schools, and communities, they can work with others to design more effective and focused programs as well as develop evaluation plans to assess whether the outcomes were met by the program or not.

Students

Student outcomes are generally presented in three major areas: social development, psychological development, and academic learning/intellectual development (Conrad, 1991). Educators have asserted that service-learning may positively influence the following aspects of student development: academic skills, problem-solving skills, critical thinking skills, ethical development, moral reasoning ability, social responsibility, self-esteem, assertiveness, empathy, psychological development, civic responsibility, political efficacy, tolerance and acceptance of diversity, specific skill acquisition relevant to the service tasks, and career goals and knowledge (Alt and Medrich, 1994). Service-learning is often expected to have other positive effects as well, including fostering a decrease in discipline problems, increased enthusiasm for school, and students serving as positive role models for other students.

The Maryland Student Service Alliance's (1992) intended, primary outcomes for students in their state-mandated service-learning programs include demonstrating all of the following:

• social and civic responsibility in service settings
• political efficacy in service settings
• proficient use of service skills
• personal development through performing service
• moral development by acting ethically in service settings
• basic academic skills in real-life situations
• increasing ability to do higher-order thinking through service
• learning by reflecting on the service experience

These outcomes are just one programmatic example reflecting the three major areas of student development associated with service-learning programs: social, psychological, and academic.

Schools

The potential positive outcomes of service-learning involvement extend beyond student effects to the teacher-student relationship, teachers' collegial relationships, and the atmosphere of the whole school. As students are empowered to take on new leadership roles, a consequent shift is created in the teacher's role. Teachers of service-learning tend to become guides, mentors, or facilitators; the quality of the student-teacher relationship changes as well when students recognize that they are partners in learning, and not passive recipients of factual knowledge. As partnerships are realized, some students may experience an increased respect for adults and increased comfort working with them (McPherson, 1989).

Teachers' collegial relationships with each other may also undergo a shift when working together on service-learning activities. In many schools, teachers are isolated in their work, perhaps only briefly discussing their classroom happenings on coffee breaks or in the staff lunchroom. When teachers collaborate on service-learning projects, they come together to engage in meaningful work that reinforces shared values and goals. Teachers often report a deep sense of satisfaction due to the collaborative nature of service-learning activities. If many teachers in the school are involved in the service-learning program, the atmosphere in the school can change to become more open, positive, and empowering for students. Recent studies have found that service-learning changes the quality of relationships and the learning environment for students, and in so doing, enhances the atmosphere of the school as a whole (Brill, 1994; Shumer, 1994b).

A third outcome for schools is the relationship formed with the community. School-community partnerships formed in service-learning programs can be very beneficial for the school. Most communities provide excellent resources for student learning. Community members may be more willing to come to the school to help with educational and social service efforts when links have been established initially through service-learning activities. Caskey (1991) described yet another important aspect of enhanced school-community relations.

> With only one fourth of American households currently having school-aged children, it is especially critical that schools find additional means to establish close ties to the community. The contributions that students make through service enhance public appreciation of young people and increase support for public education. (p. 31)

Communities

Communities benefit in many ways from students' contributions through service-learning programs. First, individuals in need receive direct aid. Seniors living alone get their lawns raked and snowy driveways shoveled. Headstart children increase their reading skills as they are tutored by older children. Immigrants are coached to pass citizenship tests. The environment is enhanced as well; parks are cleaned, trees are planted, river water quality is tested.

While these direct outcomes are perhaps the most visible, there are many other benefits for communities as well. Agencies benefit from the new ideas, enthusiasm, and extra help offered by student volunteers. In the long term, students come to see themselves as community-minded citizens and communities come to see youth as one of their most valuable resources. If service becomes an enjoyable habit and an important aspect of youth's identity, it is likely they will continue to serve their communities. As they mature, they many expand on their school-based activities to include voting, running for office, serving on agency boards, and other meaningful involvement in the social and political life of the community.

Spotlight on Outcomes

Develop a list of 10–12 intended outcomes for an environmental service-learning project included in a high school ecology class. Imagine that the project involves study and testing of a local river and is part of a schoolwide service-learning program. Which specific outcomes for students, the school, and the community would be most appropriate for this project?

WHAT CAN RESEARCH TELL US ABOUT THE EFFECTIVENESS OF SERVICE-LEARNING PROGRAMS?

Research on K–12 service-learning programs has focused almost exclusively on student outcomes. While a widespread belief exists that youth benefit in numerous ways from service experiences, Alt and Medrich (1994) noted that there is little firm evidence regarding student benefits. However, some areas of service-learning research have revealed optimistic trends. Before examining the research on K–12 service-learning programs below, the limitations of research on service-learning in general should be considered.

Conrad (1991) asserted that the primary difficulty in assessing the effects of community participation is that the term encompasses a wide variety of practices with an even wider variety of purposes. Although Conrad was writing about community-based programs in general, his critique is also valid for service-learning programs. Related challenges include: different effects from different types of participation, difficulty in identifying the appropriate independent variables and appropriate research instruments, outcomes focused on broad and stable personal characteristics that do not change quickly and are not measured easily using surveys or questionnaires, and the likely atypicality of participants in voluntary programs (Conrad, 1991). In addition, researchers may look for specific outcomes or many outcomes that a program was not designed to achieve. Relatively brief timing and duration of the service-learning program may make significant gains for students less likely than in longer programs, regardless of the objectives (Alt and Medrich, 1994).

In spite of all these problems, the limited research on service-learning has produced some promising, if inconclusive, findings in regards to student outcomes. A summary follows of the research on students in K–12 service-learning programs in three key outcome areas: (1) academic and intellectual development, (2) social and personal development, and (3) political efficacy and participation.

Academic and Intellectual Development

Research evidence for the impact of service-learning on academic learning and intellectual development is neither extensive nor conclusive. Conrad (1991) noted that researchers studying experiential programs have tended to steer away from the acquisition of facts and concepts as a focus of inquiry. A few studies, however, particularly those involving cross-age tutoring, reveal some promising effects on academic development.

In a meta-analysis of thirty-nine studies on tutoring, Cohen, Kulik, and Kulik (1982) found that students benefited from having tutored, though the differences were not large. In another metaanalysis of tutoring studies, Hedin (1987) also found tutors gained academically. Conrad and Hedin (1982) reported that students in a service program displayed better problem solving abilities than comparison students. Wilson (1975) found that students involved in political or social action became more open-minded. Shumer (1994b) noted that students in a community-based learning program improved their attendance and school grades, as compared with a control group. Williams (1991) concluded that students who participated in fieldwork had higher grade-point averages at the completion of their program.

While general knowledge of students performing service does not usually differ from that of control students, it appears that service does not reduce knowledge, even though students are spending less time in the classroom (Alt and Medrich, 1994). This finding is supported by the conclusion drawn by two studies completed during the 1970s: Engaging students in active learning outside the traditional classroom had no negative effects on academic achievement (Urie, 1971; University of Pittsburgh, 1975).

Social and Personal Development

A 1984 survey of high school–based volunteer program coordinators found that enhancing student's personal development was the most commonly cited program goal (Newmann and Rutter, 1986). Students who did volunteer work in eight exemplary school-based programs reported that social and personal outcomes such as productive relationships with others, feeling appreciated for helping others, teaching a new skill, and winning a child's trust were among the program's main benefits (Rutter and Newmann, 1989). In a study of twenty-seven school-sponsored community programs (including but not limited to service-learning), Conrad and Hedin (1981) found modest gains in social and personal responsibility as measured by the Social and Personal Responsibility Scale. Newmann and Rutter (1983), using a modified version of the scale, also found modest gains. Their overall finding was that community service programs did have a positive impact on students' sense of social responsibility and sense of personal competence as contrasted with comparison groups. Hamilton and Fenzel (1988) found significant gains on the social responsibility subscale but not on the personal responsibility subscale, though gains were greater for students involved in community improvement projects versus for those working in a child care program.

Proponents of service-learning argue that placing students in challenging situations where they will need to face real problems and consequences is an effective means of promoting personal growth. Conrad (1991) concluded that "the most consistent finding of studies of participatory programs is that these experiences do tend to increase self-esteem and promote personal development" (p. 543). Overall, the literature suggests that personal and social development are the best documented outcomes of secondary school sponsored community service programs (Conrad and Hedin, 1989; Giles and Eyler, 1994; Williams, 1991). Alt and Medrich (1994) noted that while studies of voluntary service programs tend to show only small increases in self-confidence and improved self-image, "these data confirm a consensus of opinion expressed by teachers and students about positive gains in this area" (p. 9). While not every study has been positive, numerous studies have noted gains in self-esteem, competence, or general self-worth (Beister, Kershner, and Blair, 1978; Conrad and Hedin, 1982, 1989; Hamilton and Fenzel, 1988; Hedin, 1987; Newmann and Rutter, 1983; Sager, 1973; Sprinthall and Mosher, 1978; University of Pittsburgh, 1975; Urie, 1971). Conrad and Hedin (1989) also noted that reviews of studies found evidence that moral and ego development are enhanced through service activities.

Political Efficacy and Participation

The findings on whether or not service-learning enhances political efficacy are mixed (Alt and Medrich, 1994; Furco, 1994). A study of high school students did not credit participation in service with changes in political efficacy, plans for future participation, or future social/institutional affiliation (Newmann and Rutter, 1983). Conrad and Hedin (1982) found, however, that students in service-learning programs showed larger gains in valuing community involvement than control students, though no indication was given of the magnitude of these changes and whether differences were significant or not. Hamilton and Zeldin (1987) found that students who volunteered in local government internships increased their knowledge of local government and their sense of competence in political work more than students in traditional classes focused on local government. Using Campbell's Scale of Political Efficacy, Wilson (1974) found that students in a community-based alternative school who engaged in political and social action gained in political efficacy. Button (1973) found that students who did fieldwork regarding the political structure of their city gained in political efficacy and became more interested in politics. Corbett (1977), however, in a study of a year-long community service program, did not find gains in political efficacy. One reasonable hypothesis regarding all of the political efficacy findings cited here is that certain types of programs (i.e., those focused on political issues or local government involvement) may be more likely than other types of programs to lead to increased political efficacy.

In regard to youth volunteer activities leading to future voluntary participation in the community, a series of studies by Independent Sector revealed that early community service experience is a strong predictor of volunteering for both teens and adults (Hodgkinson and Weitzman, 1992a, 1992b). Furthermore, the role of schools is critical. Among teens who reported that their schools encouraged voluntary service, 75 percent volunteered. "Regardless of race or ethnic background, if individuals are asked to volunteer they are more than three times as likely to volunteer than if they are not asked" (Schervish, Hodgkinson, Gates, and Associates, 1995). Another national survey of youth views further affirms the importance of the schools' role in encouraging community service-learning. Many teens indicated that they do not volunteer because they do not know how to get involved (74%) or simply are never asked (60%) (Wirthlin Group, 1995). As in the Independent Sector studies, the Wirthlin Group (1995) found much higher involvement in youth community service when schools placed emphasis on its importance.

Summary of the Research

Conrad (1991) notes that despite the discrepancies or vague support for certain outcomes, there is one salient finding of virtually every study of service-learning programs: "Participants, their teachers, their parents, and their community supervisors overwhelmingly agree that their programs were worthwhile, useful, enjoyable, and powerful learning experiences" (p. 545). It appears that the strongest findings are in the areas of self-esteem and further community service. Certainly, more and better research studies are needed on all aspects of service-learning programs, including the effects on schools and communities. Conrad (1991) concluded his review of the research by offering an adage from an old cartoon: "Of course none of the arguments are valid, but, taken collectively, they present a body of evidence too considerable to be disregarded." This is perhaps, for the present, the most appropriate judgment of the research on community service-learning.

HOW DOES SERVICE-LEARNING FIT WITH OTHER EDUCATIONAL REFORM EFFORTS?

Service-learning is an important movement in current efforts to reform public schooling in the United States. Reforms being implemented in many schools—such as site-based management, teacher empowerment, cooperative learning, shared decision making, authentic assessment, and portfolios, to name a few—are wholly consistent with service-learning. In chapters 9, 10, and 11, the authors note how service-learning supports reform efforts in the areas of school as community, constructivist teaching and learning, middle school philosophy, integrated curriculum, higher-order thinking, multiple intelligences, problem-based learning, and school-to-work transition.

McPherson (1989) contrasted early reform efforts' (late 1970s and early 1980s) emphasis on basic skills with the broader perspective prevalent beginning in the mid-1980s. According to McPherson, the current wave of reform includes:

• expanded pedagogy, providing equal access to education for all students
• curriculum that focuses on students' understanding "why" as well as "how" they learn

• an emphasis on higher-order thinking skills
• engaged, hands-on learning so that students retain what they learn
• flexible use of time in schools
• focusing on the individual school as the locus of decision making and change
• development of a collegial, participatory environment among students, staff, and community (McPherson, 1989).

Reviewing the definition and components of service-learning, it immediately becomes apparent how service-learning has the potential to foster all of these reform efforts.

PUTTING IT ALL TOGETHER

Service-learning is a comprehensive teaching strategy with great potential for bringing about positive outcomes for students, schools, and communities. Given the legacy of service in our democratic society and public schooling, service-learning has an important role to play in meeting the needs of communities and developing civic-minded youth. In concert with other progressive reform efforts, service-learning has the potential to bring down the wall between the school and the community, to shift our view of youth from recipients of information to creators of learning, and to transform the role of teachers in public schools across the United States.

While further research is needed to document the effects of service-learning programs on students and their communities, educators are hopeful that the promise of service-learning will revitalize both our public schools and the participatory republic in which they exist.

Challenge Activity
Write a five-minute speech that you would deliver to a group of your choice (school board, teachers' faculty meeting, classroom of high school students, community agency members, or parents) advocating service-learning. How would you define the concept? What rationale would you offer for the inclusion of service-learning in public schooling? If possible, deliver your speech to a group or your classmates.

Chapter 2

Preparation

Rahima C. Wade

Preparation is the most important aspect of quality service-learning programs. When program leaders take the time to plan each phase of the project with students and community members who will be involved, the project has a much greater likelihood of being both a successful service activity and a productive learning experience for students. Approaches to preparing service-learning projects are as diverse as the schools, individuals, and services involved. There are, however, some basic components that should be addressed in the preparation phase of most service-learning projects. The components addressed in this chapter include: choosing a project, developing an overall plan, reaching out to others, orienting students and the community, handling logistics, and evaluation. Basic components covered in subsequent chapters include: collaboration (chapter 3), service (chapter 4), curriculum integration (chapter 5), reflection (chapter 6), and building support for service-learning programs (chapter 7). Program leaders will want to read chapters 3–8 before engaging in the planning process described in this chapter.

WHAT ARE SOME APPROACHES
TO CHOOSING A PROJECT?

There are many ways to go about choosing a service-learning project. It is wise to begin with considering the parameters for the scope of the experience (Stephens, 1995). Program leaders might decide on the duration of the project, how much time will be devoted to the project on a daily or weekly basis, and which curriculum objectives are to be integrated with the service experience. In addition, some may find it helpful to consider early on the funds available for the project and the desired physical location (school site, local neighborhood, given areas of the town or city). Program leaders should endeavor to set boundaries that help participants design a workable project, yet do not limit participants' creativity in implementing ideas that might not at first appear to be feasible. In general, setting just a few parameters with regard to time and perhaps curriculum or location should suffice.

After the boundaries have been defined, all participants in the project should be involved in choosing the specific service activity. In general, there appear to be three approaches teachers take to choosing a specific service activity (Wade, 1995a). The first approach involves beginning with a community need or problem. This part of the preparation phase can involve considerable brainstorming and outreach activity. Students can gather information about community issues of concern through interviewing neighbors, conducting a community survey, and contacting local social service agencies. A representative of the local United Way or a volunteer action center may be able to provide a rich and varied perspective on community concerns.

A second approach to choosing a project begins with a curricular objective. Especially at the secondary level, program leaders may want to make sure that the service-learning project reinforces specific curricular content or skills. The curricular objective can be presented to the students along with the question How can we meet this objective through providing a service to our school or community? Students can brainstorm ideas in concert with some of the community search ideas outlined in the first approach above.

Often a program leader or student has a personal connection to a particular issue of concern. With the third approach, this connection becomes the impetus for a service-learning project. For example, in an elementary school where a student's parent had died of AIDS, a third-grade class began a service-learning project working with the local AIDS hospice. Program leaders may have a personal connection with a particular agency in the community that may lead to a productive working relationship in a service-learning project.

Whether the project choice revolves around a community issue, a curricular objective, or a personal connection, there are likely to be a number of projects proposed by students, program leaders, and community members. The next step involves actually choosing the specific project. Again, different routes may be taken. Especially with older students, program leaders may decide that different options are possible. Students could choose among those project possibilities that the planning group has deemed feasible, given the parameters for the project. If a single project completed by the group is desired, a second option involving modeling the democratic process through voting, a town meeting, or consensus decision making may be the route to take. Those involved can discuss the pros and cons for each project idea and decide on the one with the greatest potential for both making a difference in the community and contributing to student learning.

WHAT SHOULD BE INCLUDED IN AN OVERALL PLAN?

After participants have decided on a project, the next step is to develop an overall plan. If possible, all participants in the project, including community agency members and some service recipients, should have input. Inclusion of the different perspectives provided by these participants will ensure a project that meets both community and student needs (see chapter 3 for a detailed discussion on collaboration). The group that develops the plan should not be too large but should include key players in the project, their representatives, or both. For example, a middle school project planning team might consist of the three teachers who will be participating, an agency member, an agency client, and two or three students.

The plan serves as an overall skeletal structure for the project; it is a blueprint for the steps the project will follow and should be referred to often by the project participants. The plan should provide an overview of the basic project components: outreach, orientation, logistics (including funding), service, curriculum integration, reflection, and evaluation. Plans for celebrating the completion of the project can be included in the overall plan or developed later on (see chapter 7).

In addition to this information, a comprehensive plan will include a time line and lists of the outcomes and responsibilities for the project participants. McPherson (1991) recommends using a table format, encompassing both the time line and responsibilities, to indicate each task (What?), when it will be completed (When?), and who will be responsible (Who?).

Caskey (1991) notes that there are important outcomes in service-learning projects for students, teachers, schools, and communities (see list in chapter 1). Project participants should work together on specifying the outcomes for each group. For example, outcomes might be designated for students in the areas of academic skill development, growth in social responsibility, and the development of civic attitudes. Teacher and school outcomes could include the incorporation of service-learning in teachers' repertoire of teaching strategies, an increase in staff collegiality, or improved school-community relations. Community outcomes should specify the contributions students will make to problems or needs in the school or larger community. Once completed and agreed on, the list of outcomes should serve as an organizer for evaluating the success of the service-learning project.

HOW IS REACHING OUT TO OTHERS
PART OF THE PREPARATION PROCESS?

Depending on the project, the planning group may need to include outreach to administrators, parents, students, community agencies, and mem-

bers of the larger community. Outreach at this point in the preparation process may serve to recruit program participants, gain needed approval or support for the project, or inform interested parties about upcoming service
activities.

Some service-learning projects involve citizens of the community not
directly connected with a specific agency. For example, an intergenerational
project might need to recruit widely for seniors willing to come to the school to
participate in an oral history project. Or a project focused on developing minority youth leaders might require the participation of business, government, and
other community leaders of color. Many service-learning programs recruit students in the school to participate in mentoring, tutoring, or other service activities.

Outreach efforts are particularly important with projects that require
administrative approval. For example, planting trees on the school grounds or
at a public park will likely require approval from the appropriate authorities. If
the project requires additional funds from the school district, it is important to
ascertain whether the resources are available before beginning work on the
project. Program planners may also want to inform parents early on about project activities, particularly if the work site is in a part of the community unfamiliar to the students. Informing both administrators and parents about the
nature of service-learning activities at the beginning of the project may contribute to additional types of support, such as parent volunteer time, that may
prove beneficial.

As service-learning projects are always site-specific, it is difficult if not
impossible to specify all the types of outreach necessary for any project. In general, the program planning group should consider who the key stakeholders
are likely to be for a given project; whose approval is necessary; which resistors
might be converted to assistors with advance information; and which individuals should be brought on board early to ensure project success? Reaching out
to those in the school and community who are likely to have a vested interest in
the project can help to avert potential problems, thus contributing to a greater
likelihood of project success.

WHAT TYPES OF ORIENTATION ARE NEEDED?

Service-learning projects almost always require providing orientation
for student participants. Projects that take place at community sites may also
necessitate preparing the community for the students. Orientation sessions are
often more successful if conducted collaboratively with others who have knowledge and expertise on key issues of concern. For example, in a project involving people with disabilities, program leaders might enlist the help of an agency

member, a person with a disability, students with physical challenges, and the school nurse or guidance counselor.

To contribute to both student comfort and program success, students should participate in an orientation session prior to beginning their service experience. If students will be working with a population with whom they are unfamiliar, such as nursing home residents or Headstart preschool students, an initial orientation session should focus on both stereotypes and concerns they have about the group and factual information about what they are likely to encounter when working with this population.

Students are also likely to need orientation in the specific skills they will need to successfully complete the service project. Skills in cooperation, communication, and team work may need to be taught. If students will be planting trees, building bat houses, or sewing cloth books, they will need specific instructions for completing these tasks.

The orientation session might also include opportunities to brainstorm solutions to potential problems students may encounter as they begin their service experience. What if the homeless person you are eating lunch with doesn't speak to you? What if the child you are tutoring becomes discouraged? In addition to allaying fears and averting potential pitfalls, discussing the "what ifs" associated with a project helps student participants begin the reflection process so critical to effective service-learning.

A final part of the student orientation should focus on the rules at the work site and the expectations community members hold for student participation. Program leaders should not assume that students will be familiar with an unspoken code of ethics about how to behave at the work site. Safety rules and confidentiality are two key issues that may be new to students working in the community setting.

As with every other aspect of service-learning projects, inviting student input and encouraging student ownership of the orientation process are key. Ask students to give input about the orientation being planned for them. They may have requests for factual information or concerns to discuss that might not occur to the program leader.

While orientation should be focused primarily on the student participants, it may be necessary in some cases to prepare a community agency for what to expect from the students. If a nursing home, homeless agency, or animal shelter has not previously had student volunteers, especially young ones, it will be important to provide an orientation for the volunteer coordinator at the site as to what he or she can reasonably expect from the students.

Spotlight on Orientation

Plan an orientation session for sixth graders who will be conducting oral histories with the residents of a local nursing home. What information and skills are necessary to make this project successful? Who might be involved in presenting the orientation? How will you include opportunities for students to express their current views and attitudes toward seniors?

WHAT LOGISTICAL ARRANGEMENTS NEED TO BE MADE?

Logistics for service-learning projects, commonly referred to as "nuts and bolts," vary considerably depending on the site and the type of service activity. Four logistical aspects common to many projects include: scheduling, transportation, liability, and funding. Funding is addressed in chapter 8; the other three issues are discussed here.

Scheduling

Scheduling can be a particularly thorny challenge for service-learning programs, especially at the middle and high school levels. Often secondary level classes are organized in fifty-minute blocks, an arrangement that rarely provides enough time to go out into the community, complete a service activity, and return to school in time for the next class. While elementary teachers often have greater flexibility in when to conduct community activities, they too can find that service activities tend to infringe on an already overcrowded curriculum with scheduled classes in art, music, physical education, and special education.

Collaborators on the project should share the decision-making process for scheduling service activities, otherwise school personnel could end up planning for service at a time that is unsuitable for the nursing home or the day care center. If the whole school is involved in service-learning, the staff will need to agree on a suitable arrangement. Participants should consider the wide range of scheduling options available with their accompanying strengths and weaknesses before deciding on one approach.

Many creative options exist to provide students with time for service in the school day (McPherson, 1989; Stephens, 1995). Many middle schools have adopted an interdisciplinary approach, which includes team teaching and block or flexible scheduling. Others have used a homeroom or advisory period for students to plan service-learning projects. At the high school level, classes with service components can be coupled with the beginning or ending of the school day, the lunch period, or a study hall. In this way, students have more than the fifty minutes to be off campus. Another option is to use service sites that are in the neighborhood or within walking distance of the school. An additional choice is for the school staff to designate a half day each week, a full day each month, or some other predetermined time for the whole student body to devote to service activities. An added benefit of the latter method is that teachers can use the time for planning if community members or parents supervise the students at their service sites.

If all these options seem unworkable, students could complete their service activities within the school to eliminate time needed for traveling to a service site. Even if students complete the service activities outside of the school day, teachers can still connect the service experience to academic learning by including reflection activities and related course work during class time.

Transportation

How transportation is handled can have a significant effect on the success of a service-learning program. Program leaders should plan ahead for how students will be transported to service sites, keeping in mind student safety and liability issues as well as the resources the program has that can be devoted to transportation. Conrad and Hedin (1987) offered the following options for transportation in service-learning programs:

- *Student resources*. High school students may have a car to drive and can transport others. They might also be able to take public transportation on their own.
- *School district bus*. Buses may be free during school hours if the buses are owned by the school district. In some cases, parents or teachers can drive if they have a chauffeur's license.
- *Personal cars*. Program leaders, staff, or parents with appropriate insurance coverage can transport students to service sites.
- *Minibus or van*. With school district, grant, or local service club support, some programs purchase a minibus or van specifically for use in the service-learning program. If the program is small, the van could be shared with other school or agency programs.
- *Bus tokens or fares*. Often school districts can get special rates on public transportation or provide participants with identification cards that entitle them to reduced fares.
- *Used bicycles*. A fleet of used bicycles may assist energetic students riding to nearby service sites.
- *Borrowed vehicles*. Community agencies or local businesses may have cars or vans they are willing to share with service-learning programs. School-owned driver education cars might also be available.

If none of these options appears feasible, program leaders should consider sites within walking distance of the school or focus the program on school issues.

Liability

Questions about liability, insurance, or risk management are of central concern in service-learning programs that place students out in the community, particularly in sites that involve some personal risk. Liability and insurance rules vary by state and school district, thus, program leaders will need to check on the specific aspects of these issues in their regions. Seidman and Tremper (1994) provided the following suggestions in their publication *Legal Issues for Service-Learning Programs.*

Almost all instances of legal liability involving students result from negligence; thus, this is a key concept for program leaders to understand. The law considers an action or inaction to be negligent if a reasonable person would not have acted the same way. A second important concept is duty. Schools have a duty to protect their students from harm; schools also have a duty to ensure that students engaged in service programs do not cause harm to others in the course of their service activities. They also have a duty to inform students of any risks they are aware of that may be associated with the service activities. In the case of a student's doing harm to another, liability also depends on whether the student's harmful conduct was foreseeable by the program leader or staff. Unfortunately, none of these critical concepts, that is, negligence, duty, or whether an action is foreseeable, can be defined specifically; they are all subject to interpretation by a judge or jury in a particular case.

When a school and a community agency share supervision of students in a service-learning program, liability complexities increase. Anyone injured during a service-learning activity may sue both the school and the agency, as well as specific individuals who caused or contributed to the harm. In general, the less the school is involved in a program, the less likely it is to be held liable, although there are exceptions if the school should have been more involved.

Even if the service-learning program is managed so that harm ensues, the program may not be held liable if protected by one of a number of "liability shields." Liability shields vary by state; one type is "sovereign immunity," meaning that schools cannot be sued because the act of providing education to the public constitutes a governmental function. Many states have also adopted statutes that protect volunteers from personal liability. A document that provides informed consent may also serve as a liability shield. Informed consent involves apprising parents or guardians of the risks involved in the service activity. Goldstein (1990) asserts that informed consent documents are much more useful than waivers of liability, which can easily be ignored and may create a false sense of security. All types of informed consent, waivers, and releases must be developed in accordance with state law to be legally valid.

Good service-learning program management includes risk management. Seidman and Temper (1994) recommend becoming familiar with the risk management procedures in place in the school district as well as making sure that all participants know what is expected of them, that they know how to perform their duties properly and safely, and that they know when and how to report problems or suggest changes. In general, the more guidelines that can be put in writing, the better.

Program leaders also need to check into insurance coverage for students involved in service at community sites. In some cases, an additional insurance rider may need to be purchased by the program or school district.

Understanding liability issues in regard to service-learning programs is a complex matter. Program leaders should meet with their school district's legal counsel and discuss the following:

- applicability of sovereign immunity and volunteer protection laws to the service-learning program
- waivers, participation forms, and other items designed to limit liability
- liability insurance and accident insurance for students and other individuals involved in the program
- insurance coverage for the school and any independent entity participating in the programs
- policies and procedures regarding: use of school facilities, grounds, vehicles, and equipment; course credit or stipends for participating; selection and termination of students in the program; involvement of nonschool personnel; and reporting and investigation of incidents that may lead to liability
- if collaborating with another entity: responsibilities of each party in the program; letters of agreement or contracts; and hold harmless, indemnification, and insurance arrangements

Taking the time to deal with liability issues may seem like an inconvenience, yet taking steps for risk management in the preparation phase serves to safeguard the program and should also ease the concerns of the program leader, school authorities, parents, and program participants.

WHICH EVALUATION STRATEGIES ARE SUITABLE FOR SERVICE-LEARNING PROGRAMS?

Often people conceptualize evaluation as something that is carried out at the end of a course or program. Why think about evaluation in the preparation phase? If evaluation is to fulfill its intended purpose—giving feedback to program coordinators and participants on important questions and designated outcomes—then plans for gathering this information must be made early on.

The strategies used to evaluate a service-learning program vary depending on the purposes of evaluation. Evaluation may serve to gain support for the program from the community, improve program practice, or justify continuation of the program to administrators. Program leaders should consider whether the purposes of the evaluation will be best served by collecting quantitative or qualitative data. The former involves numbers, for example of students who stayed in school or percentage gains in achievement scores. The latter focuses on participants' views of their service experience in their own words, collected either on paper or in interviews. Evaluation can be complex, involving considerable time, measures, and expertise or can be as simple as documenting the events in the program. Program leaders in university communities may want to enlist the assistance of professional researchers in designing and conducting an evaluation of the service-learning program.

For most purposes, though, evaluation can be conducted by the program planners and participants. Shumer and Berkas (1992) recommended that program leaders begin a self-directed evaluation process by asking what kind of information is needed. A related question is Who will use the information? These two questions should guide the choice of evaluation strategies and the forms in which results are shared with others. Data might be gathered about the participants in the program, the people or environment affected by the service activity, products produced by participants, or organizations involved with the program (Shumer and Berkas, 1992). The evaluation should be clearly connected to the outcomes specified in the overall plan.

As part of the evaluation, program leaders and participants should document their service-learning activities. In chapter 8, I present detailed information on keeping track of the service-learning program through a paper trail, logs, journals, portfolios, photos, videos, and other "artifacts" of the program. Documentation allows others to get an insider's view into the project, to learn who was involved and how the events unfolded. While documentation is an important first step in evaluation, additional strategies are usually needed to assess whether the desired outcomes for the program were met or not. Following are additional strategies often used in evaluating service-learning programs. Helpful details on conducting program evaluations are found in Michael Quinn Patton's (1989) *Qualitative evaluation methods* and Worthen and Sanders' (1987) *Educational evaluation: Alternative approaches and practical guidelines.*

• *Qualitative evaluation of documentation data.* Much of the data collected in the documentation process can be analyzed using qualitative research methods. For example, students' reflection essays or journals could be examined for key themes such as learning about self, learning about others, and attitudes toward service. Of critical importance is a systematic approach to analyzing the data, rather than random selection of positive comments.

- *Quantitative evaluation of documentation data.* Using quantitative methods, program leaders can determine numbers of hours spent on service, students and community members involved in the program, gains in achievement levels for program participants, as well as many other types of desired information. While qualitative approaches are equally valid, often "hard numbers" can provide skeptics with convincing evidence that the program is worth maintaining.
- *Surveys and questionnaires.* Surveys and questionnaires are the most convenient strategy for gathering similar information from large groups of people. Pre- and postsurveys can be administered to students, service recipients, or agency members to assess changes in knowledge, attitudes, or services as a result of the project.
- *Interviews.* Interviewing individuals involved with the program will often lead to more in-depth information than a survey can provide. Interviewing, however, is considerably more time consuming. Program leaders should consider interviewing key participants, such as the volunteer coordinator at the community agency, as well as a small sample of student participants.

PUTTING IT ALL TOGETHER

Preparation is perhaps the most important aspect of a service-learning program. In the preparation phase, program leaders, participants, and their community collaborators choose a service-learning project and develop an overall plan that includes a time line, responsibilities of all participants, and desired outcomes for students, the school, and the community. Constructing an effective and cohesive plan necessitates the consideration of all the basic components of service-learning programs. In this chapter, I highlighted scheduling, transportation, logistics, and evaluation. With carefully conceived plans, service-learning program participants are likely to have productive learning experiences and to provide valuable services to the school or community.

Challenge Activity
Develop a plan for an elementary level service-learning project working with a local animal shelter. Fifth-grade students will be exercising the dogs on Friday mornings at the shelter, making animal treats at school, and conducting a neighborhood campaign for keeping pets safe and healthy. The project will be conducted over a three-month period; the animal shelter is approximately

five miles from the school. Who should comprise the planning team? Be sure to include in your plan outcomes, responsibilities, and a time line for the project activities. How are the logistical issues in this chapter relevant to this project? What evaluation strategies will you use to assess student learning and community benefits?

Chapter 3

Collaboration

Rahima C. Wade

Collaboration is an essential aspect of service-learning projects. School-based projects require collaboration among teachers, staff, and students. If project activities are carried out at a community site, working cooperatively with community agency members and clients is critical to the success of the project. Collaboration is only effective, however, when there is give and take, when working together benefits everyone involved. Conrad and Hedin (1987) asserted that while schools or community agencies can offer high-quality service-learning experiences for youth on their own, neither can do the job as well as when they work together.

As an example, Conrad and Hedin (1987) cited a national program in which Junior League adult volunteers work with teams of high school students to design community projects. The Junior League volunteer, with knowledge of the community and experience in volunteerism, helps students launch new projects or get involved in existing ones. The teens' expertise lies in knowing their peers and developing effective recruitment strategies for involving other high school students. The teacher integrates the students' experiences with their academic programs and ensures that students receive academic credit for their work.

The concept of collaboration often gets confused with cooperation and coordination. Mattessich and Monsey (1992) distinguished between these three terms and noted that collaboration indicates a more durable and pervasive relationship. They defined collaboration as:

> a mutually beneficial and well-defined relationship entered into by two or more organizations to achieve common goals. The relationship includes a commitment to: a definition of mutual relationships and goals; a jointly

47

developed structure and shared responsibility; mutual authority and accountability for success; and sharing of resources and rewards. (p. 7)

While collaboration provides many benefits to those involved, working together effectively is a complex challenge. In this chapter, I will discuss the many reasons to engage in collaboration, consider the potential collaborators in service-learning programs, and explore the changes in collaborative efforts over time. The chapter will conclude with an example of both the pitfalls and benefits of collaboration with two community agencies in an intergenerational service-learning program.

WHY SHOULD WE COLLABORATE ON SERVICE-LEARNING PROGRAMS?

Collaborating on service-learning activities holds many benefits for program participants, community agencies, and service recipients. Of central importance is the fact that service-learning activities should be responsive to the needs and interests of the community agencies or individuals for whom the service is intended. If teachers and students develop service-learning projects without the input of those the project is intended to help, the activities may not be appropriate. In addition, if program leaders want students to work *with* rather than *for* others—from the perspective of solidarity rather than charity—collaboration is essential. Therefore, the first reason for collaborating is to assure that service-learning projects are truly democratic. All those involved—those who are serving as well as those being served—should have a voice in the planning and conduct of the project activities.

Because collaboration takes time and extra effort, it is important to understand the variety of benefits that can accrue from working together. For teachers and students working on service-learning projects, collaborating provides skills, information, resources, and technical assistance necessary to carry out a service that meets a real community need. For community agencies, service-learning programs can provide publicity for the agency and help meet client needs that cannot be met by paid staff.

For both groups, collaboration can contribute to efficient use of time, resources, and people power, thus making services to others more effective (Mattessich and Monsey, 1992). With careful planning, responsibilities can be divided among all those involved to match capabilities and interests to specific tasks and to get more done in less time. Working with others widens our perspectives on community issues and provides a morale boost for long term change efforts. Collaboration can also help us pool important information and enhance our ability to share scarce resources. Practical ways of building meaningful ties between agencies and school-based service-learning programs include labor swaps (working on each other's projects), joint newsletters, shared training sessions, cohosted fund-raising efforts, and joint recognition events. Those who have studied collaboration note that often the process increases quality results, leads to creative ways to overcome obstacles, and has great potential for solving many difficult community problems (Gray, 1989; Mattessich and Monsey, 1992).

WHO ARE THE POTENTIAL COLLABORATORS IN A SERVICE-LEARNING PROGRAM?

Service-learning program leaders should cast a wide net when considering all the potential collaborators on a service-learning project. Of course, the specific individuals involved will vary depending on the nature of the project and the issue or concern being addressed. In general, collaborators can be found in the school, in the school district, in the school's neighborhood, and in the local community.

Collaborators in the School

In addition to the teacher or program leader involved, a primary group of collaborators should be the student participants. Engendering student input and ownership of the project is essential to its success. Students of all ages can offer their perspectives on community issues, brainstorm ideas for projects they would be interested in carrying out, and help to recruit other students or parents to help. Students can also be instrumental in helping to document and evaluate the program as well as in assisting with fund-raising and publicity efforts. Involving students in the planning and ongoing decision making of a project is one way to model the democratic process in the classroom. Through their participation, students can learn the skills of public talk: creative thinking, listening, negotiating, problem solving, and decision making.

It is likely that there are others in the school who will be interested in collaborating on a service-learning project as well. Think about what aspects of the service-learning program are directly relevant to other teachers, staff, or administrators in the school. For example, a school custodian might help with a recycling project or a school counselor could help prepare students for their first visit to a nursing home. In a health related project, the school nurse may be a valuable resource. If the service-learning project has learning goals relevant for a variety of subject areas, other teachers may be interested in taking advantage of the opportunities for learning their subject matter through service. Art and music teachers can also provide needed ideas for community or school-based projects. If your school has a service club or student council, these student groups may be interested in helping with the project.

If the project will involve publicity in the local community, the school principal should contribute to the effort. As the person most responsible for relations between the school and the community, the principal can facilitate community contacts. Principals can also lead their staff in goal setting, develop a schoolwide focus on service, or encourage teachers to integrate service in the curriculum. McPherson (1991) maintains that the vision and leadership of the principal are central to the effectiveness of a service-learning program (see chapter 16 for further information of the role of principals and other administrators in a service-learning program).

Collaborators in the School District

Many school districts have coordinators at the district level who can be instrumental in the successful coordination of service-learning projects. In particular, the coordinators of community education, school volunteers, or business partnerships may provide assistance with contacting community agencies or individuals who would like to be involved in the program.

Some school districts hire coordinators to focus solely on the administration of a service-learning program. A service-learning coordinator can provide teacher training; connect teachers with community agencies; coordinate the scheduling, transportation, and logistical aspects of service-learning projects; and work on long-term fund-raising and institutionalization of the program. Teachers working in a program with a service-learning coordinator have attested to how valuable this individual can be when trying to carry out service-learning activities in the midst of a busy school day (Wade, 1995d).

Superintendents and school board members can also be key players in a districtwide service-learning program. Their support may be helpful for getting a program started and essential for funding and continuation of the program. Superintendents are in a central position to advocate for a districtwide policy on infusing service in the curriculum or incorporating learner outcomes related to service in district outcome goals (McPherson, 1991).

Collaborators in the School's Neighborhood

Parents are an often untapped resource for service-learning programs. Research has shown that parental support and involvement enhance student success in schools (e.g., Henderson, 1989). While parents are often involved in their children's education in the elementary years, they usually become more disengaged from their children's schooling as students grow older (Buchen and Fertman, 1994). Parent involvement opportunities at the middle and high school levels occur less frequently and are of lower quality, according to parents

(Dauber and Epstein, 1993). Involvement with service-learning activities offers parents of students at all levels opportunities to contribute to the community as well as to their children's learning.

Parents can help with service-learning projects through simple tasks such as providing snacks, transporting students to community sites, and assisting with newsletters, fund-raising, or recognition events. Parents with expertise on the issue addressed by the service-learning project or community connections engendered through their jobs or volunteer work can provide valuable assistance in the planning stages of a service-learning project. Program leaders should ask students to think about the contributions their parents might make to the service-learning program and then follow up by inviting their assistance. (See chapter 20 for further information on the role of parents in service-learning programs.)

Schools can take many steps toward being a welcoming environment for parent involvement. A parent resource center in the school that provides a small space for parent volunteers to gather, socialize, hang up their coats, or take a coffee break can be one such effort. Find out what parents need and try to provide it. For example, find out when interested parents can get off work for a few hours to help with a community site visit and then schedule the event around their availability. Do some parents need child care for young children while they volunteer? Do others need small tasks they can complete at home in the evening after working all day? Communication coupled with flexibility and creative ideas will enable program leaders to structure many opportunities for parent participation in service-learning activities.

Individuals and agencies in the local neighborhood also can play a key role in programs. Have students conduct a survey of neighborhood residents to assess both skills individuals have to offer and neighborhood problems that might form the nucleus of a project. Students should also take a "walking tour" of the school neighborhood to find out about nearby community agencies. Projects that take place within close proximity to the school can diminish some of the challenges in service-learning activities with transportation, liability and scheduling.

Collaborators in the Local Community

Collaboration in the local community often begins with the attempt to locate social service agencies or volunteer opportunities. A catalogue or listing of these agencies can often be found in the phone book or obtained from a local organization specializing in tracking opportunities for service and recruiting volunteers. This organization, likely to be labeled a Volunteer Bureau or Voluntary Action Center, is a good starting point for program leaders who want a comprehensive resource that includes a variety of types of social service agencies. If your community does not have a voluntary action center, information on local agencies and volunteer opportunities might be available from the public library, the town hall, the county health and welfare council, or the local United Way.

Conrad and Hedin (1987) listed a variety of other groups and individuals that may provide valuable information at the planning stage for service-learning activities. They include city or statewide human service networks (e.g., state association of retarded citizens, council on aging, day care association, mental health association), service clubs (e.g., Rotary, Lions, Kiwanis, League of Women Voters), religious organizations, or public employees (e.g., mayor, city council, social worker, county extension agent). All of these individuals and groups can provide information on needs in the community and options for youth service activities. They can also become key players in the design and conduct of service-learning projects.

It is important to choose agency members with whom to collaborate who have a sincere interest in working with students and teachers and who value the notion of youth involvement in service-learning. After one or more such agencies have been identified, program leaders must identify who in the agency will be directly involved in the service-learning project. If agency clients will benefit from the service, one or more individuals representing this group should be involved in the design and conduct of the project. If the agency has a volunteer coordinator, that person is also a likely choice. If a parent, student, or program leader has a personal contact within the agency, it may be best to start with that person.

Private sector involvement can also enhance the success of a service-learning project. Many banks and businesses are always on the lookout for community activities they can donate funds or personnel time to support. Some businesses require their workers to donate so many hours to community service or use a certain percentage of company profits for community development. Even small grocery or department stores may contribute needed items or offer school discounts for service-related activities. Through such activities, these businesses realize that they stand to gain at least as much as they give, through positive public relations in the community.

In some school districts, businesses develop positive relationships within a school district by forming partnerships with individual schools. A business partner might provide financial, material, and personnel resources for a collaborative project between the business and the school. For example, a business partnership between a bank and an elementary school might involve bank executives coming to the school to help elementary students set up a bank account for their service-learning fundraising efforts. Espinoza (1988) notes that businesses have a vested interest in such collaborations. "Employers hold a great deal of power over the resources that enable families and schools to work together for the improvement of children's education. If that power is exercised in positive ways now, it will pay high dividends later in the form of a more skilled work force" (Espinoza, 1988, p. 62).

Spotlight on Collaborators

Who might be involved in collaborating on an intergenerational program for middle school students? Which individuals in the school and school district might contribute needed expertise? Which agencies or individuals in the local neighborhood could be involved? Which businesses, agencies, or individuals in the local community might provide support, information, and assistance with resources? Brainstorm a list of all the potential collaborators in the program.

HOW DO PROGRAM LEADERS APPROACH COMMUNITY AGENCIES WITH WHOM THEY WANT TO COLLABORATE?

Who to contact is an important strategic decision. If the program leader knows someone who works in the agency, they should begin with that person. While there are no rules about who to approach, eventually the support of both the agency members directly involved and the person in charge of the agency is needed. Conrad and Hedin (1987) recommended that if program leaders sense there may be hesitancy to involve youth in agency efforts, they should downplay their interest in a long term collaboration initially and focus instead on arranging a tour or visit for a student group to the agency site. The visit might help the program leader and students learn more about the agency and its needs, meet key staff people, and begin to build a positive relationship.

In general, it is best to approach an agency with ideas about what the service-learning program can offer them, rather than what the agency will provide. While eventually program leaders will need to make sure that the collaboration is effective for everyone involved, they can begin by addressing the needs or concerns of the agency and how student service can help. Most community agency members are overworked; they need to believe that a service-learning project will benefit their clients, especially if the collaboration will take time and effort on their part.

Program leaders should ask them about their needs and problems before trying to promote a specific project. This is especially important when seeking collaboration with an elementary school group. Agency members might balk at the question, How can elementary age students help your agency? thinking that there is no meaningful contribution that can be made by students at such a young age. Even if program leaders are inquiring about service opportunities for older youth, agency members may respond with limited offers to help with indirect service, such as mass mailings, or fund-raising efforts.

A better approach, then, is to inquire about unmet needs in the agency and then take some time to brainstorm with students about possible ways they could help. Seek ideas that meet agency needs but also allow for creativity and challenge on the part of the students. If possible, youth are likely to benefit more from activities that involve direct contact with others. If program leaders approach the collaboration with a win-win attitude—that both agency and student needs can be met within a given project—they are more likely to be successful. Once program leaders have a few possible projects in mind, they can call the agency member back and propose one or more of the ideas.

Unfortunately, it is impossible to predict how a specific community agency member will respond to a request to collaborate. Some agency members are hesitant to work with youth if they have not previously done so or are overwhelmed with trying to meet the needs of their clients and can't envision taking time for a collaborative service-learning project. Other agency members may be thrilled at the offer for assistance. A few years ago, when I contacted the director of the local animal shelter about possible collaboration with school groups on service-learning projects, she stated enthusiastically, "I've been waiting for this call for fifteen years!"

Regardless of the agency member's level of interest, program leaders shouldn't ask for too much at first. Program leaders should "test the waters" to see if this individual or agency is truly interested in collaborating and if those involved will follow through on agreed on tasks in a timely and efficient manner. (See chapter 19 for further information on the role of the community agency member in a service-learning program).

HOW DOES COLLABORATION ON SERVICE-LEARNING PROJECTS CHANGE OVER TIME?

Cairn and Kielsmeier (1991) present three stages of collaboration in service-learning programs: initiation, implementation, and institutionalization. A brief discussion of each of these stages will serve to illustrate the differences in collaborative activities throughout a long-term collaboration.

At the initiation stage, program planners should look for allies in and outside of the school system. They should also inform and include important decision makers early on, link the service-learning program to high-profile needs in the school and community, develop a clear plan and vision to guide the program, and secure administrative support.

Shared responsibility and decision making characterize the implementation stage. Community members, program leaders, and students may collaborate on orientations and trainings. Responsibilities of all those involved should be carefully defined. Every attempt should be made at this stage to also involve those who are being served in the decision-making process.

At the institutionalization stage community members, program leaders, and participants seek to gain widespread support for the program. They also meet to discuss evaluation efforts and ideas for improving the program. At this stage, program leaders may want to encourage community agencies to take on a larger commitment to the program.

An alternate view of collaboration is based on the time and energy contributed to the project by the agency. The following ideas present a continuum of involvement with a community agency, from one-time requests to ownership of the program. Program leaders could think about moving their collaboration along this continuum over time, in concert with the success engendered through working together and the specific needs of the project. The three aspects of working together on service-learning projects described below roughly correspond with Mattessich and Monsey's (1992) descriptions of cooperation, coordination, and collaboration.

1. One time requests—The agency fulfills a request for assistance with minimal time and commitment to the program.
   Program leader asks for agency materials or verbal information.
   Agency sends a guest speaker to the classroom.
   Students visit agency site to observe and learn about the agency.
2. Ongoing assistance—The agency is a cocollaborator in the program over time though the program is still seen primarily as being coordinated and owned by the school.
   Agency members and clients help to plan the project.
   Agency members provide ongoing support for the project either at the school or agency site.
   Students volunteer at the agency under agency member's supervision.
3. Ownership—The service-learning project is seen as an agency activity as well as a school generated project.
   Agency adopts the project as one of their agency activities.
   Agency contributes financial assistance or agency volunteers to the project.
   Agency coordinates the project.

A third framework for creating a collaborative relationship is promoted by the Minnesota Office on Volunteer Services (1993). The seven steps listed below embody the organization's beliefs in the importance of joint ownership of service-learning programs and the involvement of all people and organizations that will be impacted by the services youth provide.

1. Identify potential partners.
2. Identify needs that are of mutual concern.
3. Determine individuals who will serve as primary liaisons in the planning and implementation process.
4. Negotiate and agree on the desired outcomes for all involved.
5. Negotiate and agree on the expectations for all involved.
6. Determine a method for ongoing communication and evaluation.
7. Periodically redesign relationships based on changing needs and circumstances.

A fourth model for the development of a collaborative relationship is divided into four stages (Winer and Ray, 1994). They call the first stage "Envision results by working individual to individual." This initiation phase involves bringing people together, setting up a plan for meetings that builds trust, confirming a shared vision, and specifying desired results from the collaboration. The second stage, "Empower ourselves by working individual to organization," includes confirming organizational roles in the collaboration, setting up a process for resolving conflicts that arise, and organizing the collaborative effort through determining roles, deciding about staffing, and sharing resources. The second stage also involves supporting the members by establishing a decision making structure, creating a communications plan, and rewarding members of the team as well as others who have helped thus far.

In stage three, "Ensure success by working organization-to-organization," collaborators start to realize results from their efforts. At this stage, the focus is on managing the work, creating joint systems, evaluating the results, and renewing the team's effort through retiring or adding new members and celebration. Finally, in the fourth stage, "Endow continuity by working collaboration-to-community," the team creates visibility and involves more people in the community, plans and begins to make changes in "the system," and, in some cases, ends the formal structure for the collaborative effort.

The four frameworks presented here have their differences yet they all highlight the importance of shared planning and decision making. They also illustrate how joint ownership of a service-learning program can evolve from initial collaborative efforts. While program leaders may begin their contacts with community agencies looking for someone to help them, the ultimate goal is the development of a program that is equally shared between the individuals and organizations involved. Through collaboration, program planners model the processes of collaboration while student participants learn skills in communication, cooperation, and conflict resolution vital to their future participation as citizens in our democratic society.

Spotlight on the Collaboration Process
Develop a plan for how you would approach an employee of the local Parks
and Recreation Department to work on a middle school service-learning pro-
ject involving renovation and upkeep of a nature trail in one of the city parks.
Assume that the Parks and Recreation Department has not previously been
involved with school-based service-learning programs. Who will you approach
at the department? What information or questions will you provide initially?
Map out a projected plan for how you hope the partnership will progress over
a three-year time period.

WHAT CAN BE DONE WHEN CONFLICTS DEVELOP BETWEEN PROGRAM COLLABORATORS?

Conflict is an inevitable part of life. When collaborators in service-learning programs represent the diversity of individuals involved (e.g., school personnel, students, community agency members, service recipients) there are
likely to be differing needs, views, and ideas for how to proceed with the program. Winer and Ray (1994) recommended that collaborators should expect
conflict. We all bring different histories, communication patterns, and decision making styles to a collaborative effort. If we don't pay attention to the conflicts, valuable time and energy can be diverted from agreed upon goals. "For
success, conflict cannot be about right and wrong; it must be about differences" (Winer and Ray, 1994, p. 76).

Program leaders can begin to plan for conflict by taking preventive steps
such as listening to others and establishing avenues for communication and
shared decision making. Even with great respect for differing views and the best
laid plans for communicating and making decisions, however, some conflict is
likely to ensue. Program leaders, therefore, should also be knowledgeable
about conflict resolution strategies that can be used as needed. Winer and Ray
(1994) offered many insightful ideas regarding the nature of conflict in collaborative teams. They listed as among the typical sources of conflict: power
struggles, the wrong people on the team, low trust, vague vision and focus,
ambiguous desired results and strategies, and lack of clear authority. Their
recommended approach to solving conflicts during meetings involves: revisit-
ing the purpose of the collaboration, deciding who will facilitate the process for
resolving the conflict, separating the conflict from issues of right or wrong,
making sure everyone is heard, and not burning bridges that will harm the collaboration in the long run.

Shields (1994) recommended mapping conflict through the following
procedure. Write a short title in the middle of a large sheet of paper to label the
conflict. Draw a section on the map for each of the individuals or groups who

have specific needs and concerns. List all of the needs and concerns and resist the temptation to focus immediately on solutions. After mapping the concerns in some detail, examine the map carefully. Where is further information needed? Should the problem be broken down and addressed in smaller parts? Take some time to reaffirm areas of common ground and common vision on which to build win-win solutions. Brainstorm a list of possible solutions that meets the needs and concerns of those involved, then evaluate the options together to decide which one is most suitable and mutually acceptable. Finally, formulate a plan to put the solution in action. Try it out for a set period of time and meet to reevaluate whether its working or further changes need to be made. Conflict resolution is a challenging and time consuming endeavor, yet essential when problems arise. (For additional excellent ideas on conflict resolution, see Fisher and Ury, 1981 and Kreidler, 1984).

WHAT ARE THE CHARACTERISTICS OF A SUCCESSFUL COLLABORATION?

An extensive review and analysis of the research on collaboration among human service, government, and other nonprofit agencies revealed nineteen factors that influence success (Mattesich and Monsey, 1992). Three factors relate to the collaborative environment. Collaborations are more likely to work well if the participants have a positive history of cooperation or collaboration in the community, if the collaborative group is seen as a leader in the community, and if the political leaders, opinion makers, and general public support (or at least do not oppose) the group's mission.

Factors related to membership characteristics of the collaborative team seem to be especially critical: (1) members of the group must share mutual respect, understanding, and trust; (2) the group should include representatives from each segment of the community who will be affected by its activities; (3) the group members see their collaboration as in their self-interest as well as the group's as a whole; and (4) collaborating partners show a willingness and ability to compromise.

Four factors relating to process and structure are also important: (1) members need to feel ownership of both the group's process and the outcome; (2) organizations involved in the group should include multiple layers of decision making, from upper management to clients; (3) both flexibility and adaptability in the group are important; and (4) the collaborating partners need to clearly understand their roles and responsibilities.

Two factors focus on communication in the group. First, open and frequent communication greatly contributes to success. Group members need to update each other frequently, discuss issues openly, and convey necessary information to those outside the group. Second, the team needs to establish both formal and informal communication links such as phone calls, newsletters, memos, and e-mail messages.

Making goals and objectives clear and attainable is the first of the three important factors related to purpose. Second, the partners must have or develop a shared vision for their work together. Third, the mission and goals or the approach of the group should differ, at least a little, from the mission, goals, or approach of any one of the organizations involved in the collaboration. Finally, factors related to resources include having an adequate and consistent financial base and a skilled convener to organize and facilitate meetings.

COLLABORATION IN THE REAL WORLD: THE YOUTH AND ELDERLY IN SERVICE PROGRAM

The principles and practices outlined so far in this chapter, while important, do not wholly illustrate the complexity of collaboration in a service-learning program. The following example, from my own experience during the initiation stage of the YES (Youth and Elderly in Service) integenerational program, will highlight some of the pitfalls and benefits of collaborating with community agencies.

The idea for the YES program originated in the summer of 1993. As a social studies methods professor, I was looking for a service-learning project in which to involve my preservice teachers. I wanted them to learn about the local community, to develop their skills in planning enjoyable and educational activities for children, and to experience service-learning firsthand, hopefully realizing the benefits of active citizenship, the goal of social studies instruction. At the same time, I wanted a program that would meet important needs in the local community.

After phone conversations with various community agency members, it seemed that an intergenerational program would be appropriate. I found out that the local community has a large elderly population, many of whom are living alone at home, as well as a sizable number of children from single-parent families on the waiting list at Big Brothers/Big Sisters. After conversations with the local Retired Senior and Volunteer Program (RSVP) Coordinator as well as the director at Big Brothers/Big Sisters (BB/BS) of Johnson County, it seemed that the YES project could meet some of their needs as well as the goals I had for my university students. I noted in my journal at the time that my contacts with the two agency members deepened my personal feeling of connection to the community and strengthened my values about the importance of trying to create change for a better world. I worked with these two individuals primarily; though I also spoke to directors of intergenerational programs in other parts of the country, read literature on such programs, and reflected on my previous experiences with intergenerational service-learning activities.

The project looked so good on paper that it was supported financially for two years by the Fund for the Improvement of Postsecondary Education (FIPSE). With FIPSE support, we could provide funds for project supplies, transportation, community agency presentations in my classes, and evaluation. The agency members and I were excited about the potential of our collaboration; the next step was recruitment of the seniors and children from single parent families who would be involved.

The RSVP director thought we could recruit the seniors easily by putting flyers under the doors of the two senior high-rise apartment buildings located in the downtown area. There were a total of 160 seniors living in the buildings and we only needed 37 for the YES project. What neither of us anticipated was that the managers of these buildings would not allow us to distribute the flyers. Posting the flyers on bulletin boards netted us only two volunteers (both of whom dropped out early on in the project).

The RSVP director provided moral support and much of her time and energy to helping me continue our recruitment effort beyond this first attempt. Early on in our planning, she realized that YES volunteers could be counted as RSVP volunteers as well. This was an ideal arrangement for both of us as the seniors' participation could be covered by RSVP's insurance and their volunteer hours could be reported in RSVP's reports. As RSVP volunteers, they were also entitled to receive the agency's mailings and were invited to annual recognition events. Organizing the program in this way also allowed both of us to share ownership and to value putting time into our collaboration.

Despite these benefits, however, recruitment was very slow going. Initially we had hoped to include isolated and homebound seniors in the project. However, senior center agency members working with homebound elderly would not give us phone numbers or mailing lists to contact them; the agency workers felt that our program would be a burdensome request that frail elderly would not be interested in. I tended to think they were right when we sent out about 100 flyers through the Home Delivered Meals program and no one responded. Finally, after hundreds of mailings and phone calls, numerous trips to retirement residences, and the additional support of a graduate student working on the project, we finally reached our goal of thirty-seven seniors. Personal meetings and phone calls with many seniors allowed us to hear their concerns and to modify the project accordingly.

Recruiting the children was an easier task, yet problematic in different ways. BB/BS caseworkers helped recruit the children for the project by going through their caseloads and choosing children they thought would do well in the YES program. While the original idea, discussed between the BB/BS director and myself, was to include only those children on the waiting list, many of the children the caseworkers chose already had a Big Brother or Big Sister. Numerous children thus remained on the waiting list without either a Big Brother or Big Sister match or participation in the YES program. At first, I felt the agency was doing these children a disservice. However, after talking with the agency director about this issue and watching the project unfold over two years, I have come to see that the caseworkers were probably right. Most of the children on the waiting list are older boys and, in general, older boys who have participated in YES have either been dissatisfied with the program or dropped out midway.

An additional difficult aspect of my collaboration with BB/BS was the screening my university students would need to undergo to work with the children from the agency. Initially, the BB/BS agency director had said that references would suffice, but eventually the BB/BS agency staff decided that the university students would need to submit their names for police record checks, a standard procedure for other BB/BS volunteers. While I was initially worried about both the expense and the outcome of the screening procedure, it has not proved especially problematic. Only a few students have been unable to participate in the program because of an arrest in their past. The benefit to having the university students go through this screening is that they are then considered volunteers for BB/BS and, along with the children, are covered by the agency's insurance while participating in YES.

LESSONS LEARNED

While the story above focuses only on the initial stage of collaboration, it serves to illustrate the complexities involved. For example, program leaders and agency members do not always agree on the best ways to structure a project. Indeed, there can be disagreement within the agency itself as there was with both the Senior Center where RSVP was housed and BB/BS of Johnson County. Agency members at both locations differed about who should be recruited; the focus of the project changed as a result. Key lessons I learned in regard to this change were to listen to community agency members' concerns carefully, to acknowledge their expertise, and to modify the program as needed.

This initial attempt at collaboration could have been greatly improved with more time and advance planning. Our efforts could have been more successful if we had taken more time at the planning stage, had staff meetings involving more community agency members, consulted with more program participants (particularly university students, children, and their single parents), and first piloted the project with a small number of participants.

On the positive side, the YES program story highlights many of the benefits that can be gained through developing agency input and ownership of the program. Both RSVP and BB/BS decided to include YES as one of their agency's programs. This act involved benefits for both the agencies (larger numbers of volunteers and services provided to clients) and to the program (insurance coverage, assistance with recruitment). We accomplished more by working together and our camaraderie through mutually shared values and goals provided needed moral support and the energy to carry us through difficulties in the initial stages of the program. Ultimately, we continued the program on a smaller scale after FIPSE funding was terminated by each agency taking a share of the work in recruiting and managing the project.

PUTTING IT ALL TOGETHER

Effective collaboration involves many elements. While collaboration is at times complex and unpredictable, program leaders who approach collaboration with the best interests of both their program and the agency in mind are more likely to be successful. Collaboration takes time, but with creativity and persistence, working together can help service-learning partners actualize the adage "many hands make light work." Effective collaboration not only gets the work done more efficiently but provides those involved with the important personal benefits of camaraderie through shared ideals, similar values, and common goals. Through collaborating we are challenged to listen to other perspectives, to expand our notion of the "right" way to do something, and to model the democratic process in our schools and communities.

Challenge Activity
Imagine that you are the director of the YES project. How would you further develop the collaborative effort described in this chapter? What plans would you design with those involved to enhance communication, decision making, problem solving, evaluation, and ownership of the program? In what ways could you and the two agencies involved share resources for mutual benefit? How could you work together to sustain the program beyond grant funding?

Chapter 4

Service

Rahima C. Wade

"I slept and dreamt that life was joy. I awoke and saw that life was duty. I acted and behold, duty was joy!" This quote from the great Indian poet Rabindranath Tagore reveals some of the mystery behind the practice of service. Service is, of course, the foundation of service-learning, yet it is an illusive concept to define. In this chapter, I explore the nature of service, the rationale behind serving, and what happens through the process of giving one's time, energy, and creativity to address a problem or need. Next I discuss different types of service experiences, from indirect service activities such as fund-raising and canned food collecting to advocacy efforts focused on changing local laws or getting a proclamation passed. Finally, I present numerous examples of specific service activities, categorized by common issue areas in the field of service-learning.

WHAT IS SERVICE?

Most people think of service as a caring act in response to a need or problem. Synonyms for the word "service" include all of the following: aid, assistance, help, ministration, and usefulness, among others. Service is action with intention. Ideally, service should result in a better world, less suffering, a healthy environment.

Yet if we look deeply into the nature of service, we find that service is more than an action. Service is also an attitude, a relationship, and a way of being in the world. "We can help through what we do. But at the deepest level we help through who we are" (Dass and Gorman, 1985, p. 227). In fact, we may not be truly serving others if we act without compassion, engagement, and a willingness to be "with" rather than just "for" another. Instead of seeking to do something with people, too often we have sought only to do something for them (King, cited in Albert, 1994).

There is an important distinction to be made between service and charity, a distinction that is often lost in service-learning programs. Charity involves a distance between the server and the served. In a charitable act, one person is clearly doing something *for* someone else, usually with some feeling of pity. While charity can help others, it can also emanate from an attempt to alleviate one's guilt or a desire to feel superior to others. If we act primarily out of fear, loneliness, guilt, or a need to feel important, we may be less likely to hear what others feel they really need. "One should be wary of the personal satisfaction of helping witnessed in a number of do-gooders and philanthropists. It escalates into patronizing, making people feel indebted to one's generosity, having strings attached to one's beneficence, and it culminates in sheer crass egotism" (Khan, 1985, p. 1).

Thoreau (1948) reminds us of further dangers inherent in charity in his statement, "If I knew . . . that a man was coming to my house with the conscious design of doing me good, I should run for my life" (p. 55). Charity can actually be painful to the one being "helped." Stated one beneficiary, "But when you're talking about what really hurts, and about what I'm really not getting from those who're trying to help me . . . that's it: that feeling of not being seen as whole" (Dass and Gorman, 1985, pp. 27 and 28).

With service, compassion should replace pity and separateness should be transformed into community. Instead of doing something one decides is needed for an "other," service involves working alongside people in ways that assist them in defining and helping to fulfill their own needs. Some have argued that we actually do those in need a disservice if we simply give to them in ways that create or continue disempowerment (Lappe and Dubois, 1994; Neusner, 1988; Olasky, 1992). For example, some service-learning projects focus solely on providing goods for individuals who are poor, hungry, disabled, or non-English speaking without asking them to become involved in working together to address the problems that beset them. Service must be envisioned as empowering individuals to work on their own behalf as much as it is to provide food and shelter. "The real issue," asserted Khan (1985), "is helping people to convince themselves that they can do something useful by giving them a chance to find an activity that is not too challenging, yet moderately rewarding" (p. 1). Lappe and Dubois (1994) maintain that instead of providing handouts to others, citizens should all work together with an attitude of "relational self-interest"— the perspective that we all share in community problems and therefore that working together on them is in *all* of our best interests.

With true service, the question of Whose problem is this, anyway? fades away. Service involves a connection between the helper and the helped that eventually dissolves the distance between the two.

Our service, then, is less a function of personal motive and more an expression of spontaneous, appropriate caring. We're not so much helping out, then, because it's "me" needing to tend to "you." We're helping out because it's "Us." The more we understand and dwell in that truth, the more we serve simply in the way of things. If one of "Us" needs help, if one of Our arms gets caught in a door, naturally we use the other of Our arms to set it free. (Dass and Gorman, 1985, pp. 49, 50)

While the bond of community formed through service is ultimately rewarding, people are often hesitant to reach out to others in this way. "When our hearts do open in empathy, all too often we close down quickly, frightened by the intensity of our feelings; we substitute denial, pity, or other defense mechanisms for the spontaneous response of the heart" (Dass and Gorman, 1985, p. 222). Khan (1985) further explicates reasons why we often fail to serve.

The trouble is that we feel our generosity runs counter to what we believe to be our most dire needs, or more so, those of our families. Moreover, we are rightly afraid that once we get ourselves involved in helping others, we shall be drawn further and further into sacrificing our needs since the demands appear to be much greater than we had first suspected. (p. 1)

Unfortunately, there are no easy shortcuts in serving others. "There can be no community without involvement; there can be no involvement without vulnerability; there can be no vulnerability without risk" (Joseph, 1990, p. 30).

What is service? Service is wonderful and challenging, heart wrenching and heartwarming, a simple action and a comprehensive way of being in the world. Most important, service is a process of working *with* others not just *for* them. Through service, we address needs and problems of mutual concern in hopes of creating a better world.

WHERE ARE THE ROOTS OF SERVICE TO BE FOUND?

Service is not a new idea; the roots of service can be found in all times and cultures. The Jewish mitzvah and the Cherokee *gadugi* call the people to help others in their times of need. The African saying, "It takes a whole village to raise a child" embodies the principle of service in a way of life for all community members. Asian, Latino, and many other cultures worldwide live out an ethic of service in their family and community relations.

For the early colonists of the United States, service to others was a necessity. Raising a neighbor's roof, providing enough food for community members during a long winter, and caring for the sick and elderly were tasks that had to be shared by many. Service has continued its legacy throughout U.S. history in the abolition of slavery, the women's suffrage movement, and the civil rights movement, as well as through government programs such as the Peace Corps and Volunteers in Service to America (VISTA). During the Depression, President Franklin Roosevelt created the Civilian Conservation Corps, putting thousands of unemployed youth to work in their communities.

In 1990, the National and Community Service Act was established to provide program funds, training, and technical assistance to states and communities to develop and expand service opportunities. Most recently, the legacy of service continues through programs sponsored by the federal Corporation for National Service, established through the National Service Trust Act of 1993. The Corporation oversees the Americorps youth volunteer program and provides funds and technical assistance for service activities in K–12 schools, institutions of higher education, and communities nationwide. (See Chapter 1 for a brief history of service and service-learning in the United States.)

WHY ENGAGE IN SERVICE?

In the ideal human community, we would all have the resources and abilities to respond effectively to our own problems. However, for varied and complex reasons, we do not all have those resources and thus it is imperative that those of us who can help, do so. We don't just help for the sake of others, though; we also do it for ourselves. "When we hear the cry, in order to live honestly with ourselves and others, we want to respond" (Dass and Bush, 1992, p. 7). We act for a number of disparate reasons: because we care, because we can't avoid it, because we feel guilty, because it helps fulfill our lives.

The boundaries of who is served and who is serving become blurred when we work with others, rather than just for them. Indeed, it is often difficult to determine who benefits more. Those who truly serve find themselves nurtured through the process and connected to a deeper sense of their own identities. Gardner (1965) noted that happiness is not found in desires fulfilled or entertainment, it is found in striving toward meaningful goals and seeking to fulfill one's purpose through the use of one's skills and talents. People by their nature seek meaning in their lives, and life has meaning in not only what we accomplish for our own benefit but also in how we contribute to others. Service is a vehicle through which we reach a deeper understanding of ourselves, others, and life (Dass and Gorman, 1985).

Studies have shown that many people engage in service primarily because it feels good (Serow, 1990, 1991). Yet those who give of their time and energy needn't be seen as self-centered. Satisfaction is a natural byproduct of helping. "I serve more . . . and I find myself more in love. What is wonderful is that the love lies not outside as a reward, like a gold star for being a good helper, but within the act itself" (Dass and Bush, 1992, p. 130). Jackson (cited in Albert, 1994) asserted that there is power in service, a power that does not deny the self or ego, but rather affirms their fulfillment in the highest and best manner.

Another reason many people engage in service is their recognition of responsibility as an essential aspect of life in a democracy. Barber (1992) and others have noted that participation in a democracy is not only a right but also an obligation. If we are to uphold and guarantee the individual rights that have been afforded to many of us by our forebears, then we must actively exercise these rights in the public sphere. Furthermore, in recognition of the many people who are disenfranchised and still not granted basic rights, we must all work together to secure these rights for all citizens.

WHO CAN SERVE? WHO CAN BE SERVED?

Martin Luther King, Jr. once stated, "Everyone is great because everyone can serve." Helping is not some special skill reserved for those eighteen and older. It is not confined to a single domain of our lives. There are as many ways to serve as there are individuals and needs and moments in a day.

The best time to begin teaching the practice of service is in childhood. Children must be actively guided to do good, to share, to be helpful. Children who are coached to be helpful are more likely to help again when a situation presents the opportunity (Joseph, 1990). Eisenberg and Mussen (1989) observed that the classroom is an ideal learning laboratory for helping behaviors. "Caring should be modeled and taught as a way to approach self, group, community, and society, and it will be internalized as a value and demonstrated by the behaviors of young people" (Chaskin and Rauner, 1995, p. 673).

If children engage in service when they are young and continue to help their communities as they grow older, they are more likely to see service as the province of all people and all times. As all individuals can serve, so can all at one time or another be served. In one phase of life, we may be able to give a lot to others; later on we may fall on hard times and depend on the generosity of our community. Cultures with an ethic of service recognize this fact and accept the changing roles that life may bring.

Nel Noddings (1992), in her pioneering work on caring in the school curriculum, observed that it is challenging to develop real caring toward those who are not present. Thich Nhat Hanh, the Vietnamese Buddhist monk and philosopher, also advised us to focus our service efforts on those in our immediate environment.

We talk about social service, service to people, service to humanity, service for others who are far away, helping to bring peace to the world—but often we forget that it is the very people around us that we must live for first of all . . . The word service is so immense. Let's return first to a more modest scale: our families, our classmates, our friends, our own community. We must live for them—for if we cannot live for them, whom else do we think we are living for? . . . How can we live in the present moment, live right now with the people around us, helping to lessen their suffering and making their lives happier? (1975)

The question posed by Thich Nhat Hanh is an important one. Being present is an essential aspect of service. Effective service with others should lessen suffering; indeed this can be one of the ways to measure if an activity is actually a service or not.

While we commonly think of service as addressing the needs of people in the immediate community, service can also be extended to the natural world. Animals, trees, and other aspects of the environment are often the focus of service projects. Caring for the environment is an important aspect of civic responsibility. Including animals, plants, and trees in our understanding of "who" can be served can expand the possibilities for problems that can be addressed through service activity.

WHAT ARE THE DIFFERENT TYPES OF SERVICE?

While service projects come in all shapes, forms, and sizes, most can be categorized into one of three types: direct, indirect, or advocacy. In general, most service-learning projects fall into one of the first two categories. Advocacy projects are an exciting and important form of service that is currently underutilized in schools.

Direct service involves working with people or the environment. This type of service can be the most rewarding for students, because they can see the results of their efforts. A smiling face, a heartfelt "thank you," a growing tree, or a clear stream provide immediate feedback during the process of helping. "Direct service teaches students to take responsibility for their actions. Students also learn that they can make a difference" (Dunlap, Drew, and Gibson, 1994, p. 9).

Indirect service experiences channel food, clothing, funds, and other resources to those in need rather than working directly with individuals or the environment. Schools commonly include indirect service projects, in part because they are easy to organize and usually do not involve students leaving the school site. Unfortunately, many indirect service projects are not true service as defined in this chapter; they are very often carried out with little sense of solidarity with the recipients. If indirect service projects are to be more than guilt reducers, two important challenges need to be addressed. First, program leaders must be careful to design an indirect service project with others so that it is not just an act of charity. Second, students need to reflect on how their service activity is making a difference for others, even when they don't see the benefits firsthand.

A third type of service experience is advocacy. Advocacy requires students to engage in social action, to assess not just ways they can help others through existing structures but how they can work to eliminate the causes of a problem or inform the public about the issues involved. Advocacy projects can involve lobbying public officials, getting proclamations or resolutions passed, changing local laws, or organizing a campaign. Students can research a community issue through conducting interviews or surveys with others, or collecting data through observation, then publicizing the results. For example, they might count how many cars per hour pass by a busy intersection and then lobby the city council to pay for stop signs. Advocacy projects often involve working on controversial issues or "taking on city hall." It is likely for this reason that teachers do not include advocacy in the curriculum as often as direct and indirect service activities. However, advocacy projects hold great potential for students to learn how to effect change in the community through civic participation. Students also learn to present their concerns clearly, collaborate to come up with feasible plans for change, and recognize the rights and responsibilities of all citizens in working for social justice.

WHAT ARE SOME EXAMPLES OF SERVICE ACTIVITIES FOR YOUTH?

Teachers, students, and community members have come up with many creative means for addressing problems and issues in their schools and communities. The following list of service project ideas is divided into thematic categories typically used in K–12 service-learning programs: intergenerational, environmental, animals, health and safety, poverty and hunger, arts and humanities, and in-school community service projects. This list provides an overview of a variety of service options for youth.

Intergenerational

Projects teaming young people and the elderly have been some of the most popular in service-learning programs. The old and the young have a natural affinity with each other. Given the pleasure derived by both groups, it is often difficult to determine who are the givers and who are the receivers. Stephens (1995) makes a strong case for the importance of intergenerational relationships for youth.

> As the average life span increases, it is ever more crucial that young people have contacts with elders to establish realistic concepts of aging, to accept each stage of life as normal with pleasures as well as problems. Additionally, such contacts provide the young with an understanding of the past and of their heritage. Unfortunately, in our mobile society, many children have limited contact with their grandparents. (p. 139)

Intergenerational projects may involve frail senior citizens in nursing homes, capable retirees in apartment housing, or active seniors who enjoy volunteering in their communities. Activities between seniors and students help to break down stereotypes each group may hold of the other and reveal the joy of discovering the similarities people share regardless of age. In intergenerational service projects, students can:

- help with chores (i.e., raking leaves, shoveling snow, cleaning gutters, painting fences, sweeping walks or driveways, washing windows, landscaping, shopping errands)
- conduct oral histories—document seniors' lives so that they may share them with relatives and friends (be sure to give a copy to the senior)
- provide companionship—visits, pen pal letter writing, making small gifts, crafts, placemats, holiday decorations, phone pals
- conduct a service project working alongside seniors to benefit the poor, hungry, or the environment.
- landscape the grounds at a nursing home, senior center, or retirement residence
- develop and lead an exercise class for seniors or sponsor a dance
- adopt-a-walk mate—children and seniors walk together once a week or month for companionship and exercise
- invite seniors to the classroom to enrich history lessons
- collect food, clothing, and supplies for a homeless shelter that serves the elderly
- have an elder fair—invite seniors to set up tables (science fair style) on their interests, hobbies, or displaying antiques or memorabilia
- include seniors on student council—invite seniors from the neighborhood to come and talk to the student council about neighborhood problems and what can be done about them
- produce a newsletter for a senior center or nursing home

- make picnic tables for a nursing home and make a picnic meal for an inter-generational lunch
- write letters to the editor about local issues affecting seniors in the local community
- help organize an intergenerational lobbying group that can work to promote better living conditions for seniors in the local community or state
- research laws and codes affecting nursing homes in the state and then write letters to managers of nursing homes to inquire about their compliance with these regulations
- research a national issue affecting seniors in the local community and write to state legislators or congressional representatives to inquire about any pending legislation on this issue

Environmental

Environmental projects are often favored by teachers just beginning service-learning activities. Activities focused on environmental problems and issues can be short or long term, conducted on the school grounds or in the community, and related to any subject area. Students of all ages can understand the importance of caring for the natural world and will eagerly dive into tackling pollution, monitoring water quality, cleaning up parks, and advocating for recycling and conservation programs. In environmental service-learning projects, students can:

- plant trees or flowers at a local park, in the school yard, or at a senior center
- start a recycling program in the school or community
- plan and build a public recreation path or nature trail
- plant a rooftop community garden
- organize a litter campaign
- clean up a beach, a park, a river, or other nature area
- coordinate a schoolwide can and bottle drive, donate the proceeds to an environmental organization
- study a local river and publicize findings on the water quality
- rid the schoolyard of fire ants, research which trees and flowers will aid in this effort and plant them
- help a community that has been effected by a natural disaster such as a flood, tornado, or hurricane
- plant a butterfly garden
- study the waste from school lunches, publicize the findings and develop a plan (different menu, à la carte selections, compost bin)
- rake leaves or shovel snow for seniors in the neighborhood
- plan a neighborhood clean-up day

- paint trash cans for the community
- organize a graffiti white-out (paint out the graffiti)
- plant marsh grass along a seashore to prevent beach erosion
- advocate for pesticide-free foods at local grocery stores
- raise funds to purchase and preserve acres of rain forest
- organize a community forum on environmental issues, invite media coverage of the event
- make reusable lunch sacks from scrap material
- decorate recycled paper grocery sacks with environmental messages, return them for use at local grocery stores
- organize a car pool system for high school student drivers
- lobby for curbside recycling in the community
- write letters to public officials offering ideas and political solutions to environmental problems
- reclaim a vacant lot and convert to a garden or playground
- participate in a forest restoration project
- investigate waste disposal in the community and publicize the findings
- use trash and recyclable items to create a miniature golf course
- assist with the recycling of Christmas trees
- make hand-rolled logs from newspapers for heating purposes and distribute to low-income families
- make and sell a recipe book of healthy foods or environmentally sound household cleaners
- research xeriscape (drought resistant) plants and urge officials to use them in dry land regions
- sell rain forest snacks at a community event (made of fruits, spices, and nuts grown in the rain forest), donate the proceeds to an organization working to save the rain forest
- protect the further destruction of wetlands areas through a community campaign, fund-raiser, or lobbying public officials

Animals

Youth's love for animals can contribute to strong motivation to engage in a service-learning project. Animals are everywhere: in our neighborhoods, backyards, farms, woods, and parks, as well as at local agencies such as veterinary clinics, animal shelters, and wildlife rehabilitation centers. Gandhi once said, "I hold that, the more helpless a creature, the more entitled it is to protection by man from the cruelty of man." The following ideas will help students join the community of those who respect and care for animals enough to take action on their behalf. Service-learning projects that help animals include activities in which students can:

- write to companies to protest the testing of beauty products on animals
- ask city council members to pass an ordinance banning the sale and keeping of exotic wildlife except for rehabilitation purposes
- participate in a call-in radio show and talk about an animal issue
- make and sell animal rights buttons or bumper stickers
- collect food, newspapers, cat litter, old blankets, and towels for a local animal shelter
- make dog bones or catnip toys for the shelter
- exercise the animals at the shelter
- convince the local newspaper to run photos of the animals who are up for adoption at the shelter
- form a friends of the shelter committee to lobby and raise funds
- review a book about animal rights for a school newspaper or local publication
- make and sell ID tags for dogs and cats
- distribute leaflets in the neighborhood educating about neutering and spaying pets
- volunteer with a veterinarian
- take cats to visit with seniors in a nursing home (make sure its allowed first)
- refuse to dissect animals in school and form an animal rights group
- build a bat house
- adopt a whale, manatee, or other endangered animal
- organize a neighborhood campaign for the birds, encourage others to cap their chimneys, put up bird baths and bird feeders, and remove kite string from trees
- write congressional representatives asking them to cut off funds for military deployment of dolphins
- boycott fur, toys and items made with fur, and stores that sell fur products
- support animal protective legislation in the community or state
- organize a lost animal search group
- ask local grocery stores to stock tofu and other vegetarian foods
- raise funds for or volunteer at a wildlife rehabilitation center
- launch a stop-the-balloons campaign (balloons released for school projects and other events often kill wildlife)
- make bird feeders from recycled containers and maintain through the winter

Community Health and Safety

From elementary school children biking to school to teens driving and drinking, safety is an important issue for students of all ages. Service-learning projects focused on health and safety issues are most effective when students choose an issue of concern to them in the present or a problem they are likely to encounter in the future. Health and safety projects vary greatly depending on the age of the students involved and the location of the community. For example, many of the ideas presented here would be well-suited to a high school project in an inner city, but might not be appropriate for other ages or settings. In health- and safety-related service-learning projects, students can:

- participate in a neighborhood safety program in cooperation with local police and fire departments
- set up crime prevention groups to patrol neighborhoods, escort people to their cars, and watch out for crimes
- sponsor self-defense workshops
- create a booklet showing people how to effectively use the 911 phone number
- write a letter to the editor about ideas for reducing crime in your community
- lobby for better police protection, better lighting in public places, better supervised public parks
- create a presentation to show how to handle crime emergencies, present for other students or community members
- lobby for keeping bushes trimmed along pedestrian paths
- create and present a proposal for establishing a bike trail in the community
- set up regular meetings of Alcoholics Anonymous or Narcotics Anonymous at the school
- volunteer to rock drug-addicted or boarder babies at a hospital nursery
- start a SADD (Students Against Drunk Driving) chapter at school
- solicit support from businesses for drug treatment centers and halfway houses
- design a puppet show about avoiding drugs and present to younger children
- conduct drug abuse awareness and prevention campaigns
- organize and maintain a safety patrol for a park or playground during busy play times, students can assist youngsters, clean up the area, and contact authorities if troubles arise
- coordinate an after-school hotline for latchkey children
- volunteer as an aide at a local library or summer recreation program to provide support for at-risk youth
- make quilts for AIDS babies
- complete a Red Cross course in basic aid training in order to help out in a crisis or emergency
- organize a bike rodeo for young children emphasizing safe biking techniques and the importance of wearing helmets
- design bookmarks about safety issues and distribute to young children or through the local library
- write and publish a newsletter on safety issues of concern to students, distribute through the school or the local library
- develop and teach a baby-sitting course focused on safety issues
- design a community smoke-detector survey, distribute in the neighborhood

- conduct an inspection of the playground and school grounds looking for safety hazards, make a list of the problems and submit to the school custodian
- identify intersections that are sites of frequent accidents, lobby community officials for stop signs, traffic lights, and cross walks
- develop and present a training on AIDS, what it is, how it is contracted, and how it can be prevented
- research the effects of smoking and secondhand smoke as a national health issue, publicize the findings
- make posters urging students not to drink and drive
- coordinate an alcohol- and drug-free prom night event
- organize a community health fair in the school, at a local mall, or at a senior center
- help with hearing and vision tests at a local elementary school
- create books on tape for visually impaired seniors or children in hospitals
- participate in "Jump for Heart," a jump-roping event to raise funds for the American Heart Association

Spotlight on Service Projects

Choose one of the thematic categories of service-learning projects presented in this chapter. Divide the projects into categories in two ways. First, list which projects are direct, indirect, and advocacy. Second, list projects that would be most suitable for elementary students, middle school students, and high school students. Compare your list with another person. Discuss the similarities and differences in the ways you grouped the service activities.

Hunger and Poverty

Projects focused on hunger, poverty, and homelessness are most often indirect service activities. Often agencies serving those who live in poverty are concerned with keeping the identity of their clients confidential and thus may not allow students to volunteer directly with those who are served. Program leaders need to be especially mindful, therefore, of inviting community input in these projects and creating opportunities for students to go beyond charity to solidarity with those who are in need. Poverty and hunger are such pervasive and serious problems in our county that advocacy is an especially important component of working on these issues. Hunger- and poverty-related service-learning projects give students opportunities to:

- set up a food donation bin in a local grocery store; ask the management to match shopper's donations
- organize a drive for coats, warm clothing, shoes, gloves, and other needed items for shelter residents or low income families

- put together housewarming packages for families moving from shelters to permanent housing
- become a big buddy to a child in a shelter
- put together infant care packages for low income or teen mothers
- plan and serve a meal at a local soup kitchen
- plant a garden for individuals who are homeless; donate the produce to local food banks and free meal programs
- build or renovate housing through Habitat for Humanity
- bag groceries at a local food bank
- organize a canned food drive at the school
- organize a benefit sporting event between students and teachers; use funds to purchase sports equipment for a local shelter
- establish an ongoing relationship with one organization serving people who live in poverty; assist with agency programs, fund-raising, and public relations efforts
- hold a story hour at a local Headstart preschool or shelter
- develop a partnership with one low-income preschool; each month buy or make birthday cards and gifts for children celebrating birthdays
- make colorful placemats and table decorations for use on tables at a soup kitchen or shelter
- make bookmarks with the names and phone numbers of agencies serving people who live in poverty; distribute through schools, churches, libraries, neighborhood centers, and grocery stores
- conduct a demographic and economic impact study of those who are homeless; publicize the findings through the local media
- interview community agency members who work in agencies that address poverty and hunger; develop a plan for taking action that addresses the root causes of these problems
- lobby a state legislator to find out what he or she is doing about poverty and hunger; share specific concerns about poverty and hunger in the local community
- collect nonperishable items such as soap, toothbrushes, and combs for a local shelter
- collect stuffed animals and donate to children at a shelter
- set up a book corner for children and adults at a shelter
- participate in a weekly or monthly meals-on-wheels route
- assist at the Department of Social Services to help people fill out forms
- set up and staff child care at the Department of Social Services
- provide baby-sitting, transportation, or errand services for people on fixed incomes
- write to local officials or state legislators supporting legislation that assists those in poverty

In-School Service

Community service activities can also happen in the school community. Students can be involved in identifying the specific problems that beset their school through observations, interviews of other students, and questionnaires distributed to faculty, staff, parents, and students. The projects below not only resolve issues of concern in the school but they also go a long way toward building a supportive atmosphere in the school, thus enhancing students' feelings of belonging and their motivation to learn. School service projects give students opportunities to:

• make school supplies packets for low income children
• start a reading circle for parents and children
• organize a voter registration event in the high school
• provide mentors, child care, and tutoring for teen moms returning to school
• create a directory of services or a newsletter for teen mothers
• open up the school as a community space; invite nonprofit groups to hold meetings and events at the school when not in use for classes
• tutor younger children
• set up a program for peer counseling or tutoring
• create a school newspaper focused on issues of concern to the school community
• set up a senior-freshman buddy program in which seniors help freshman with the transition to a new school and offer support and advice
• volunteer as a student aid in an adaptive physical education class for students with physical or mental challenges
• make get well cards once a month for all students and students' family members who are seriously ill or in the hospital
• learn sign language in order to communicate with students in the school who are deaf
• develop a peer-run conflict mediation program
• interview the school principal or PTA officers about issues effecting the climate of the school and develop a plan to address one of them
• conduct a survey among a sample of the students to determine the types and frequency of sexual harassment occurring at the school, develop a campaign to alleviate the problems learned about
• review the books in the school library on people from minority cultures; suggest removing books with biases and purchasing new books for updating the collection
• develop welcome kits (map of the school, coupons for shared lunches and playing together, bookmarks, etc.) for new students and good-bye kits (picture of the class, stamped envelope, etc.) for students who are moving

• attend a school board meeting and make a brief presentation on a critical issue affecting the school
• lobby the superintendent about establishing or expanding a districtwide service-learning program
• raise funds, design, and help to construct playground equipment
• create a program to prevent vandalism and emphasize school pride
• beautify the school grounds, pick up litter, plant flowers and trees

PUTTING IT ALL TOGETHER

There is no shortage of problems and needs to be addressed in our communities. Service activities focused on working with rather than just for others have the potential to lead to shared responsibility and the empowerment of all people to help each other create a better world. As the barriers between giver and receiver dissolve, we can discover the true nature of service. When what was "their problem" becomes "our problem," the transition transforms a mere association into a community. Our democratic way of life depends on its citizens being willing to engage in acts of service, with each other, for the good of the whole.

Challenge Activity
Choose one of the service projects that you feel would be most beneficial for your community. For which grade level(s) would this project be best suited? How would you ensure that this is a service activity in the truest sense of the word and not just an act of charity?

Chapter 5

Curriculum Integration

Rahima C. Wade

The twofold mission of public schooling in a democratic society is to help students learn the skills, knowledge, and attitudes they need to (1) live healthy, happy, and productive lives as individuals and (2) participate as responsible citizens of their communities, states, and nation. One could argue that service has no place in the public curriculum if it does not contribute to student learning. Indeed, much of the argument revolving around whether service is a legitimate requirement for high school graduation points to the question of whether or not students learn needed skills and knowledge from their service experience. Before considering how to infuse service in the academic curriculum, therefore, it is necessary to consider the case for doing so.

WHY INTEGRATE SERVICE IN THE CURRICULUM?

As educators increasingly demonstrate that adding service to the academic curriculum not only meets community needs but also enriches student learning, the legitimacy of service-learning's role in the curriculum will also increase. Some schools, in fact, have adopted service-learning primarily for the inherent learning potential. As one example, consider the definition of service-learning included in the South Carolina Department of Education's curricula: "Service-learning is an educational method which engages young people in service to their communities as a means of enriching their academic learning, promoting personal growth, and helping them to develop the skills needed for productive citizenship" (Dunlap, Drew, and Gibson, 1994, p. 196). This definition focuses almost exclusively on academic and personal outcomes for students by framing the service activity as a means to enhance student learning.

When service is integrated with the academic curriculum, students not only meet important community needs, they also have the opportunity to learn academic skills and content in concert with helping. Many program leaders have observed that the service activity brings meaning to academics. Students' motivation to learn skills and content in math, science, social studies, and other school subjects increases when they realize that they will need to use the knowledge to help others or to improve the environment. "It gives the student who cannot see the need to learn, a new focus for learning. For students who are eager to learn, service-learning gives them a way to expand their knowledge and develop more fully the talents and skills they already have" (Dunlap, Drew, and Gibson, 1994, p. 10). Through applying academics to service activities, students readily learn that school knowledge is relevant in the real world. Because we retain more of what we learn through experience than what we just read or write about, academic achievement may be enhanced through adding a service component to the curriculum.

HOW SHOULD SERVICE
BE INFUSED IN THE CURRICULUM?

There are many approaches to infusing service in public schooling, some of which do not connect service with academics. Many high schools have service clubs or offer credit toward graduation for volunteer hours. Some schools offer a class specifically in community service or service-learning. Others, usually elementary or middle schools, incorporate service activities as a schoolwide activity. Increasingly, community agencies are contacting the schools to invite students to participate in volunteer opportunities on weekends, school vacations, and during the summer.

While clubs and other cocurricular activities are valuable experiences in their own right, service activities that are not connected to subject matter courses or lessons miss the opportunities discussed above for enhancing academic development. In this chapter, I will highlight examples of service-learning projects that reinforce the objectives of typical K–12 school subjects. While these projects could be carried out in a variety of curricular or cocurricular formats, each could also be integrated in the curriculum by a single teacher interested in adding service-learning to the curriculum as a way to enhance instruction and student learning. (Many more ideas for service activities can be found in chapter 5.)

In some middle and elementary schools, teachers are working together across subject matter boundaries to infuse service in a number of subject areas. Most of the service-learning projects presented in this chapter could be taught using a thematic or interdisciplinary approach. Considering the consequences of a project for past, present, or future citizens connects the activity with social studies. Many projects can be incorporated with science instruction through either systematic scientific study in the project or consideration of the environmental effects of the activity. Almost all projects incorporate language arts skills such as speaking, listening, reading, and writing. If a project involves use of funds, building items, or managing time, math skills are easily incorporated.

One important strategy that can be used in any subject area is tutoring. When students tutor their peers who need extra help or younger children in their own or a neighboring school, both the tutors and the tutees learn valuable academic skills and content. Cross-age and peer tutoring programs have generally led to strong academic gains for both those students working as tutors and those receiving the help (Conrad and Hedin, 1991).

WHAT ARE SOME IDEAS FOR SERVICE-LEARNING PROJECTS IN SCHOOL SUBJECTS?

Social studies, with its goal of active citizenship, may be the most obvious content area within which to teach civic responsibility, yet many subject areas can benefit from a service component. Ten subject areas are included here: language arts, math, science, social studies, fine arts, physical education, foreign language, life skills, computers, and industrial arts.

Language Arts

The skills and knowledge of the language arts are essential for student success in all areas of the curriculum. Language arts as a subject area includes reading, writing, and English instruction as well as the study of literature and the development of listening and communication skills. As a result of language arts instruction, students should be able to read, comprehend, evaluate, and use written material; write standard English; use spoken language effectively in formal and informal situations; understand various forms of literature representative of different cultures, eras, and ideas; and understand how and why language functions and evolves. Following are some service-learning projects that integrate language arts skills.

Multicultural book reviews. Working with the public library, identify a set of ethnic children's books in need of updating, for example, African-American children's books. Review the books based on appropriate guidelines. Recommend deleting books that are outdated or stereotypical in content. Review newer books and recommend that the library purchase some of these books to update their collection. Produce a brochure of the new and existing books. Hold a story hour to share some of the newer books. Create a display of the books at the library to publicize both the books and the project.

Language arts curriculum connections: reading ethnic children's books; knowledge of guidelines for ethnic children's books; writing skills; read-aloud skills.

Careers video. Create a video library highlighting different career options. Do some background reading on different careers and develop questions to ask. Interview workers in a wide range of occupations and create short five-minute tapes on each career. Be sure to include diversity among the interviewees in terms of gender, physical ability, race, ethnicity, and social class. Tapes can be distributed to guidance counselors, the public library, and local job service organizations.

Language arts curriculum connections: nonfiction reading; interview skills; listening skills; video production skills.

Short stories. Read novels or stories about children with different problems. Decide as a class on a group of children for whom to write stories (i.e., children with chronic illnesses, children living in a homeless shelter, low-income preschoolers). After instruction in writing short stories, write stories about topics of interest to all children (e.g., animal stories, mysteries). Present or send the short stories to other children and invite their responses. Continue pen pal relationships if they are initiated by the recipients of the stories. If interest exists, pen pals could write additional stories together.

Language arts curriculum connections: reading novels or short stories; knowledge of how to write a short story; writing, editing, and publishing skills; letter-writing skills.

Math

Mathematics provides essential computation and problem-solving skills applicable to a wide range of everyday situations. As a result of mathematics instruction K–12, students should be able to perform computations using whole numbers, integers, decimals, and fractions; understand and use ratios and percentages; make and use measurements; solve problems using algebraic equations; understand and apply geometric concepts; understand and use methods of data collection and analysis; and use mathematical skills to estimate and predict outcomes. Following are three service-learning projects that specifically focus on the development of math skills.

Canned goods. Contact a local food pantry or crisis center about what types of canned goods are needed in the coming months. Collect canned goods from families and neighbors and bring to school. Count and sort the cans and keep a graph of types of canned goods contributed. Analyze the contents of the cans and develop recipes using the canned goods and a few other basic food items. Include recipes with the canned goods delivered to the food pantry. Compile a booklet of the recipes to be distributed free of charge at locations accessible to low-income people. Sell copies of the recipe book to raise funds for the food pantry.

Math curriculum connections: counting, sorting, and measurement skills; creating graphs and charts; money skills.

Community survey. Assist a local nonprofit group with a survey of the community. Assess the cost of conducting the survey, including copying, mailing, and staff time. Learn about the agency's funding sources and annual budget and how this survey will contribute to their efforts to help the community. Analyze the survey results using a computer program and produce a brief report that the agency can use in publicizing their findings. The report could also be distributed free-of-charge through the public library.

Math curriculum connections: knowledge of budget and fund-raising issues in a nonprofit organization; understanding of cost analysis; ability to use a computer statistical program.

Traveling grocery display. Working with senior citizen volunteers, create a traveling demonstration of unit pricing on grocery story items. The display can travel to different grocery stores, senior centers, and nursing homes. Together, select items that can be compared and featured. For example, a consumer advocate counted the raisins in different brands of raisin bran cereal and found that private label brands had more raisins than the advertised national brands and were about one dollar per pound cheaper (Stephens, 1995). In the display, include a shelf of products as well as posters and handouts that compare prices for name and local or generic brands. Offer other seniors assistance with comparison shopping by including a handout in the display that gives the times and days when assistance is available from the student or senior volunteers.

Math curriculum connections: skills in counting, averaging, price comparison, computing cost per unit or pound; ability to use a calendar; time-management skills.

Science

Science instruction provides a conceptual framework for understanding the natural world and the causes and effects of its phenomena. As a result of science instruction, students should be able to understand the concepts and basic vocabulary of the biological, physical, and environmental sciences and their application to life and work in contemporary society. They should also be able to apply the principles of scientific research to simple research projects and recognize the social and environmental implications and limitations of technological development. Here are some service-learning project ideas that teach science skills and principles.

Soil testing and landscaping. Study climate and landscaping in the region. Learn how to do soil testing and what to add to improve the soil for plants and trees. Using this knowledge, help landscape the grounds of a nursing home, homeless shelter, or other community agency with residents or agency members. Develop a plan together for how the new plants will be maintained by residents, employees, or both at the site.

Science curriculum connections: knowledge of climate, plants, trees, and soil in a given region; ability to perform scientific experiments in soil testing; skills in developing the soil and landscaping using suitable plants and trees.

Waste reduction. Conduct a scientific analysis of the waste produced by the school within a set period of time. Include items that can be or are recycled (such as paper products) as well as trash and school lunch refuse. Develop a plan to reduce the amount of waste the school produces. The plan might include a recycling effort, building a compost bin, reusing certain items, or revising the school lunch program. Keep graphs and charts each week on the waste produced to evaluate the success of the reduction activities. Publish the findings in a neighborhood publication or local newspaper along with recommendations for how others can reduce waste in their homes and workplaces.

Science curriculum connections: knowledge of recycling, composting, reuse of materials, and other aspects of waste; research skills, experimentation skills, graph and chart-making skills.

Public safety partnership. Study various weather conditions and the safety precautions needed for specific weather hazards in the region. Learn about plans and procedures at the local public safety department for possible natural hazards. Assist with working on a project that will help meet the needs of individuals who may be faced with a weather hazard (such as making sandbags for potential flooding). Find out about a recent environmental disaster in another part of the country or world and take action to help. Discuss the advantages and limitations of what people and technology can do in the face of weather-related disasters.

Science curriculum connections: knowledge of weather conditions and natural disasters; knowledge of the public safety department and its role in dealing with weather-related events; understanding of the advantages and limitations of technology in natural disasters.

Social Studies

Social studies provides students with an understanding of themselves and others and prepares them for active, civic involvement in our democratic society and pluralistic world community. Social studies typically encompasses instruction in history, geography, economics, political science, anthropology, psychology, and sociology as well as the arts and humanities. As a result of social studies instruction, students should be able to demonstrate a knowledge of the basic concepts of the social sciences and how these help to interpret human behavior; apply their knowledge of the social sciences to decision making in personal and civic situations; and participate in the social and political lives of their communities. Following are three examples of service-learning projects that specifically address social studies objectives.

Community history. Research what types of community history publications are currently in existence. Contact the local historical society and find out if there are significant periods of history, local events, famous individuals, or historic buildings that have not been written about. Write a history of one aspect of or period in the community's history. Interview prominent community leaders and senior citizens. Advertise a search for "artifacts" connected with the topic being written about. Compile a community history booklet that can be donated to the public library or sold to fund-raise for historical restoration projects in the community.

Social studies curriculum connections: knowledge of the community and local history, knowledge of periods of U.S. history, research skills, interviewing skills, understanding history through diverse perspectives (community leaders and senior citizens).

Voter registration campaign. Contact the local voter registration headquarters to obtain statistics on how many citizens are registered to vote. If possible, obtain age, gender, and other types of demographic data on the voter pool. Research national trends in voting and the history of voting in the United States. Develop and carry out a plan for educating others about the importance of voting and how to register to vote. If possible, include presentations to groups who are typically underrepresented in the voter pool (i.e., young adults, people in poverty, minority populations). As one part of these presentations, dialogue with those attending about their personal views on the advantages and disadvantages of political participation.

Social studies curriculum connections: knowledge of the history of voting in the United States, analysis of demographic data, understanding the voter registration process, valuing political participation, developing an awareness of diverse perspectives on political participation.

Service with immigrants. Contact a specific group of immigrants in the community or an agency that works with the group. Learn about their culture and values. What were their lives like before coming to the United States? What differences between that life and life in the United States are proving to be difficult? Find out what needs and concerns they have as they adjust to life in the community. Based on their issues, develop projects together that help them meet specific needs. For example, students could: tutor immigrant adults to help them pass their U.S. citizenship tests, work with young children while their parents look for jobs, assist with a cultural fair or fund-raising event, or help immigrant families learn about the services and organizations in the community.

Social studies curriculum connections: knowledge of the lifestyle, history, and values of a cultural group; understanding diverse perspectives on the local community; other objectives as determined by the specific service activities.

Spotlight on Interdisciplinary Teaching
Choose one of the social studies service-learning projects above and develop a plan for use of the idea in interdisciplinary teaching. What other subject areas could be incorporated with the project you chose? Write down at least three subjects in addition to social studies and list at least two curriculum objectives associated with each subject that could be taught or reinforced in the service-learning project.

Fine Arts

The arts give students the means to express themselves creatively and to appreciate the artistic expressions of others. Included in the fine arts are music, visual arts, theater, and dance. As a result of instruction in the arts, students should be able to describe the unique characteristics of each of the arts; identify processes and tools required to produce visual art, music, theater, and dance; and demonstrate the basic skills necessary to participate in the creation and performance of at least one of the arts. The following service-learning projects allow students to use and develop their artistic skills.

Graffiti white out and mural. Identify a wall in the city that (1) is covered with graffiti, (2) is large enough for a mural, and (3) is in a safe and publicly visible location. Obtain permission from the appropriate authorities to paint a mural on the wall. White out the graffiti with white paint. Design a mural that celebrates a positive image of community. Paint the mural on the wall. Call a local newspaper to take a photo of the mural and interview the student and community artists about their work.

Fine arts curriculum connections: design and painting skills; awareness of the public benefits of art.

Senior concert. Contact the local senior congregate meal site and talk with seniors there about what songs and instrumental compositions they enjoy. Develop a show incorporating these musical pieces. The school choir, band, and/or orchestra members could be involved. Invite any seniors who would like to be in the performance to come to practices at the school. Perform at the congregate meal site as well as at local retirement residences and nursing homes. Make a video of the performance to share with other students at the school and performers' families.

Fine arts curriculum connections: knowledge of new songs and instrumental compositions; skills in singing and playing instruments; recognition of the value of public performance.

Traveling troopers. Write and produce a play based on the theme of accepting others. Make sure that students with disabilities and students of color are involved in the development of the play as well as in the cast and crew. Attempt to identify skills of students who are usually left out or ostracized by their peers and incorporate their contributions into the play. Travel to community sites, especially locations with young children, to present the play.

Fine arts curriculum connections: play-writing skills, play-production skills (directing, lighting, costume design, etc.), performance skills.

Physical Education

Physical education instruction enables students to acquire physical fitness, coordination, and leisure skills. As a result of physical education, students should be able to: demonstrate basic skills and physical fitness necessary to participate in a variety of conditioning exercises or sports; plan a personal physical fitness program; and understand the physical development and functioning of the human body. Following are three service-learning projects that can be integrated with physical education courses.

Special Olympics mentors. Connect with a local or state Special Olympics program months in advance. Form mentor relationships between able-bodied students and Special Olympics participants. Pairs can practice the skills to be used in the Special Olympics events. The mentor can provide additional "training" in regards to nutrition, stress, rest, and so forth. Special Olympics students can teach their able-bodied mentors about their disabilities and the challenges they face and overcome to participate in sports activities. On the day of the Special Olympics, mentors are there to help out as needed and to be coaches and cheerleaders for their partners.

Physical education curriculum connections: large-motor-skill development, sports skills development, knowledge of the development and functioning of the human body, development of coaching skills.

Youth recreation program. Organize a recreation program for younger children in day cares, after school programs, at the local YMCA, or "on the streets" for dropouts or latchkey kids. Consult the students about what types of games and sports they would like to play. Approach school districts and local sports businesses for donations of new or used equipment. Develop a plan for staffing the program on a rotating basis so that each student volunteer works at the program one or two days a week.

Physical education curriculum connections: knowledge of sports and games, large-motor skill development, sports skills development, awareness of sports-related businesses.

Bikeathon. Develop plans for a community bikeathon. Determine fees to be charged (if any), events, location, and needed supplies. Involve other organizations and agencies as possible. For example, local police could set up booths on registering bicycles or traffic safety. Raffle off a bicycle helmet or lock donated from a bike store. Set up a bike maintenance and repair booth. Decide which organization to support with any funds raised.

Physical education curriculum connections: knowledge of bike maintenance and safety; valuing of educating the community about the importance of exercise and safety

Foreign Language

Most secondary schools provide foreign language instruction, typically in at least French and Spanish. Some schools provide instruction in other languages as well, such as Latin, Russian, Japanese, Chinese, or German. As a result of foreign language instruction, students should be able to communicate verbally in the language under study; read and write the language under study; and possess an understanding of and an appreciation for the place of their own culture, language, and historical-ethnic heritage, as well as those of others, in a pluralistic society.

ESL assistance. Provide English as a second language (ESL) instruction for students or members of the community who need English tutoring. Offer a service whereby students can accompany the ESL community members to doctors' and lawyers' offices and to other community locations to help with English and interpreting. At the same time, student volunteers can learn more about the language and culture of the ESL community members.

Foreign language curriculum connections: ESL tutoring skills; practice in a second language; knowledge of another culture.

Bilingual brochures. Talk to ESL community members about community information they would like to have access to in their own language. Work together on translating information from English to another language. Distribute the brochures in the appropriate locations and in the ESL community.

Foreign language curriculum connections: translating skills; writing skills in a second language; awareness of ESL community members' needs for information.

Cultural contacts. Find ESL students and community members who would be willing to visit foreign language and social studies classrooms to enrich students' understanding of languages and cultures. Develop a plan together for publicizing the availability of the volunteer service (use multiple languages in the brochures), for coordinating the visits, and for evaluating the program. Talk to foreign language and social studies teachers about their particular needs and develop a data bank that can be distributed to potential ESL volunteers.

Foreign language curriculum connections: speaking skills in a second language; writing skills in a second language; collaboration with ESL students and community members.

Life Skills

Education in life skills, often the focus of health and home economics instruction, provides students with the knowledge and attitudes to live healthy lives. As a result of life skills education, students should be able to understand the physical structure and development of the human body; understand the principles of nutrition; exercise efficient management of emotional stress; develop a positive self-concept; be mindful of drug use and abuse; know about the prevention and treatment of common illnesses; understand basic concepts of growth and development, sexuality, family life, and parenting; develop basic skills in sewing and cooking; and understand consumer health and safety, including environmental health. The following service-learning projects can be included in a life skills curriculum.

Nutrition education. After learning about good nutrition, consider the different groups in the community that might benefit from this information (i.e., senior citizens, younger children, teen mothers, low-income families). Develop a partnership with a community agency to conduct nutrition education workshops with one or more of these populations. Be sure to acknowledge differences in nutritional needs and desires based on both individual and cultural differences.

Life skills curriculum connections: knowledge of nutrition; knowledge of groups in the community that can benefit from nutrition education; awareness of consumer issues in regard to nutrition.

Home emergency skills. Contact agencies that deal with emergency assistance, such as the fire department, police department, and the Red Cross. Produce a play for latchkey elementary school children on how to deal with emergencies that may come up when they are home alone. Develop a brochure with illustrations for the latchkey children to take home to remind them what to do.

Life skills curriculum connections: awareness of health and safety issues; knowledge of child care concerns in working parent families; knowledge of local agencies working on emergency assistance.

Fund-raiser for a health organization. Find out which organizations in the community have fund-raising events planned in the next few months (e.g., American Heart Association's Jump Rope for Heart). Help the agency with a community mailing about the event and publicize the fund-raiser in the school newsletter. Plan to participate in the actual fund-raiser or organize an event to coincide with the fund-raiser (such as a healthy food booth or a fun run). Keep track of how much money is raised and learn about how the money is being used to work for change.

Life skills curriculum connections: knowledge of community agencies focused on health issues; awareness of the importance of fund-raising in supporting efforts to improve people's health; improving one's own health through participation in a fun run, healthy food booth, or jump rope event.

Computers

While computers can be integrated in any course, many schools offer separate instruction in the use of computers. As a result of computer instruction, students should be able to understand the capabilities of the computer and use it as a creative learning tool; use keyboarding skills to input data into a computer; use data base management skills to organize information; use word-processing skills to convey ideas; use spreadsheet and graphing skills to express ideas quantitatively; and understand that computers and other technology are tools in the hands of the learner.

Intergenerational computing. Use word processing skills to type invitations to senior citizens to come to the school for computer collaborations. Some seniors are experts on computers and might like to teach younger students computer skills. Other seniors might want to learn how to begin or further their use of the computer. Find out what types of skills they would like to develop on the computer (word processing, spreadsheet, data base). As students work with seniors on computer skills, discuss the differences between computer use and other ways of accomplishing the desired tasks.

Computer curriculum connections: word processing, data base, and spreadsheet skills; awareness of advantages and disadvantages of different forms of technology and writing.

Nonprofit agency computer assistance. Identify one or more nonprofit agencies that would like to update their agency operations using computers. Help them identify their needs and assist as requested with any of the following: choice of computer, software or both for purchase; word-processing, data base, or spreadsheet instruction; developing promotional materials using graphics; developing needs assessment surveys.

Computer curriculum connections: word-processing, data base, and spreadsheet skills; awareness of benefits of computer use in nonprofit agencies; knowledge of ways to use computers for agency promotion and surveys.

Global electronic pen pals. Find out about one of the electronic mail networks connecting students around the world. Communicate with students in other countries about the problems and issues in their communities. Where possible, assist with global projects by sending funds or needed items. Publicize the information learned about youth concerns in other countries in the school or local newspaper.

Computer curriculum connections: word-processing skills, electronic mail skills.

Industrial Arts

Industrial arts courses have changed greatly due to advances in technology. While the traditional wood and metal shop activities are still featured in many schools, many districts offer students opportunities to learn about computer-assisted design and encourage them to consider energy sources and environmental issues in the completion of a wide variety of construction projects. As a result of industrial arts instruction, students should be able to work with a variety of materials and processes in the field of construction; develop an awareness of various careers in the fields of construction, communication, manufacturing, and transportation; evidence safe and appropriate use of machines, tools, and technological equipment; and develop knowledge about materials, products, processes, uses, and developments in the field of construction in a technological society.

Building ramps. Study construction techniques for building ramps to serve as access to buildings for people with physical disabilities. Learn about the different disabilities of children attending a local Headstart preschool or Child Development Center. Research the legal requirements and restrictions that apply to ramps. Build ramps for an agency serving children with physical disabilities. Have a celebration at the site and invite students, parents, and teachers from the school and members of the community agency.

Industrial arts curriculum connections: skills in computing angles, inclines, and measurements; skills in planning and building ramps.

Repairing seniors' homes. Contact the local senior center to find out about low income seniors who need housing renovations. Send letters to all eligible seniors and then meet with those who are interested about what types of renovations and repairs are necessary. Make out a list of needed supplies and tools and procure these items. Work on the seniors' homes; seniors serve as consultants and advisors on the projects.

Industrial arts curriculum connections: skills in assessing repair needs in homes; knowledge of tools and supplies needed for specific repair tasks; skills in making home repairs and renovations.

Cooperative appliance and auto repair. Have one day a month when low-income individuals can bring their cars, engines, or small appliances to be repaired at the school. Individuals interested in using this service would need to call in advance to schedule a time for the repair and also be willing to help either by assisting with the repair or performing small tasks in the repair shop (sweeping, organizing supplies, helping with a mailing about the project, taking photos for publicity purposes). Charge only the cost of the equipment/supplies needed for the repair.

Industrial arts curriculum connections: skills in repairing cars, engines, and small appliances; knowledge of tools and supplies needed; skills in organizing a repair business.

PUTTING IT ALL TOGETHER

Service-learning projects can do much more than address school or community needs. They can also provide valuable, hands-on learning experiences for students that give them practical reasons to learn academic skills and knowledge. With increased motivation and opportunities to apply academics to real world issues, students are more likely to internalize and value what they have learned in school. Any subject in the curriculum can be invigorated with the inclusion of service activities. Through including service in the curriculum, the original mission of public schooling for citizenship is fulfilled while students also learn valuable skills and knowledge they can use in living productive, successful lives.

Challenge Activity

The Community School, a public (elementary, middle, high—choose one) school in a major city, has chosen a schoolwide theme, Across the Generations, for the upcoming school year. Develop a plan for intergenerational service-learning projects that could be completed within at least eight of the subjects included in this chapter. Which objectives will be taught in each subject? How will the projects complement each other? Which agencies or individuals in the community will be included in the planning?

Chapter 6

Reflection

Rahima C. Wade

WHAT IS REFLECTION?

Reflection is a common aspect of everyday life. When we drive to work, walk the dog, take a shower, or wash the dishes; we mull over the events of our lives, evaluate our actions, and consider our next steps. When we meet a friend for lunch, chat with a colleague in the hallway, or telephone a long-distance family member; we continue the reflection process by sharing aloud the myriad thoughts and feelings we carry with us about our experiences. These simple forms of reflection are important to our personal growth and well-being. They have the potential to help us process our experience in ways that we can learn from. We use what we learn through reflection to improve our lives and our interactions with others.

While almost all of us reflect intermittently throughout our days, privately and in conversation with others; few of us set aside time specifically to reflect. Nor have many of us studied reflection in an effort to improve our ability to learn from our experience. Reflection, like any other skill, is a process that benefits from mindful practice. In this chapter, I address specific methods and guidelines for encouraging conscious student reflection within a service-learning program. While it might be said that one cannot teach reflection, service-learning program leaders can facilitate the development of reflective thinking through planned activities coordinated with goals and objectives for student learning.

Conscious reflection begins with a focus on experience. Experience is the substance of reflection. Reflection is a means for reliving or recapturing our experience in order to make sense of it, to learn from it, and to develop new understandings and appreciations. The root of the word *reflection* comes from the Latin *reflectere*, which means "to bend back." As a mirror reflects a physical image, so does reflection as a thought process reveal to us aspects of our experience that might have remained hidden had we not taken the time to consider them.

While reflection involves a separation or stepping back from experience, it is also a connective process. As we reflect, we discover links between different aspects of our life experience. Past experiences must be reconsidered in light of new information. We put our values and beliefs to a reality test. Reflection allows us to draw conclusions about our past experience and develop new insights that we can apply to our future activities.

There are many words used to represent the reflection process; debrief, process, consider, ponder, weigh, evaluate, and analyze are just a few. While each of these terms vary slightly in meaning, they all include some core components of reflective thinking. First, reflection is a deliberate thinking process that is applied to an experience, idea, or issue. Second, reflection takes time and the more time we can devote to reflecting on an experience, the greater potential for learning and insight. Third, reflection can lead to cognitive growth. Reflection should result in new understandings and appreciations. Finally, we reflect to inform our future actions.

According to Dewey (1916), reflection is an ethical undertaking. People's reasonable and responsible behavior rests on their ability to reflect on their prior acts and make informed choices about their subsequent behavior. Dewey saw reflective thinking as an intentional attempt to discover specific connections between our actions and their consequences. He believed that reflective thinking would improve students' problem-solving skills and increase their ability to learn from their experience.

WHAT IS THE ROLE OF REFLECTION IN SERVICE-LEARNING?

The service-learning literature is unequivocal in asserting that reflection is an essential element of good practice. However, the word "reflection" is becoming, like many educational terms, a concept that means many things to many people. The diversity of views on what reflective thinking is indicates a confusion in the field about reflective thinking, how it should be taught, and what types of learning outcomes can be reasonably expected from including reflection activities in service-learning programs. Clearly, additional study and exploration are needed to provide a more comprehensive understanding of the role of reflection in service-learning.

To begin, why is reflection necessary? Studies by Gary Phillips (cited in Silcox, 1993) revealed that retention of knowledge is connected to human senses that are stimulated in learning. Phillips has found that we remember about 10 percent of what we hear, 15 percent of what we see, and 20 percent of what we see and hear. However, we retain 60 percent of what we do, 80 percent of what is done actively with reflection, and 90 percent of what we teach others. Thus, if we want students in schools to learn, our efforts will be more successful if learning is experiential and offers opportunities for reflection on experience.

David Kolb (1981) also found that reflection is a key element in learning. Kolb's cycle of learning begins with concrete experience, followed by "reflective observation"—being able to reflect on and observe one's experiences. Following this stage, learners should be encouraged to create concepts and integrate their reflections into new theories. The final part of Kolb's cycle of learning involves active experimentation, during which learners use their new ideas to solve problems and make decisions. In Kolb's view, reflection enables the learning cycle to continue so that learners continue to develop and change.

Kolb's work alludes to the fact that reflection is essential because we do not automatically learn from our experience. Many of our daily acts are experienced unconsciously and never emerge for review in the forefront of our minds. Without reflection on our experience, we do not learn from it and we cannot glean lessons from our actions to inform our future efforts. Cognitive scientists tell us that the brain deals with thoughts, feelings, and attitudes simultaneously. As we learn, we take in information both consciously and subconsciously, at the same time. Thus, without focused reflection experiences, we leave to chance what students will learn from their community service experience.

The potential benefits for student learning from service are too important to omit reflection as a planned component of service-learning programs. McPherson (1991) cited the following potential outcomes of reflection on service: effective problem solving strategies, life-long learning skills, increased sense of personal power to create change, higher-level thinking on the root causes of complex issues, and ideas for improving the service activity and the overall program. Perhaps one of the greatest benefits of reflection on service is recognition of how service is central to effective citizenship in a democratic society.

Silcox (1993) maintained that the different reflection methods leaders use will lead to different types of outcomes. For example, Silcox views journal writing as most effective for fostering self-understanding and directed writing activities as more conducive to bringing about cognitive growth and academic development. This list of potential outcomes of reflection also includes overcoming personal stress and anxiety, group bonding and trust, leadership, citizenship, critical thinking skills, and problem-solving skills. A "Reflection

Chart for Evaluating Learning Outcomes" has been developed by Silcox (1993) to help leaders coordinate the reflection method with the desired learning outcome.

Cairn and Kielsmeier (1991) asserted that there are five essential elements of quality reflection in a service-learning program. First, reflection activities need to emanate from clear objectives and goals for student learning from the service experience. These goals will undoubtedly vary based on a multitude of factors including students' ages and developmental levels, the type of service, the academic context, and the time devoted to reflection. Second, quality reflection involves structure. While service-learning program leaders do need to be flexible enough to capitalize on unforeseen opportunities for reflection, most reflection activities should be planned according to the situation and the participants.

Third, reflection should be an engaging and ongoing process. Opportunities for reflection should be integrated throughout the service experience, not just at the end. Fourth, reflection should be integrated in students' course work. Using reflection activities, teachers can teach academic skills and content that will inform the service activity. They can also apply the lessons learned from service to the study of academic material. Finally, it is important to use a variety of reflection methods, both to tap into the diversity of students' experiences and to respond to different learning styles and abilities.

Reflection in service-learning programs is critical if we want students to learn from their service experience. While service programs that neglect the reflection component may provide valuable assistance to service recipients, the tremendous opportunity for student learning is overlooked. Indeed, service-learning programs can and should benefit both those receiving and those providing services. Focusing students' conscious awareness on what they are learning while serving is essential if we hope to develop students with values, knowledge, and skills that will contribute to their future efforts to serve the community.

WHAT TYPE OF CLASSROOM CLIMATE SUPPORTS REFLECTION?

Before we consider the many methods that can be used to encourage student reflection in service-learning programs, a brief discussion of the essential elements of a classroom climate that supports reflection is in order. Establishing a classroom environment in which students feel psychologically and physically safe to express their views is a prerequisite for effective reflection sessions. Students are more likely to be interested in engaging in the reflection process in a classroom that includes all of the following:

1. *Respect for students' ideas.* Program leaders should express appreciation for students' contributions and honor the differences in their perspectives. If students recognize that the program leader cares about them as individuals and does not expect similar or specific responses, they will be much more likely to share their views.

2. *Student-to-student talk.* Most discussions include more leader than student talk. If leaders share their ideas sparingly, students will be more likely to believe that their contributions should form the substance of the discussion.

3. *Room arrangement that facilitates student-to-student interaction.* If students sit in rows facing the program leader, they are less likely to direct their comments to each other. Group discussions focused on student to student talk are best facilitated by placing chairs in a circle.

4. *Mutual respect and caring among students.* It is not enough for the program leader to model respect if classmates are disrespectful to each other. Students may need to be taught skills in affirming others' comments, in disagreeing with someone's idea without putting down the person, and in accepting different perspectives on an issue of common concern.

5. *Planned reflection activities and openness to unexpected opportunities.* It is important to prepare reflection activities guided but not inhibited by the goals and objectives of the program. At the same time, students' service experiences may present spontaneous opportunities for powerful and meaningful reflection.

6. *Reflection sessions throughout the service-learning project.* Reflection should occur before the students begin their service experience, at intervals throughout the service activity, and at the conclusion of the service project. As with any skill, proficiency in reflecting will increase if students engage in this type of thinking on a regular basis.

7. *Adequate time for reflection.* Students will realize the value the program leader places on reflection if debriefing opportunities are not rushed. It is important to allow sufficient time for students to not only think about their own service experiences, but to engage in helping each other explore the deeper issues connected to their service work.

8. *A balance of different reflection methods.* Research on learning styles and multiple intelligences have made educators aware of the different ways students learn. Personality and ethnic identity also influence whether students prefer to reflect individually or in a group, through writing or discussion, in activity or through the visual arts.

9. *Challenging, relevant, and fun reflection activities.* Learners should look forward to opportunities for reflection in service-learning activities. Students can be involved in designing both the focus and strategies for reflection sessions.

10. *A leader skilled in facilitating student reflection.* As program leaders conduct reflection sessions, they should reflect on their own experience. Lead-

ers would do well to make a note of which methods and issues seem to be particularly effective in helping students learn from their experience, draw conclusions, and apply their knowledge to future service activities.

WHAT TOPICS ARE RELEVANT
FOR STUDENTS' REFLECTIONS?

One of the challenging aspects of guiding reflection sessions is choosing the topics to form the basis for student reflections. Endless possibilities can prove daunting to some leaders who either leave the topics solely up to students or ask such vague questions that any response is possible. While it is important to ask open-ended questions to encourage meaningful reflection, program leaders should also structure reflection activities to foster learning consistent with the program's goals and objectives.

At the heart of any reflection session is coming up with a suitable topic or specific questions to guide student thinking. Sample questions are provided here for six areas of focus: events, self, others, service, societal issues, and citizenship. Program leaders should think carefully about the goals for student learning in choosing which topics and questions to incorporate.

Events

It may be most suitable for students to begin reflection sessions by pondering the events in their service-learning projects. Reflecting on the service events that took place includes problem solving and decision making for upcoming weeks. Thinking about what happened this week at the service site is an effective entry point into reflecting on many of the other topics listed here. Following are some useful questions to guide student reflections on the events of their service-learning projects.

• What happened at your service project this week?
• How did people respond to you?
• What problems did you experience?
• How did you respond to the problems?
• What successes did you experience?
• What is your biggest challenge in this project?
• What are your plans for next week?

Self

Most service-learning programs include students' increased awareness of themselves, their skills, values, and beliefs, as important goals. Reflecting on oneself provides essential information for building self-esteem and self-efficacy. In thinking about their skills, interests, and abilities, students can make more effective plans for improving their service efforts and working on issues of importance to them. Due to personality, culture, or religious background, some students will be less comfortable than others reflecting on themselves. Program leaders should allow for individual differences and respect students' privacy. Following are reflection questions designed to enhance students' self-awareness.

• How did you feel participating in your service activity this week?
• What skills did you use in helping others?
• How did you make a difference this week?
• What aspects of the service activity did you find most interesting?
• What aspects of the service activity did you find most challenging?
• What additional skills or knowledge would increase your ability to make a difference?

Others

Service-learning programs that involve direct service with others often include goals of developing respect, empathy, and solidarity. If students do not reflect on the people with whom they are working, they may retain the stereotypes or patronizing attitudes they held prior to the service experience. Most program leaders do not want to foster "do-gooding" or charity among their students, but rather, working alongside others to make the world a better place for us all. Questions that can be used to guide reflection on others in service projects include the following:

• Who are the people with whom you are working?
• What are their values, beliefs, hopes, and dreams?
• What do they have in common as a group?
• How are they different as individuals?
• How do they perceive their needs and problems?
• How do they work for change in their lives?
• What forces limit their effectiveness?

Service

Program leaders can help students learn about both the negative and positive aspects of serving their communities by focusing their reflections on the act of serving. Students can learn valuable lessons through these reflections for both their present service involvement and their future efforts to make a difference. Following are key questions to guide student reflection on service.

• What do you gain from helping others?
• How do others benefit from your efforts?
• Is making a difference easy or difficult? How?
• What or who helps you to make a difference?
• What or who makes it hard for you to make a difference?
• Do you think everyone should help their communities? Explain.
• What values or beliefs are most consistent with serving others?

Societal Issues

Some service-learning programs do not focus on direct service to others. Environmental projects, advocacy efforts, and projects focused on state, national, or global issues involve students working for change on societal issues rather than with a specific population in need. The following questions are important for students in these programs to consider in order for them to realize that their efforts are making a difference. The questions are applicable to programs that focus on direct service to others as well. Students working in these programs should also reflect on the societal issues that effect the human needs to which they are responding.

• What issue is your project addressing?
• If your project is successful, what difference will it make for people?
• What new knowledge have you learned about this issue?
• How is this knowledge informing your actions?
• What human needs or problems are created by this issue?
• What historical events have been connected with this issue?
• What are the current political, economic, and social contexts influencing this issue?
• What are the best means in your opinion for trying to create change about this issue?

Citizenship

Reflecting on the role of service in democratic citizenship is important for all students. Even kindergarten children can begin to understand how communities thrive when everyone helps. Young students can observe this phenomenon in their families, classrooms, and in the local community. Following are questions for students of various ages to consider in reflecting on the relationship between service and democratic citizenship.

• What is a good citizen?
• What type of citizen do you think you will be when you grow up?
• What are the ways that citizens help their communities?

• How does a democracy depend on civic participation?
• What would happen in our democracy if everyone helped?
• What would happen in our democracy if no one helped?
• Is community service an essential aspect of being a good citizen? Why or why not?

Spotlight on Reflection in Young Children
At our annual service-learning awards ceremony, I asked a fourth-grade boy if
there was any difference between his service-learning project and the other
classroom subjects he studied. "Oh yes!" the young man answered quickly.
When I asked him what the difference was, I expected he would talk about
how service-learning helps people or takes place in the community. Instead he
answered, "Well, service-learning is fun, and then there's reading and math
and all that other stuff." What does this elementary student's response tell
you about reflection with young children? What might you as a program leader
ask this child to encourage him to reflect more deeply on his service involve-
ment?

WHAT METHODS CAN BE USED
TO ENCOURAGE REFLECTIVE THINKING?

There are a wide variety of methods program leaders can use to encourage reflection in service-learning projects. Reflection activities will vary
depending on the ages of the students, the goals of the program, the time and
materials available, and the topic on which the students are reflecting. The following methods are presented under four headings: discussion, writing, presentations, and the arts.

Discussion Activities

Some educators maintain that it is only the verbalizing of our ideas and
the social processing we do in conversation with others that allows us to formulate our views and beliefs. Others assert that reflection is primarily an individual process, but that it can be assisted by social activity. Discussion is the
most frequently promoted means for fostering reflective thinking in the classroom. It is also one of the most important skills used in civic participation;
effective meetings, debates, and public hearings all depend on participants'
expertise in discussion and deliberation. Following are a number of activities
that incorporate speaking with others as the central form of reflection:

1. *Think-Pair-Share.* Present the topic or question for reflection and have students deliberate silently for a minute or two. As they think, they can also

write down a few notes. Then each student pairs up with someone sitting nearby and they discuss their ideas. Finally, provide an opportunity for the whole class to share.

2. *Numbered Heads.* Divide students into groups of five. Students number off in their groups from one to five. After the leader presents a reflection question, each group discusses the question for a few minutes. The leader then chooses a number card randomly from a stack of cards labeled one through five. Only the students with that number are invited to respond to the question in a whole class discussion. The activity proceeds with new discussion questions until each number has been called and every student has had the opportunity to speak at least once.

3. *Quote responses.* The leader puts some of the quotes below on the blackboard or gives them to students on a handout. Students are encouraged to discuss their service experiences in light of one or more of the quotes that has meaning for them. Some quotes to use in this activity are the following:

"Anyone can be great because anyone can serve. You don't have to have a college degree to serve. You don't have to make your subject and your verb agree to serve . . . You only need a heart full of grace, a soul generated by love."—Martin Luther King, Jr.

"There are no passengers on spaceship earth. Everybody's crew."—Marshall McLuhan

"Unless someone like you cares a whole awful lot, nothing is going to get better. It's not."—Theodore Geisel (Dr. Seuss)

"Of all the teachings we receive, this one is the most important: Nothing belongs to you of what there is. Of what you take, you must share."—Chief Dan George

"What matters is that you are not cruel or wasteful; that you don't keep the truth from those who need it, suppress someone's will or talent, take more than you need from nature, or fail to use your own talent or will."—Gloria Steinem

"Ask not what your county can do for you, ask what you can do for your country."—John F. Kennedy

"The value of experience is not in seeing much, but in seeing wisely."—Sir William Osler

4. *Fishbowl.* A small circle of four or five chairs is assembled in the middle of the room. Students form a large outer circle around this inner circle. The leader presents a question or topic for reflection and those interested in discussing it move to the inner circle. As students finish their comments

they move back to the outer circle and new students may then enter the inner circle. When sitting in the outer circle, students remain silent observers.

5. *Positive/Negative*. In a whole class or small group discussion, students are asked to talk about the negative aspects of their service experience. They then list the positive outcomes of their service activity. Brainstorming may follow to both build on strengths and come up with potential solutions to problems.

6. *Metaphor Making*. In this creative thinking exercise the leader poses a question in the following form, "In what way is serving in the community like _____?" For example, in response to the question "In what way is serving the community like climbing a mountain?" students might respond that it takes a lot of effort, that you have to keep going sometimes when you're tired, or that you get a great feeling of accomplishment. Here are some other phrases that could be used metaphorically to stimulate students' creative reflection on their experiences.

> baking a cake
> hugging a friend
> reading a good book
> running a race
> planting flowers

7. *Yes/No/Sometimes/Not Sure*. Signs with each of the terms in the title are placed in the four corners of the room. The leader reads a statement such as "Service in the community is an important activity for all citizens" or "Service takes too much time out of the school day to be included in the curriculum." As a statement is read, students move to the corner of the room with the sign that best indicates their views. The leader can ask students who are willing to state briefly why they chose the responses they did. This activity stimulates controversy and critical thinking.

8. *Student Facilitated Discussion*. Students sit in a large circle. The leader begins the discussion by presenting an issue or question and calling on a student who wants to respond. After stating his or her views, that student then calls on the next student who wants to speak. The discussion proceeds with each student who speaks being the one to call on the next student. This discussion strategy is excellent for limiting teacher talk and encouraging student to student interaction. The activity can also be conducted in small groups.

9. *Talking Stick*. Students sit in a large circle. In order to speak, an individual must be holding the talking stick. The stick can be passed around the circle or randomly. If the stick is passed around the circle, students should be informed that they can pass. This activity limits teacher talk and encourages everyone to express their opinion on a given issue or question.

10. *Circle in a Circle.* Students form two concentric circles of equal number facing each other. The leader asks a question or poses a topic for discussion and each pair of students facing each other talks for a minute. Before the leader asks the next question, the inner circle moves to the left so that everyone is facing a new partner.

11. *Opposing Views Lines.* Students form two straight lines of equal number facing each other. The leader presents a question or issue that is likely to encourage diverse views. The students in the left line must address the issue in a positive light while the students in the right line must discuss the issue from a negative point of view. The leader can have one line move so that students face a new partner for each question and/or have students switch sides so that they are discussing issues from different perspectives.

12. *Individual Conference.* Leaders can hold conferences with each student involved in the service-learning activities. Conferences can include a standardized set of questions asked of all students or can be conducted on a more informal basis.

13. *Discussion with Community Members.* This activity can be used before the service experience begins, during the project, or as a culminating lesson. Community agency members working in the area of the students' service activity are invited to class to discuss their views on key issues of concern. Students should prepare for their visit by developing a list of suitable questions to ask. Students can also share their own opinions and hear the responses of those working in the field.

WRITING ACTIVITIES

Reflection strategies that involve writing provide a viable means for teachers to assess what students are learning from their service experience. Writing activities serve the added purpose of integrating skill development in the service-learning program. Students can use their writing abilities in many types of civic activities now and in the future, such as letters to the editor, petitions, surveys, newsletter articles, and so forth. Following are some of the many reflection strategies program leaders can use that involve writing.

1. *Journal.* Probably the most frequently discussed reflection strategy in service-learning is journaling. Students can write daily or weekly entries recounting their experiences, feelings, reactions, and opinions. Leaders can also structure journal entries by providing students with specific questions to answer in their journals. It is important for leaders to read student journals periodically to make sure that students are employing higher-level thinking skills in their writing and not merely recounting events. Cairn

(1993) cautioned that students be advised that they do not have to disclose private feelings they might be uncomfortable sharing with others.

2. *Dialogue Journal.* In a dialogue journal, students write journal entries to another classmate or the program leader. The reader of the journal entry then writes back and the dialogue continues in this manner over the life of the service-learning project. Readers should respond with their own views as well as encourage writers to explore their ideas in greater depth. Students can be partnered so that they are writing to the same person throughout the project, or journals can be shared randomly for a more diverse set of responses.

3. *Learning Log.* In a learning log, students write about their service experiences on a regular basis and also include drawings, charts, and photos to illustrate their service experience. Leaders should provide specific questions and scheduled writing time for students not used to the discipline of keeping a learning log. Cairn (1993) recommended that leaders encourage students to go beyond a merely factual description of the service activities and include how leadership was taken, how problems were solved, who helped, and students' feelings about the service experience. (See chapter 7 for further information on learning logs.)

4. *Creative Writing.* Students can write poems, stories, songs, cartoons, and essays about their service-learning activities. Following reflection on a lesson learned from their service experience, students can write their own version of Aesop's Fables with the lesson or moral at the end. Leaders can encourage students to begin with actual experiences and then use their imaginations and additional ideas to embellish their writing. Carefully chosen creative writing activities can help students meet curricular goals as well as have some fun with the reflection process.

5. *Persuasive Letters.* Letters to the editor of a local newspaper or to a Congress person can be the motivation for students to reflect on the essential aspects of their experience and their resultant opinions about action on an issue. Students should be encouraged to draw on their personal experiences as well as do some research on the issue they are addressing to inform their positions. Students must carefully edit and proofread their letters before mailing them.

6. *Concept Map.* A concept map is a diagram of the multitude of components and their connections concerning a concept. For example, the student could place the word "service" in the center of a piece of paper and then draw an interconnected web of the many ideas related to the concept of service. Concept maps can be created at the beginning and end of the service-learning project to assess students' development.

7. *Publicity.* Students can write newsletter or magazine articles about their service-learning projects. They can also design brochures or other promo-

tional materials for recruiting future participants. All of these activities require students to reflect on the important or appealing aspects of their service-learning activities and to consider how this information can best be presented to others.

8. *Evaluations.* Students may write an evaluation of their service-learning project taking into account the following: their own efforts and feelings, the benefits to the community, the strengths and weaknesses of the program, and ideas for improving the program. Group discussion or interviewing of program participants preceding the writing of the evaluation will assist students in drawing on information beyond their own experience.

9. *Guide for Future Participants.* Developing a set of guidelines for future participants in the service-learning program will require students to evaluate their own experiences and to assess the next steps for the program. Students can work on guidelines for specific parts of the program (i.e., recruitment, training, problem solving, celebration) and then assemble their work into one product.

10. *Directed Writing.* Directed writing assignments require students to address specific content chosen by the teacher. This type of writing "tends to be highly cognitive and oriented toward subject learning" (Silcox, 1993, p. 56). For example, students might answer questions about their service-learning activities focused on the specific behaviors of effective citizens in a democracy. Silcox (1993) asserted that directed writing, with its focus on a particular topic or problem chosen by the teacher, can foster discipline and work-study habits that are not present in other forms of reflection.

11. *Writing in the Curriculum.* A particularly useful form of directed writing is the assignment that can be integrated in the academic curriculum. For example, if a language arts teacher needs to instruct children on how to write a business letter, students could write letters to local businesses to raise funds for their service project. A math teacher could have students develop story problems based on the service activities and a science teacher might have students devise a hypothesis and subsequent experiment to test a potential outcome of the service activity. Creative program leaders will seek out ways to encourage student reflection and academic development at the same time.

ARTISTIC EXPRESSION

Artists by their nature reflect on the world and create a means of representing their ideas to share with others. While most schools tend to value the three R's more highly than artistic skill, artwork can be a very suitable outlet for creative reflection in service-learning programs. Including options for artistic expression in service-learning reflection sessions can also help program leaders meet students' learning-style needs. Often artistic products or presentations are effective ways to share about the service-learning activity with others. Following are some of the many ways students can express their learning through art:

1. *Visual Arts*. Students can draw, paint, or sculpt their service experiences. A diversity of experiences can be represented in a collage or a quilt. A diorama or shoe box scene can offer students the opportunity to depict a key event or turning point in their service project.
2. *Music*. Students can write songs or compose instrumental pieces to represent what they have learned from service. Along with this activity, students could learn about how music has accompanied social change efforts in our nation's history. Leaders can encourage students to share their music publicly to inspire others' involvement in their communities.
3. *Theater*. From skits and role plays to dramatic productions or musicals, students can reflect on their service experience through the theater. Producing a play will likely involve writing, discussion, and artwork (creating props, scenery, costumes) as well. Students who are kinesthetic learners will benefit from using their strengths in theatrical productions. As with many other art forms, theater is a particularly effective way to share with others about the service experience.
4. *Dance*. Another suitable mode for the kinesthetic learner, dance is an exciting means for students to represent the feelings, values, and ideas resulting from their service involvement.
5. *Technology*. Students can document their service activities in photos, a slide show, or a video essay. Reflection comes into play in editing and organizing the images to tell a story. More recent technology such as interactive computer programs, CD-ROMs, and laser disc, can provide an additional challenge and a fascinating reflection experience for students.

PRESENTATIONS

When students share what they have gleaned from their service-learning project with others, they must first reflect on which parts of their experience to include and second how to represent that experience in a way that communicates effectively to those who have not participated in the project. As mentioned previously, teaching others about a topic is one of the best ways to instill learning. Also, students will have many opportunities as community citizens to make presentations at school board meetings, public hearings, city council meetings, and so forth. Students who engage in some of the presentation activities below will not only reflect and learn from their reflection but they will also be continuing to make a difference as they inspire others to service.

1. *School Display/ Presentation.* Program leaders can build awareness and support for their service-learning activities in the school while fostering student reflection through student displays and presentations. Displays in shared spaces such as the library, lunchroom, gym, and hallways will be seen by most of the people in the school. Students can schedule informal lunch time talks on their service activities or offer to give brief presentations in other classes. Presentations for the school's parent-teacher organization might help to develop parent support or garner additional funds for service-learning activities.

2. *General Public Presentation.* Students can present what they have learned publicly at the local library or recreation center. Public presentations of service-learning activities may reach more people if offered in conjunction with existing events such as parades, community fairs, or candidates forums. Where an event is held may greatly influence who attends.

3. *Community Agency Presentation.* Following a service-learning project, students could present what they have learned to the agency members with whom they worked or other agencies who work with a similar population. For example, students who completed an intergenerational oral history project might invite the activity directors from all the local area nursing homes to a presentation on their project. In this way, new agencies might become interested in service-learning collaborations.

4. *Policy Presentation.* Students could present on their projects at a local school board or town council meeting. This type of presentation should be integrated with a proposal the group is considering, for example, to fund a districtwide service-learning program or to set up a homeless shelter. Students should prepare carefully for such presentations as it is likely their presentation time will be limited to a few minutes. It is important that their presentation offer valuable information relevant to the policy being considered and not just a "cute" example of students helping others.

5. *Conference Presentation.* Presenting a workshop or session at a conference is a terrific opportunity for students to reflect on their experience and to develop their presentation skills. Some conferences, notably the National Service-Learning Conference sponsored by the National Youth Leadership Council (see Appendix), favors proposals that include student presenters. If the local service-learning program is large enough, students could organize a local conference with a variety of student presentations.

6. *Training Presentation.* Students can assist with training future service project participants by presenting at a training. (This activity could be combined

effectively with the students' development of guidelines for a service-learning program listed under the Writing Activities section of this chapter). Their presentation should be focused to include specific information or skills relevant to participating in the service-learning project.

Certainly this is not an exhaustive list of the ways that students might reflect on their experiences in service-learning programs. The ideas presented here, however, do address the different needs for reflection activities in service-learning programs. Collectively they take into consideration different learning styles, various stages in the service-learning project, students' differing developmental and ability levels, different skills to be developed through reflection, and various topics or issues to address.

HOW ARE REFLECTION SESSIONS STRUCTURED AT DIFFERENT POINTS IN THE PROJECT?

In addition to the topics and methods that form the substance of reflection activities, program leaders must also consider the "when" and the "where" of reflection sessions. As mentioned previously, it is important to plan for reflection throughout the service-learning activity. While the many topics and methods for reflection could combine in endless ways, the following guidelines are helpful in thinking about structuring reflection sessions at different points during the project.

1. *Reflect on assumptions, stereotypes, and other preconceived notions* before *the service activity begins.* If students are going to be working alongside people with whom they are unfamiliar, it is important to assist them in exploring their stereotypes and prior learning. For example, students who will be working with senior citizens can think about grandparents and other elderly people with whom they have had contact. What views do they hold about seniors as a result of these experiences? How might these views influence their service-learning activities?

Students will be entering the service site with a host of feelings and beliefs about themselves and the act of serving as well. What do they expect to accomplish? What skills do they fear they may be lacking in their service efforts? What prior experiences have they had in trying to "make a difference" in their personal lives, schools, and communities? Helping students assess their ideas about themselves as service providers may lead to realizations about unrealistic expectations or limited views of their own capabilities. Program leaders can respond to students' needs in these areas more effectively when they understand students' thinking.

2. During *the service activity, help students process their feelings and experiences.* As students engage in service, they will come face to face with problems, successes, and challenges they could not have foreseen. Students should evaluate how they are effectively making a difference and where their efforts need more attention or a different approach. Problem solving and decision making are key reflection activities during this phase of the service-learning project. Reflection at this stage can help students identify their own values, personal skills, and knowledge base.

It is important to guide students' realizations as they come up against the assumptions they held before beginning the service activity. Which of their prior beliefs appear to have held true? What aspects are different than what they had expected? How have they changed their views based on this new information?

While students are involved in service, they should also begin to place the lessons they are learning about themselves, others, and the act of serving within the context of what it means to be a citizen in a democracy. Depending on the ages of the students and the situations in which they are serving, they can begin to think about the root causes of the problems they are addressing and brainstorm ideas for future service activities to effect greater change.

3. At the end *of the service-learning activity, encourage students to draw conclusions and apply their new knowledge to future service projects.* Reflection at the conclusion of a service-learning project should focus honestly on what was accomplished and what goals were not reached. Students can explore the range of personal, social, and societal issues that may have limited their good intentions. Reflecting after the project is completed, students can organize, compare, contrast, evaluate, and summarize their experience. Students should also be encouraged to recognize new skills, values, and knowledge resulting from their service activity. The focus of reflection sessions at the end of a service-learning project should be on applying students' new understandings to their future service involvement.

When students have completed a service-learning project, they are ready to consider some of the larger questions as to how service fits into their view of a good citizen. Drawing on their feelings and experiences, students can form opinions about the importance of service for themselves, others, and society.

In considering the "where" for student reflection, the classroom is probably the optimal site in most cases. However, if the service-learning project is coordinated outside of the regular academic program this may not always be possible. Program leaders can also engage students in reflection on the bus as they travel to and from the service site or in a separate meeting area at the service site. Many program leaders give students reflection exercises as homework, such as writing in a journal or learning log. The location of the reflection session is not as important as making sure that reflection is a planned and integrated component of the service-learning program.

PUTTING IT ALL TOGETHER

Leaders who establish effective reflection experiences for students in their service-learning programs realize that there are many considerations that must be taken into account when planning reflections sessions. Decisions must be made about which reflection methods are most suitable for specific topics and phases of service-learning activities. The following checklist can be used to make sure that all the essential components have been included.

Reflection Planning Checklist

Reflection activities:

_____ are planned for the beginning, middle, and ending of the service-learning project.

_____ may also occur spontaneously to fit the needs of students.

_____ use varied methods to meet different learning style needs.

_____ are integrated with academic skills and content.

_____ take place within a classroom climate supportive of reflection.

_____ focus on topics (events, self, others, service, societal issues, citizenship) consistent with the goals of the program.

Challenge Activity

Design a reflection plan for a middle school service-learning program that involves forty seventh- and eighth-grade students working once a week for two hours with children in a homeless shelter. The students service-learning activity is part of their social studies class. What goals do you think such a program would have for student learning? How will a classroom climate supportive of reflection be established? What topics and methods will you choose? How often will students reflect? Where will the reflection sessions be held? Make sure you are able to explain why you designed your reflection plan as you did.

Chapter 7

Building Support for Service-Learning

Rahima C. Wade

Planning and carrying out an effective service-learning project can be a rewarding experience for all involved. Building on a positive experience, program leaders can enhance the future success and growth of service-learning activities by considering ways to strengthen support for service-learning in the school and community. The focus of this chapter is on building support for service-learning programs through documenting, celebrating, publicizing, and fund-raising for project activities. All of these efforts are critical to ensuring the success and longevity of service-learning programs.

While some program leaders prefer to approach administrators and community members for money and commitment to service-learning *before* they begin projects, my experience leads me to believe that a better approach involves demonstrating the benefits of service-learning through carrying out a small project and sharing the results with others. In this way, potential supporters can see for themselves the powerful effects of service-learning for students and communities.

Building support for service-learning programs really begins in the planning stage, not as an afterthought to a successful project. In chapter 2, I discussed evaluating service-learning activities. Evaluation data should be used in concert with the strategies outlined in this chapter. While discussed separately in this chapter, in reality, documentation, celebration, public relations, and fund-raising often overlap and all serve to enhance building support for service-learning.

WHY DOCUMENT SERVICE-LEARNING PROJECTS?

Documenting service-learning projects serves at least four important functions integral to building support for programs. First, documentation enables program leaders to share the project with others. Perhaps a parent is curious about the learning component of the project or a colleague wants to try the project in his or her classroom. Documentation enables others to get a more detailed view of the project as a whole.

Second, documentation assists program leaders in their efforts to evaluate the program. (See chapter 2 for further details on conducting program evaluations.) Keeping track of the steps that were taken and the results along the way is useful in reflecting on one's own practice, in analyzing what worked and what didn't, and in considering how the program can be improved in the future. Adequate documentation also allows program leaders to complete the same project again without reinventing it anew.

Third, the items saved in documenting the project are useful in guiding students' learning from their service. Students can use photos, papers, and other materials saved to reflect on their service activities and draw conclusions about themselves, others, and the act of making a difference.

Fourth, documentation of the project is central to publicizing and celebrating the service activities. Program leaders can use many of the items saved in displays and presentations. Photos can be provided to local newspapers to accompany articles written about the service-learning project and students' reflections can be shared with parents at conference time.

HOW DO PROGRAM LEADERS DOCUMENT THEIR SERVICE-LEARNING ACTIVITIES?

Documentation procedures will vary depending on the type of project and the energy invested in the process. Program leaders should think about their goals for documenting the project and choose documentation activities that will support those goals. For example, if community presentations for fund-raising purposes are in the plans, make a slide show or a video of your project. If program leaders want to do the same project again with a new group of students, keeping a paper trail will help. With some guidance, students can also assist in the task of documenting the project. Following are some possible documentation activities for service-learning programs.

1. *Paper trail.* Keeping a paper trail on the project involves saving copies of papers associated with the project. These might include: the program leader's planning sheets and notes, correspondence, students' written work (journal entries, class assignments, reflections, etc.), and publicity on the project. A specially marked folder can be used to place copies of all papers associated with the service-learning activities; the papers can be sorted and organized periodically for an ongoing project or at the end for a short-term project.

2. *Journal.* Program leaders will benefit by keeping a journal on their involvement with service-learning. If students are journaling as part of their reflective process, program leaders can journal at the same time and model the importance of reflection. The journal can be a private place to record feelings of frustration and fulfillment as well as a space to jot down ideas for next steps or future activities. (See chapter 6 on reflection for further ideas about journals.)

3. *Project log.* The project log is a place for the program leader or student participants to record the date, time, and activity for each aspect of the service-learning project. For example, an early entry in a log might read as follows: "9/12/95–3:15 p.m. to 4:00 p.m.—Planned for student reflection activities." A later entry might be listed as "11/29/95–1:00 p.m. to 2:30 p.m.—Field trip to local recycling center." The log is a useful tool for documenting the time spent on different aspects of the service-learning project. The project log can be used to record the total hours served by program participants as well as all service completed (i.e., number of people served, number of students providing service, total trees planted, etc.).

4. *Learning log.* Cairn (1993) advocated students keeping learning logs to document their service-learning experiences. The learning log serves a number of purposes beyond documentation, including developing written communication skills, fostering reflective thinking, venting feelings, recording data, and referencing content and resources for future writing. Program leaders should clearly outline the expectations for students' work in learning logs and set aside time periodically to review the logs and write back to students. Students should be encouraged to write after every service experience, to describe their experiences (including date, time, names, location, challenges, and summaries of activities), and to include drawings, charts, or photos to add to their descriptions.

5. *Letters of support.* Program leaders may want to solicit letters of support from community leaders, community agencies involved in the service-learning activities, parents, and individuals who have benefited from the service project. These letters of support may prove useful in future fund-raising efforts or in gaining administrative support for service-learning programs in school districts. If you want to be able to quote from these letters in fund-raising solicitation letters or in news articles, indicate this in your initial request for the support letter.

6. *Photos, slide shows, and videos.* If you can, take photographs throughout the service-learning project. As the saying goes, "A picture is worth a thousand words." Photos can be useful for reflection, publicity, and celebrations and they may be able to tell the story of your project better than any other means. If you plan presentations on your project for large groups, consider having students document their efforts in a slide show or video.

7. *Artifacts.* Often projects will include concrete materials or products. Saving an example of the craft project completed with seniors at a nursing home or a bat house built for a local nature center is an important means of documentation. When it is not feasible to save an example of the project, take photographs.

8. *Site visits.* It is important to conduct site visits to the service location and document some of the activities there. Documentation activities on-site might include some of the ideas above, for example, taking photos or videotaping, as well as interviewing agency members, distributing surveys to program participants, or conducting focus group discussions. Kendall and her associates (1990) suggested setting up a site visit after becoming clear about the goals for this visit. Questions program leaders might attempt to answer through a site visit include the following:
   • Are students meeting their service and learning objectives?
   • Have students made any notable contributions?
   • What problems have been encountered and what steps are being taken to solve them?

9. *Portfolios.* Many of the above can be combined and assembled in a portfolio. Creating a program portfolio involves collecting program documentation, reflecting on the items and information of greatest importance, and selecting those items to arrange in a three-ring binder or other format. Portfolios offer their developers a sense of both personal history and future; students' portfolios "collect and document who they were, who they are now, and who they want to be" (Sunstein, 1992, p. 37).

WHY CELEBRATE SERVICE-LEARNING PROJECTS?

Celebration serves many important purposes in service-learning projects beyond simply "having fun." Celebrating is a means for saying "thank you," affirming our connections, honoring our efforts, and renewing our commitment to service. Many of the items and papers saved in the documentation process will be useful in celebration events at the end of the service-learning project. McPherson (1991) advocated that celebration be included in service-learning projects both for renewing participants' enthusiasm and for sustaining support for the service-learning program. Celebrating one's efforts with others can be a fun aspect of civic life. Following are some of the potential benefits celebration can provide for students, community members, and the service-learning program itself.

1. *For Students.* It is important for students to see that their service efforts are valued by the school and community. Celebrations that recognize student

success can contribute to students' self-esteem and self-efficacy. "They should be public affirmations by parents and other adults recognizing a transition marking the significance of youths' contributions to others" (Cairn, 1993, p. 58). Through celebrations, students can acknowledge that they really did make a difference.

Service activities are not always easy; nor do students always accomplish all they set out to at the beginning of the project. Celebration can serve as a reflection tool and an energy booster for students. In addition to acknowledging success, students can recognize where the project fell short of their initial goals. The energy and support engendered by celebration can contribute to renewed commitment to further service.

It is important, however, to keep celebration in perspective. The material rewards for involvement in service should not outweigh the internal satisfaction of helping others and making a difference. Celebration activities should serve to affirm students' efforts yet not be the primary motivator for participating in service.

2. *For Community Members.* Celebration activities should also recognize the efforts of community members who participated in the service-learning project. Celebration is an important way to say "thank you" to those who have invested a great deal of time and energy in the service experience, such as an agency member who coordinated students' activities on-site. Such individuals should receive special attention at a celebratory event. For community members, celebration can be an acknowledgment of the network of parents, teachers, students, and community members who have collaborated together to help others. Celebrations can also give those community members with minimal involvement a chance to learn more about the service activity and encourage them to continue to participate.

3. *For the Service-Learning Program.* Finally, celebration is an effective way to publicize the service-learning program. When students and community members are being recognized for their efforts in a festive atmosphere, parents and others from the community are likely to want to attend. If program plans include recruiting new students or community participants, ask those attending to bring friends and consider opening the event to anyone in the community who would like to attend. Be sure to invite local newspaper reporters and community members connected with potential sources of funding as well.

WHAT ARE SOME OPTIONS FOR DIFFERENT TYPES OF CELEBRATIONS?

Celebrations vary greatly in size and type. When coordinating a celebratory event, program planners should consider the potential benefits outlined above and invite input from all program participants. Following are some suggestions for celebrating, from small, student-oriented events to large public gatherings.

1. *Celebrating Student Success.* Celebrations that focus predominately on recognizing students' efforts can be as simple as a pizza party, a special field trip, or an extra recess. Ask students themselves what they would value as acknowledgment of their service involvement. Elementary students might like to eat popcorn and watch a video. High school students might prefer certificates or mention of their names in the local newspaper. Simple gifts such as a button or T-shirt that says "I made a difference" might be appropriate as well. Pencils or note pads with the program's logo can serve as mementos for students leaving the program.

   The advantages to student-focused celebrations include being generally easier to organize, less time consuming, and less costly than larger events. However, both students and programs may miss out on the public recognition that can be gained through larger events. If the celebration includes only students, make sure that thank you notes or small gifts are sent to community members who participated in the service-learning project.

2. *Celebrations for Program Participants.* Celebrations that include all of the participants in the service-learning program can affirm the collaboration and community spirit created through serving together. Depending on the total number of program participants, these events can range in size and scope. If funds are lacking for a large gathering, consider having students make decorations and plan a "potluck" approach to providing refreshments.

   Celebrations with more than fifteen or twenty participants should be carefully organized. Think about providing name tags, a mixer activity to help everyone get acquainted, and a set agenda for the event. If plans include refreshments and socializing, a group activity, and time for giving out awards or recognizing participants' efforts, sixty to ninety minutes is probably adequate.

   Even though the focus is predominately on program participants, consider inviting just a few additional people, such as a school district administrator or a local newspaper reporter. Including three or four other people will probably not hurt the group spirit of the event and may enhance your efforts to build support for the continuation of the program.

3. *Large Public Events.* If the program needs additional funding, new participants, or a stronger base of support in the school or community, a public celebration is probably the best choice. Public events can be exciting experiences for students and their parents as well. While large events have many advantages, they take considerable time, energy, and sometimes funding to coordinate. Plan a large event carefully, with an eye for making it an enjoyable and productive experience for everyone involved.

Sometimes a number of service-learning programs can collaborate together on one large event. For example, the university–public school service-learning program I coordinate puts on a "Service-Learning Fair" each spring at the local public library. Representative students and their teachers from ten schools set up displays on their projects and receive award certificates and ribbons to take back to the classroom. While in some ways similar to a Science Fair, we eliminate the competitive aspect and honor all students' efforts equally. The Service-Learning Fair has proven to be an effective vehicle for publicizing service activities to parents and community members as well as for helping students expand their ideas about how they can serve the community.

Spotlight on Celebration
Second graders in Ames, Iowa, have a special awards ceremony on completing a year-long partnership with residents in a local nursing home. The evening event held at the school includes the seniors, students, citizens, parents, school personnel, and community agency members. Students are given individual certificates and refreshments are served. How do you think the second graders feel when participating in this event? What other purposes does this recognition serve in terms of building support for an ongoing program?

WHY PUBLICIZE A SERVICE-LEARNING PROJECT?

Publicizing a service-learning activity is not only a way to celebrate students' accomplishments, but can also be a means to inspire others to engage in service. When students plan the publicity for their project, it gives them an opportunity to reflect on the most meaningful and interesting aspects of their work, who might be interested in learning about the project, and the best opportunities for getting their message out to the audience they have in mind. Again, publicity should be designed with an eye toward the goals of the program and future recruitment and funding needs.

WHAT ARE SOME OPTIONS FOR PUBLICIZING SERVICE-LEARNING PROJECTS?

Publicizing a service-learning project can be both fun and educational for students. Depending on the goals and needs of the program and the time program leaders want to invest in publicizing their projects, one or more of the following options might be suitable.

1. *Local Newspapers.* Students can write letters to the editor about their project. As the "Letters to the Editor" section is one of the most widely read features in most papers, this is a great way to get information out to a large group of people (Fleisher, 1993). Make sure that the name and address of the letter writer is included as most newspapers won't print anonymous letters. Another approach to getting into the local newspaper is to write a short article on the project. If possible, send along a few black-and-white photos with the article. (Be sure to obtain permission from those included in the photo for it to be printed in the newspaper.) A third approach program leaders might also consider is to take out a classified ad to recruit new volunteers or to request a listing in the Volunteers Needed section of the newspaper.

2. *Public Service Announcement.* A public service announcement, or PSA, is a short radio or television announcement of a community event. Both radio and TV stations are required to read PSAs every day. To increase your chances of getting your PSA on the air, write a twenty- to thirty-second script for the announcer, make sure the PSA contains all important information about the event, identify your organization and contact person clearly, and mail to the public affairs director two to three weeks before the event (Fleisher, 1993). Program leaders should also consider making follow-up phone calls to the station to make sure the announcement was received and to inquire about when it will be aired.

3. *Public Access Television.* Cable television companies are required to have a public access channel where anyone who has a presentation to make can do so. Program leaders could videotape service activities or associated learning in the classroom, organize a talk show on the service theme, or tape interviews with program participants. In some cases, public access programs do not reach many people. If program leaders want bigger audiences, they should publicize the broadcasts with fliers and posters, by word-of-mouth, or through an announcement in the local newspaper.

4. *Leaflets.* Handing out leaflets on a busy street corner can be a way to reach many people in a short amount of time. While some people will not read the flier and the audience one reaches is random, leaflets can be an inexpensive way to get out the word about a program and to experience an important aspect of the democratic process. (The Constitution ensures everyone's First Amendment right to express their opinion by handing out information in public places.) If the program hopes to recruit more students, consider handing out leaflets in the lunchroom, at a schoolwide assembly, at a dance, or at a sports event.

5. *Brochures.* A brochure highlighting the components and benefits of the service-learning program can be handed out like a leaflet or mailed to a specially identified audience. For example, brochures on an intergenerational project could be mailed to nursing homes, retirement residences, and local

agencies that provide services to seniors. Brochures should be simple yet eye-catching. Encourage students to reflect on the most important points to include in a brochure on the project and to include intriguing graphics or photos of project participants.

6. *Posters*. Many public places and private businesses will put up posters on their premises, particularly if the poster is advertising a public event. Program leaders may want to enlist the help of the art teacher in guiding students' creation of posters that are well-designed and carefully crafted. Encourage students to choose potential locations for posters and to share in the task of requesting to have them put up.

7. *Art display*. A display of drawings, paintings, sculpture, or photos with relevant captions can be an exciting way to publicize a service-learning program. Suitable locations for such a display would include the local mall, the public library, a bank, a restaurant, a laundromat, a hospital, a community agency, or the local post office. Program leaders should consider who they want to inform about the project in choosing a suitable location for the display.

8. *Newsletter*. Articles in school and agency newsletters will publicize the program to key audiences. School newsletters will let parents know about the project; agency newsletters will inform both employees and clients. In writing newsletter articles, students should include the basics—who, what, when, where, why—of the project. As with newspaper articles, students should include photos to accompany the article if possible and carefully proof before submitting.

9. *Publicity "event."* A special publicity event could feature a guest speaker, a video, or a slide show. Consider combining a publicity event with other program needs, such as celebration or fund-raising. For example, a publicity event on a hunger project could feature a simple soup and bread meal in addition to a video on the project. By charging a small amount for the meal, the event can serve as a fund-raiser for the project. Other possibilities include a fun run fund-raiser for a health-related service-learning activity or a car wash for an environmental "clean up" project.

10. *Information Table*. Similar in some ways to leafleting, students can set up an information table on their project at school or community events. Craft fairs and county fairs draw large crowds and some communities feature annual volunteer fairs to attract new participants. At some of these events, students may have the option to sell snacks or project souvenirs (pencils, note pads, mugs, T-shirts) to assist with fund-raising efforts as well.

These are just a few of the many ways program leaders can involve students in publicizing their good works. Additional ideas, such as conducting workshops or conference presentations, are included in the list of reflection activities found in chapter 7.

Spotlight on Publicity
A middle school service-learning program focuses on improving the local environment. Recently during a water test of a local stream, students found that pollutants were at a dangerous level. What publicity techniques would be the best strategies for the students to get the news out to many people quickly? What techniques might build support for the school's service-learning program?

WHY FUND-RAISE FOR SERVICE-LEARNING PROGRAMS?

Most service-learning programs have a need for some operating funds. Even if staff and training costs are covered by the school district, programs usually need some type of ongoing support for transportation and supplies associated with service-learning activities. While small group projects can probably support themselves through fund-raising events such as fun runs, bake sales, car washes, dances, and movie viewings, districtwide programs may need external sources of funding. Fund-raising is an important civic activity, especially when working with social service or other nonprofit agencies.

WHAT OPTIONS EXIST FOR FUND-RAISING FOR SERVICE-LEARNING PROGRAMS?

Fleisher (1993) recommended considering the following categories when choosing a fund-raising option: level of difficulty to carry out, planning time needed, number of organizers needed, start-up costs, potential return, informational value, and particular advantages and disadvantages in the approach. In addition, answering the ten questions below will aid program leaders in choosing the best strategy for their program.

• How much money do we need to raise?
• For what purposes will that money be used?
• About how many people are available to help organize a fund-raiser?
• About how many volunteer workers are available to help work at our fund-raising event?
• How much community support is there for our issue?
• What special connections—to businesses, entertainers, churches, etc.—does our group have?
• Right now, if we had to choose between raising lots of money or informing lots of people about our issue, which would be more important?

• What fund-raising strategies have we tried before? Which were successful and which were not?
• What fund-raising events are our group members most interested in doing? (Fleisher, 1993, p. 157)

Program leaders should begin the fund-raising process by establishing clear goals for the program and an accompanying budget of anticipated expenses. Careful attention to fund-raising and money management is critical to the success and longevity of service-learning programs; responsible funders will not contribute to programs that do not have clear goals and an explicit budget. The list of fund-raising ideas below begins with small-scale efforts and ends with activities focused on obtaining substantial external support.

1. *Small-scale events.* If students are fund-raising for a specific project with a budget of a few hundred dollars or less, a small-scale event can raise the funds, build group cohesion, and develop collaboration skills in the process. Typical examples of such fund-raisers include the following: car wash, bake sale, fun run, walkathon, school dance, movie viewing, yard sale, carnival, or spaghetti supper. These events can take considerable time to coordinate and do not assure a specific level of income. However, they enable students to have fun while taking ownership for funding their service-learning project.

2. *Selling items.* Some programs publicize their activities and raise funds at the same time by selling T-shirts, mugs, pencils, note pads, buttons, bumper stickers, or other items with the program's logo. Sometimes local businesses will produce these items at a reduced cost as a way of making a contribution to youth service in the community. Using a variety of math skills, students can get involved in obtaining estimates for the products, evaluating the best deal, and figuring out how much to charge for each item so that reasonable costs and profit margins are achieved. Students might sell items at school or community events; setting up a concession stand at school sports events or local fairs can also be profitable. Operating a business, such as a school store, thrift shop, or used book store, is also a good way to raise money.

3. *Performance.* Encourage students to use their own skills and talents to raise funds for the program by producing a play or concert. Tickets can be sold and if the performance is held at the school, there will be little overhead for such events. They can, however, take a great deal of time to coordinate. With some thought and creativity, plays and concerts can be used to inform the audience members about the focus of the program or the specific service activities.

4. *Bowling or Skating Party.* Another type of "fun-raising" event is a party at the local bowling alley or roller skating rink. This event only works as a

fund-raiser if the business involved agrees to split the profits gained. While this type of event is generally less work than a performance, success depends on getting the word out early to those who are most likely to attend.

5. *Speakers*. Who in the community would a large number of people pay to come out and hear? This is the question that program leaders should think about when considering having a speaker as a fund-raising event. The speaker could be a popular community figure such as a college sports star, local politician, or television celebrity. Another possible approach would be to invite a speaker who is an expert in the issue area that the service-learning program addresses. A third possibility is for students to set up a speaker's bureau through which they could speak to community groups for a small fee.

6. *Workathon*. The workathon fund-raiser involves having individuals or businesses in the community pledge a small amount of money for each hour of student service incurred during either the project as a whole or on a single day of service. For example, patrons might pledge one dollar per hour students spend working one Saturday at the Special Olympics. The workathon is a cost-free way to raise funds and also to inform donors about the civic efforts in which students are involved. The success of the workathon depends on extensive publicity and students being willing to ask others to make pledges on their behalf.

7. *Business Sponsors*. Depending on the nature of the service-learning project, program leaders should consider asking a specific business in the community to become a partner for a project. For example, a grocery store might be invited to sponsor a project focused on feeding the homeless or a medical supply business might be interested in forming a partnership on an intergenerational or health-related project. Before inviting a partner, think about which businesses might benefit from the publicity associated with the project and develop a proposal that includes ideas for how the partnership will benefit the business as well as the community.

8. *Signature Ad*. Businesses and service clubs in the community can each make a donation to the program and then have their names featured in a signature ad in the local newspaper. This type of fund-raiser is good publicity for both the donors and the service-learning program. Be sure to find out how much the newspaper charges for different size ads as this will need to be deducted from the donations to figure the profit. Consider asking the newspaper to be a patron as well by donating some of the cost of the ad and having their name included.

9. *Raffle*. Seek out businesses that will be willing to donate items for which raffle tickets can be sold. Larger items will lead to more ticket sales. Sell

tickets for fifty cents to a dollar; a higher cost will deter some potential supporters. An alternative approach is to have students raffle off an item they
have made, such as a quilt; or services, such as baby-sitting, mowing lawns,
or raking leaves. The success of a raffle depends on student interest; they
must be willing to approach others in the school and community to sell tickets.

10. *Auction.* An auction may be a more profitable approach than a raffle if
program participants have obtained many donated items. Silent auctions
involve providing a sheet of paper next to each item on display where people can write down their bids. This is a generally less time consuming and
easier to coordinate approach than an auction where the audience must sit
through public bidding on each item. Consider having a silent auction at an
event that is sure to draw a large crowd such as a Back-To-School Night or
a community fair.

11. *Direct Mail/Phoneathon.* Both direct mail campaigns and phoneathons
seek to obtain support from a large number of individual donors. Program
leaders using one of these approaches should think carefully about who to
solicit and who will provide the time to conduct these activities. Direct
mail can be expensive and may result in only a small percentage of
responses (Flanagan, 1982).

12. *In-kind Donations.* Many service-learning programs can benefit from
donated space, services, and items. For example, a local print shop might
donate the cost of printing a brochure on the program or the city transportation system might provide free rides for students who need public
transport to their community service sites. Community businesses and
organizations may also be able to help with the people power and physical
space needs of service-learning programs. Program leaders should consider which businesses and local agencies might provide the types of in-
kind contributions most suitable for the projects. Also, parents can often
obtain contributions from their workplaces or agencies with which they
are involved. Skillful attention to obtaining donated services and materials
can greatly reduce the need for other types of fund-raising.

13. *Grants.* Many federal and state agencies and private foundations are currently supporting service-learning activities. In general, grants are highly
competitive and are awarded to larger programs that can demonstrate innovation, experienced leadership, and fiscal responsibility. Some foundations are willing to provide seed money with the understanding that the program will become self-sufficient within a few years (Bobo, Kendall, &
Max, 1991). Carefully research grants and foundations to determine the
conditions of their grants; many give only within a specific geographic or
issue area. An excellent resource on grant funding opportunities for service-

learning programs is the *Service-Learning Planning and Resource Guide* published by the Council of Chief State School Officers in Washington, D.C. For further information on grant funding, see also Corporation for National Service (1995) and Mellon Bank Corporation (1985).

14. *Issue-oriented Funds.* Some service-learning programs have been able to take advantage of funds earmarked for special efforts in the schools such as dropout prevention, drug prevention, and literacy initiatives. Program leaders should check with their state department of education to find out what reform efforts provide funds in their states and how service-learning programs might support the goals of these initiatives.

PUTTING IT ALL TOGETHER

Program leaders might understandably find the list of strategies for documenting, celebrating, publicizing, and fund-raising for service-learning activities daunting, given the time it takes to coordinate a service-learning program. The key to building support for service-learning programs in a time efficient manner is to focus on how singular efforts can serve multiple purposes.

For example, at the conclusion of an intergenerational project that involves university students, senior citizens from the local Retired Senior Volunteer Program, and elementary age children from Big Brothers/Big Sisters, we have a party to celebrate all of these volunteers' contributions. We also build support for our program through the following: inviting local media personnel to attend and subsequently publicize the event, inviting parents and potential new volunteers, and inviting members of community agencies and service clubs who might want to become further involved in the program or contribute funds. We also take photos at the party and keep records as to who attended, planning time involved, cost of supplies, and activities held. The party is largely planned and coordinated by university student volunteers. Thus, through this event, we not only celebrate the program, but also enhance student leadership skills, publicize our program, recruit new participants, and broaden our base of support and potential financial donors.

Challenge Activity
A high school social studies class has been studying the disability rights movement as part of their focus on the history of U.S. citizens' rights. After studying the laws on access for people with disabilities, the class conducted a survey of six community buildings to determine whether they are in compliance with federal and state regulations. They found one building that needed some changes to improve accessibility, specifically raised numbers and braille in the elevator and a ramp into the building. How can the students raise funds for

these renovations? How could their fund-raising efforts be combined with publicizing their survey results? What strategies should they use to document their service-learning project? How can they celebrate their efforts when they are finished with the renovations? Develop a coordinated plan for the class to accomplish all of these results.

Part 2

Service-Learning in Schools

This part of the book focuses on the practice of service-learning in public schools. In chapter 8, the author proposes that the concepts of "community" and "diversity" can serve as a focus for service-learning programs and that programs should encompass four key components: intellectual understanding, participation skills, civic attitudes, and civic participation. The following three chapters focus on service-learning practice in elementary, middle, and high schools, respectively. Each chapter situates numerous examples of service-learning programs within the context of schooling and youth development at that level. Finally, chapter 12 explores the critical role of the classroom teacher in service-learning activities, highlighting the benefits and challenges as perceived by teachers in their attempts to meet community needs and provide their students with rich academic experiences.

Young and old collaborate for mutual benefit.
Photo Credit: Jean Jordan

In a midwestern environmental project, students seed a prairie.
Photo Credit: Kevin Eans

Chapter 8

Service-Learning in a Democratic Society: Essential Practices for K–12 Programs

Richard M. Battistoni

Over the course of this semester I have become a citizen of New Brunswick. It could be argued that I was a citizen here well before registering for the course, but I did not feel as if I were one. Having taken the course, I now know why I must work for change, and never accept the status quo—things can always be better. I am now aware of what is happening around me. New Brunswick extends beyond the [campus] bus route. It is filled with people who need aid, people who give aid, people who cannot be bothered to give aid, and people, who, like me, don't realize they are citizens at all. I cannot even say, for sure, that my work at my service site brought about this change in perspective for me. One of the most instrumental facets of my experience was simply my walk to the building [where I worked] each day. Every time I went I became more aware of my surroundings. I now see the city differently. I'm no longer scared walking to the site—far from it. I feel like I know that small portion of the city now. Now when I pass people on the street, some say hello to me, and call me by name. Through my work . . . I've gotten to know individual people, and they've gotten to know me. I enjoy my community service. It has opened my eyes as to the role I play as a citizen in my community.[1]

The above quote comes from a college student, but the sentiment underlying it just as easily could come from a high school or middle school student. My experience with service-learning programs at all levels has been that when democratic citizenship is at the foundation of a community-based learning experience, students come away feeling more a part of their communities, and with a better and more critical understanding of these communities and of their own roles in them. Previous chapters have explored the key aspects of service-learning and have provided ideas for good practice. The chapters in Part 2 take a programmatic perspective, describing service-learning at elementary, middle, and high school levels, and exploring the challenges service-learning poses for teachers and students at each level. This chapter will focus on the essential components of a democratic service-learning program. If service-learning is to be a method of teaching young people about their roles and responsibilities as citizens in a democratic society, then content and strategies must model and support democratic principles. There are three primary approaches to developing a democratic service-learning program; all are essential. First, the program should focus on key democratic principles. Two are emphasized here: community and diversity. Others that should contribute to a foundational core are equality, justice, freedom, and responsibility.

Second, a democratic service-learning program must incorporate the basic components of effective civic education outlined in the introduction to this book: intellectual understanding, participation skills, civic attitudes, and direct participation. Third, in light of the strong influence of the hidden curriculum on student learning, democratic principles must inform the ways program leaders make decisions about pedagogy, program design and structure, and partnership with the community. Following a brief comparison of two ethical foundations of service, each of these essential components is discussed.

THE ETHICS OF SERVICE

Advocates of service-learning argue that community service experiences enhance teaching and learning in all subject areas. If we are concerned with service-learning's contribution to education for democracy, however, we need to look beyond enhancing learning in distinctive subject areas. In addition, service-learning should be valued as a method of developing in students an other-regarding ethic appropriate to democratic citizenship.

There are two distinctive ethical foundations for service-learning: philanthropic and civic. While they may be mutually reinforcing in certain ways, the two nonetheless pose contradictory choices and yield different pedagogical strategies. The philanthropic view emphasizes service as an exercise in altruism: the nurturing of giving either in terms of "paying back" or "gratitude" (Buckley, 1990); or in terms of a kind of noblesse oblige of people lucky enough to be where they are. This approach is in the tradition of nineteenth-century thinking about charity and emphasizes character-building and a kind of compensatory justice where the well-off feel obligated to help the less advantaged.

The civic view, which informs this book, emphasizes mutual responsibility and the interdependence of rights and responsibilities; it focuses not on altruism but on enlightened self-interest. The idea is not that the well-off "owe" something to the less fortunate, but that free democratic communities depend on mutual responsibility and that rights without obligations are ultimately not sustainable. Here the focus is on the nurturing of citizenship and the understanding of the interdependence of communities (Barber, 1992; Bellah, Madsen, Sullivan, Swidler, and Tipton, 1985; Kemmis, 1990). The civic approach also encourages an educational partnership between school and community, with the community actively involved in defining its own capacities and needs as well as the role service will play in the education of students.

Where a philanthropic, charity-based model lacks a focus on the larger society and its needs, the civic approach's connection to the political sphere may be viewed as more controversial in the public school setting. Given that study after study shows that young people especially lack confidence in the public realm and in their own political efficacy, it is vital to emphasize political participation as an integral component of service-minded civic behavior. Unfortunately, some see service as an antidote to politics rather than a method of learning how to participate politically as a citizen. One approach to reconciling the reality of political cynicism with a desire to educate for citizenship through service-learning is to focus on two key concepts: community and diversity.

Community

I have found that a focus on the less provocative concept of "community" can be a particularly effective response to this concern. By connecting students' service to the concept of community, student learning can be expanded beyond the objectives of the particular project in question. Younger children can be encouraged to describe "their" community or take photographs of important landmarks or leaders in "their" community. Older students can be asked how their service work affects the community, and what community is being served by the project. With "community" as the broader theme, students can be encouraged to think critically, and all academic subjects or disciplines can contribute to the idea of community. Moreover, students can bring different conceptions of community and citizenship to the understanding of their service work. For example, "my community" can be defined geographically, institutionally, or culturally. Students can thereby define community quite differently, and yet have a shared, civic reflection on their service.

Diversity

In addition to assisting students' learning about community, service-learning programs in elementary and secondary schools can be effective teachers about diversity. One of the greatest concerns in our democracy today lies in the increasing divisions among our people—divisions based on race, class, gender, and culture. While not a panacea, service-learning projects where students work together in teams and reflect seriously on their service work can be opportunities for students from different backgrounds to join in common cause with adults, other young people, or both in the larger community, themselves reflecting a diversity of cultures and interests.

Where the school or classroom itself reflects a diverse student population, community service integrated into the curriculum can be an effective device for understanding one's own identity in relation to community and for engaging with other students from diverse perspectives. Where the school does not reflect the diversity of our larger pluralistic society, as is true of too many of our public school systems, service with members of the larger community can be an effective way of engaging students with people of diverse backgrounds. At the very least, service can promote the integration of young people with adults from different age groups and walks of life. A number of studies (Conrad and Hedin, 1977; Carnegie Council on Adolescent Development, 1989) have criticized educational institutions for keeping students in school full-time, thereby isolating them from adults (who might serve as their mentors) and from the "real world" of the community around them.

For example, middle or high school students can work with senior centers on oral history projects, which can accomplish the threefold tasks of providing companionship and service to the residents, contributing a resource to the community-based organization that paid staff would not be able to produce, and promoting intergenerational learning for the students involved.

Focusing on both community and diversity can produce an overarching substantive framework for students' civic education tied to community service experiences. In addition, the introduction briefly highlighted four essential components of civic education that must be addressed specifically within the context of service-learning programs: intellectual understanding, participation skills, civic attitudes, and direct participation in schools and communities. In this chapter, I explore each of these areas in more detail.

Intellectual Understanding

Intellectual understanding comes first. Since the report of the famous Committee of Ten in 1893, which said that the chief purpose of education was "to train the mind," the main thrust in American education has been cognitive development. The "thinking citizen" is still one of the aims of civic education today. We want to develop citizens who can use a variety of methods, theories, and models to examine the world and evaluate facts, in order to reach conclusions. Service-learning programs should aim at developing students' critical thinking skills; experience in the community can reveal challenges to our working cognitive assumptions regarding human nature, society, and justice. The students' ability to analyze critically is enhanced by confronting ideas and theories with the actual realities in the world surrounding them. For example, students who gain experience interacting with the guests in a homeless shelter are both able to put a face on "the poor" and test their own and others' theories about poverty, public policy, and democracy against their actual observations and the real-life stories of those with whom they interact in the shelter.

The discussion here about using service-learning to achieve greater intellectual understanding is not meant to minimize the possible tensions between the affective goal to socialize students into patterns of responsible civic behavior and the cognitive aim to develop in students critical thinking skills. Given the powerful emotional experiences young people experience though service, service-learning programs may be more tempted than most to adopt an hortatory or even celebratory tone. This is one of the most important reasons why service-learning needs to be infused in the core curriculum, where critical inquiry, deliberation, and discussion are the rule. In this regard, Lappe and Dubois' (1994) concept of "relational self-interest" may help balance the more vague idea of community as the content core of a democratic service-learning curriculum.

Participation Skills

Intellectual understanding, while essential to democratic citizenship, must be accompanied by participation skills that can be developed through service-learning. Alexis de Tocqueville laid out most clearly the argument for participation in community-based organizations, from an early age, as essential to maintaining democratic institutions and to educating people for citizenship. He argued that in democracies, "all the citizens are independent and feeble; they can do hardly anything by themselves, and none of them can oblige [others] to lend their assistance. They all therefore become powerless if they do not learn voluntarily to help one another" (Tocqueville, 1945, p. 115). Participation in civic associations educates people to overcome this powerlessness and isolation, since through this participation members of associations learn "the art of pursuing in common the object of their common desires" and of "proposing a common object for the exertions of a great many and inducing them voluntarily to pursue it" (Tocqueville, 1945, p. 115). More recently, Robert Putnam (1995) echoes Tocqueville's argument, lamenting the decline in voluntary associations and the subsequent loss of "social capital," the foundation of our democracy.

Essential to participation in civic associations are communication skills. Democratic citizenship certainly requires clear thinking about public matters, but it also involves the communication of our thoughts and actions, both vertically, to our leaders and representatives, and horizontally, with our fellow citizens. The goal of any democratic service-learning program ought to be to develop students' persuasive speaking and writing abilities, in order that they might better communicate and deliberate in the public arena.

Speech, argument, and persuasive communication are all important elements of democratic literacy. Perhaps even more important is the lost art of listening. In a democracy, citizens need to be able to listen to each other, to understand the places and interests of others in the community, and to achieve compromises and solve problems when conflict occurs. The overriding images of our democratic culture tend to involve talkers: great communicators like Thomas Jefferson, Daniel Webster, Martin Luther King, Jr., and Ronald Reagan; representatives giving speeches or talking on C-SPAN; or lawyers persuasively arguing in the courtroom. Perhaps the truer image of democracy exists on the other side of the courtroom, among the members of the jury, both listening to the arguments and testimony and to each other in deliberation. An effective congressional representative delivers persuasive speeches on the House floor yet also listens carefully to constituents at public hearings. Education for citizenship must involve the development of the ability to listen as part of communication skills.

Service-learning programs that employ appropriate reflection strategies heighten students' communicative abilities. Through reflecting on service-learning experience, students are called on to give an account of themselves and their thoughts in classroom discussions, in oral or artistic presentations, and in their writings. The community service experience also teaches students to listen to the stories and needs of others. When visiting an elderly person, doing an oral history, or tutoring another student, young people learn, in a tangible way, the art of listening.

Civic Attitudes

A service-learning program in elementary or secondary school aimed at civic education should also develop students' moral dispositions of civic judgment and imagination. By civic judgment I mean the ability to use publicly defendable moral standards in application to the actual life and history of a community. There is currently a debate among moral philosophers about whether politics can generate ethical or moral standards, but there is no debate about whether such standards are necessary for the individual citizen's judgments about how to choose and act in the political world. Democratic service-learning programs should try to develop capacities for public judgment.

Imagination is also crucial. Imagination involves the ability to think creatively about public problems. Moreover, to put oneself in the place of others requires imagination. Prejudice and bigotry may be connected to the absence of imagination. Imagination is also present in the ability to project and embrace a vision for the future, to think about oneself and one's community in ways not tied to the past; to "dream things that never were and say, 'Why not?'" as George Bernard Shaw put it.

The practical experience students gain in service-learning programs allows them to set and reset their standards of judgment, and it may cause them to modify their political judgments in reaction to the world they observe and with which they interact. Their visionary abilities should also be heightened, by enlarging their sense of who they are and enabling them to use their imagination to join together in working toward a common goal with people who have different backgrounds, values, and life stories.

Civic Participation

Democratic citizenship is also about taking action, both individually and together with members of one's community. Community service-learning projects cannot neglect the importance of getting even the youngest students to engage in direct action to meet school or community needs. The acts of planting a garden, testing a local stream, recycling, or working to solve traffic control problems near the school are tangible reminders to young people of the importance of direct public participation. Through projects in which students take action and see the results of their efforts, students have the best chance of developing a commitment to civic participation. Knowing that they are able to make a difference and can enjoy doing so, students will naturally continue to participate in school and community life, provided that their school programs encourage them in this pursuit.

Providing opportunities for students to engage in direct service, however, is no simple task. In fact, finding a suitable activity and coordinating the logistics of student participation in the community may be the most challenging aspects of service-learning. It is no surprise, then, that many public school teachers choose to end a unit of civic study with having students discuss how they might solve a community or national problem, without ever actually giving them the chance to try to effect change. While this approach may be tempting due to constraints on time, energy, and funds, direct civic participation has the greatest chance of not only motivating students' lifelong participation in their communities but of enhancing their interest in learning academic skills and content as well. Service activities are not just the "icing on the cake" in service-learning programs, educators must remember that service provides the program's raison d'être, and allows students to connect academic learning with activity that has meaning and relevance in the here and now for themselves and others in their community.

So far the discussion has centered on the democratic principles and civic education practices most consistent with a citizenship emphasis in a service-learning program. To focus exclusively on appropriate civic content and skills, however, is to miss the important role that pedagogy and institutional relationships plays in how students learn, even in an experiential, community-based learning program. Many educational writers (Bowles and Gintis, 1972; Illich, 1972; Silberman, 1970) have described the presence of a "hidden curriculum," arising out of the school's organizational imperative that there be order, hierarchical control, efficiency, and organized competition among students. Richard Merelman (1980) summarizes the argument about the hidden curriculum by saying that "students cannot learn democracy in the school because the school is not a democratic place" (p. 320). If an education for democratic citizenship is the ultimate aim, then we must also look to transform the classroom and the relationship between students and teachers in the classroom, as well as the relationship between the school and the larger community, all in line with a model of community characterized by democratic equality and participation.

Classroom Pedagogy

Democracy demands equal participation and voice by all citizens. The classroom, on the contrary, often mirrors hierarchy: what Paolo Friere (1970) termed the "banking model of education," with the teacher "depositing" information into the minds of passive student–ATM machines. Moreover, in most classrooms, even those with experiential components, students do their work and are judged as individuals. A citizenship education model for service-learning that does not reform the traditional pedagogy is not modeling what students need to learn about democratic community, and more important, may not contribute to student learning in ways those in the service-learning movement intend. Long ago, John Dewey (1916) argued that under this kind of individualistic, "mechanical learning," students'

> seeming attention, [their] docility, [their] memorizing and reproductions, will partake of intellectual servility. Such a condition of intellectual subjection is needed for fitting the masses into a society where the many are not expected to have aims or ideas of their own, but to take orders from the few set in authority. It is not adapted to a society which intends to be democratic. (p. 305)

Dewey contended that any educational regimen consisting of "authorities at the upper end handing down to the receivers at the lower end what they must accept" was an education "fit to subvert, pervert, and destroy the foundations of democratic society" (1916: 133). Even a conservative like Michael Oakeshott (1967) felt that "the activity of the teacher is specified in the first place by the character of his partner" (p. 156), necessitating a view of the teacher's role that pays serious attention to the student's needs and interests as well as those of society, which wants to bequeath to him or her its "history of human achievements, feelings, emotions, values, and beliefs" (p. 176).

Teachers who wish to incorporate democratic pedagogy in their service-learning courses should, to every extent possible, include discussion formats; encourage "dialogue journals" (students writing back and forth to each other) or other group-oriented written reflections, such as end-of-semester group projects and presentations; and attempt to organize students in their service placements into small teams or crews. Many community service programs are organized around individual service placements. However, when program leaders make the experience of democratic community a part of the organization of the class and of the service team, students get a better sense of the meaning of group responsibility, reciprocity, interdependence, and cooperation (or conflict). Students in teams are able to share and compare their service experiences, supplementing the teacher-student and community-student learning environment with a peer education experience.

Program Design and Structure

Chapter 3 presents several good reasons why student participants should be given adequate input into and ownership of a school-based service-learning program. The focus on participatory democracy and equal citizenship should also cause educators to make genuine student input central to the service-learning program's design and management. Students should play an active role in planning the program and serve as leaders in it, not only because students have good ideas and can recruit and organize other students, but also because active participation and involvement in service-learning can help students learn the lessons of democracy. When students participate actively in the design and structure of educational programs, they learn about decision making and civic responsibility in ways that overcome the most dangerous effects of the hidden curriculum. Research findings have shown (Beck and Jennings, 1982; Boyer, 1983; Battistoni, 1985) that students who have participatory experience in school policies and activities are more likely to exhibit "democratic" attributes. "These students have been found to be more likely to be informed about how political decisions are reached and the alternative ways of reaching them, to have more self-confidence, and to be more actively 'participatory' in motivation and more skillful in the art of weighing opinions, negotiating, dissenting, and discussing issues of mutual concern" (Battistoni, 1985, p. 122). Aside from the obvious effect on student empowerment and citizenship education, institutionalizing student participation creates a more suitable climate for operating a service-learning program.

Teachers must also play an active role in the integration of service-learning into the curriculum. There has been a tendency among those in the service-learning movement, as has been the case with other educational reform movements on all sides of the political spectrum to exclude classroom teachers from the design of curricula.[2] Some service-learning advocates, at both the state and local level, have tried to design "model" service-learning projects or curricula for use in the schools, in effect bypassing the classroom teacher. There may be a few good reasons for this, ranging from teacher unfamiliarity with service-learning to the time burdens on teachers of adopting this pedagogical approach; but we cannot bypass individual classroom teachers, who know best how to integrate particular projects into the daily life of their classroom, and whose thinking is ultimately invaluable to the success of a service-learning program. We must realize that the bureaucratized, routinized, or "bypassed" teacher will not be the agent of an education befitting active democratic citizenship. Recognizing this fact, some curriculum development projects have been based largely on teachers' efforts.[3]

Community Partnership

Chapter 4 also makes detailed mention of collaboration with parents and the local community. An emphasis on democratic citizenship should cause any educators in service-learning programs to reexamine the school's relationship with the larger community. When service is understood as an educational tool for our students to learn about democracy and citizenship, parents and organizations in the larger community can be approached as partners in education rather than as clients to be served. Partnership underscores mutual interdependence and helps create an understanding of community—among students, teachers, staff, and administration—not as those with problems but as the group to which we all belong. The town comes to be seen as a "text," and neighborhoods reciprocally gain the opportunity to reclaim their schools as centers in the community (see Lappe and DuBois, 1994). It is no small coincidence that community-based service-learning often goes hand in hand with site-based school management reforms, where parents, community members, and teachers play an active role in running the school and determining its curriculum.

IN CLOSING

Community service-learning can be a particularly effective method of civic education; developing a strong participatory citizenship is a necessary condition for our democracy's survival. This chapter identified essential practices in the areas of content, method, and program design, for educators wanting to use community-based learning in the service of democratic civic education. Readers are encouraged to keep these components in mind when reviewing the service-learning programs discussed in the next three chapters.

Hannah Arendt, writing about what she saw as the crisis in American education, declared that "education is the point at which we decide whether we love the world enough to assume responsibility for it and by the same token save it from that ruin which, except for renewal, except for the coming of the new and young, would be inevitable" (1962, p. 196). She saw education as the process of preparing our children "in advance for the task of renewing a common world" (Arendt, 1962, p. 196). Service-learning can be the vehicle by which we fulfill this task, but only if we consciously construct our programs with the education of democratic citizens in mind.

NOTES

1. Quoted from journal entry with permission of student.

2. For further discussion of this issue, see Battistoni (1985).

3. See, for example, Cairn, 1993; Dunlap, Drew, and Gibson, 1994; Kinsley, 1991; Stephens, 1995.

Chapter 9

Elementary School Programs

Carol Kinsley

This chapter will focus on the organization of elementary schools and examine the educational foundations for community service-learning. It will also show how community service-learning supports the academic and social growth of elementary students, how community service-learning becomes an instructional strategy in elementary classrooms, and the resultant changes in the role of the teacher, the assessment process, and the school culture. Finally, the chapter will respond to the challenges that elementary level community service-learning program leaders face as they move from coordinating traditional community service extracurricular experiences to developing community service-learning as a method for teaching and learning.

Community service-learning enlivens learning and engages elementary students in a way that makes schooling fun, relevant, and meaningful. Through community service-learning experiences, students become motivated and more connected to their school and neighborhood communities.

Service-learning projects at the elementary level cover a wide variety of themes and subject areas. Consider the following examples of community service-learning in elementary schools:

• After learning about the alphabet, children in a kindergarten class each designed and contributed a page to an alphabet coloring book. The class book was presented to preschoolers in a Headstart daycare.
• A first-grade teacher had her students interview elderly members in their community and then chronicle these histories in a book for the town and school libraries.
• First- and second-graders learned about team work and service while reading stories about quilts and subsequently sponsoring a quilting bee to collect

quilts made by parents and students together for babies with AIDS. A connection with math was made as students measured and cut the material into accurate squares as they prepared the quilt for the babies.

- Third- and fourth-graders learned about hunger and homelessness while growing a vegetable garden in the backyard of an elderly center. Students and a senior partner worked together on their plots. Part of the produce went to the senior partner, the other to a homeless shelter.
- Fifth-graders explored the topics of animal habitats, soil, and recycling natural resources in science class. To complement this learning, they spent a class day creating a conservation area in a former ravine, making trails, planting shrubs, and developing a sledding area.
- Fifth-grade language arts class partnered with students in the school's developmental skills class and learned about their partners' physical and mental disabilities. Assisting the special needs students with classroom assignments, the language arts students recorded their experience in a log, which was later used to create picture books about the partnership. (Laplante & Kinsley, 1994)

ELEMENTARY SCHOOL SETTINGS

A variety of values, philosophies, and practices guide elementary education. The range varies from traditionalists who focus on basic skills, structure, and "drill and practice" to those who advocate and practice progressive, integrated, constructivist education. Community service-learning can be integrated into schools based on either point of view.

For example: in the traditional classroom, teachers may view community service-learning as an extracurricular activity not directly connected to the learning process, yet affirm that it may be beneficial for students, supportive of a positive school climate, and helpful for the community. The constructivist approach, emphasizing that children should create their own learning through active, participatory methods, supports community service-learning experiences in which students develop their knowledge and meet many curriculum requirements.

Today, elementary school organizations range from the self-contained classrooms, to nongraded situations, to team teaching structures. In some schools, organization has been effected by community groups, businesses, and parents as they have sought more influence and involvement in decision making. A recent initiative in many schools is the formation of site-based teams comprised of the principal, teachers, parents, and business and community representatives to determine the school structure and curriculum. In schools adopting site-based management, the principal becomes a facilitator within the school, sharing with parents and community members in the decision-making process.

When community representatives are also included, schools become less isolated and more integrated with the local community. Through these external contacts, real needs and resources can be identified that can be used as the basis for developing community service-learning experiences.

In the current school reform literature, schools are being asked to examine how they can become communities: communities of learners, collegial communities, caring communities, inclusive communities, professional communities. Thomas J. Sergiovanni (1994) explores these concepts in his book, *Building Community in Schools*. He suggested that in order to become any of these communities, first and foremost, schools need to become purposeful communities.

> They must become places where members have developed a community of mind that bonds them together in special ways and binds them to a shared ideology. Schools cannot become caring communities, for example, unless caring is valued and unless norms are created that point the way toward caring, reward caring behaviors, and frown on noncaring behaviors. (pp. 71–72)

A key question then is How does community service-learning support the notion of creating community within the school organization? In 1989, Virginia Anderson, then principal of Chestnut Middle School in Springfield, Massachusetts, observed students involved in community service-learning and remarked that it brought a positive climate to the school. She said, "When students learn to care for others, they learn to care for themselves."[1] When schools organize around a philosophy of developing a caring community and provide opportunities for youth to "learn to care for others and themselves," they will reinforce the belief system within the school, create a more positive environment and school culture, and add to the ingredients necessary to produce the desired sense of community in schools.

Margaret Ells Elementary School in Springfield, Massachusetts, is just one example of a school creating community through the inclusion of service-learning. The school has adopted as one of its three major school improvement goals "developing positive attitudes through community service-learning." Principal James Walsh indicates that the school decision making team believes that when students work together on community service-learning activities, they develop relationships with each other and the faculty that results in a more positive learning environment.[2]

EDUCATIONAL THEORY TO SUPPORT THE DEVELOPMENT OF ELEMENTARY STUDENTS

"All children can learn" has increasingly become a fundamental tenet of elementary education; practitioners are translating this slogan into actions to support our youth in their growth and development. Ideas of how we view students range from research that describes stratified developmental stages to John Dewey's philosophy that children build their knowledge bases on their experiences at various stages, "namely that children are overflowing with impulses and that they want to interact with the environment and people around them because these interactions create experience, and experience is what creates people" (Ruenzel, 1995, p. 36).

Ralph Tyler and Hilda Taba have reminded us that when students become engaged in real activities, they learn more effectively and efficiently, and retain what they learn. They simply suggest that "learning occurs through the active behavior of the student" (Kinsley, p. 41). They believe that it is what [the student] learns, not what the teacher does that is the key to learning (p. 41). This view finds support in Piaget's work, where he identifies "real learning" in which the teacher helps students construct their knowledge. Richard S. Prawat (1992) describes how in this process, teachers need to "guide students toward a more mature understanding, which frequently means challenging students constructions" (p. 11).

He suggests that cognitive psychologists have identified that "the former experience is the most important predictor of a child's conceptual understanding" (p. 11) and that ". . . the learning that people do outside of school frequently surpasses what they can do in the classroom" (p. 12). Prawat then identifies elements of out-of-school learning as meaningful experiences and shared activity that help the teacher build a learning community. He suggests that we look at the classroom as just one place to educate students and that "clearly, we should no longer consider the classroom the prototype of effective learning" (p. 12).

Jacqueline and Martin Brooks (1993) in their book, *In Search of Understanding: The Case for Constructivist Classrooms*, provide a thorough examination of the roles of teachers and students in constructivist learning. Table 9.1 describes the delineation between traditional and constructivist classrooms (Brooks and Brooks, 1993, p. 17). Note the similarities between Brooks and Brooks's description of the constructivist classroom and the column I have added to describe community service-learning.

NEEDS OF ELEMENTARY STUDENTS

How can community service-learning help meet the needs of elementary students and assist youth in developing the meaning of citizenship? Literally, all students can participate in community service-learning: special needs students, regular education students, gifted students: students of all ethnicities, all socioeconomic levels, and all grade levels.

Michele Hebert, fifth-grade teacher at Liberty School in Springfield, Massachusetts, approaches service-learning as a method for reaching all stu-

Table 9.1

Comparing Traditional and Constructivist Classrooms with Community Service-Learning

Traditional Classrooms*	Constructivist Classrooms*	Community Service-Learning
Curriculum is presented part to whole, with emphasis on basis skills.	Curriculum is presented whole to part with emphasis on big concepts.	Curriculum is presented as a unit based on a general theme, usually as an interdisciplinary unit.
Strict adherence to fixed curriculum is highly valued.	Pursuit of student questions is highly valued.	Ideally, the theme emerges based on students' research and interests. Thinking skills are a primary process used in implementation.
Curricular activities rely heavily on textbooks and workbooks.	Curricular activities rely heavily on primary sources of data and manipulative materials.	Unit is based on learning by doing.
Students are viewed as "blank slates" onto which information is etched by the teacher.	Students are viewed as thinkers with emerging theories about the world.	Thinking skills and inquiry are used as primary tools to examine issues. Reflection occurs throughout the process.
Teachers generally behave in a didactic manner, disseminating information to students.	Teachers generally behave in an interactive manner, mediating the environment for students.	Teachers use community service-learning as another way to become facilitators of learning.
Teachers seek the correct answer to validate student learning.	Teachers seek the students' point of view in order to understand students' present conceptions for use in subsequent lessons.	Units begin with students' interests and their reflections are encouraged throughout the process. Making learning relevant is a primary goal.
Assessment of student learning is separate from teaching and occurs almost entirely through testing.	Assessment of student learning is interwoven with teaching and occurs through teacher observations of students at work, through teacher observations of students at work, and through student exhibitions and portfolios.	Assessment occurs by identifying outcomes, teachers' observation, learning logs, reflections, and exhibitions which can be included in portfolios.
Students primarily work alone.	Students primarily work in groups.	Students (primarily) work in groups.

*(Brooks and Brooks, 1993:17)

dents in her classroom. Michele has used community service-learning as a teaching tool for the past seven years. She uses themes such as citizenship, conflict resolution, peace, and intergenerational relationships as focal points for interdisciplinary academic units of study and as a motivating force for her students. Based on her experiences, she believes that community service-learning addresses the needs of her students and helps her teach to the individual needs of her students.

If we are to be successful we must find ways to invite each and every student to participate in learning how to be a productive citizen. That is the end product of a student's school career and has been for generations. That goal of education has not changed. If we are to consider community service-learning as a pedagogy, then it behooves each of us to ask ourselves, "What has changed?" In my experience, basic needs of students often are not met before they enter the door of the classroom every day. Some need to be fed, some need to be hugged, and some need to be in a place that is safe. All are required to be educated! Community service-learning helps me meet these multi-faceted needs.[3]

Those immersed in research about good teaching reinforce the need to reach all students and urge the connection of community and schools. Jarolimek and Parker (1993) write:

Teachers who make a difference are the ones who see the potential for success in all students. Such teachers set challenging but realistic expectations and provide a strong supportive environment for students. . . . These teachers help students sense a linkage between their school experiences and their lives outside of school. In this way students learn that their schoolwork can both help them cope with conditions in the larger society and help them achieve meaningful life goals for themselves. (p. 21)

CREATING COMMUNITY SERVICE-LEARNING CURRICULUM

How do Ms. Hebert and hundreds of other educators provide the student-centered learning that responds to the needs of their students and to the school community? How does community service-learning become a way for teachers to put into practice elements of the constructivist philosophy? The answers to these questions are not simple. For many educators, this method challenges the way they have been teaching for years. It challenges their levels;

it also challenges the authority of standardized tests used by school systems and state educational agencies. It challenges the traditional method of the teacher as the authority, the dispenser of knowledge. As one seventh grade student said when asked why he felt more teachers did not use community service-learning as a method, "They are afraid to take a risk."[4]

Despite these challenges, elementary teachers can readily incorporate community service-learning in their classroom. For example, the standard elementary social studies curriculum usually includes the topics of family and community. Efforts to incorporate community service-learning into units on these topics is not difficult, especially when students have been visiting the fire station and the police station or learning about their grandparents. Unfortunately, students are rarely asked to help the community or their grandparents in a consciously reflective way.

Consider the following example of how a service-learning component could enrich a field trip to the fire station. Linking a visit to the fire station with an issue such as fire safety provides an opportunity for students to participate in learning about fire safety, to think about what it means and what we all need to do to make sure our environments are safe, and then to compile this information and share it in an appropriate way. The class might investigate fire safety by participating in an information-gathering trip to a local fire station, not just hearing about what the fire fighters do. Before their field trip, they would research and develop the questions they would ask the fire fighters. They could role play being newspaper reporters. Their findings could be compiled and distributed to other classes in the school, their families, or the outside community. Using this process, students would use language arts skills, thinking skills, organizing skills, and presentation skills (Laplante and Kinsley, 1995, pp. 4, 5). Students could reflect on their service by drawing pictures, writing about their thoughts, or responding to questions in a discussion.

Elementary level community service-learning curricula can form the basis of an interdisciplinary unit or connect to a single content area. The process often used and developed by the Springfield, Massachusetts Community Service-learning Center is based on the convergence of Dewey's thinking with Tyler's learning theories, Hilda Taba's approach to curriculum development, and Paolo Friere's theories of community development. The process of developing a unit includes the following components, although the sequence of steps used may vary. Reflection is encouraged as part of preparation, implementation and planning as well as in a follow-up to the service experience. (The procedure here highlights many of the important aspects of preparation discussed in chapter 2.)

• Determine the best way to involve students in the planning
• Establish goal(s) of the unit
• Establish learning outcomes and the assessment process

• Identify a school/community/global need and develop a theme
• Identify student interests
• Select core curriculum and service activity
   —match with student interests
   —connect a service theme with core subject areas to build an interdisciplinary unit (see diagram below)
   or
   —identify a single content area and determine how a service experience can enhance understanding of specific learning objectives
   or
   —select a service experience and build a unit around it
• Connect with community partners/recipients
• Organize learning experiences/activities, including:
   —student orientation to community service-learning project
   —problem-solving, multicultural experiences, active learning, critical thinking, etc.
   —evaluation/assessment
• Plan for the reflection process throughout the unit, in preparation, implementation and as a follow-up activity
• Organize celebration.

The following web (Figure 9.1) illustrates how the theme of homelessness and poverty and associated learning objectives can be linked in an interdisciplinary unit.

The following intergenerational unit illustrates how elementary students could be come involved and build relationships with the elderly population. Activities were drawn from different schools and ideas generated by several educators.

The description here follows the previously described *process* used to create a community service-learning curriculum. Using the process, each school activity evolves in its unique way based on the community's needs, the talents and interests of the students, and the resources of the community.

INTERGENERATIONAL
COMMUNITY SERVICE-LEARNING[6]

School: Kindergarten through Fourth-Grade School

General Theme: Develop a relationship with older adults in a nearby nursing home to enable students to accept and understand older adults, and to help older adults to feel joy and have faith in the future. Following student prepara-

Figure 9.1
Community Service-Learning Interdisciplinary Web[5]

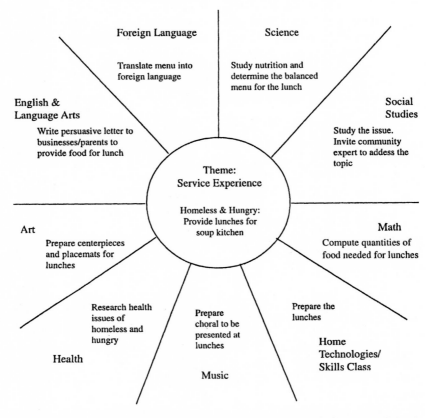

Based on 1991 community service-learning project at Mary G. Pottenger School, Springfield, MA.

tion, each grade level will provide a service-learning project and interact with the residents at an appropriate time of the year. The projects will be followed by a time for reflection on the meaning of the service activities for the students and the older adults.

Determine School or Classroom Objectives

1. Develop caring relationships between students and older adults to counter age segregation.
2. Help students gain a sense of responsibility for older adults.

3. Develop within students an understanding of how older adults are treated and cared for in our society.
4. Develop within students an empathy and sensitivity for older adults.
5. Help students gain a sense of their own self-worth as they serve others.
6. Develop opportunities for interaction between students and older adults.

Select Content and Learning Experiences:

- *Social studies:* Depending on the school's curriculum guides, children can learn about families and roles grandparents play in the family structure. Compare the roles of the children, parents, and grandparents within a family. Compare the way older adults are cared for in various cultures. Interview elders to learn about their school experiences, early family life, major occupation. Develop interview questions with the class. Discuss why it is important to help older adults. Establish a list of ways students can help in school, at home, in the neighborhood, and in the community. Reflect on the services offered by students.
- *Language arts:* Develop a list of library books about older adults that can be read aloud to children. Establish a pen pal program between children and older adults. Children and older adults are given the same homework assignment and then come together to share their writing with each other.
- *Mathematics:* With older adults, compare cost of food items in 1940 and 1990. Present the concept of "fixed income" and budgets.
- *Science:* Grow plants from seeds to share with older adults on a special occasion.
- *Health:* Study the importance of exercise as people grow older. Select one of the parts of the body, e.g., the heart, and research what preventive health care and dietary measures are needed to maintain good health. Analyze the use of medication by youth and older adults.
- *Art:* Children in different grade levels provide artwork to decorate the older adults' center at different times of the year. Create cards to send to the residents.
- *Music:* Children present musical programs for older adults at appropriate times of the year. In school, children learn songs of various eras to gain a sense of the past. Songs, with the theme of community, caring, sharing, and loving, help create a feeling for the service-learning project.

Identify Major Learning Objectives

- *Skills:* academic, communication and citizenship skills, creative expression and social development.
- *Affective outcomes:* a deeper sensitivity toward others, a stronger sense of self, the meaning of helping others and a sense of purpose and usefulness.

Develop an Action Plan for the Service-Learning Project

- Survey teachers to determine current service activities.
- Meet with teacher/students to brainstorm possible service activities. Determine the curriculum content to be included.
- Meet with the social service coordinator at the nursing home to determine appropriate activities, responding to seniors' needs. If the older adults are able, you may also be able to determine ways they can volunteer in the school.
- Meet with the principal to organize timing and scope of the project.
- Orient teachers in the building, requesting their assistance and support.

Sample Project

Introduce the intergenerational theme by inviting older adults to participate in a special "Read Aloud Day" in the school. Create a bulletin board in a central location announcing the theme. Ask students to draw pictures of a grandparent or older adult neighbor that can be displayed on the board. Or, ask the nursing home to take Polaroid pictures of residents who would like to become pen pals with students. The photos and selected letters could be displayed. Book jackets of read-aloud books could be used. Older adults could assist in creating the bulletin board.

Class Activities

- *Kindergarten:* Ask some older adults to volunteer in the classroom. Children can create special flowers, cards, or favors for special occasions, which can be shared appropriately.
- *First grade:* Following the study of the family, honor grandparents with a special day. Discuss what older people bring to the family and why older adults are considered to be wise.
- *Second grade:* Working with older adults, create a "Then and Now" book around the themes of childhood games, school, work. Have the children and older adults discuss what life is like without television.
- *Third grade:* Grow plants in science class (marigolds or begonias) and share them with older adults in the spring. If social studies has an international component, discuss how older adults are treated in other parts of the world. Invite older adults from a variety of nationalities or ethnic groups to discuss family traditions.
- *Fourth grade:* As part of a writing process project, give the same assignment to older adults and students to write an essay on "Memories of Childhood." Bring the writers together to read their essays and to discuss the commonalities and differences in their experiences.

Time Line

This will depend on the scope and depth of the project. Some schools choose to extend the service projects throughout the year, others feel a defined time is more appropriate.

Reflection

Reflection is a critical part of service-learning and brings meaning to the service activities. Through discussion, writing prose or poetry, music and art, students internalize and understand the value and importance of caring, sharing, responsibility, and community. Journals and diaries can be kept by the very young as well as high school students. Going through the motion is not enough, the process of thinking and understanding needs to take place.

Evaluation

If there is a research department within the school system, work with the director to determine the appropriate process of evaluation; a variety of informal evaluations can take place:

- A pre- and postsurvey can be conducted to determine attitudes toward each other (community partner and students).
- A panel discussion of older adults and children can be held to discuss how each has changed and what they have learned from each other.
- A joint scrapbook can be created, focusing on the discoveries and highlights of the experience (Kinsley, 1989).

Using this planning process, community service-learning becomes a regular part of schooling as it is integrated into the curriculum. The integration takes place as a

> natural extension of the content and skills already being developed in the classroom and does not distract but rather enhances existing curriculum. Teachers may either take an existing unit and identify where community service-learning fits into it or they may pick a new theme and build service and academics around it. In this way community service-learning becomes unified with the learning process, instead of an extra task for teachers to add to an already busy day. This approach allows educational content objectives to be achieved through active learning as well as traditional learning methods. (Laplante and Kinsley, 1994, p. 5)

CITIZENSHIP THROUGH COMMUNITY
SERVICE-LEARNING: A CASE STUDY

In 1989, Lincoln School in Springfield, Massachusetts, demonstrated how a theme adopted for community service-learning activities could unite classrooms, the school, and the community to support academic and social development.

Lincoln School is located in a largely Hispanic neighborhood that is isolated from the surrounding community. Few parents were involved other than to bring their children to school. Staff identified as their need "building a sense of community" and adopted "citizenship" as their theme. Leadership for the project came from the principal, who gave her permission for the activities, and a small team of teachers who reached out to other staff members for suggestions. Michele Hebert, quoted earlier in this chapter, was the community service-learning coordinator for the school.

Teachers met to determine how to connect the theme to their academic work and make learning about citizenship active and fun for the students. Each class used the theme in a way that connected it to their curriculum. The teachers helped the students gain a sense of the meaning of citizenship through discussions and by exposing them to a wide variety of examples from literature and history.

The first schoolwide activity, a "good citizen contest," was held to help make the meaning of citizenship relevant and to encourage the students to reach out to the community and discover good citizens there. In order to record the nominations, a giant "Wall of Fame" was set-up on a wall in the basement of the old school, replete with a giant model of Uncle Sam. Children from each class wrote or drew about why they selected their particular "good citizen" nominee. The list of nominees was long and among them included parents, grandparents, foster parents, social workers, teachers, neighbors, older brothers and sisters. Each class then discussed their nominees and elected the one that best exemplified the meaning of good citizenship. According to teacher Carolyn Price,

> Through participating in and reflecting on these activities, the children learned that good citizens are everywhere. They come from a variety of ethnic backgrounds and socioeconomic levels. The common denominator that makes these citizens special is that each of them is a caring, sharing, and loving individual. (Anderson, Kinsley, Negroni, & Price, 1991, p. 763)

Following the class elections, the entire school community joined together to hold a "Good Citizens on Parade" celebration. By this time the

North End Citizens' Council learned of the event and offered to purchase Lincoln School T-shirts and banners and balloons for the event. (This was the first time the school and the Council had worked together on a project.) On the day of the parade, the children dressed in their green-and-white T-shirts organized to march to a nearby park led by Springfield's Mounted Police, the drill team, and the school's fourth-grade band. The community was widely represented, with Mayor Richard E. Neal, the superintendent of schools, the state representative, and the neighborhood leaders greeting and honoring the children and each recipient of the "Good Citizen Contest." Following a celebration at the park, the children were treated to a concert and ice cream donated by a neighborhood group.

The activities described here formed the backdrop for a series of service activities. Several thematic units were created and implemented. In conjunction with their studies, students served the elderly, children at local hospitals, neighborhood organizations, and the school community. Ms. Price observed that,

> As the school reached out to the community, the response was overwhelming. A cadre of volunteers from neighborhood organizations came forward to share their expertise with the children and to help them expand their vision of community. A school/business partnership with the local power company focused on the concept of community service-learning. The partnership pays for materials, equipment, and transportation for community service-learning projects. (Anderson et al., 1991, p. 763)

The children gained a sense of citizenship and community that would be difficult to learn from a textbook. For this learning experience the neighborhood and neighbors became the "text." The outcomes? Ms. Price observed

> By integrating CSL into this instructional approach, the school has created a learning environment that is exciting, stimulating, and motivating—in short, an environment that works for students. The rewards for the school are both intrinsic and extrinsic.
>
> Children's self-esteem has grown, and this heightened sense of self-worth has led to improved academic achievement. . . . The climate of the school is orderly, friendly, open, and warm. Negative behavior is rare, and children routinely choose to be helpful, kind, and caring. They have been given the opportunity to develop in a setting and structure that focus on the intrinsic rewards that come to those who support and serve one another and the community. (Anderson et al., 1991, p. 763)

CHALLENGES FOR ELEMENTARY SERVICE-LEARNING PROGRAMS

Current literature indicates a growing trend toward embracing character education that will help our students learn the values of caring and sharing.[7] Recent school improvement strategies include recommendations for teachers to use student-centered, participatory methods of instruction to make learning more relevant and active.

Some of the reform literature indicates community service-learning is a way for teachers to address this need, but for the most part the majority of articles and reform initiatives do not mention community service-learning as a vehicle to help students grow and learn. Furthermore, those who are uninformed about service-learning's place in the curriculum see service activities as typical of what teachers in schools have done for many years: provide their students with an activity to raise funds or participate in an extracurricular project for a good cause. Thus, one of the central challenges is to move beyond the perception of community service-learning as an extracurricular activity to viewing community service-learning as a helpful and useful *process* to implement as a teaching strategy.

Several other challenges face elementary educators in order for community service-learning to be understood and implemented. Educators need to realize how community service-learning provides a vehicle to educate students in a wholistic way so they develop social skills and self-esteem as well as academic meaning. They must also understand how community service-learning sets the stage for student-centered learning. By involving the students in determining the community needs that will be addressed, relating activities to their skills and talents, and building on their interests, teachers can create meaningful learning experiences.

A further challenge is to identify relevant learning outcomes for community service-learning units and use assessment tools such as portfolios, journals, and exhibitions to measure students' growth. The effects of service-learning in the elementary school are not readily determined through the use of teacher-made or standardized tests. Indeed, students who participate in the same service-learning project may have completed very different tasks, developed different skills, or learned varied content. In the face of this complexity, educators must develop appropriate and flexible modes of assessment and resist the temptation to avoid trying to assess student learning from service. Assessment strategies suitable for service-learning programs are vital to counter critics' assertions that service-learning is simply a "feel good" activity.

Organizationally, major challenges exist to provide the *time* in the elementary school day for planning and implementing community service-learning. Some schools designate a common planning time for teamed or similar grade level teachers, making organizing service-learning activities a natural part of curriculum development. As teachers recognize the academic value in tying service experiences to content areas, time during the school day can be allocated for the implementation of community service-learning.

Experience tells us that community service-learning motivates students, provides active learning experiences, and builds a positive classroom and school climate. Yet, one of our greatest challenges is to develop reliable research to validate what we already know from our experiences and to respond to the need for greater understanding of the implications for the infusion of community service-learning into elementary education.

IN CLOSING

Community service-learning motivates students in elementary schools. It provides a way to develop curriculum that activates learning, enables students to learn more about themselves, and builds a sense of community within classrooms and neighborhoods. Service activities in the school and community provide students with a meaningful reason for using their reading, writing, and mathematics skills. Through service-learning experiences in the elementary years, students have the best chance of developing a concept of themselves as caring and active citizens of their schools and communities. In essence, a natural connection exists between community service-learning and elementary education that can enhance both teaching and learning.

NOTES

1. Quote from the video *Making a Difference* produced by the Springfield Public School District (1989).

2. Interview with James Walsh (1995).

3. Interview with Michele Hebert (1995).

4. Comment made by Jesse Sharrad at a meeting of the Springfield Public School District's Community Service-Learning Task Force, 1991.

5. Based on 1991 community service-learning project at Mary G. Pottenger School, Springfield, MA.

6. This section is from *Developing an elementary service-learning curriculum: The unit method*, by C. W. Kinsley. Copyright © 1989 by Springfield Community Service Learning Center. Reprinted with permission.

7. See, for example, recent issues of *Phi Delta Kappan* (March and May 1995) and *Educational Leadership* (May 1995).

Chapter 10

Middle School Programs

Felicia George

We think that every young person should have a chance to serve the community because you can become more responsible and have fun while you're at it. I discovered I had the power to take time out to talk to the most vicious kid in the classroom and keep him calm.
I learned to try harder because we only learn from our mistakes.[1]

These are the voices of young people engaged in service. These voices attest to the power of service learning as a viable teaching strategy with particular relevance to the emotional and intellectual needs of young adolescents. Service learning is an ideal method for engaging the physically active, self-involved early adolescent in stimulating experiences that challenge intellectual development and satisfy personal questions of self-identity. Recognition of the developmental stage of early adolescence and the subsequent emergence of the middle school movement have led to increasing interest in service-learning as a viable teaching approach for early adolescents.

The developmental issues that ten- to fifteen-year-olds face and the restructuring of the educational setting to better meet their unique needs calls for a strategy that can forge a link between student need and instructional purpose. In order to understand how that is accomplished, a number of questions should be considered. What needs and particular challenges does the early adolescent contend with in the twenty-first century? How does service learning address these needs and challenges? Are there existing examples of programs to which we can look for guidance? How do they operate and what do they provide to the youth involved? Answering these questions will lead to a picture of what service learning at the middle school level is and an understanding of what this emerging methodology can accomplish for early adolescents and their communities.

In this chapter I examine the unique relationship between service and middle school student beginning with a review of the development of middle schools and an overview of the features and characteristics of this developmental stage. I then present specific examples to illustrate the elements of quality service-learning programming and the effectiveness of this instructional strategy in educating young adolescents. Finally, I propose recommendations for advancing the service experience in middle schools and advocate for its institutionalization in schools throughout the nation.

THE MIDDLE SCHOOL

Middle schools are a recent phenomenon in the history of schooling in the United States. It wasn't until the early 1920s that the concept of an intermediate period between elementary and high school evolved with the emergence of major publications on the junior high school. Educators began to talk about the unique characteristics and needs of this age group and the resulting requirement for a different educational approach (Lawton, 1989).[2] They recognized the difficulty students face in moving from the child-centered, nurturing quality of the elementary school to the subject-centered, academic focus of the high school.

The junior high school was formed to bridge the link between elementary and high school but in fact, as the name implied, they adopted the look and feel of the high school and did not provide significantly different instruction. The typical junior high follows a departmentalized schedule, much like the high school, with the addition of a slightly longer home room period and greater guidance resources.

The first middle school in the U.S. opened in 1950. By 1971 the number of middle schools had grown to more than two thousand (Doob, 1975).[3] These schools were established in an effort to "better meet the important educational, personal, and social needs of intermediate level students" (Doob, 1975, p. 1).

The middle school has no more than five grades and no less than three grades, always including grades 6 and 7. In theory, the middle school is distinguished from the typical junior high by: an emphasis on guidance and human relations; individualized instruction; exploratory courses and activities; interdisciplinary team teaching; home based teachers; a mixture of teacher certification—elementary as well as subject area secondary certified teachers; flexible scheduling; and less competitive and sophisticated social activities—school dances, inter- and intramural sports (Educational Research Service, Inc., 1975, pp. 2, 3). The child-centered focus in the middle school allows for a gradual transition from the supportive personal atmosphere of the elementary school to the more departmentalized academic focus of the high school (Educational

Research Service, Inc., 1975, p. 4). Support for the middle school concept grew as a result of two pivotal events—the creation of the National Middle School Association in 1973 and the publication of *Turning Points* in 1989. The middle school philosophy became clearly articulated and codified into a unifying image of what middle school education should be.[4]

Educators' support for a distinct instructional format for young adolescents underscores that the ten- to fifteen-year-old is substantially different from the sixteen- to twenty-year-old and therefore will be served better in a different educational setting. Middle schoolers have not yet developed a level of abstraction suited to the instruction that takes place in departmentalized courses fashioned after the college lecture hall. Advisory periods, teaming of teachers, interdisciplinary curriculum and other middle school features support *how* children learn and take precedence over *what* they are learning. The true middle school model seeks to continue the supportive feeling of the elementary school while introducing students to the more rigorous academic demands they will face in high school.

Whether schools are named "middle" or "junior high" school, in practice the school setting for most young adolescents remains unsuited to their developmental needs. Research has shown that the move to a different school comes at a time when the child is most vulnerable; the change often has a negative effect on the student's development. In reporting on research documenting the difficulty young people experience in the move from elementary to middle school, Hillman, Wood, Becker, and Altier (1990) stated that the settings are described as

> characterized by increases in the size of the school and student body, ability grouping, both competitive motivational strategies and normative grading standards, greater rigor in grading, teacher control, and discipline. At the same time [there are] decreases in opportunities for student autonomy, reduced close personalized contact between students and their teachers and between students and their peers, and fewer opportunities for higher-level cognitive problem solving. (p. 44)

The school change is often negative because it is in conflict with students' developmental needs. "At a time when students are preoccupied with issues of self-esteem, peer relationships, and identity formation, schools emphasize increased competition, social comparison and ability assessment" (Hillman et al., p. 44).

More recent research indicates that there has not been much change in the specialness of middle schools or in the education for young adolescents. In the January 25, 1995, edition of *Education Week* the "Focus On: Research" feature presented the case for positive middle school environments to help smooth the transition from elementary school for the young adolescent. The author, Debra Viadero (1995), cited a national longitudinal study completed by Midgly and Eccles in 1993 who found that instruction in schools designed for young adolescents was similar regardless of whether students attended a junior high or middle school. As in the earlier study, schools for young adolescents are still "larger, less personal, and more formal than the elementary schools from which their students came" (p. 28).

Despite efforts to codify education for middle school youth, no two middle schools or junior high schools look alike. A school may have any combination of features characteristic of the middle school model. A typical school day sees the students involved in some type of guidance grouping known as advisory, core class or homeroom. This is the time of day when the school staff attend to the students' emotional and social needs, when issues related to attendance, health, family, and relationships are addressed. The rest of the day may be divided into forty- or forty-five-minute periods of specific subject area classes or blocks of time in which interdisciplinary or teamed subjects are offered. Most schools following the middle school model will offer a number of alternative instructional strategies that include teaming, a house structure (in which a group of students remain together through all three grades with the same set of teachers), and a wealth of noncompetitive social activities and special interest programming (art, music, athletics, foreign languages, and clubs).

THE EARLY ADOLESCENT

What are those unique needs of early adolescents and what makes this stage of growth so different from any other period in the lives of youth? When posing the question, "Who is the middle school student?" we are asking a question central to early adolescence, that is, "Who am I?" The answer is as varied as there are students and different times in the day! This volatile period of human development has been referred to as "the age of raging hormones," and likened to a traumatic illness.

Joan Schine (1991), Founding Director of the National Center for Service Learning in Early Adolescence stated:

Until quite recently the developmental literature failed to differentiate between the early and later years of adolescence. Although there is overlap, and some generalizations do apply, early, middle, and late adolescence do differ in important ways, even though they have much in common. Moreover, even within any group of early or late adolescents there will be differences.[5]

A teacher described the experience of meeting her new eighth grade class each fall. "All I can predict with any certainty about any class is the widest imaginable range of abilities, problems, attitudes, and levels of maturity" (Atwell, 1987, p. 27). Walk into any eighth-grade classroom, and you will see students (most often girls) who could pass as high school seniors and others who could as easily be in the fifth grade. But they're all thirteen years old. John Mitchell, a Canadian researcher of adolescent development, maintained, "The most consistent error that adults make is to treat early adolescents as if they were more mature and self-directing than they are, and to treat late adolescents as if they were more juvenile than they are" (1986, p. 93).

Mitchell (1986), in *The Nature of Adolescence*, suggested that "the adolescent is similar to the preschool child who, upon encountering a world beyond mother, grapples with new roles, expectations, and rules. The adolescent replays the sandbox drama to learn afresh the roles and rules of adolescence" (p. 17). Hormonal changes and the lengthy and more uncertain time span of the adolescent stage adds to the difficulties for middle schoolers and the adults who work with them. Schine (1993) described early adolescents in terms of contrasts:

> No single adjective will do the job . . . They are energetic/lazy, self-centered/altruistic, fat/skinny, almost adults/still children, pimply/handsome, scatterbrained /purposeful, sullen/giggly, conscientious/irresponsible, risk-taking/fearful, enthusiastic/apathetic, loyal/fickle. If all this sounds unsettling and confusing to us, it is even more so for these youngsters. These middle schoolers are changing so quickly, are dealing with so many choices—not just the obvious ones that get so much press these days, but numbers of difficult choices that may determine the course of their lives well beyond the middle school years.[6]

At this stage of development the focus on affective development should be preeminent as youth face the emotional issues of identity formation and separation from family. The affective issues related to self-esteem—"Am I liked? What do others think about me? What do I look like to the outside world? How should I behave? Why do bad things always happen to me and only me?"—predominate as the young person struggles to acquire confidence and become a competent adult. Joy Dryfoos (1990) described the early adolescent in this way:

> [Y]oung adolescents are egocentric. They are looking inward, probably for the first time, to form a consciousness of self, to confirm their indi-

viduality. At the same time, there are emerging self-doubts and a growing need for reinforcement from the social group. On one hand, they search for autonomy and, on the other, they are very dependent on support from their friends and families. (pp. 24, 25)

Peer group relationships are also more important in early adolescence than they have ever been before, and more important than they will ever be again. Young adolescents relish the opportunity to work together but also suffer the challenges of shifting loyalties and redefining friendships.

According to Dryfoos (1990), the tasks that psychologists see as critical for achieving responsible adulthood include a search for self-definition and a personal set of values; the acquisition of competencies such as problem solving and decision making; becoming emotionally independent of parents, finding the balance between achievement and acceptance by peers and experimenting with a wide array of behaviors, attitudes, and activities.

The challenges in accomplishing these tasks that face adolescents today are more perilous and their choices have graver consequences. Many young teens, whether in urban inner-cities or rural settings face a daunting array of temptations and risks: drug and alcohol abuse; early pregnancy and parenthood; violence; disillusionment with school; homelessness and abuse. Increasingly young adolescents are estranged from families and are without the support that once served as a buffer during this critical time. In the best cases, traditional institutions have been replaced with specially created programs to ensure that developmental needs are met. Hechinger (1992) noted that

The sad reality is that young adolescents at every economic level are very often neglected by adults—even within their own families—or get lost in the mass, victims of large institutions that undermine their healthy development. Many young people attend schools that ignore their needs and capabilities. They return from school to empty homes and suffer the consequences of anonymity—a scourge of modern society and a condition that makes people, young and old, behave at their worst. (p. 26)

With all these changes and uncertainties, and without the reservoir of successes that sustain many adults when they confront new situations or roles, young adolescents need experiences that will give them the skills and the confidence to move ahead. Service learning can do all of this and more. It can be a vehicle for fostering positive growth and a means for connecting youth with the adult guidance that is so scarce.

SERVICE LEARNING IN THE MIDDLE SCHOOL

Service learning is a teaching strategy that can help young adolescents mature into responsible adults. Through service, young people are making positive contributions, engaging in activities that give them real responsibility and calling on the adults in their world to recognize their competence. In taking responsibility, realizing that others depend on them, and following through, young adolescents begin to see themselves as capable of making a positive difference, to be change agents, even to see a future in which they can have a place as active citizens.

How does service-learning address the developmental tasks of adolescence? Service-learning allows the early adolescent to take risks within the limits of a well-planned structure. Young adolescents, volatile and changing, respond more positively to projects where the outcome is fairly immediate. Reflection activities allow them to prepare for situations they will meet while onsite and thus increases their chances of being successful. The structure provided by a well-planned program makes it possible for them to succeed and achieve.

Young adolescents need to be guided through reflection exercises that will help them examine their behavior and feelings while serving—what they did, how they felt, what was good or bad about it, what they might do differently a second time around.

Service can provide an opportunity for the young adolescent to have some autonomy and to practice responsible decision making. Students can make decisions within the framework of a carefully crafted program such as, decisions about what type of activities to plan for a service site, a choice from among a selection of predetermined service placements, a way to say "goodbye" to the group or what to prepare as a remembrance of involvement.

Community involvement also puts the young adolescent in contact with a number of adults outside of home and school from whom they can learn and begin to make connections. It provides that all-important adult model of what may be possible in their future and gives them examples of options. It helps to dispel the isolation and sense of aloneness that haunts many adolescents, particularly in large impersonal inner-city environments.

Service learning allows for recognition and rewards, for young people to have their competence recognized by others. Reinforcement of positive behaviors at this stage may have lasting effects that will reach far beyond the teen years. And, one hopes, these rewards for competence will be internalized to encourage positive behavior for its own sake.

MODEL SERVICE PROGRAMS

In 1991 the National Center for Service Learning in Early Adolescence (now known as the National Helpers Network, Inc.) set up a Clearinghouse of information and resources pertaining to service learning for young adolescents. One of its goals was to document the existence of viable service programs and collect program descriptions that could be used by other schools and agencies as a template for developing their own service models. The Helpers Network recognizes the following critical elements:

- an overarching goal or perceived purpose for the service;
- a skilled, understanding adult facilitator (Program Leader);
- genuine responsibilities for the young adolescent and a means for holding them accountable;
- training and ongoing reflection, *with guidance*, to provide students with the skills, knowledge, and understanding they will need to meet their responsibilities;
- a clear understanding among young people, the school or sponsoring organization, and the placement site about the young people's responsibilities and the obligations of site supervisors;
- the opportunity to perform services recognized as "real" by both young adolescents and those they serve;
- opportunities for youngsters to practice decision making and problem solving, individually and collectively;
- opportunity to engage in an ongoing service project allowing youngsters to engage in a sustained relationship with service recipients and adult supervisors;
- group development and trust building among peers; and the program's position as a firm element in the school's or community-based organization's schedule; not a "hit-or-miss" program.[7]

The individual programs that are highlighted in this chapter cover a spectrum of possible service models, including settings in which service learning is central to the school and implemented in one or more grades; individual classes or teachers who lead service projects; programs that represent collaborations between school and other community agencies; and programs in which students are engaged in a variety of service activities or programs that involve students in a single project. Examples are taken from urban, suburban, and rural settings and represent all types of students. Some of the programs described have been established in the last few years with support from government or private funds. Others have been in existence for ten years or more.

Shoreham-Wading River Middle School, Long Island, New York

One of the oldest service programs with strong links to the overall school program is the Shoreham-Wading River Middle School Community Service program. At this suburban middle school on eastern Long Island, students have an opportunity to engage in service experiences at every grade level beginning in the sixth grade.

Shoreham-Wading River's Community Service program began modestly with one class in 1973. Since then, the program has grown to become not only a pioneer among middle school service-learning programs, but also an integral part of the education of every one of the school's approximately five hundred sixth- through eighth-graders. Service activities take place as part of eight to ten week units of study by one class, or in a team of two classes. These units include in-class assignments in addition to the learning that takes place on-site. Many students participate in short-term projects, such as hosting preschool children at the school and its adjoining farm, teaching adults computer skills at the school's computer lab, and working on environmental issues.

The Community Service Program's goal is to enable its participants, nearly all white and from working- and middle-class families, to understand those different from themselves. Students work with young children, children with handicaps, and the elderly, to provide needed and valued service and to form new relationships.

No teacher is required to offer a service opportunity, although practically 90 percent of the teaching teams do. Students are required to participate; it is part of their class. Class size ranges from twenty to twenty-five students and the two classes in a teaching team usually participate in the same type of service. Groups of about forty students are taken in minibuses driven by the teachers and the assistants to the service site. While at the site, the students are supervised by a teacher and several assistants.

Service experiences generally last from six to ten weeks and are conducted during a double period, allowing time for traveling to and from the site and about an hour for working with groups at the site. Generally, students visit the site once a week, spend one period prior to the visit on preparation and one period afterwards to discuss and evaluate what occurred at the site.

Because service is integrated into the school program, there is a Service Learning Office staffed by a full-time coordinator and three teaching assistants. This staff is responsible for logistical and program arrangements. Working closely with teachers, Community Service staff handle such necessary but time-consuming tasks as locating agencies for placements, working out details with agency staff, scheduling transportation, and finding appropriate classroom materials. They also maintain regular communication with agency staff during each project. In addition, all site visits and some small group work are handled by the Community Service staff. This allows the classroom teacher to focus on preparing students for the on-site work and ensures that each project goes smoothly and is useful to both the students and agencies involved. Planning is done during the summer when teachers choose the type of service for their classes. The Community Service Office then schedules the sites and buses based on how many classes are participating in each type of service.

A typical example of a service project is a seventh-grade team who works with children with disabilities. The math/social studies teacher teams with a language arts/science teacher in guiding their seventh-graders to plan cooking, crafts, and games for a group of youngsters with disabilities. The activities used are designed to reinforce learning goals for the children with disabilities. For example, the game telephone is played to reinforce communication skills. Sometimes the service project is the crux of the curriculum and other times it is not. In one instance, seventh-graders used measurement and geometry skills to determine how much square footage is needed to accommodate a class of young children with disabilities, given the required square foot per child.

Dr. Bell, Principal of Shoreham-Wading River Middle School, stresses that there must be support from both teachers and administration in order for a service program to work. The teachers must accept the idea and the administrators must provide the support (resources, planning time, assistance) for the teachers to implement the program.[8]

Community Service Academy, New York City

With a majority population of Black and Latino youth from lower-middle class and poor families, the Community Service Academy of the IS 218 Salome Urena Middle Academies represents an urban program in which service learning is an integrated component of the total school program. IS 218 is an ideal of service learning in action—a middle school based on the theme of community service in which service and reflection occur once a week at a scheduled time, where staff and youth design service projects based on their interests and expertise, and where small groups of young people are guided by caring and enthusiastic adults.

The Community Service Academy (CSA) integrates community involvement with academic excellence. In a model of school/community partnership, each subject teacher works with a small group of students in advisory periods and a community organization to plan and implement a service project. Advisory groups decide on a service project, choosing from among the community organizations that will accept young volunteers. All of the teachers and staff in the Community Service Academy participate in the service program. In the 1992–1993 school year, twenty-three teachers lead twenty-four advisory groups. Each teacher is responsible for maintaining a positive relationship with their group's placement site, but the initial placements were arranged for and established by Lydia Bassett, the assistant principal.

One afternoon is set aside for service and reflection. Students spend time in the classroom preparing materials, learning about the groups they will serve and working on their projects once a week. After working at their placement they return to their classrooms to reflect on their experiences.

Service projects cover a wide range of activities from traditional helping in child care centers and neighboring elementary schools to specially created projects such as advocating for immigrant rights at the Victim's Services Agency; setting up and running a Children's Corner at a local welfare office; and improving community–police relationships, through a variety of joint projects between the student PEACE Team and the local precinct, such as the students teaching police officers the colloquial Spanish of the major Latino population in that community.

Young adolescents also take important neighborhood action, most notably through the Neighborhood Action group and the PEACE Team. The Neighborhood Action team worked for an entire school year on getting the appropriate city authority to take responsibility for a subway tunnel that had deteriorated physically and was dangerous. The persistent research of these sixth-graders forced the Transit Authority and Borough president to recognize their responsibility for maintaining a safe and attractive subway entrance.

The young people at the Community Service Academy are communicative and caring in a way that few young adolescents are—in fact, they are comfortable with themselves. And one can see why. The Community Service Academy is *their* school, its halls are covered with their words, its teachers work hard to shape meaningful programming, and its principal believes strongly in their voices. Bassett says, "We need to make students feel powerful, important, needed, and effective *now*—not ten years from now. Community service does that. There is a sense of well-being and goodness that comes from knowing you contribute to your world."[9]

Turner Middle School, Philadelphia

At Turner Middle School in western Philadelphia, the students of a school-within-a-school configuration work on health-related issues with the assistance of staffs and students from a neighboring university, community agency, hospital, and health center facilities. The Neighborhood Health Promotion and Disease Prevention Program, as the service program is known, is run out of the Turner Middle School and administered by the West Philadelphia Improvement Corps (WEPIC). Ninety-eight percent of the students at Turner are African-American and the school is a Chapter 1 school, 50.3 percent of the students are from families whose incomes fall below the poverty level. Service is fully integrated into the curriculum for students in grades 6, 7, and 8 enrolled in the WEPIC Pod. Of the seven hundred students attending the Turner Middle School, one hundred students are in this school-within-a-school program.

The project grew out of a school and community revitalization effort spearheaded through the collaborative efforts of a community based organization, WEPIC (a subdivision of the West Philadelphia Partnership); the University of Pennsylvania's Penn Program for Public Service and the Philadelphia School District. This unique service program originated in 1985 with a goal of creating a university-assisted, staff-controlled and -managed community school. Community advisory boards are involved in guiding special projects at the school and in the outcomes of the planning. The University's assistance is determined by community leaders and serves the community's real needs.[10] WEPIC provides the administrative support, the School District provides the school structure and the University provides students and staff from various departments, including the medical school, to lead health surveys and share expertise.

Young adolescents in this program address different aspects of the community's health needs determined by a questionnaire administered by students during a summer institute. In the 1991–1992 school year, the sixth-graders addressed nutrition needs, the seventh-graders worked on general concepts of health and wellness, and the eighth-graders worked in a hospital or local health clinic as part of a school-to-work transition program.

While these examples of schoolwide service programs are notable, service learning need not involve an entire school to be effective or worthwhile. A number of schools who see service as a viable teaching strategy have begun with a single service learning course or have involved one grade in service activities. This programming configuration entails fewer administrative and logistical challenges. Not as many placements are needed, fewer staff are involved, transportation needs are reduced and scheduling can be accomplished more easily. However, the basic steps to establishing a program and the issues that need to be addressed are the same whether the program is schoolwide, gradewide, or an individual class.

A. McArthur Barr Middle School, Nanuet, New York

In a middle-class suburb thirty miles outside of New York City, the A. McArthur Barr Middle School of Nanuet, New York, has redesigned its required Home and Careers class to include service involvement for all eighth-graders. The purpose of this program is to offer service to their community; provide students opportunities to apply skills and knowledge learned in Home and Careers in real life situations; and create opportunities for students to be recognized and show leadership. Beginning in the fall of 1993, thirty-five students at a time have been serving at thirteen different sites. The Home and Careers teacher, Marion Thorley, oversees the coordination of the program and the relationship with the sites with the assistance of eight teachers and the support of the administration.

Students select their site in the spring term of the seventh grade. They are given an interest inventory and asked to check their choice of sites in order of preference, usually receiving their first choice. Students work at day care centers, nursery schools, elementary schools, nursing homes, or a school for physically and mentally handicapped children.

In the day care centers, students help supervise the younger children and art activities, read to the children and oversee hygienic care (washing hands, brushing teeth, etc.). In the elementary schools they assist the teachers with whole class activities, one-on-one tutoring, art activities, book making, and media productions. Students who work in nursing homes help with transport, serve lunch, play games, draw sketches of the seniors, and engage them in conversation. At the Jesse Kaplan School for Children with Physical and Mental Disabilities, the helpers assist with exercise, eating, puppet shows, academic work, and socialization.

During their stay at the sites, students' school schedules include at least two periods of reflection a week. With the assistance of eight teachers trained in service-learning, students are encouraged to think about their experiences and formulate conclusions about the effects of their service-learning activities on themselves and those with whom they worked. In addition, each student is required to complete a project related to his or her work at the site; these projects are evaluated by Mrs. Thorley, the site supervisor, and the student.

Students receive academic credit for community service as part of their Home and Careers class. Both the classroom teacher and the site supervisor write letters that are placed in the students' files. Parents receive a copy of the letter and the project evaluation described above; the note "see anecdotal" is written on students' report cards. Thus, students receive two personal evaluations rather than a letter grade for their service-learning experience (Winokur, 1995).

Paoli Junior-Senior High School, Paoli, Indiana

In rural Indiana, the Paoli Junior-Senior High School has responded to a statewide recommendation that service learning be integrated into the curriculum by instituting a service-learning elective. Paoli is a small community in the hills of southern Indiana, not far from the Kentucky border. Students in grades seven through twelve attend one Junior-Senior High School with an enrollment of about 820. The major industry in the area is furniture manufacturing; there is high unemployment. The school reflects the community, in that there is very little ethnic or racial diversity. Though income levels are mixed, a large percentage of families would be considered low income.

In 1993, Paoli Junior-Senior High School and the Orange County Child Care Cooperative received a major three-year grant from the Lilly Endowment to support school restructuring. One aspect of the restructuring proposal was the implementation of a service-learning program for students in junior high grades. Staff of the Cooperative and a consultant from the Endowment researched service programs and were assisted by the National Helpers Network, Inc. (then known as the National Center for Service Learning in Early Adolescence) in developing the course.

The initial class consisted of thirteen seventh-grade students. After a six-week introduction to the program and some class work on child development and volunteerism, the students worked three days a week at nearby Throop Elementary School. Every Monday students had a study–discussion session and every Friday they wrote in their logs about their experiences. By the second semester, eighteen students were enrolled in the course.

For the first semester, nine students were placed in first grade classrooms tutoring in reading and math, two were placed in a fourth grade, helping in the computer lab and tutoring, one worked in the art class, and one worked one-on-one with a fifth grade student who was identified as being emotionally disabled. Placements the second semester were similar, with students who had reenrolled continuing in their original placements. Students who are tutoring generally work with no more than two or three children. Students are placed in teams so that they can be mutually supportive.

Students tutor three days a week for one forty-five-minute class period each day. They meet twice a week to talk about their experiences and plan for the next visit. The course meets one period every day for a semester; each placement lasts about twelve weeks. Students have the option to take the course again, and those who do may continue in the same placement. The course is offered on a semester basis only. Students who sign up in the fall work with Wee Care, Headstart, and First Chance preschoolers. Students who register for the spring semester work in the original tutoring program at Throop Elementary School.

The program has been well received. The supervising teachers' evaluations have been very favorable. One teacher commented that she had been concerned that one child in her first grade class might be retained, but she was reconsidering that recommendation based on the progress he had made with the help of his tutors. This teacher was particularly impressed with the patience of the two seventh-grade boys who worked with the child (Bruce, 1994).

Nespelem School, Washington

The Intergenerational Service Learning Unit: How Can We Help Our Elders? is the creation of Sheri Edwards, a sixth-grade teacher at the Nespelem School in Nespelem, Washington. Nespelem serves a Native American population who live on a reservation, and come from homes that have a high rate of unemployment, domestic violence, and drug and alcohol problems.

Since fall of 1991, students choose their service project and Edwards integrates it into the curriculum, knowing that "the programs will have a better chance of success if the students do what they want to do." Students are involved throughout in the decision-making process. They make checklists of what they want to accomplish with elders, and how they want to behave. In reflection they assess if they have accomplished what they had expected of themselves. They also participate in a variety of activities aimed at preparing them for and helping them understand their service experiences.

At first glance, the Intergenerational Service Learning Unit looks like other intergenerational programs where sixth-grade students serve convalescent residents. What sets it apart is that the students not only gain experience interacting with elders, but that they also investigate the aging process in a yearlong comprehensive unit. By studying nutrition, physical and mental health, and drug and alcohol prevention, students set goals for their own lives and apply what they have learned to their understanding of their friends at the convalescent center.

During the year, students focus on five core values: family, trust, caring, respect, and responsibility. By reflecting on their lives and those of the elderly, students begin to see what effects the choices one makes have on one's life. Throughout the program there is a strong emphasis on understanding and dealing with emotions. The interdisciplinary unit combines science, social studies, humanities, the arts, health, study skills, and language arts. Edwards's cognitive and affective outcomes for the year include: language arts skills of writing, oral communication and reading, social studies knowledge of the needs and characteristics of older Americans and practice of citizenship behaviors, information about science facts related to nutrition and health, respect and empathy for older adults, and an understanding of the influence of present-life choices on later health.

The effect on the students as well as the community, has been impressive. Edwards sees students becoming more caring, concerned individuals. She hears them comment on the kind of future they want for themselves and how they can make choices to positively affect their physical and mental health. The quality of their academic work has also improved; and the community, aware of the value of the students' service, strongly supports the program (Friesem, 1994).

St. John Boscos, Parma Heights, Ohio

Another cross-age service experience is provided for the seventh- and eighth-grade science students at St. John Boscos in Parma Heights, Ohio, a homogeneous middle-class community. Science teacher Patricia Kenzig developed this program in response to a request from primary teachers who wanted to provide laboratory experiences for their students.

In 1990, the first group of seventh- and eighth-grade homerooms planned a separate Sunshine Day for the first through fourth grades. Fall and spring activities are focused on the environment and take place in the Metropark area (the woods behind the school). The winter activities take place indoors and are centered on physical science. The students' training as "teachers" or "guides" takes place in science class but the actual activities are conducted during several classes in the school day.

The students spend one week before the science day preparing a program of activities for first- and second-graders and another for third- and fourth-graders. The "guides" lead younger students to the locations where different activities are taking place. The "guides" also assist the young "teachers" with activities aiding individual students who need additional help. A few days before the event, the science classes go to the woods and select locations for the different activities and the science teacher instructs "guides" in how they can assist with the activities. In the fall, for example, students in grades 1 and 2 receive help in building birdfeeders and students in grades 3 and 4 participate with their helpers in a study of the topsoil found in an area of the Metropark.[11]

Felida Elementary, Vancouver, Washington

Felida is a Generator School, one of a number of schools throughout the nation that serves as a demonstration model of educational reform through service learning sponsored by the National Youth Leadership Council. In addition to NYLC's support, the district also received a fifteen thousand dollars Learn and Serve-America grant, the largest awarded in Washington State, that has helped get programs started.

Felida's program shows how service-learning opportunities can be enhanced by technology. Judy Smith, fifth-grade teacher, uses computers to connect her fifth graders with seniors at the nearby Kamlu Retirement Center. Students practice writing and communication skills in many subject areas as they develop a sense of pride, responsibility, and friendship. Principal Lani Gordon alludes to one program goal and the power of service in her statement, "We want to make the kids better citizens, more compassionate. We feel it's important for children to reach out and help others. We need to instill those kinds of values."

The program started in the fall of 1992; ideas, supplies, and enthusiasm grew rapidly. Two out of three fifth-grade classes at the school are involved in the "Kamlu Connection," communicating via computer with residents at the Center. The communication, however, does not end at the computer terminal as was originally expected; the "pen pals" have chosen to augment their electronic relationships with personal visits and shared experiences. What started out as a fifth-grade project now encompasses students in many grades, as well as the school principal. High school students teach the seniors how to use the computers, younger students make holiday decorations for the retirement center, and the principal has a "Lunch Bunch" twice a month, taking four students at a time to Kamlu to share lunch with their new friends.

The Kamlu Connection extends learning far beyond where traditional curricula can reach. Kamlu residents have a wealth of experiences and knowledge to share. Many are retired from nursing, teaching, or engineering professions. Kamlu resident Marie Sork said, "What our generation remembers—the second World War, the Depression, the Kennedy years, crystal radios, the first automobiles—these are things we can share that are not coming out of a book."

Smith noted that she initially spent much of her own time to get the program going. She began by scheduling visits, organizing programs, making calls, delivering letters, taking students to visit, and planning. In addition, she put time into both holding fund-raisers to underwrite sending student representatives to conferences, and getting ready for the presentations. She estimates that she devotes only half-an-hour each week outside of school to the program now (Friesem, 1993).

Oregon Graduate Institute's Saturday Academy, Oregon

Occasionally community agencies develop and bring individual schools into the service community. One model for agency involvement in school-based service learning is the Student Watershed Project, a program developed by the Oregon Graduate Institute's Saturday Academy in which middle and high school students analyze basic scientific data on the health of local rivers, streams, and surrounding watersheds. By means of a special computer network, accessible from classroom computers, this data is made available to a committee of participating scientists from regional universities and city, county, and state land-use planning agencies. Students generate scientifically credible and reliable information—from far more locations and with greater regularity than could otherwise be afforded—on which state and local jurisdictions can base land-use decisions. Beginning in the 1993–1994 school year curriculum materials have been tested in fourteen classrooms in nine different school districts, all in the Tualatin River watershed, a tributary of the Willamette, Oregon's major north-south river. In the pilot year the fourteen participating classes were intentionally varied. Some were required earth science classes, others were advanced electives which students selected knowing the Watershed Research Project was part of the course.

Steve Andrews, former director of the project, noted, "This has been a dream of mine ever since I was the statewide education coordinator for the Department of Fish and Wildlife." In that role, Andrews developed a program called, "The Stream Scene: Watersheds, Wildlife, and People," that focused primarily on teaching students about salmon and trout habitat and spawning areas. The Stream Scene led students to identify problems in fish habitat that needed attention, but Andrews believed it did not prompt students to seek solutions or provide youth with a means to act on what they learned. In addition, according to Andrews the original program lacked scientific rigor. Since the project is now part of science classes students receive credit for their contributions. In part, the project is designed to expose students to real science and to interest them in pursuing a science career (Dreyfuss, 1993).

CHALLENGES FOR MIDDLE SCHOOL SERVICE-LEARNING PROGRAMS

Effective service-learning programs can be implemented at the middle school level to enhance the educational learning experience for youth involved. However, for service-learning to reach a greater number of students and schools the middle school climate needs to become more conducive to the implementation of this unique methodology. The administrative staff, from the building principal up through the superintendent's office, need to provide the resources that will enable classroom teachers to implement this innovative teaching strategy. Teacher training institutes need to include service-learning in their preservice instruction to allow new teachers to adopt the philosophy and attitude that support the service learning approach. Policy makers and funders need to support initial efforts with increased funds and secure ongoing revenues for sustaining programs. Community agencies need to provide opportunities for young people to serve their clients. Parents need to know what their children are capable of and work with the schools to promote service experiences.

While programs may vary tremendously, effective service learning requires several essential ingredients. As noted earlier there must be a clear reason for using the service learning process that is understood by everyone involved; a skilled, understanding facilitator knowledgeable about early adolescents and sensitive to their needs to serve as Program Leader; sustained involvement; collaboration and ongoing communication among all the different groups involved such as young people, administrators, educators, youth workers, site persons, and parents; and a clear understanding among all involved about the young person's responsibilities and the obligations of each party. In addition, students should be provided with training and ongoing reflection, with guidance, to ensure that they have the skills, knowledge, and understanding they will need to meet their responsibilities.[12] Time for planning and developing a program that addresses the particular needs of the young adolescents and their community is also essential.

Funding middle school service-learning programs is a significant challenge, especially given that early adolescents cannot drive themselves to community sites. Although the Federal government through its Corporation for National Service initiative has provided some funding for service learning at the K–12 level, much of this money is for start-up and schools are expected to identify sources for sustained funding. It is anticipated that once service catches on the school district will include it in their budget. Where service is integrated into subject areas as part of the coursework, the financial support is likely to be there. However, in many instances service learning is still an add-on—an elective or after school program. In the event of budget cuts, these configurations are often the first to go. Even in instances where service is institutionalized and integrated into the entire middle school program or required coursework, there is a danger that reduced funding can eliminate some of the supports that make a difference in the effectiveness of the program. The coordinator or bus transportation may be just the ingredient that makes it possible for young adolescents to work in optimal service sites. Thus, the argument for community-school collaboration is as important at the middle school level as it is for other levels. It is one mechanism for insuring continuous financial and staff support for programs that may be jeopardized by cuts in education and social service.

While these and other challenges must be met to establish long-term quality programs, educators must not forget the importance of these pursuits and the benefits of service-learning for middle school students. "By providing community service, young adolescents will practice skills they already have and take on responsibility for their neighbors and their environment, reviving a tradition of cooperative effort that is essential for the survival of a democratic society (Schine, 1989, p. 35).

IN CLOSING

Service learning has great potential for transforming the education of middle school youth. It can be a mechanism for making instruction real and for connecting abstract academic learning to practical on-the-job information. It also can be a catalyst for transforming a community from a conglomerate of isolated institutions to one in which school and social and government agencies work in partnership to address the concerns that effect them all. It can forge connections between generations, and ethnic and social groups, as well as give young people new status among their families and neighbors. For service learning to accomplish all of this, it takes great care and effort on the part of everyone involved. The young adolescent cannot do it on his or her own, nor can society leave it up to educators alone.

There is an ethic of service that is part of this nation's heritage. It is endemic to our moral foundation as a republic in which each individual is responsible to every other for the shared governance of our democratic society. Coupled with the schools' mandate to educate young people to build a future for the generations to follow, educators have a particular responsibility to prepare their students for this charge. Service learning can be the key to fulfilling this mandate.

NOTES

1. Remarks by Helpers at the National Center for Service-Learning in Early Adolescence's Ninth Annual Convention of Helpers, May 13, 1994.

2. Edward J. Lawton, *A Journey Through Time: A Chronology of Middle Level Education Resources* (Columbus, Ohio: National Middle School Association and National Association of Secondary School Principals, 1989), pp. 1 and 2.

3. *Research Brief: Summary of Research on Middle Schools* (Reston, Virginia: Educational Research Service, Inc., 1975), p. 1.

4. *This We Believe* (Columbus, Ohio: National Middle School Association, 1982 and 1992).

5. Schine, J. Remarks at the Early Adolescents Helper Program's Annual Autumn Workshop, September 26, 1991

6. Schine, J. Remarks at the National Center for Service Learning in Early Adolescence's Annual Autumn Workshop, October 7, 1993.

7. *Critical Components of a Quality Program* (New York: National Helpers Network, 1995), Handout.

8. "Community Service Program: Shoreham-Wading River Middle School," in *Clearinghouse database* (New York: National Helpers Network, 1994).

9. "Community Service Academy: I.S. 218 Salome Urena Middle Academies," in *Clearinghouse database* (New York: National Helpers Network, 1993).

10. "Neighborhood Health Promotion and Disease Prevention Program: Turner Middle School," in *Clearinghouse database* (New York: National Helpers Network, 1993).

11. "Science in the Sunshine—St. John Boscos School," in *Clearinghouse database* (New York: National Helpers Network, 1993).

12. *Critical Components for a Quality Program* (New York: National Helpers Network, 1995), Handout.

Chapter 11

High School Programs

Don Hill and Denise Clark Pope

Service-learning is a promising instructional strategy for improving education in American high schools and strengthening community life. In this chapter we take a critical look at contemporary secondary education in America and examine how and why many educators and students are discovering the power of combining public service with academic study. We begin the chapter with a brief overview of the diverse and compelling needs of adolescent youth in the 1990s. In the second section, we offer a snapshot of the high school setting and reflect on the widespread criticism of secondary education in the United States by leading researchers. The third section of the chapter explores the difference between voluntary community service and service-learning and then provides a representative sample of high school service-learning programs operating in both traditional and restructuring schools. We conclude with a preview of the challenges ahead that will determine whether service-learning becomes a fundamental educational reform or a brief, exciting blip in educational history.

As we conducted our research for this chapter, we read descriptions of hundreds of service-learning programs and surveyed secondary school service-learning leaders throughout the country. The programs we describe represent a wide variety of high school settings and innovative approaches toward infusing service into the academic curriculum. While we have left out far more quality programs than we have included, we hope that the descriptions we offer here stimulate educators to consider many possibilities for service-learning programs at the high school level.

THE HIGH SCHOOL STUDENT

In *Horace's Compromise*, Ted Sizer (1984) describes adolescents as a diverse lot:

They come in all sizes and shapes. There are good ones and bad ones, saints and liars, bores and inspirers, quick ones and dullards, gentle ones and brutes. Besides their age, they have in common the vulnerability that comes from inexperience and social status bordering on limbo. They are children, but they are adults too. Many are ready and able to work, but are dissuaded from doing so. They can bear children, but are counseled not to. They can kill, and sometimes do. They can act autonomously, but are told what to do. . . . We adults too easily talk of these adolescents as an undifferentiated blob of people . . . (pp. 32, 33)

Over a decade later, evidence of the diversity of adolescents persists. Notice the two different worlds embodied by the following youth. First, an inner-city gang member explains how adolescents view their experiences in the high school in his neighborhood:

Some kids . . . they be really wantin' to go do school. . . . But their parents are hooked on drugs and that be bothering them when they be in school. They mind don't be focused on books. And they'll stop going like that too. . . . These kids got nobody to do all this [school or sports with]; they's mind full of worries, so they jus' think why try. (McLaughlin, Irby, and Langman, 1994, p. 208)

Contrast this student with a ninth grader from an affluent neighborhood who also talks about the stress she feels in school:

Look, I have to get good grades. Not like B's, but A's. I want A's in every subject so I can go to a good school. I will spend hours and hours on homework if I have to. I can stay up pretty late now without getting really tired. I just tell myself it has to get done. But the assignments seem to never end. Then the next day, I might miss a kick in soccer and I get really, really annoyed, because I want to play my best, but I know I don't have the energy and I have another night of homework ahead. (Katie, personal communication, May, 1990)

The current literature on adolescents and secondary schools offers numerous reasons to explain why both of these students' minds are "full of worry." Though most youth struggle to form an identity, achieve autonomy from primary caretakers, define gender roles, prepare for future occupational and family roles, and hone reasoning skills during the high school years; many of today's high school students face a wide range of challenges due to particular socioeconomic status, culture, family background, and other factors that may interfere with their adolescent development (Feldman and Elliott, 1990).

In addition to the myriad biological and social transformations that occur during adolescence, researchers document a variety of problems that influence high school students today and affect their ability to find meaning and value in what they learn at school. Studies show that more children live in poverty and in single-parent homes than ever before; that teenage drug abuse, pregnancy, and suicide rates continue to rise in certain communities; that youth violence persists in many urban and suburban neighborhoods and schools; that intense pressure to succeed may lead to serious psychological and physical disorders; that large numbers of students drop out or tune out of high school, and that linguistic differences, socioeconomic status, and cultural barriers may significantly affect school achievement (Phelan, Yu, and Davidson, 1994).[1] Given these sources of stress and the hardships many adolescents face, educational researchers continue to explore questions such as What role should the high school play in assisting these youth? and How can educators design and implement secondary school curriculum that best serves the students' needs?

THE HIGH SCHOOL SETTING

In the 1993–1994 school year, 2,255,095 students graduated from approximately 16,000 American high schools (United States Department of Education, 1993). Most of these schools were four year high schools, grades 9–12, but some students graduated from schools with other configurations including grades 10–12, 8–12, and K–12. Many factors impacted the nature of the students' high school experiences, including size of school, geographical location, socioeconomic make-up of the student population, and amount of money spent on their respective educations.

While no two high schools are exactly the same and many are implementing significant changes, most high schools share a number of traditional characteristics. The normal school day is divided into six or seven class periods that meet for approximately fifty minutes. Instruction is presented in specific content areas that are organized by departments including English and language arts, math, science, social studies, business/vocational arts, creative arts, and physical education. Students normally repeat the same cycle of classes every day of the week for the entire semester. Although educators have recently advocated interdisciplinary instruction in high schools, there has been very little change. High school teachers tend to have a strong commitment to their area of academic training and see themselves as teachers of a specific body of knowledge (Johnson, 1990a).

The student course of study is strongly influenced by graduation requirements that vary from state to state and even from school district to school district. The general pattern, however, resembles the 1990 requirements of Kansas and Pennsylvania described in Table 11.1 below.

Table 11.1
Typical High School Graduation Requirements

	Carnegie Units Required	
Course	Kansas	Pennsylvania
English/language arts	4	4
Social studies	3	3
Math	2	3
Science	2	3
Physical ed	1	1
Arts/humanities	2	
Electives	9	5

(U.S. Department of Education, 1993, pp. 145–47)

Students are usually assigned courses according to ability level and preference. Although there has been much criticism of tracking students by ability, most high schools continue the practice. They commonly offer an honors or advanced placement track, an academic or college track, and a general and/or vocational track within each subject area. Some high schools have responded to the criticism of tracking by limiting the practice in the ninth grade, eliminating it in one subject area such as social studies, making it easier for students to change tracks, or simply renaming the general track; but most use some system for sorting students by ability level. There are also separate programs designed to help students with special needs, though most states strongly encourage "mainstreaming" or placing special needs students in regular classes.

Most high schools are led by an administrative team that includes a principal, one or two assistant principals, and one or more counselors. The department chairs typically serve as an advisory group for the principal on curriculum and budget issues. This structure is often balanced by a school site council that has broader parent, teacher, student, and community representation. It is difficult to make meaningful generalizations about how different administrative organizations operate in high schools across America. Most observers continue to report, however, that the high school teacher remains a rather independent, isolated person when the classroom door is closed and tends to play only a minor role in the administrative process.

High schools located in many of the major metropolitan areas face unique challenges because of the impact of increased immigration on student populations and the pressures of urban poverty. Under these conditions, traditional teaching strategies often fail to work, forcing schools to try to develop new approaches at the same time that class sizes are increasing and resources are being cut. Teachers, administrators, and students in some of these schools live in a crisis environment shaped by physical fear and a sense of hopelessness (McLaughlin, Irby, and Langman, 1989).[2]

Though this sense of severe crisis fades as you move away from the cities, widespread criticism of American high schools that accelerated in the early 1980s continues unabated. The broadly researched judgment featured in a number of influential books affirms that there are far too many American high schools "where significant numbers of students are unmotivated, where unacceptable numbers drop out, and where those who graduate may not have even the basic skills needed for either higher education or the workplace" (Cawelti, 1994, p. 1).[3]

Gordon Cawelti, in his introduction to *High School Restructuring: A National Study* (1994), restates seven critical views of high schools emphasized in national studies conducted within the last decade:

1. Low student achievement, both on tests of basic skills and on tests of general knowledge in core subjects.
2. The need to move beyond only teaching basic skills and factual information to developing higher-order intellectual skills such as critical thinking and problem solving, and to . . . help students derive their own meaning from learning.
3. Curriculum fragmentation, which prevents students from seeing the connections between school subjects and life.
4. The impersonality of many large high schools in which many students feel little or no sense of belonging to the institution.
5. The failure to impart learning experiences that provide students with the skills needed for transition to meaningful jobs in the work world after graduation.
6. The predominance of students as passive learners and the failure to actively engage them in the learning process.
7. The failure to provide the challenging curriculum needed by language minority students and a culturally diverse student population. (pp. 1 and 2)

In his study, Cawelti assesses efforts to restructure high schools in light of such severe criticism. He organizes the analysis of restructuring efforts into the categories of curriculum-teaching, school organization, community outreach, technology, and monetary incentives. Survey data indicates that a significant percentage of schools are working in one or more of these areas, but that very few have adopted a systemic strategy that includes all five. This reality helps explain why secondary school observers continue to report, even when they visit schools with reputations for success, that very little has changed in most classrooms. The seven critical views mentioned above continue to serve all too well as a general description of most American high schools in 1995.

Nonetheless, we do see glimpses of hope in current reform efforts at the secondary level. Many reformers are diligently working to address the changing needs of high school students and to make their high school experience more meaningful. The reformers utilize strategies to increase student motivation for learning, such as showing students the relevance of subject matter and "empowering" youth by encouraging student choice and decision making within the curriculum. Other strategies include addressing individual learning styles and multiple intelligences, relying on cooperative learning techniques, and offering interdisciplinary or problem-based curricula. As Phelan, Davidson, and Cao asserted (1992), the students' views of how they learn best seems to match those of recent educational theorists who advocate active and integrated learning. One student remarks: "I want to feel like I'm really being educated rather than just memorizing facts and forgetting them the next day. I'm not learning anything by that" (p. 699).

Though no one strategy will miraculously help all high school students succeed, these reform efforts address individual needs of the youth and strive to make high schools meaningful to the wide variety of students who attend them. Service-learning represents one such effort which exemplifies almost all of the characteristics mentioned above. In service-learning programs, students work cooperatively to address real community needs and to use content knowledge to work through real-life issues. Often, the students play an integral role in shaping the curriculum and use many of their multiple intelligences as they grapple with community problems. Through service-learning, curriculum can be interdisciplinary, challenging, and alive. The rest of this chapter will describe how service-learning is working today in American high schools and sketch its potential for tomorrow.

HIGH SCHOOL SERVICE-LEARNING PROGRAMS

Service-learning has evolved in American public high schools from two different influences that shape its local character. In order to better understand the high school service-learning programs described below, we need to look at these formative forces.

First, there is a long tradition of voluntary community service in some form on almost every high school campus in America. Students have been encouraged to provide community service as members of honor societies, clubs sponsored by business service organizations, 4-H clubs, and by student governments. Activities have ranged from organizing food drives for the needy to running errands for housebound seniors. Schoolwide projects at Thanksgiving and Christmas have also been commonly organized to help others in need. Many high schools have designed service reward systems to recognize student volunteers on their school transcripts and at graduation. The *service* of service-learning, therefore, is definitely not a new concept for American high schools.

Second, American high schools have also regularly offered opportunities for students to learn through direct experience. Writing and publishing the school newspaper, directing and acting in school plays, constructing projects in woodshop, and participating in school field trips, all allow students the chance to be actively involved in the learning process. This kind of learning, called experiential education, enables students to test theories and knowledge through hands-on applications. This kind of education motivates most students to become more engaged and enthusiastic with their schoolwork. Service-learning represents one form of experiential education. The *learning* of service-learning, therefore, is also not a new concept for American high schools.

Service-learning has started to move to the foreground as a powerful instructional strategy for promoting active student learning in part because it builds on these two foundations and directly tackles the challenges embedded in the seven critical views outlined earlier. We begin this section on high school service-learning programs with a few words of definition. Service-learning is not voluntary community service—although hundreds of teachers and schools use the terms interchangeably, and some have simply retitled their community service programs "service-learning programs" to help secure funding.

The Service Learning 2000 Center at Stanford University has developed a quadrant diagram (Figure 11.1) to help clarify the differences between community service and quality service-learning.

This diagram uses two intersecting spectrum lines to create four quadrants. At the Unrelated Learning point on the horizontal line, there is no connection between service and what is being taught in the classroom. At the Integrated Learning point on the horizontal line, service is tightly woven into the goals of the curriculum. At the Low Service point on the vertical line, there is either little or no service at all. At the High Service point of the vertical line, the service is well organized and meets a very important need. The ultimate goal is to develop projects that fit in quadrant II in the top-right corner of the box because they promote "high service" and are "highly integrated" into the curriculum. In essence, the level and quality of curriculum integration, therefore, determines the difference between community service and service-learning.

While many educators understand the value of helping others and the power of learning through experience, relatively few understand how to use these values to help students learn traditional curriculum and develop academic skills. It is not surprising, therefore, that many programs described as service-learning turn out, on closer examination to be community service programs that do not fit in quadrant two. For example, many schools give service-learning credit to students who perform a set number of hours of vol-

Figure 11.1

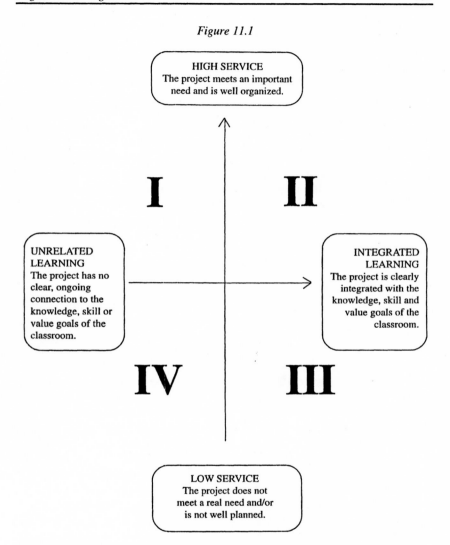

HIGH SERVICE
The project meets an important
need and is well organized.

I   II

UNRELATED
LEARNING
The project has no
clear, ongoing
connection to the
knowledge, skill or
value goals of the
classroom.

INTEGRATED
LEARNING
The project is clearly
integrated with the
knowledge, skill and
value goals of the
classroom.

IV   III

LOW SERVICE
The project does not
meet a real need and/or
is not well planned.

untary service regardless of integration of the service into the curriculum. Other
schools, responding in part to the principles of quality service-learning developed by service-learning organizations that suggest the need for a reflective
component, now require that students submit a written reflection when they
complete their voluntary service (Honnet and Poulsen, 1989). This reflection,
however, can be a perfunctory assignment that does little or nothing to assure

that a student has derived meaning from his or her experience. What seems to be crucial is how well the reflective component connects the service experience to the particular curriculum.

SERVICE-LEARNING THROUGH CURRICULUM INFUSION

Quadrant II service-learning requires that service be integrated or infused with existing curriculum to maximize the value for students. For most high schools, this means infusing service-learning into courses offered by traditional subject matter departments that tend to dominate the organization of instruction. Teachers have accomplished this elusive goal with an incredible variety of service-learning approaches.

Cross-Age Tutoring

One of the most common and most productive approaches is cross age tutoring. Teachers have rediscovered the power of the old adage that the best way to learn something is to teach it to someone else. Through cross age tutoring service-learning projects, students from all levels of ability and areas of society are achieving remarkable success in helping others learn. What is more striking, however, is how this experience has transformed the values and skills of the student tutors. Some of the most impressive programs rely on student tutors and tutees considered to be high risk. For example, students doing poorly in high school English classes have been effectively organized to provide reading instruction for at-risk elementary school students in Redwood City, California (Service Learning 2000, 1994, p. 10). Similarly, the Literacy Corps in Philadelphia High Schools including Kensington, Olney, and Central send hundreds of high-risk students to effectively tutor elementary school students (John Briscoe, personal communication, March 11, 1995). Programs like this across the country are recording dramatic improvement in academic skills for both the tutors and the students receiving help. These programs also demonstrate profound impacts on the personal attitudes of tutors about self-worth and the value of personal effort. One Redwood City high school student explains, "I think this was the first time in school that anyone asked me to do something that seemed to me to be really important" (Service Learning 2000, 1994, p. 1).

Civic Education

A second common approach for infusing service-learning is in the social studies curriculum, especially within the area of civic education. Government teachers, for example, may require students to do ten or more hours of community service outside of class time and then ask the students to write brief descriptions of what they did to receive credit. Classroom instruction may be enhanced by bringing in speakers from the community to inform students about local issues. This teaching strategy may well strengthen the connection between the community and the school, but it does not quite fit the definition of quality service-learning unless teachers are making use of the students' service experiences to enhance classroom learning.

The Constitutional Rights Foundation and the Close Up Foundation, pioneers in civic education efforts for many years, have jointly developed Active Citizenship Today (ACT), which strives to build quadrant II service-learning programs by emphasizing the study of public policy and the role of policy in finding solutions to public problems (Constitutional Rights Foundation, 1995). Instead of identifying a problem in a community such as joblessness, homelessness, or pollution, and jumping in to tackle it, students analyze how and why the problem arose in the first place, what kind of policies are already in place to help solve the problem, and who makes the policies. This analysis and evaluation of current policies leads the students to productive action plans. The ACT project in Omaha, Nebraska, for instance, involves over 300 middle and high school students supporting a series of service-learning projects that range from improving public attitudes toward politicians and curbing youth violence to integrating special needs students into school communities. Variations of this type of policy education approach have been developed by civics teachers across the country as they strive to help students learn the skills and values needed to make our democracy work.

In another approach to civic education, Kent County, Michigan, has established 162 positions on 29 different community boards, commissions, and municipal councils for high school juniors to serve year terms (Jennie Boyer, personal communication, February 13, 1995). This program enables students to learn about local government while participating in the governing process. Opportunities range from regional authorities and municipal councils to nonprofit agencies like the Kent County Council for the Prevention of Child Abuse and Neglect and commissions like the Cable Television Board and the Housing Appeals Board. For example, since 1988, more than 20 students have participated on the City of Grand Rapids' Planning Commission and Zoning Board of Appeals. A typical student experience includes being part of an inspection committee that visits each site two days before a scheduled hearing and assists in presenting the committee report to the Board. Through direct experience in these government positions, students have a chance both to serve their community and to enhance their knowledge of the government process.

Community Service Writing

A third example of service-learning infused in a particular curriculum is community service writing. English and Language Arts teachers have developed two powerful strategies for using service-learning to improve student writing. One strategy involves students engaging in important writing tasks to serve a variety of community needs. As part of their regular course work, students create newsletters, design publicity media, write reports, seek funding, and analyze issues for short-handed community agencies. Instead of writing only for the teacher, students write for a real audience where the quality of their work has real consequences. Students at Birchwood High School in the small, rural community of Birchwood, Wisconsin, began publishing a monthly community newspaper in October, 1994, because there was no town paper in Birchwood (Jim Connell, personal communication, February 8, 1995). This service-learning project, led by an English teacher and a business education teacher, has enhanced the curriculum while enabling students to apply their skills to benefit the entire community. Recognizing that this project is almost like an in-house apprenticeship program, Birchwood is using School to Work grant money to help support it, emphasizing a program connection that deserves more attention.

Similarly, students at Woodside High School in California, upset with negative newspaper descriptions of youth in general and their high school in particular, decided to create a publication that featured positive stories about unsung heroes in the youth community (Susan Miller, personal communication, March 1, 1995). Springfield Central High School in Springfield, Massachusetts uses a tenth- through twelfth-grade writing lab class to generate service-learning projects. In one class, the students decided after much discussion to create a class project on writing for the environment. This project, like many service-learning efforts, sparked unexpected spin-offs. The students started a schoolwide "Earth Action" club that involved special needs students in all of its activities. Writing for class became writing to create Earth Action programs and document activities that included launching a recycling program, contacting elementary schools to work with Springfield students, planning and advertising Earth Day activities and writing editorials and letters to promote different kinds of environmental awareness. Personal reflections on the project were recorded regularly in journals. One student pointed out how much "had been accomplished during the year with real people and real experiences which all had started simply with documents on disks in computers in writing lab" (Bettie Halen, personal communication, March 8, 1995). Other community service writing projects include writing history books for elementary school children and writing stories about local immigrants to increase cultural understanding.

In the second strategy for using service to improve student writing, teachers ask students to use their rich, compelling service experiences to serve as the springboard for both creative and critical writing assignments. Many teachers discover that students with no apparent interest or skill in writing become enthusiastic and skilled when they try to capture the meaning of their experiences in words. Teachers also encourage their students to use their service experiences as sources of information when writing research papers and to draw on facts and opinions gathered at the service site to augment research collected from library books and more common sources.

Science and Environmental Education

A fourth subject area often including service-learning is science and environmental education. High school students, working in collaboration with government and private agency personnel, learn about key issues such as the need to protect watersheds and then apply their knowledge to promote environmental awareness and contribute to watershed health. Almost one hundred Selinsgrove Area High School students in Pennsylvania in a course on environmental science are measuring the quality of Susquehanna River water, analyzing insect larvae and plants from local tributaries, and studying the effects of sewage treatment on plants and air pollution in valley waterways (Central Susquehanna Intermediate Unit Information Services, 1995). Service connections include teaching elementary school students about the environment and planning water clean-up projects. The teacher, Bill Bechtel, reports,

> The kids' enthusiasm has been amazing. We're accommodating various ability levels and interests - some students will be building fences to keep farm animals out of streams; some are doing chemical testing on Susquehanna's electron microscope. This is a unique opportunity for us. The students not only can study environmental protection, they can initiate a conservation program. (Central Susquehanna Intermediate Unit Information Services, 1995)

In the Moshannon Valley School District located in rural Houtzdale, Pennsylvania, Tom Marcinko coordinates another environmental program centered in an introductory science class in the tenth grade (Kay Yannaccone, personal communication, January 30, 1995). Students provide services that include soil and water testing, stream surveys, and park and cemetery restoration.

Environmental service-learning projects have been particularly successful in building broad-based partnerships and sharing expertise. For example, the St. Louis River Watch Project, which is coordinated by Jill Jacoby of the Minnesota Pollution Control Agency, is a partnership that connects Wisconsin and Minnesota school districts, universities, and government agencies (Jill Jacoby, personal communication, March 4, 1994). This joint effort, influenced by the River Watch Network in Montpelier, Vermont, has served as a catalyst for developing service-learning curriculum in earth science, biology, chemistry,

English, and civics. It has also sparked the development of an interdisciplinary curriculum around St. Louis River Watch activities at Cloquet High school where, according to Jacoby:

> The history teacher is teaching the history of the St. Louis Watershed (including timber harvesting, iron ore mining, Native American communities, fur trapping, etc.). The English teacher is helping the students write both scientific reports and creative writings that grow out of their experience of the river. And the shop teacher is teaching students about hazardous waste disposal. (Urke & Wenger, 1993, p. 23)

Jacoby highlights the developing sense of river stewardship among students in the service-learning programs: "Kids say, 'The river's in my backyard, but I never knew anything about it. Now I want to protect, clean it up, deal with it'" (Urke & Wenger, 1993, p. 25).

Foreign Language Education

Another fertile area for service-learning is in the foreign language curriculum. Although foreign language service-learning tends to be dominated by cross age tutoring programs, language teachers have developed many other effective approaches. In Gig Harbor High School in Washington, the third- and fourth-year Spanish classes become partners with the Hispanic community center to share cultural posters and piñatas with the center (MacNichol, 1993). The Spanish classes write and translate children's stories into Spanish, and the drawing class illustrates them. These books are then donated to the Martin Luther King Shelter for homeless families to assist the program director in encouraging Hispanic parents to read aloud to their children.

In another program, at Sequoia High School in Redwood City, California, the Advanced Spanish class adopts an adult education literacy class for recent immigrants (Service Learning 2000, 1994, p. 12). The students interview the immigrants in Spanish to create written histories of their immigration and life experiences. Students then use computers to write up the life stories in Spanish and add photographs and other graphics. The final product is a class book which is presented to all members of the literacy class and students' parents.

Special Education

Service-learning has also proved to be an effective strategy for special needs students. Many service-learning projects generated by individual students or classes have invited the participation of special needs students and used the shared experience to increase understanding. Special needs teachers have also designed collaborative projects where regular program students help the special needs students accomplish a task that they could not do on their own. For example, a California project integrates regular program students and students with limited intellectual ability to work on a school garden (Service Learning 2000, 1994, p. 16). The regular program students help the students with special needs design, plant, monitor, and harvest a vegetable and flower garden behind a biology classroom. Both groups of students deliver garden produce to St. Anthony's Dining Room, a local dispenser of free food to the needy, prepare soup for a faculty lunch, and deliver flowers to teachers and staff on special days of appreciation. The garden is used as a central, experiential focus for classroom instruction of the special needs students, leading to learning about life skills at a level that was not previously thought possible.

SERVICE-LEARNING IN RESTRUCTURED SCHOOLS

Although service-learning is much more difficult to implement in traditional high schools, our attention has primarily focused there because that remains the dominant reality. Service-learning is, however, a soul partner to high school reform efforts and often serves as a "Trojan horse" for change. Successful service-learning programs stir up pressures to change school schedules, improve school-community relations, form teaching teams, develop curriculum connections, and create new, authentic assessment strategies. Restructured schools, therefore, encourage more extensive service-learning programs than probably could exist in traditional schools.

Central Park East Public Secondary School in New York City, for example, transforms a typical volunteer community service program into a quadrant II program by the way it connects the service to the school goals and to curriculum objectives (Anne Purdy, personal communication, February 3, 1995). At Central Park East, the service-learning coordinator selects and trains agency personnel to work with students in a number of areas, including the art of reflection. Students volunteer weekly as part of their regular school schedule and participate in organized reflection in small advisory groups. In addition, they are required to develop student service-learning portfolios to help meet an "authentic performance" graduation requirement and are encouraged to discover and write about ways to connect their service experiences with curriculum in academic classes. All of these components enable the Central Park East School to act on its belief that service-learning requires thought-provoking analysis and reflection as well as a powerful service experience. Champlain Valley Union High School in Hinesburg, Vermont, represents another example of a school that illustrates the symbiotic relationship between interdisciplinary instruction and service-learning. Cynthia Parsons reports that the principal, Valerie Gardner, has "every single student involved in service-learning in imaginative and interesting ways" that enable the school to move toward full interdisciplinary instruction as students make the connection between their service experiences and many different subject areas (Cynthia Parsons, personal communication, January 30, 1995).

Efforts to reform high schools have increasingly focused on creating smaller schools that are designed to meet individual needs of the students. These needs range from helping at-risk students who have failed in the regular high school to offering magnet schools designed for special purposes such as the study of technology or the arts. Service-learning often plays a pivotal role in these alternative settings. For example, the Media Academy in Oakland, California, was highly praised in the book *Reducing the Risk* for its success in engaging at-risk students. The authors wrote:

> How unlike traditional school to have at-risk students in active roles, producing useful products such as a Spanish/English language paper for a local community and creating public service announcements and commercials for radio and television. How unlike school to have students working cooperatively on a group project and at the same time becoming competent in the necessary academic skills of reading, writing, speaking, and critical thinking. How unlike school to engender a sense of school membership through academic rather than extracurricular activities such as sports and music. (Whelage et al., 1989, p. 190)

The media projects are designed as service-learning projects, and therefore foster the kind of motivation and academic success that would not be possible for many of these students in traditional schools.

This overview of service-learning programs reveals only a tiny sample of what is being accomplished today in high schools and just scratches the surface of what is possible in the future. In the next section, we examine some of the challenges high school service-learning educators grapple with today and offer some modest suggestions for enhancing effective practice in the years to come.

CHALLENGES FOR HIGH SCHOOL SERVICE-LEARNING PROGRAMS

Most informed educators will agree that what we describe as quadrant II service-learning programs offer constructive, effective learning experiences for students. But service-learning educators face a number of critical challenges ahead. Service-learning remains largely on the periphery of the majority of American high schools and will likely fade from the educational scene unless a number of concrete issues are addressed. Many of these challenges stem from the nature of the reform itself—the difficulty of building school-community partnerships, the logistical obstacles such as securing financial resources and arranging transportation off campus, and the problems inherent in connecting service experiences to classroom curriculum. In addition, three specific aspects of American high schools pose special hurdles for service-learning implementation.

First, most high schools are still organized by subject matter areas. Teachers have been trained as experts in one particular field and are often segregated on high school campuses in individual departments. This structure may impede successful collaboration among teachers and makes interdisciplinary planning especially difficult. Since quality service-learning often relies on teacher collaboration and on interdisciplinary curriculum, the traditional high school departmental structure proves challenging.

Second, high school students must adhere to strict time schedules. Many classes meet for approximately fifty-minute periods, which makes scheduling service experiences on or off campus particularly challenging unless teachers schedule the class to meet at the end of the day or couple it with a lunch period or study hall.

Third, high schools face pressure from institutions of higher education and local businesses to graduate students who meet high academic standards. Many high school teachers feel burdened by the overloaded curriculum and the emphasis on traditional academic subject areas. Consequently, service-learning at the high school level has been criticized as representing "just another add-on" that may undermine traditional academic learning.

Though these challenges are significant, high school teachers across the country still manage to have high levels of success as they implement service-learning programs on campus. They offer the following advice: start with small and simple projects, rely on colleagues for help, and involve all participants in the school and community in the planning.

IN CLOSING

While the examples and recommendations provided in this chapter will prove useful to program facilitators, all the practical advice in the world will not help high school teachers decide to take the first step. To encourage that first step, service-learning teachers must share more broadly the magic of their experiences. They must talk about student enthusiasm and motivation to learn. They must tell how service-learning enriches their professional lives. They must explain to department colleagues that service-learning is not another useless reform or unbearable add-on. They must share the secret that service-learning is an educational innovation that actually works.

NOTES

1. See also M. LeCompte and A. Dworkin, *Giving Up on School: Student Dropouts and Teacher Burnouts* (Newbury Park, CA: Corwin Press, 1991).

2. See also LeCompte and Dworkin, *Giving Up on School;* and G. Whelage, R. Rutter, G. Smith, N. Lasko, and R. Fernandez, *Reducing the Risk: Schools as Communitities of Support* (London: Falmer Press, 1989).

3. See also Ernest Boyer, *High School: A Report on Secondary Education in America* (New York: Harper and Row, 1983); Arthur Powell, Eleanor Farrar, and David Cohen, *The Shopping Mall High School: Winners and Losers in the Educational Marketplace* (Boston: Houghton Mifflin, 1985); John Goodlad, *A Place Called School: Prospects for the Future* (New York: McGraw Hill).

Chapter 12

Teachers of Service-Learning

Susan E. Seigel

This chapter focuses on classroom teachers who engage their students in service-learning activities. There are at least two significant reasons to address teachers' roles in service-learning programs. First, teachers who function as change agents are central to the process of school reform (Flinders, 1988; Paris, 1993). Therefore, institutionalized change in the field of service-learning depends on the degree to which teachers are able and willing to implement service-learning into their curriculum. Second, teachers have a significant impact on the quality of student learning. Within the context of the classroom, a teacher ultimately decides what is taught and how it is taught. The success of a service-learning project largely depends on the knowledge, skill, and creativity of the classroom teacher (Nathan and Kielsmeier, 1991).

The potential benefits to students who participate in service-learning are well documented (Conrad and Hedin, 1991; Newmann and Rutter, 1983; Halsted and Schine, 1990). Service-learning can promote students' personal growth and self-esteem, increase students' intellectual development, and assist in students' social growth and development. Teachers are central in helping students learn from their service experiences. As with other curricula, unless a teacher deliberately includes a specific purpose or learning outcome (ability to take responsibility, basic academic skills, or developing more positive attitudes about working with people from diverse backgrounds) student learning is limited to a "hit-or-miss" basis.

By providing students with appropriate orientation information and activities, teachers can help students prepare both academically and emotionally for the service experiences ahead of them. For example, most students need preparation to understand the limitations of the elderly before visiting a nursing home and engaging in activities with older individuals who have disabilities.

Similarly, students need to understand some of the reasons why individuals are homeless and unemployed before they help at a homeless shelter. It is the responsibility of the teacher to prepare and guide students through the learning process of their service experiences.

In recognition of this important responsibility, this chapter addresses the backgrounds, experiences, and perceptions of teachers in service-learning programs. The data taken for this chapter comes primarily from two qualitative studies focused on ten public school teachers in the midwest (Wade, 1995d) and six middle school teachers in the northeast (Seigel, 1995). An additional study (Shumer, 1994a) on a small group of teachers in grades 5 through 7 plus a teacher who taught a high school service-learning class provided additional confirmation for the findings in the other two studies. All three of the studies centered on the beliefs and practices of individual teachers in service-learning programs. Their stories provide insight into the day-to-day practice of service-learning in the public school curriculum and illustrate how service-learning is a complex pedagogy that requires time, creativity, and flexibility in its implementation.

TEACHERS IN SERVICE-LEARNING PROGRAMS

There are many reasons why teachers today are involved in service-learning programs. Some teachers have engaged their students in service-learning projects long before it was placed on the national agenda for education reform. Recently, the numbers of teachers involved in service-learning nationwide has mushroomed since the passage of the National Service Trust Act in September 1993. For example, during the 1994–1995 school year, $404 million was distributed to schools across the country providing funding for staff and program development, transportation costs from schools to service sites, and other materials related to service-learning projects.

In some school districts service-learning programs were mandated by the administration, and teachers were told that they had to include service-learning as part of the ongoing curriculum. For example, in one urban middle school, all the sixth-grade teachers were informed that they would have to do a service-learning project with their students during the school year. As one teacher described it:

> I was just told that we would do community service and what would I like to do? Would I like to go to a school or a nursing home the first year? Then I said, "Well, let's go to a nursing home." So we went. (Seigel, 1995, p. 145)

In most cases, however, service-learning involvement has depended on the interest of the individual teacher. This chapter centers on those teachers who choose to include service-learning to meet the needs of their students and communities. Who are these teachers? How do they perceive themselves as educators? What beliefs do they have about the ways students learn? What do they see as significant about their service-learning experiences?

Teachers Who Choose Service-Learning

There are many reasons why teachers choose to engage their students in service-learning activities. Factors such as a teacher's past experiences with community service, beliefs about teaching and learning, and knowledge about service-learning as pedagogy play a significant part in determining the teacher's interest level and ability in implementing service-learning activities in the curriculum.

Teachers' decisions to engage in service-learning may also be influenced by the structure of the school. For example, it might be easier for an elementary teacher to fit a service-learning project into his or her curriculum because of a more flexible time schedule. At the high school level, a teacher might have the advantage of students who are able to drive themselves and others to a service site, even if time for service is limited during the school day. Middle school teachers often struggle with transportation issues but may be assisted by team teaching arrangements in implementing community-based service projects.

A supportive administration is key in helping teachers with their efforts. A school principal who fully understands how service-learning enriches student learning is likely to provide the necessary time for teachers to plan and implement their projects. A supportive administrator will also allow teachers the necessary freedom and flexibility to develop curricula combining the learning needs of students with the genuine needs of the community.

Motivation to Include Service-Learning within the Curriculum

Teachers cited many reasons when asked why they decided to include service-learning in their curriculum. Some teachers emphasized the importance of instilling a sense of caring, social responsibility, or self-esteem in their students. For example, Rachel, a sixth-grade science teacher explained that her attraction to service-learning predominantly centered on another way to connect with students, who she perceived as having many personal and social needs:

> I am drawn to things like community-service learning, because I see a huge need for kids to be able to feel like they belong. Because there is so much alienation with these kids . . . I have never seen . . . so much alcohol abuse, drug abuse, emotional, physical, or sexual abuse in the home. (Seigel, 1995, p. 171)

In some cases, teachers became involved because they knew other teachers in their schools who had successful experiences with service-learning. For example, Carla, a sixth-grade social studies teacher, became interested in community service learning through her connections with other teachers at her school.

> I feel like we [the team] began to think about getting the kids out of the classroom . . . we did it in more recreational ways as a team . . . I'm trying to think how I really got hooked onto this. It was definitely through some chatting with Gregory. (Seigel, 1995, p. 166)

Carla's attraction to community service learning was consistent with her individual beliefs about student learning and the needs of early adolescents. She believed that it was difficult for these students to be confined within a classroom throughout the entire day. As she explained, she wanted to be able to provide more for them:

> I guess it was part of my own feeling [that] there really needs to be something else we need to be doing with kids beyond the experience in the classroom and feeling as though, you know, frustration that middle school kids probably spend too much time sitting at desks all day. . . . Kids need to be more connected with their community in a greater way than what we [teachers] do. You know we talk about it [the community] in sort of laboratory situation in the classroom. . . . I think that kids get a chance to have a real connection with something—a real experience instead of a laboratory experience. (Seigel, 1995, p. 167)

Some teachers stated that they have been doing service-learning for years without knowing the term. For these teachers, their perceptions of teaching and learning coincide with the philosophical foundations of experiential education and service-learning. Moreover, these teachers perceive service-learning as another teaching method that offers many possibilities for students to develop "self-growth." A sixth-grade social studies teacher explained that

> students get to learn something about themselves from giving to others. I think it isn't just the experience of what we give and [that] someone is either pleased or displeased; but I think there is some learning that takes place about oneself, your capacity to give, your abilities, your talents, the fact that someone cares that you have something to offer, that you do have something to offer. (Seigel, 1995, p. 172)

The most common responses centered around the compatibility between service-learning and teachers' beliefs about teaching and life. One teacher noted that service-learning is important for junior high school students because, "they are really starting to show some empathy and concern for [the] community" (Wade, 1995d, p. 10).

The notion of developing individual "pride" was emphasized by several teachers. Karen, a midwestern elementary school teacher–guidance counselor commented:

> I think there's a lot of pride that kids can get from making a contribution back to a school or community . . . It's exciting to see kids as a member of society . . . and in contributing ways . . . I just think there are lots of opportunities in this community and we need to be teaching kids about what they are and how they can take advantage of them. (Wade, 1995d, p. 10)

When asked about the learning outcomes for students participating in service-learning, Carla responded:

> one of our first goals was [to develop a sense of] pride in [the school]. This is a particularly rundown building. . . . I think there has been a lot of effort in the last year particularly to try to generate student pride for the school and . . . one of our goals [was] to help kids feel like they owned a little piece of this and that they could contribute to the beautification, if you will, of [the school]. (Seigel, 1995, p. 169)

For Carla, "school pride" meant building school community. She saw a need for students (and faculty) to be connected to each other in more constructive and respectful ways. By participating in an activity that would improve the appearance of the school, Carla believed that students might feel more ownership of it and therefore develop a sense of "community" within it.

Although Carla's teammate Rachel didn't elaborate on building school community, she did comment on students' ability to make a difference within their school through "a sense of pride in having accomplished something that beautified the front yard. And a feeling of ownership. This is our school, we just made it better" (Seigel, 1995, p. 170).

Because some teachers emphasized that their primary responsibility is attending to student learning (over serving the community), they noted the importance of students' academic development from their service-learning experiences. A middle school language arts teacher pointed to the significance of service-learning in meeting academic goals:

> It made so much sense that part of growing up as thinkers and listeners, that they be linked somehow with the community . . . One of the things

that I talk with them [the students] about is the fact that I cannot provide . . . within the context of the classroom, the kind of language experience that will be useful to them in interacting with the community and the world outside these walls . . . [Service-learning] is a springboard for a lot of the writing. (Wade, 1995d, p. 11)

Patrice, a sixth-grade ESL teacher also noted that her Cambodian students participating in service-learning gained academically from their experiences at a nursing home:

Well, for my kids it forced them to use English. . . . I didn't feel like I was wasting time because the kids were there speaking English to people they really had to explain things to. [These old people couldn't hear them, and they didn't understand half the time what they were saying, so my kids really had to dig down and use what English they had. . . . They also don't get much time to really speak English because they shop in Cambodian stores; they play with Cambodian kids; they live in Cambodian neighborhoods. So they never really have any genuine practice with Americans. And I thought it was just great just going. And we always tried to spend most of the time just in kind of conversation with them. (Seigel, 1995, p. 146)

Prior Community Service Experience

Many teachers who choose to be involved with service-learning have had prior community service experience. Wade (1995d) found that most of the teachers she studied indicated that they had some prior service experience as a child in their family, in their community, from schooling, or as an adult. Many teachers indicated they were involved in community service experiences through their families, church groups, or other organizations such as 4-H or Girl Scouts. One elementary school teacher reflected on her childhood and how much she appreciated being included in her community's service effort:

I remember very clearly my whole town building a swimming pool . . . and being able to be involved. People were not telling me, "You can't help" because I was a kid. The town raised money and then just with whatever expertise the people in town brought, we built the swimming pool . . . I remember tying reinforcement rods in the bottom of the pool together with these little wires . . . I wanted to swim in the swimming pool . . . as bad as anybody else. I didn't think it was something that just the adults had to have their fingers in. Fortunately, they let me help. (Wade, 1995d, p. 8)

One sixth-grade science teacher perceived her childhood community service experiences as clearly influencing her teaching practices in relation to service-learning:

> My dad is a minister. I was doing community service learning from the time I was hatched! Only no one called it that. And when I was in school we would . . . go to the local nursing home and we'd do something or other . . . Maybe the chorus would sing. Maybe we'd go to the hospital and every so often during the year we'd do something . . . There was any number of things that happened when I was a student myself. So this is very natural to me to have kids doing this, because I did it myself. Only we didn't have a fancy name for it. (Seigel, 1995, p. 166)

Several teachers mentioned that they had tutored others during their high school or college years. A high school teacher who facilitates a service-learning program involving students in cross-age tutoring activities, recalled her own experiences tutoring.

> When I grew up, I went to probably the very last country school in Iowa. For nine years. [For] a couple of years I was the only girl, and other years there were just two of us. So for all those years, I was the teacher for everybody else. So . . . I grew up tutoring. I guess you could say that was service because I did a lot of that. (Wade, 1995d, p. 9)

The data suggest that teachers' past experiences with community service likely contribute to their current beliefs and willingness to participate in service-learning projects with their students.

TEACHERS' EXPERIENCES WITH SERVICE-LEARNING

While service-learning can be rewarding for teachers who see their students motivated to learn while helping others, it can also be problematic. Service-learning takes time, commitment, creativity, and flexibility. One middle school science teacher recalled the amount of work she put into doing a service-learning project with her students. "It was also a lot of work. But almost anything worthwhile ends up being a lot of work. I think it was positive. I think the positive things definitely outweighed the negative things" (Seigel, 1995, p. 172).

Several components need to be considered in a discussion of teachers' experiences with service-learning: how teachers plan service-learning projects, the kinds of collaboration a teacher has with others that are needed to successfully implement a project, and the support that a teacher receives from his or her school administration for service-learning. In addition, a consideration of the rewards and challenges teachers encounter as they engage in service-learning will further illuminate an understanding of teachers' experiences.

Planning Service-Learning Projects

There are basically three approaches that most teachers use to develop service-learning projects. Some teachers plan the project themselves, selecting the service, making contacts, setting dates, preparing instructional materials, and then informing students how they will participate. Other teachers engage their students in a collaborative planning process that often includes investigating community issues and making decisions about what service project they will do and how they will do it. Some teachers include other faculty and community members in the planning of service-learning projects. The different planning approaches "appear to be connected to many factors including teaching style, age of students, type of project, extent to which the teacher is integrating the project in the curriculum, time spent on planning, and time allotted for service-learning during the school day" (Wade, 1995d, p. 11).

Teachers select service-learning projects using a variety of criteria. A project is often selected based on how the teacher perceives that it will "fit" or "connect" with the existing curriculum. Sometimes projects are selected because community sites are in close proximity to the school, therefore eliminating transportation expenses. For example, an intergenerational project was selected by a second-grade teacher because the care center was near the school, she was good friends with the director, and she saw the connections between service to senior citizens and her language arts curriculum. A seventh-grade science teacher selected a recycling service-learning project at a hospital because it was within walking distance to the school, and the topic of recycling was included in his science curriculum.

Regardless of how a project is initiated, many teachers recognize the importance of student ownership to the success of service-learning activities (Wade, 1995d). Students who are included in decision-making processes within their service-learning projects are much more likely to be motivated and engaged in the service activities and related learning (Conrad and Hedin, 1991). In fact, in most of the service-learning projects studied, even those selected by teachers, students were given options and choices during implementation. For example, the second-grade teacher described above allowed her students to decide what activities they would do with the senior citizens during their monthly visits. After attending a three-day service-learning workshop two enthusiastic sixth-grade teachers, recognizing the importance of student ownership in service-learning, raised the question, "We know what *we* want to do for our service-learning project, but how do we get our students to think that it was their idea?" (Wade, 1995, personal communication).

The following experience of two sixth-grade teachers further illustrates the importance of student decision making and ownership in service-learning. Rachel and Carla decided to involve their students in a collaborative service-learning project, in which a flower garden would be planted on the lawn in front of their school. Carla explained the process they used to select their project:

> I think it was the idea that many of us in the building feel like we're not sure kids really feel part of the [school] community . . . and generally just . . . trying to get kids involved in making this seem less than an institution and more of their place. And the grounds have always seemed to me as though they have not been particularly well cared for and they have a rather austere look . . . The idea was getting them involved in some project that would be outside the classroom, something really different. We thought a project that would be hands-on, moving, digging, that there would be some physical activity associated with it, which I thought would be a good break from the kinds of things we usually do and to spruce up the grounds, give it a face lift. (Seigel, 1995, p. 170)

She also described how the students were maneuvered so *they* would suggest that a flower garden was a school need:

> We . . . brought them outside before we told them what we were doing and said, "Take a look around. What do you see? What is it you don't see? What are your feelings?" They came up with the garden idea, then we brought them in and said, "Guess what?" (Seigel, 1995, p. 175)

This tactic had limited effectiveness, however. The lack of students' enthusiasm and the number of continuous behavior problems were perceived by Carla as resulting from "the fact that these kids did not choose this particular project" (Seigel, 1995, p. 176). Providing students with choices is fundamental for successful teaching practice. Carla further stated:

> I am sure that you can't come up with the learning project that interests everyone but I think that ideally it should be something that can be planned on and discussed with the kids. I think that that's critical. I see that as problematic in what we have done here . . . if [an activity] is something kids choose to do, their investment is so much greater. (Seigel, 1995, p. 176)

Even though the flower garden project was not initially selected by the students, it did involve some student choice. Both of the teachers emphasized that students made important decisions throughout the project. For example, in Carla's class, students brainstormed the design and kinds of flowers they would ultimately select to plant in the garden. In Rachel's class, students chose where they would place certain flowers based on a set of criteria. Rachel's comments suggest that students might have been more connected to the project as a result of their individual contributions and choices:

> they went out there and admired it [the garden] the other day. They were really glad they had bothered to choose what went where, and that it looked somewhat symmetrical, although we got a lot on one side and not enough on the other side. (Seigel, 1995, p. 177)

Both teachers agreed that the major problems they had with this project resulted from three factors. First, too many students were involved in the project and were difficult to handle. Second, many students seemed disconnected from the activities, suggesting that the length or nature of planning and creating a garden may not have been appropriate for these students. Finally, because students did not select this project, their involvement in a decision making process that enlisted them in identifying community needs was missing from the experience.

At another middle school, the service-learning project strongly emphasized student decision-making. Here the students were encouraged to choose and plan their own service-learning project. The teacher explained her belief in giving students' choices about what and how they learn: "You try as much as possible, because you know that if they choose it, you'll get more cooperation than if you assign" (Seigel, 1995, p. 89).

Service-learning projects can also emerge spontaneously as students proceed through the regular curriculum. Teachers who are creative and flexible take advantage of student enthusiasm as a springboard for learning. For example, a fourth-grade teacher described how her students picked up on a topic for a service-learning project:

> My kids read the book, *Fly Away Home*, by Eve Bunting [about the homeless] and they got to talking and they said, "Let's do something!" They had just read about the man last year who died in the dumpster . . . A lot of kids clipped this story and they were really concerned about it . . . It was just a whole combination of things, and I had a calendar sitting out from the previous year that the kids had done, and they wanted to do a project, too. It just kind of evolved that way. (Wade, 1995d, p. 12)

A critical factor influencing teachers' development of service-learning projects is time. Most teachers reported that planning for service-learning projects generally takes more time than courses centered around textbooks or mandated curriculum guides. However, some teachers found the creative aspects involved in planning for service-learning stimulating:

> I guess in terms of certain steps and procedures we went through, it felt very similar to what I would think about if I were beginning a unit or organizing a unit . . . There was a lot of brainstorming that went on in different stages and that was really fun and exciting! (Seigel, 1995, p. 165)

More often than not, teachers applied their creative skills to construct a service-learning project that would fit into their existing curriculum. For example, a junior high school teacher recalled, "I took some of the things from here, put a sheet together, and spent a lot of time brainstorming ideas" (Wade, 1995, p. 14) to develop a service-learning program in her health class.

Collaborating with Others

Because effective service-learning necessitates collaboration, teachers often find that involving other individuals can be most helpful. Teachers' efforts can be supported by other school faculty and staff, community members, parents, and individuals with particular expertise relevant to the project.

School faculty and staff. The following example clearly illustrates how a variety of personnel from one school can collaborate on one service-learning project:

> A fifth-grade service-learning project at a nursing home involved the school guidance counselor (in preparing the students for interacting with seniors), the music teacher (who taught the students some "old time" songs to sing to the seniors), the art teacher (who helped the class prepare a craft project to make with the seniors), and the school principal (who videotaped the participants and served ice cream at the last visit of the year). (Wade, 1995d, p. 13)

Making connections and depending on others are often new and challenging activities for teachers, many of whom have taught in isolated conditions for most of their careers. However, teachers often reported that they benefited by collaborating on service-learning projects with others in the school. In Carla's and Rachel's case, collaboration was supported by a fundamental level of professional trust and respect for each other's work combined with a desire to try something different. Nevertheless, Carla described both positive and negative aspects of working with another teacher on a service-learning project:

It was different to work with another teacher. It was different to be constantly going back and forth to get consensus on different issues, so that was a stretch . . . for me personally, stepping out and trying this for the first time, it was very important for me to have another adult there who I could bounce ideas off of. I am generally the type of person that steps very carefully onto new ideas. I am often much more timid than I need to be, and if there is somebody there to kind of help me along then I say, "Yeah, I can do that." or "We can do that." or whatever. So I think that process of working with someone else was important in getting me engaged initially and feeling like I could probably handle this. (Seigel, 1995, p. 165)

While Rachel's assurance helped Carla gain the confidence to attempt a service-learning project, Carla's organizational skills and commitment provided Rachel with a level of security during the implementation of the project. As Rachel explains:

I would like to still work with another adult. I think that's really, really helpful. . . . Carla and I had each other, and that was really helpful. When she couldn't do something, I could, and vice versa. It was alright. It's like we covered for each other. (Seigel, 1995, p. 165)

Parents helping teachers. Teachers involved with service-learning often depend on parents for help with providing transportation, gathering materials or supplies, or supervising students. For example, one seventh-grade teacher described how parents helped with transporting students to a wastewater treatment plant:

It would be great to have a bus at our disposal . . . You know, during the class period everybody could jump in the bus and go up to any part of the river and clean it up.. Just to go down to the wastewater treatment plant next week would cost sixty-five dollars. Just to drive . . . two miles down the street. So instead we're getting parents to do it. (Seigel, 1995, p. 130)

Parents also help with obtaining materials and supplies needed for service-learning projects. For example, in the flower garden project mentioned above, one of the participating student's parents owned a nursery and provided bulbs and flowers at a discounted cost. (See chapter 20 for further information on parents' involvement in service-learning programs.)

Community agencies and businesses. As teachers become involved in community-based service-learning projects, they must collaborate with individuals from local agencies and businesses. Teachers often include these individuals in the planning stages for their service-learning projects (e.g., nursing homes, soup kitchens, Headstart programs, or elementary schools). Communication is key to the success of these projects. For example, Patrice, a sixth-grade English as a second language teacher explained her difficulty connecting with a teacher from another elementary school for a cross-grade tutoring project. According to Patrice, the teacher

> had an unlisted number and she called me one time but she never offered her number and they wouldn't give me her number at the school, so I never had any way of contacting her to figure out what we were going to do the next week. (Seigel, 1995, p. 150)

While some teachers have difficulty finding time during the school day to make community contacts, most find that their collaboration with community members enriches their service-learning activities and helps to overcome the isolation from other adults that can sometimes accompany classroom teaching.

The service-learning coordinator. Some teachers are fortunate to have a districtwide or school service-learning coordinator whose responsibility is to help teachers with the connections they need to make within the community for their projects. Five teachers from a district with a full-time coordinator agreed that the coordinator played a significant role in the planning and implementation of their projects. One teacher remarked, "She does a previsit. She comes out with slides . . . She arranges everything" (Wade, 1995d, p. 14).

In Massachusetts, one middle school funded a service-learning coordinator through a CNS "Learn and Serve America" grant. This individual was a parent who was well-connected with the community. She had time to make phone calls for teachers, attend workshops and meetings, and make connections with the local media developing public relations with the school. Her assistance greatly enhanced the implementation of the service-learning program.

Administrative Support

More often than not, the school principal is key to teachers' efforts for service learning. School principals are instrumental in teachers' efforts to learn about service-learning through their support or encouragement of faculty attendance at in-service workshops. Teachers feel acknowledged when their school principal provides positive feedback on their efforts. Wade (1995d) found that most school principals were eventually (if not initially) supportive of the teachers' efforts. "Iris' principal, who initially questioned her decision to take her students monthly to the local nursing home, ended up videotaping their last visit of the school year and helping serve ice cream to the residents" (Wade, 1995d, p. 16).

In one middle school, the principal participated in a "Walk for Hunger" fund-raising effort with the students. Connecting service-learning with school reform, another middle school principal wrote,[1] "I strongly feel that CSL (community service-learning), and the sense of community and enthusiasm it has created here over the past two years, will help us tremendously in the restructuring project we are currently involved via *Turning Points*."

The support of school administrators can make a difference for teachers who put their efforts into service-learning projects. However, these administrators also need to understand the educational implications behind service-learning in order to support it. Thus, community service-learning training for all school faculty, including administrators, is essential.

Rewards of Service-Learning

According to Cohn and Kottkamp, "Rewards, like purposes and means, are at the core of the task of teaching" (1993, p. 54). Satisfying aspects of service-learning reported by teachers include: increased student motivation and learning; opportunities for creativity in developing curriculum; positive recognition from administrators, faculty, and parents; public attention through the media; and the benefits provided to the community. However, the most rewarding aspect of service-learning is the changes teachers observe in their students. In line with research on the rewards of teaching in general (Cohn and Kottkamp, 1993; Feiman-Nemser and Floden, 1986; Fullan, 1991; Lortie, 1975) many teachers of service-learning expressed great satisfaction observing their students' enthusiasm and motivation to learn. The words "excited," "enthused," and "proud" were common among teachers' descriptions of students engaged in service-learning projects (Wade, 1995d).

Teachers are particularly rewarded when students with behavior problems change as a result of participating in a service-learning project. For example, a sixth-grade teacher described how one apathetic student was affected:

> I have one kid that no matter what you say to him he says, "Who cares? So, who cares?" That is his constant refrain . . . Yet, the "who cares kid," once we got into problem solving and saying "Oh well, what could we do?" and kids had all kinds of ideas; he was one of the ones who had some ideas, too. (Seigel, 1995, p. 181)

When a student feels that members of a community care what he or she thinks, that student is more likely to become engaged in the activities of the community (Newmann et al., 1992). Service-learning can be instrumental for drawing students into the learning process.

As Johnson (1990b) noted, "It is no news that teaching is short on recognition" (p. 290). However, for many teachers of service-learning, positive recognition from colleagues, administrators, and parents is a more common occurrence. One reason for this may be connected to the fact that teachers involved in service-learning collaborate with others. Another reason may be the visibility of service-learning activities that take place outside of classrooms, schools, or both.

Challenges of Service-Learning

Although most of the teachers in the study cited numerous personal rewards for being involved in service-learning projects, several issues were raised as they reflected on their practices. The challenges reported by teachers include: finding time during the school day for service-learning; managing large numbers of students outside of classroom settings; setting up transportation for students to service-learning sites; obtaining adequate funding for materials and supplies; and dealing with a lack of support from administrators, colleagues, or parents.

Limited Time

By far, the largest issue facing teachers was the lack of time for service-learning. Teachers often cited the difficulty of finding time for planning service-learning projects as well as implementing them during the school day. As one sixth-grade teacher described, ". . . I'm not saying that [service-learning] is not a valuable thing, but I don't know if the day is long enough as it is to take the time out to do it" (Seigel, 1995, p. 144).

Because service-learning activities differ from traditional classroom instruction, three significant issues are raised for teachers affecting their time: curriculum development; collaboration with others; and conditions outside of classroom settings which might not be easily controlled by the teacher. In terms of developing activities for service-learning, teachers must depend on their expertise as curriculum planners. They cannot follow traditional curricula guides as they might do for teaching other subjects. Teachers must be able to establish educational goals or objectives; incorporate activities for reflection that are specifically focused on the students' service experiences; and develop assessment tools. The process for developing service-learning curriculum takes time.

Often teachers must make connections with individuals who are outside of the school. Without access to telephones, and having a demanding schedule, many teachers find it difficult to collaborate with people in the community. Finally, Wade (1995d) noted that "service-learning activities often involve some unforeseen problems or surprising events" (p. 17). A late bus transporting students to a nursing home for a luncheon could mean that their planned activities have to be revised. An unexpected assembly might cause a cross-grade tutoring project to be postponed, causing teachers to deal with disappointed students as well as a changed schedule.

Managing Large Numbers of Students

While many teachers are accustomed to managing twenty-five or more students in their classrooms, this can become an issue for teachers doing service-learning outside of their classrooms. For example, Carla explained that the large number of students participating in a school garden project resulted in many incidents of behavior problems:

> The numbers of students are too high for the nature of this project. Supervision is an issue when we actually had to do the planting. I felt like me out there wasn't enough to supervise behaviors when kids had to wait. And again, if the numbers were smaller, I just think there wouldn't have been this sort of bouncing off of each other that happens out there. (Seigel, 1995, p. 173)

Again, this is where parents, other teachers, aides, or student teachers could be helpful. Moreover, additional planning might also alleviate some of the problems with having too many students engaged in one activity.

Transportation, Funding, and Support

Transportation is often more of an issue for elementary and middle school teachers than it is for high school teachers. Some teachers rely on parents for transporting students to service sites. Hiring buses can be costly as noted in one teacher's description above. Some teachers have looked for service-learning projects in or around their school buildings as one solution.

Funding for supplies and materials is another challenge. Service-learning projects often require materials not typically found in the school supply closet. For some teachers discussed in this chapter, grant money was available to cover expenses. Often local business partners can help offset costs for service-learning or small fund-raising efforts can help teachers obtain needed materials.

Support for service-learning projects is crucial for teachers. However, some teachers reported that they did not feel supported by administrators, colleagues, or parents. Educating others about the benefits of service-learning and outlining specific learning objectives can help others perceive that service-learning activities can be valuable for the academic, social, and personal development of children and young adults.

IN CLOSING

Despite the challenges mentioned by teachers involved in service-learning, most recognize the vast benefits for students participating in service-learning activities. As a complex pedagogy, service-learning takes time, creativity, and knowledge of its application. School administrators and teachers must understand both the practical and the theoretical framework that creates effective service-learning programs, the educational theories supporting service-learning, and the components of successful service-learning projects (Cairn & Kielsmeier, 1990). Teachers who choose service-learning care about their students as learners and value the benefits of student service in the school and community. They are willing to take the time to plan and implement curricula that not only connect students with real-world issues, but also combine community service with personal, social, and academic growth.

NOTE

1. Letter written on June 17, 1994, in support of the school's participation in a "Learn and Serve" grant proposal.

Part 3

Voices from the Field

Highlighting the importance of collaboration, the experiences and recommendations of many different participants in service-learning programs comprise this part of the book. The chapters in Part 3 are devoted to each of the following roles: classroom teacher, student, administrator, school program coordinator, inservice trainer, community agency member, parent, and statewide coordinator. A wide diversity of views are presented; the authors live in various locations around the United States and range from experienced professionals to those new to service-learning. Each chapter begins with the author telling "my story" of working with service-learning programs. The authors then offer their reflections on issues and challenges for collaborators in service-learning programs and conclude with recommendations for others who share their roles.

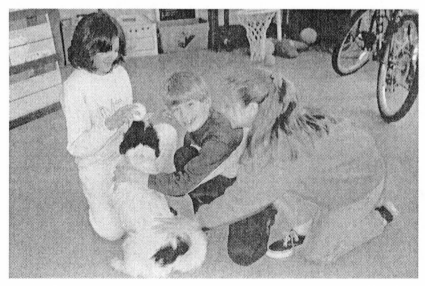

Children exercise a dog at the animal shelter.
Photo Credit: Jeff Haig

Environmental learning area.
Photo Credit: Scott Norris

Chapter 13

Classroom Teacher

Donna Boynton

MY STORY

I am a former teacher at Sky City Community School and a member of the Acoma Pueblo. Located on the Acoma Pueblo Reservation, Sky City is a Bureau of Indian Affairs–operated school serving Acoma Pueblo students in grades kindergarten through 8.

I was first introduced to the term "service-learning" just a few years ago, but community service is a familiar aspect of life in my community. "Hauba Taani" is a term used to express our community work; our pueblos for generations have performed services involving the whole community. As members of a community, we are responsible for the preparations necessary for certain social and religious events. For instance each spring, the male members of our community clean the irrigation ditches in preparation for planting, even though all of the members may not farm. The role of female members is to provide food and water for the participants in many of the traditional tribal functions that occur throughout the year. I have been raised with a deep sense of community pride and responsibility, feelings I had hoped would be continuously nurtured and passed on for generations. But like many of our neighboring Pueblos and communities, change has come with time. Some changes are good, but not at the expense of losing our culture and language. I have found that we are not immune from the social problems that affect many of today's youth. It was not until I returned to my community after being away for three years that I came to realize how much and how rapidly our young people were beginning to change.

It was at the first PTA meeting in the fall of 1991, that some parents and staff voiced their concern about a number of issues regarding adolescent behavior in our school and community. They repeatedly mentioned students' lack of respect for others and their property; their lack of responsibility; some signs of gang activity; and an increased rate of early teen pregnancy.

Three years prior to coming home to teach middle school at Sky City Community School, I had taught second grade in Naples, Florida. It had been six years since I had taught middle school, and I did not have very much time to switch from my primary-level teaching practices to teaching middle school again. As I was driving home after the PTA meeting, I prayed for ways I would be able to cope and for ideas to provide an environment that would motivate and challenge my seventh- and eighth-grade students. I continued to think of ways that I could provide an atmosphere conducive to learning and at the same time still address those issues of concern at the PTA meeting.

It was at this moment that my ideas for Buddy Works began to emerge. While teaching in Naples, my second grade class teamed with a kindergarten class for regularly scheduled sessions of shared activities in reading, writing, cooking, art, and music. I expanded this idea into what became Buddy Works. Although the Buddy Works program was initially developed out of a need to specifically address those issues of concern expressed by the parents and staff at our first PTA meeting; it was later identified as a service-learning project. This was the beginning of my formal introduction to and involvement with service-learning.

I coordinated Buddy Works for three years, while teaching at Sky City Community School, with the assistance of a Special Education aide, Harold Chino, and the kindergarten teachers. Harold Chino was instrumental in educating me about the current concepts of service-learning in our school and community; he continues to be my mentor in this area.

The basic goals for Buddy Works were as follows: (1) transfer responsibility to seventh- and eighth-grade students to help in their own development of social and academic skills; (2) develop seventh- and eighth-grade students' understanding of the responsibility of child rearing; (3) provide a tutoring program for the kindergarten students in an environment conducive for the development of readiness skills; and (4) promote seventh- and eighth-graders' career interests in the field of education.

Buddy Works was designed as a cross-age tutorial program for kindergarten students and seventh- and eighth-grade students. By building and strengthening the older students' individual responsibility, and by expanding the development of their social and academic skills, these students became aware of the great responsibilities involved in child rearing, and they became aware of the nurturing required for the development of happy and healthy individuals. My aim in Buddy Works was to guide the older students in assisting the kindergarten students to go beyond the enrichment of kindergarten readiness skills. Our goal was to improve the kindergartener's progress in the developmental areas of auditory, receptive, and expressive language, fine motor skills, gross motor skills, visual discrimination, and visual memory. Thus, we hoped that Buddy Works would be an early preventer of school failure.

Initially, the format for Buddy Works was as follows: (1) a one- to two-week introduction on the developmental stages of five-year-old children; (2) instruction in the purpose of lesson planning and lesson plan forms; (3) design of a lesson plan form which included the developmental skills to be expanded, the activity to be presented, the objectives of the lesson, the method of instruction to be used, and the materials needed to teach the activity; (4) selection of the appropriate level and types of children's literature for kindergarten students; and (5) random selection and assignment in the pairing of the seventh- and eighth-grade students with kindergarten buddies.

Once our initial preparations were complete, we moved into the following activities. Each week, the seventh- and eighth-grade students planned and prepared activities for three or more of the developmental areas identified. The students prepared lesson plans using our adapted format. Sometimes the students used themes, holidays, or literature to plan activities. Then, the students would tutor their kindergarten buddies from thirty-five to fifty minutes during the week. This time included picking up and delivering kindergarten buddies to and from class. After each tutoring session, the seventh- and eighth-grade students gave rewards of a sticker and a note with a message complimenting the younger student's participation and behavior. Once a month, we would celebrate with refreshments and a special activity. It is important to note that the older students and I provided the refreshments, rewards, and gifts for the kindergarten students and the kindergarten students reciprocated with cards and gifts for their seventh- and eighth-grade buddies during holidays, birthdays, and graduation.

While the components of the program remained consistent during the three years that I coordinated Buddy Works, the scheduling of Buddy Works into the seventh- and eighth-grade students' daily schedule changed each year. During the first year, the program was part of the seventh- and eighth-grade Language Arts. Two days were spent planning and preparing activities for Buddy Works, two days of instruction in our regular class of literature and grammar, and the students tutored their buddies on Friday. During the first year of Buddy Works, I emphasized the use of children's literature, writing stories, and bookmaking. A part of the seventh- and eighth-graders' final grades was publishing a big book for their kindergarten buddies. It was an exciting way to reinforce and enrich language arts skills. I found the majority of my students eager and motivated to complete their regular class assignments, so they could devote more time to their Buddy Works activities. It was often self-assigned homework, taken home to add the elaborate details of colors, designs, illustrations on books, game boards, game cards, or holiday greetings. The students said it was a simple and fun way to get credit for their language arts class, and I told them that it was an enjoyable way for me to assess the results of their efforts.

Due to programmatic changes in the second year, I also included the sixth-grade students into the Buddy Works program. Buddy Works was then offered as an elective. I didn't know how or where I was going to fit thirty or more students into my classroom. Our team of four middle school teachers and one primary teacher designed a program that would allow each of the sixth-, seventh-, and eighth-grade students to be registered in Buddy Works for one to two quarters. In addition to Buddy Works and their regular classes, they were enrolled in physical education, arts and crafts, computers, and public speaking. How I had the energy to coordinate all the big buddies and little buddies during that second year escapes me to this day. I just remember the experience to be long and, at the same time, very rewarding.

In the third year of Buddy Works, seventh- and eighth-grade students were required to participate for the entire school year. This was the best schedule by far. It allowed more time to plan, review teacher resource guides, gather information, and develop activities. The results of many of the activities were outstanding; the creativity and effort put into them were exceptional.

The students would reflect in their journals regularly about their experiences in Buddy Works, especially after their tutoring sessions. In the last year that I coordinated Buddy Works, the students shared their reflections with each other. The seventh- and eighth-grade students used their reflections to discuss any problems which might have occurred during tutoring. They also used their reflections to suggest to one another ways to handle discipline and to give ideas of activities to reinforce particular developmental areas. They also suggested ways to strengthen their tutoring techniques and shared their successes. Reflection became a means of giving support and encouragement to one another.

The most significant educational benefit of Buddy Works for the seventh- and eighth-grade students was being able to provide a variety of enrichment activities to enhance the kindergartners' readiness skills. The experience provided an environment conducive for the early prevention of school failure for the kindergarten students and the program gave the seventh- and eighth-grade students an opportunity to experience teaching and to explore the field of education as a possible career choice. Although I designed and implemented Buddy Works, it was the students who made it work, and they were the ones that made it special. They were the ones who read the books and wrote the stories with their kindergarten buddies. They were the ones who observed their kindergarten buddies growing physically, socially, and academically. Another benefit of the Buddy Works program was the fact that it was nonthreatening for those seventh- and eighth-grade students with special needs. Tutoring their kindergarten buddies raised their self-confidence and helped to strengthen their reading, writing, and communication skills. In addition, all of the seventh- and eighth-grade students demonstrated patience and genuine care for their kindergarten buddies. The relationships the students established have been positive and heartwarming. Even after four years, many of these students still refer to one another as buddies.

Another service learning program at Sky City is Parent Works, a program designed to help parents of kindergarten students to become active participants in the foundation of their child's formal education. In conjunction with Buddy Works, I wanted to assist kindergarten parents in sharing the beginning years of their child's formal learning as an enjoyable and meaningful experience. I had the idea for Parent Works about the same time as Buddy Works. I had written up the program the second year; but I did not implement it until my third year at Sky City. I believe part of my delay in getting Parent Works started was due to time, energy, and the fear of having poor attendance or receiving no response. Of course, the parents who did attend regularly proved me wrong. The two primary goals for the program were: (1) to promote parent assistance in helping children learn to read; (2) to assist parents in sharing with the seventh- and eighth-grade students about the responsibilities of parenting and nurturing young children.

I met with the Parent Works group once a month, in the evening for about two hours. Each month I had about fifteen to eighteen parents and grandparents who attended regularly. This accounted for about one-third of the total kindergarten parent population. This number made it easier to get around to assist almost everyone. I involved the parents in minilessons on the developmental characteristics of a five-year-old, reading-aloud, proper book selection, writing stories, handwriting, making games and puzzles, and bookmaking. Before the end of each session, the parents would reflect in their journals and sometimes the parents would share their stories, books, or whatever they made or learned that evening. The students in Buddy Works would volunteer to assist with the minilessons or mind the children that the parents brought with them. It was a very worthwhile experience to share time with these parents. They were the ones responsible for making Parent Works successful and enjoyable. This was a good example of parental involvement and working together in the interest of kindergarten students.

Neither Buddy Works nor Parent Works would have been possible without the strong support of the administration of Sky City Community School. Our principal, Charlotte Garcia, gave her assistance to both programs, which helped make them a success.

ISSUES FOR CLASSROOM TEACHERS IN SERVICE-LEARNING PROGRAMS

One of the major concerns that many of the Sky City Community School teachers had about service-learning was time; they felt they could not do any more than the things they already had to do. However, when the teachers understood service-learning, they soon realized that this teaching method could be a way to reinforce and enrich the learning taking place in their classrooms. Service-learning can be a catalyst in bridging content areas across the curriculum. There are many things teachers do in their classrooms that can be identified as service-learning. By simply adding a component to a daily lesson it could become a small service-learning project. For example, in language arts activities such as writing letters, stories, or poems, students' written work can be shared within the school, with other schools, nursing homes, or other agencies in the community or across the country. Student work can be shared through mail with pen pals or through e-mail on the computer, or they can read their work to other classes in their school, neighboring schools, or to other agencies serving school-age children. Cross-age tutoring can occur within a school, with all areas of the curriculum being implemented, and there is minimal cost to the teachers, students, or school. A science lesson on plants can be extended into a service-learning project. Stories and poetry written about plants or books made about plants could be shared with many people. Planted flower or vegetable seeds can be transplanted in the school yard, in a community garden plot, or at a nursing home. There are numerous possibilities for service-learning activities emerging from class lessons.

Teachers' energy for doing service-learning projects comes from the personal belief that the outcomes from doing service far outweigh the effort. Writing a story or letter to share with someone in a nursing home or with someone across the miles is much more rewarding than sitting in the classroom naming the parts of a letter or underlining the parts of speech from a grammar lesson. The most rewarding service-learning projects are those the teacher and students particularly enjoy; thus, selecting a project that is related to a teacher's expertise or strength is helpful. A teacher with a strong background in social studies or history might enjoy having the class do an oral history project. A teacher effective in science might to do a service-learning project on recycling, soil conservation, or preserving the community's ecosystem.

The usual questions asked regarding service-learning are the following: How can we account for student learning? How can we get staff support? By including the project in lesson plans, objectives from the curriculum can be used to support a project as it relates to a lesson. If assessment is required, there are a number of possible methods. Learning through service can be evaluated by using teacher and peer observation, oral presentations, written summary reports, illustrative reporting, group presentations, publications in a school newsletter or local newspaper, or making a book on the project. Teachers can be as creative as they want to be, or simply use the old paper-and-pencil test. If assessment is necessary, then students should be given some kind of credit or grade.

The most difficult challenge to do is to get fellow staff members to engage in service-learning. For those staff members reluctant to buy into service-learning, service-learning advocates must continue to help them understand the concept and believe in the benefits service-learning offers. The teacher, a team of teachers, or students and teachers could determine whether their service-learning projects should be required or voluntary. Educators involved with service-learning in their school or community should play a central role in determining the course of their projects. It is important that the people overseeing the projects feel that they are doing something worthwhile and believe that the outcome and rewards of service-learning will far exceed the time and energy spent on them.

RECOMMENDATIONS FOR CLASSROOM TEACHERS IN SERVICE-LEARNING PROGRAMS

1. *Choose a project that addresses an issue both you and your students care about in the school or community.* There are many problems and needs you can focus on in a service-learning project. You and your students can do a needs assessment of problems and issues in your school and community to help narrow down the choice(s). If both you and your students work collaboratively in choosing a problem in which you both share an interest, you will both enjoy the project more and feel better about putting time into it.
2. *Involve your administration, other staff members, and parents.* It is important to have administrative and parental support for your service-learning project. The more informed you keep parents and administration about your project, the easier it will be to justify your program and your accountability of student learning. Involving other staff members in your project gives them experience with and knowledge about service-learning; they could become your greatest supporters.
3. *Select a service-learning project that is realistic.* If you do not have the financial resources available, then start small. A needs assessment will help to prioritize projects and help determine which projects you can afford to establish. Dreams are good, but sometimes projects cease to exist as quickly as they begin when the needed resources are not available.
4. *Use a time line and other charts to track long-term projects.* For a long-term project, a time line is helpful in determining the progress of your project. A time line is a good visual aid, if reporting of projects is necessary. Charting the data the students have collected is a good technique to use to reinforce or enrich graph and charting skills.
5. *Know your school curriculum and the objectives of the content area in which you teach.* Being familiar with your school curriculum and objectives will

simplify integrating content areas across the curriculum. If service-learning is included in your daily lesson plans, it helps justify its inclusion.

6. *Keep student profiles on service-learning projects to justify accountability.* Using student profiles as a record-keeping technique for service-learning projects can be an essential tool for assessment. Teacher, student, and peer observations of service-learning participation can be recorded and kept in portfolios. Data and newspaper clippings of the project can also be collected and kept in the portfolios.

7. *Gather a list of resources and agencies that are available in your community.* Having a list of available resources and agencies in your community that support service-learning projects is helpful. It is your "yellow pages"; this list will save you time and leg work. Compiling a book of these resources and agencies can be one class's service-learning project. Native American communities and schools should especially be aware that the National Indian Youth Leadership Project (NIYLP) is the Native American Technical Assistance Center for the National Clearinghouse on Service Learning. NIYLP (see appendix for listing) has Native-specific materials on service learning and years of experience with service in Native settings.

IN CLOSING

These recommendations are ones that I have used in my own service-learning projects. As my Acoma Pueblo people would say, *ba trə dra we'e,* good luck with your effort.

MY STORY

Can you imagine the shock of twenty high school students on the first day of our junior year when we were asked to take on the toughest challenge of our high school career? With our faculty advisers Marc Ferguson and Jill Olsen-Virlee, and in cooperation with Fred Easker of the Granger House, a Marion historical museum, our service-learning experience varied from the traditional English class. Our class condensed, edited, and revised a 1600-page, five-volume journal, *The History of Marion, Iowa 1838–1927*, written by Marvin Oxley.

To do this, we divided into five groups of four, each group being responsible for researching various topics and events that were covered in their assigned volume of the journal. The group was also responsible for editing and revising the text that has been transferred to computer disk and correcting any errors that were made.

As a class, we went on history walks through the downtown business area, residential Eighth Avenue, and through Oak Shade Cemetery. In groups we searched for information at the Marion Carnegie, Cedar Rapids, and Masonic libraries. Going beyond the traditional sources, we also contacted The History Center, the Iowa State Historical Society, the local newspaper office, and various Marion businesses.

Additional help has been given to us by the community. Mentors volunteered their time, information, and sometimes personal resources to help in the completion of this project. Our mentors were people who had researched the history of Marion or were lifelong residents of the community and were willing to share their time and expertise with us.

Local businesses were partners in our service-learning project as well. Financial aid was provided by Farmers State Bank for the funding of the publication and we received a grant from U.S. West as well. Rockwell volunteers took the time to scan the original journal and transfer it to computer disks. French Studios helped us scan the original photographs for publication.

We prepared the journal for publication using PageMaker software to edit and add notations to the text. Further research was done and information added to update the contents of the journal. After the journal was edited, we created a finished layout including photographs.

The first semester dealt with going out and learning about the community while acquiring information to be added to the text. In the second semester the real work began. As students, we learned a lesson of tolerance and patience as we worked with the computers. Long mornings of editing and revising the contents took a toll on us. Frustrations began to run high, until we all finally realized that the goal was in reach and we were really making progress that we could see.

Presenting and sharing our experiences with the community, students, and teachers from all over the country was an enriching experience. The presentations gave us a sense of accomplishment and helped us know that people were interested in all of our hard work. At times we had forgotten that what we were doing would have a real impact on our community. The presentations not only reminded us but encouraged us and gave us the motivation to finish the project and not give up. As further testimony to our project's impact we were nominated and voted by the citizens of Marion the 1995 Marion Citizens of the Year.

I asked for the help of my classmates in compiling this account of our trials, tribulations, and successes experienced this year. We felt it necessary in order to maintain the meaning and unity that has brought us all together to reach our goal. We all have had different experiences, feelings, and perceptions. What follows then are responses from my classmates pertaining to their unique experiences.

When I first heard about this class, in my opinion, it sounded like a slack-off class because they were leaving school to go on history walks and to different libraries in the area. Also they would have people coming to their class to talk to them, while in the other English classes we were having to read books and take tests. Other students, who had just heard about the class and were not a part of it, may have shared the same opinion that I had. Now I know differently and don't think that way at all. All of those things that they were doing needed to be done in order to begin the project and keep it going. The class is not a slack-off class because this is an ongoing project that requires a lot of work and a strong commitment. The idea that we had to commit to something like this probably makes some of us grow in the area of commitment and prepares us for the commitments that we may encounter later on in the workfield.

I feel that this project is very important because with only four copies of Marvin Oxley's *History of Marion* in existence, it makes it hard for the people of the community to access this historical information. Now, we are able to make this information available to the community at an affordable price, and they will have their own copy of this journal and be able to appreciate the information it contains and the effort we put into this. After someone knows about the history of where they live, I feel that it might give them a greater appreciation for their surroundings.[1]—Nancy Chiafos

When the other English classes heard about my class, they were jealous, yet some were glad that they weren't faced with the responsibility. I felt that taking a class and incorporating service-learning into it was a great idea. The project gave me numerous opportunities to interact with our community. I especially spent many hours at the cemetery, creating a map of war soldiers, locating important people from my volume, and searching for Marvin Oxley's grave. From that experience I learned that cemeteries have stories to tell.

One day the class was scheduled to take a walk down the streets of Marion. I learned about the houses from the 1800s and the families that had lived there. I even went and talked to a lady at an old house that had once been the site of a horse carriage barn. I believe that talking with the community is the best part of our project. Some of the business owners we have tried to get information from haven't been so friendly. A local barber and a dry cleaner owner were too busy to talk to some of the students, but said they would gladly be interviewed after business hours.

I hope future students have the same positive experience with service-learning and will consider doing a similar project. I know I will be there to support them.—Scarlett Canady

On my first day I found that the class had split into five groups and I would be joining the group working with Volume IV. The class was currently working on getting notations for items of information that were unclear in the original text. I was surprised at how much freedom the students were given to complete what needed to be done. I was told that the class was self-directed, students setting their own goals and timetables, problem solving for themselves, as well as evaluating themselves. We were allowed to leave the building during the class period to work on our research. We would go to libraries, city hall, or interview the people of Marion. One time my group even went to Iowa City to collect fire insurance maps. The maps showed all the businesses at the time they were taken. Of course, this trip took the whole school day and we were required to make up our work beforehand.

We went through hard times, when everyone wanted to give up and leave the project. Somehow we always got through them though. I guess I always thought about how I didn't want to let anyone down. I am so proud of the work we have done and will continue to do as we pass it down to next year's students. I hope that many other classes can take on a similar project and feel the rewards of helping their community.—Julie Erkel

When I was asked to attend the National Service Learning Conference in Philadelphia with my teachers, I agreed. I thought it would be fun, as I had not been to that area before, and I had not been to a conference like this. At the time of our arrival I was really surprised that over 1200 participants would actually be at a Service Learning Conference because it was quite new to me.

One of the purposes for our going was to present our class project at a workshop. It was a learning experience to work with my teachers and be a part of this presentation. Even though our audience was not very large we had considerable feedback. Examples of this are receiving some help from UNI because of an instructor in attendance, and an Illinois teacher wants us to role model and help him get started on a project for his hometown.

All in all, I realize this has been a real positive experience for me. It has helped me see that we can share learning from and with others. That there are many who give and receive both benefits though service-learning. I am very glad that I was able to have this experience.—Christine McGlaughlin

Many people may say that teenagers couldn't possibly take such a valuable part of our community and create a book that will be treasured for many years to come. But those many people haven't sat in our computer lab watching us at work. They haven't had the opportunity to experience the setbacks and the moments of satisfaction when a once unreachable goal is completed.

The determination, self-discipline, and the goal setting are the main keys to this book. Without these three, this project would seem just about impossible. Although the stress, frustrations, and the setbacks are everyday adventures, the students' dedication to this book overpowers all of those feelings.

This book is taken very seriously by these twenty teenagers who have put in one school year's worth of hard work and dedication. *The*

History of Marion will be available for the public to enjoy in September 1995, and we have made that a class goal.—Carrie L. Peiffer

An honor we have received recently is being named a National Demonstration School for Service-Learning (by the federal Corporation for National Service). Several of us from the class presented our project and other service-learning projects to the selection committee. Our school was chosen as one of two Iowa schools, along with two schools each from Wisconsin and Minnesota. Each school was awarded a twenty-thousand dollar grant and will act as a model school for other schools across the tri-state area. They can visit or contact us through computers to learn about our programs and how to start their own.

We received publicity from KGAN (a local news station) who did a special show on service-learning. Our project was one of three featured. Also the local *Marion Times* and *Cedar Rapids Gazette* have written many articles about our involvement in service-learning, making the community more aware of our project.

As you can see, we have been in the public eye because of this project. It has helped us realize that young people are important members of this community and can make a difference.—Amy Bulman

ISSUES FOR STUDENTS IN SERVICE-LEARNING PROGRAMS

Many students have yet to realize what service-learning is. Frequently students have not found opportunities for or been introduced to serving the community. According to The National Education Goals Panel (1994), less than half of high school seniors performed any community service in their sophomore and junior years. Most have not been encouraged to understand the responsibilities of citizenship. Less than half of eighteen- to twenty-year-olds voted in 1992. *Democracy's Next Generation* (Fowler, 1990), a study conducted for the organization People for the American Way, suggests that we, as a nation, need to strengthen our commitment to preparing young people for informed, active citizenship. When asked to rank order seven life outcomes, study respondents ranked "being involved in helping your community be a better place" dead last—well behind "career and financial success," "a happy family," and "enjoying yourself and having a good time." Seventy-two percent of the youth in the survey agreed with the perception that young people seem less involved these days than in the past (Fowler, 1990).

Students may learn to take on a task that involves service but many need support and guidance to get started. All students have the capability and desire to reach out to help someone. Forty-five percent of youth surveyed in the People for the American Way study (1989) agreed that there is a lack of parental encouragement to help the community; no one taught these students how to get involved. Many projects that have been started and completed by students would never have come to be if someone hadn't asked them to help. Students realize that through service-learning they can make a difference in other people's lives. This fact is evidenced through student reflections from service-learning programs across the nation.

A student who volunteered at the Jewish Home and Hospital in New York City provides one example of learning to appreciate the value of making a difference to others.

> My most critical incident this year is when I was in charge of the activities for the elderly in Sutro 3 which is the right side of the building. The decisions w(h)ere up to me. So I decided to play bowling with them. It was about 12 residents. I didn't realize how important I was to them until they started talking and opening up to me. It was a great experience that my supervisor let me do it a couple more times. Well the bowling went great and the residents staying there have much history and stories to tell. These people were actually a part of history that I wasn't even around to know about. I feel that my job is important because I'm helping the residents live and recognize that they are in fact very important.—Lohattis Hayden, Central Park East Secondary School, New York, New York

Finding the meaning of life, that's what most students are searching for on a daily basis. Jodi Lebow, a hospital volunteer, found meaning through volunteering. She describes her feelings about service:

> To me volunteering is a way of life. I am much happier giving than receiving. People often question why I would choose to work without pay; but I am paid by the treasures within people . . . I feel students benefit so much from a volunteer experience. They give something back to our community as well as gaining self respect. They leave with a sense of pride and self worth. Through my volunteering I have gained a stronger sense of leadership and communication . . . After spending so much time at a major hospital in my area, I have decided to pursue a career as a physician.—Jodi Lebow, Hopkins High School, Minnetonka, Minnesota

Students recognize that they learn a great deal from service-learning. Self-esteem can improve, knowing that they are doing something that will benefit others; they also learn the responsibilities involved in citizenship. Students have an opportunity to explore and learn about topics that they don't have a chance to in schools. The following students' stories illustrate the variety of learning outcomes associated with service-learning.

> We learned independent thinking, goal setting, problem solving, and worked as a team. It gave us the opportunity to experience and understand various segments of society and explore future career opportunities. We learned biology, ecology, sociology, education and many other subjects in a hands-on way that we would not be able to learn in classrooms. We also learned to reflect and write better because we were required to write a two page journal after each service-learning day. Most important of all, we all gained invaluable social skills and it gave us such a tremendous sense of pride and satisfaction when we felt we could make a difference by helping others and our environment.—Jonathan Wai, Whatcom Middle School, Bellingham, Washington

> The most significant moment this year for me has been when I went to give a speech at the White House mini-conference on aging. It was held in City Hall and I got to meet many other people who were interested in what I was doing. This was important because I got to tell everyone what I thought. It's not very often that the leaders of this City ask a teenager what they feel. I also feel that every time I meet a new person is important to me because I learn about other cultures and other people. I've learned that growing old is not such a bad thing if you are happy. Often these people are happy when they have our company so that makes me feel good. I want to grow old gracefully and have something to say to kids when they come to visit me.—Peter Arbelaez, Central Park East Secondary School, New York, New York

> Having been at my placement for nearly the entire school year, I have received many phone calls, some disturbing and some marvelous, all of them being educational. Somewhat towards the beginning of my placement, when I was still very confused about what we did or didn't deal with, I took a call from a woman placed in a nursing home. She explained to me that she wanted to leave the nursing home hospital because she was being treated cruelly by the staff and other patients. She started crying to me that "they" stole her clothing and her money, and listening to the confession was extremely hard. Being a very sensitive person, I almost started crying, especially when I learned that nursing homes were private institutions and therefore, did not include the range of people we assisted. This was very upsetting to me because I couldn't help a woman that had wasted her only phone call on calling the Public Advocate's Office, and was crying and pleading with me. It made me realize the disadvantages of

the office's service, we can't help everybody no matter how much we may want to. We have no jurisdiction over private institutions and must turn away people like this woman regardless of how severe the situation may be. I wish I could help everybody and that the Public Advocate's office didn't have these restrictions but private is private and it is not the City's place to intervene.

There have been many calls that have helped me to appreciate and more than occasionally, strongly dislike the public. Previous to the placement I had limited experience with the public. I feel this is one of the most valuable assets my placement has provided me with. I have had people that have called up and started conversations off like "do you actually do anything down here? Or do you just sit there all day and do nothing? or "I don't expect you to understand any of this but . . ." These phone calls have given me the chance to develop my ability and tolerance to work with people, especially over the phone when people are frequently bolder than in person.—Sarah Wuchinich, Central Park East Secondary School, New York, New York

Through service-learning, students begin to learn and appreciate the differences between themselves and others. For example, Lohattis Hayden learned that elders are still full of life and emotion that they are willing to share with students:

I began to look at the residents (as) more than just old people. I think through this year I have changed in the way I look upon life. I don't feel that I've matured any because I feel I'm already very mature for my age. Before I worked with the elderly I always had something bad to say about them like: they smell, they complain too much, they look funny and so on. But now I understand the reasons. So I guess I changed or grew up more due to the understanding of things I didn't know.—Lohattis Hayden, Central Park East Secondary School, New York, New York

Students don't always have an adult at school or at home who they can confide in. The adults of the community can make a difference to students and encourage them to follow the right path, keeping kids off the streets, away from drugs, and in school.

Working with Jenny in the Health Education Center taught me a lot of things. For one, Jenny always told me things like, "Shantiese, get your degree, and further your education until you feel like you've accomplished what you've wanted." Jenny was one of the major influences in my life that worked with the hospital, also including my other boss, Lynnee Porter, whom I share my future ideas with. The only difference now, is that Jenny is gone. I remember one time, when we sat and talked for about two hours straight. Both of us are road runners with our mouths, so it was fun. I also asked her for advice, and she sometimes related her life to some of the things that might happen in mine. Her favorite words to me were, "Shantiese, you are a beautiful girl. Don't let anyone tell you what to do or what not to do. Finish school so you can do what you want to do." I miss Jenny, but her words always stick in my mind when I think about not doing my homework, or missing school because of an unmajor problem.

I feel that working at this placement has given me a major sense of maturity and responsibility. I have people there who influence my life greatly and would hate to see me fail. I look forward to every community service day to see what new thing I can learn and how I can apply it to my life. I think that this placement has helped me to grow mentally, and take my career goals much more seriously that I have taken them in the past.—Shantiese Brown, Central Park East Secondary School, New York, New York

During the time that I've been volunteering at El Museo del Barrio, I have encountered many memorable experiences. One particular incident that was significant to me was when Frederico Ruiz, the supervisor of the museum, helped me overcome my fear of heights. I told him one day that I was afraid of heights and that I have been ever since I was a little kid. So, one day he told me to climb to the top of the ladder and not be afraid because he would be right behind supporting me. Then, he asked me to sit at the top of the ladder and look around. I felt hesitant at first, but as time went on I got used to being at the top of the ladder, and before I knew it I was sitting at the top, looking at everything below me.—Jorge Rosado, Central Park East Secondary School, New York, New York

Skills learned by students through service-learning are going to be very valuable as they grow up: skills to work with all types of people, patience, a good work ethic, and technology. These skills are becoming increasingly valuable in the workplace.

What I feel that I will take on with me for the rest of my life and I hope to learn more about is e-mail. I have been working with e-mail in the Youth Can conferences for three years now. I listened to people talk about it and show me how to use it but I never really understand what it was until one day I went to community service by myself and I had a one on one chance with my supervisor to learn e-mail and I understood it. The next week my supervisor wasn't there so I had to try and remember what I did the week before. It took me about two hours but I did it and I felt proud. I found that all I needed was someone there to teach me one on one and for me to believe in myself.—Shauna Sobers, Central Park East Secondary School, New York, New York

I have also gained another invaluable asset, initiative. Many times I possess the ability to take initiative but rarely do I act on it. This is one of the first times where I have been encouraged by the staff to make my own conclusions and refer people accordingly. I am extremely grateful to my supervisor and the other case workers at the Public Advocate's that have given me this chance, since it has provided me with a lot more confidence in myself and my ability.—Sarah Wuchinich, Central Park East Secondary School, New York, New York

Students have the brightest imaginations from which wonderful ideas are formed. They need to be heard, to share their ideas, to suggest changes and solutions, to voice their frustration.

Although I love what the Public Advocate's office does, there is one area that they should improve on, training volunteers and interns. When entering my placement, I had some general knowledge of city agencies and procedures, but not enough to deal with all the cases I was confronted with. I learned many things along the way but it would have been much easier to have knowledge of them when I started. Interns should be informed on the way to deal with calls concerning private institutions or difficult constituents, etc., beforehand. People would be referred quicker and accurately and on the whole, make things a lot nicer and easier for both the constituent and the person dealing with the call.—Sarah Wuchinich, Central Park East Secondary School, New York, New York

If I were on the Board I would see to it that the seniors got more involved in their own lives. Often times you will see a person who doesn't even know their rights because someone else is doing everything for them. I think a certain number of elderly people should be on these Boards.—Peter Arbelaez, Central Park East Secondary School, New York, New York

I would change the security because in my opinion they do not do a good job of protecting the beautiful art the museum portrays. The security personnel do not watch the people who go in and out of the building. People can take anything they want because the security is poor. I would hire professional security officers to replace the ones who are not doing a good job. I would also talk to those officers that are presently employed and inform them on how important it is to take care of our museum.—Jorge Rosado, Central Park East Secondary School, New York, New York

Finally, it's important for teachers to remember that *all* students can benefit from being of service to others. Gretchen Wise is a high school student with a rare handicapping condition, Dandy Walker Syndrome. While Gretchen is in a special education class and receives many services herself, she also benefits by sharing herself and her love of poetry with seniors. One of her journal entries reads,

> Instead of handing out coupons, I helped Crystal read off the bingo numbers. I would first say the bingo number and then Crystal would repeat it to the bingo group. I also recited one of my Hi-Q's [haikus]. The Hi-Q that I shared with the bingo group was
>
> > Violets are blue,
> > To my surprise, you're nice
> > Through my flower blue eyes.
>
> As always everyone at the Saturday morning bingo session enjoyed it. I gave Doris a copy of the three poems that I recited to the bingo group last Saturday and she liked it.

Toward the end of her service-learning project, Gretchen reflected on the value of her experience.

> I think that my Saturday morning visits to the nursing home have made a big difference to both the nursing home residents and to myself. The way that I have made a difference to the people at the nursing home [is] by sharing all my poems and all of the other unique and fun things about me. I think that the way that the visits to the nursing home have made a big difference to me [is] by learning how old people think of life and love it. I also think I sort of taught the people at the nursing home something magical which is me, in general, and my poetry because I think that the old people at the nursing home didn't really have the wonderful experience of reading and writing poetry like Mrs. Wolf and Mr. Hogan have taught me.

Gretchen summed up what she learned about the elderly in the following poem.

Old People

People say "they don't want to do that."
People say "they don't have fun.
They just sit there til the day's done."
I disagree, I think they like me,
I say, hoping to find a way
To educate, make people appreciate,
To make them understand all the
Wonderful charming people,
Young people, in old
wrinkly bodies.

—Gretchen Wise,
Finger Lakes Secondary School,
Rushville, New York

RECOMMENDATIONS FOR STUDENTS IN SERVICE-LEARNING PROGRAMS

1. *Be willing and dedicated.* Don't let yourself just be forced to do community service. You won't enjoy yourself and you probably won't do the best job you can possibly do. You want to be able to get the most out of the experience. Do it for yourself and those that you are helping will benefit.

2. *Form a support group within the community.* Have at least one person at the service site who is able to answer your questions and support what you are doing. You'll need someone there that will support, encourage, and possibly reward you. If you're feeling frustrated, this person can remind you of the impact you are having in the community.

3. *Get things started as soon as possible.* Get others involved from the beginning, it's difficult to get involved in the middle of a project. Develop a sense of comfort within a group and you'll learn how to work with each other.

4. *Get some background information.* Know what you are getting into. Find out what you will be doing, what has to be done when, and with whom you will be working. Make sure you'll enjoy the work; it shouldn't feel like "work" all the time.

5. *Make sure all rules and goals are clear.* Know when you are supposed to be there, what needs to get done, and what you can't be doing. Don't goof off! It will set progress back and cause frustrations with others who are doing what they are supposed to be doing. Get everything done that you can.

6. *Don't procrastinate.* Don't put things off until tomorrow if it can be done today. This will leave time in case problems do arise and you can deal with them. You won't have to rush to finish when deadlines approach.

7. *Have a weekly group discussion and planning session.* Let others know of any problems or changes. Get information from them and ask for any suggestions or solutions they might have.

8. *Be prepared to deal with any problems.* Once a problem arises get it solved as soon as possible. If the problem has to wait, it may get worse or be forgotten. Find a solution. This will save time in the long run. If you're having a lot of trouble, ask for help.

9. *Be prepared to spend extra time on projects.* Many times projects will take longer than expected due to problems that you have to conquer. It's never clear sailing and progress is often set back.

10. *Be willing to share your experience with others.* This will get others involved and let them know how they can get involved in the community. Let others know of your accomplishments and encourage service-learning.

11. *Pat yourself on the back!* You deserve it; you've worked hard to reach your goal. You have helped the community, take the credit. Let others congratulate you too!

IN CLOSING

Service-learning may be hard work, but it's worth it in the end. As Jodi Lebow of Hopkins High School in Minnetonka, Minnesota writes, "The purpose of life is, above all, to matter, to count, to stand for something, to make a difference that you lived at all."

NOTE

1. All student quotes in this chapter are from journal entries or reflection essays written during the 1994–1995 school year. Quotes appear in their original form without editing or grammatical changes.

Chapter 15

Administrator

Carolyn S. Anderson and Judith T. Witmer

OUR STORIES

There may be no such thing as "an administrative perspective" on service-learning, if we are any standard for comparison. Carolyn is currently an assistant superintendent in a high school district; Judith is a former district administrator in a K–12 district. Our jobs have been in different settings and in different positions. We have both worked with coordinators, helped to plan service-learning programs, and been personally involved in community service over the years. Our stories differ, although the threads that tie them together are our beliefs that all students can learn, if learning is meaningful; that experiential learning is the best way to make learning meaningful; and that service in the community, properly structured, is a powerful vehicle for experiential learning. We also agree that administrators, both at the building and district level, can make or break a service-learning program. They help to make a program successful through effective planning, implementing, and monitoring; they can undermine a program by ignoring it, cutting funds, or failing to establish appropriate management procedures.

Carolyn's Story

The term *service-learning* only entered my vocabulary two or three years ago. For much of my life the concept of community service was also unfamiliar, although I engaged in community action and volunteer work. Every school district in which I have worked—as teacher, building administrator, district administrator, or consultant—has provided opportunities for students to give service to others. These schools have ranged from elementary to middle and senior high, from poor to wealthy, from urban to suburban, from monocultural to multicultural. Two types of programs were most common. One type provided one time opportunities for service outside the school; a day in the soup kitchen, for example. Another type gave students opportunities to help other students within the school, such as National Honor Society tutoring.

I drew a number of conclusions from these experiences. I discovered that the service part of community service-learning is not radical, nor is it limited to certain types of schools. What is uncommon is structured reflection time, or the learning part. My experiences also showed that field-based experiences are motivating to students, and cause them to ask questions and look for answers. Additionally, I learned that service experiences have benefit, with or without classroom discussion. However, without the reflection component, many students will miss the connections both to the classroom curriculum and to causes and solutions for social problems.

Working in a district of two high schools, I have supported proposals to expand opportunities for service-learning. My support was based on the success of the volunteer clubs at both buildings that help students provide service. Both in numbers and quality, these clubs were improving each year, showing that outlets for service are needed. In addition, I was looking for programmatic opportunities to address a district goal for self-esteem. As I have watched the club sponsors work, I am reminded that individual teachers have always been the people who make a difference—not the curriculum, not the policy book, not "how to" service-learning manuals.

However, I know that individual teachers can only move a program so far. Key administrators need to gain the commitment and involvement of other administrators and the school board. Several years ago, the district's curriculum advisory group studied what was then called community service. We conducted extensive research, including visits and consultants, and involved many staff members in extensive dialogue. We were the textbook case of preparedness. Our report to the school board was a multileveled approach to service-learning, with four proposed programs, incorporating course assignments, special classes, and an expanded volunteer club.

Unfortunately, as sometimes happens, "the best laid plans" do not work. The proposals were supported by a large number of faculty when they were taken to the school board. They generated much discussion among the board members, and an endorsement of volunteerism. But in the end the votes were there to pass only the expanded volunteer club proposal. Our proposals for a service-learning course and required service assignments within certain courses were not passed. The school board was not convinced of the value of requiring service-learning in public schools or the appropriateness of giving credit for service, and we had not resolved concerns about cost or liability. We also did not have on our side certain administrators whose support was needed. Clearly we had failed to anticipate all the concerns of key players.

I concluded from this experience that, while most people think service to others is a worthwhile venture, they may differ dramatically in their views of *how* or *if* to implement such opportunities in schools. This experience led me to explore the literature on service-learning, to seek advice from service-learning practitioners, and eventually to coauthor some publications on the topic, including *How to Establish a High School Service-learning Program* (Witmer and Anderson, 1994). I had learned, in short, that service-learning means many things to many people. Gaining a common picture before proceeding is critical and, in fact, may be the administrator's most important contribution.

Judith's Story

My early experiences were much like Carolyn's. Except for Girl Scouts, I had no experience with community service. As an educator and curriculum administrator I was at first skeptical about placing service in schools—service-learning suggested a euphemism for an easy way out of academic rigor. I envisioned "do-gooders" who dabbled in carrying trays and reading stories, expecting these activities to substitute for classroom content. With my focus on educational excellence, I could not see a place for this upstart program.

Then, in the fall of 1992, I became involved with a Pennsylvania Department of Education program that combined the concept of service with the school reform movement. Inspired and influenced by the work of John Briscoe, then director of PennSERVE (a division of the Pennsylvania Department of Labor and Industry), I read everything I could find on the subject. One of my assignments was to design a summer institute on service-learning. In this planning, I began to talk with those in the field including Carol Weiss, a classroom teacher and a PennSERVE Fellow. I also began a dialogue with the facilitators, presenters, and school district teams who were invited to participate in the summer institute. What I discovered among those involved with service-learning was a common thread of excitement, devotion, and real understanding of students. The people who implement service-learning programs see, on a daily basis, the effects of these programs on students' lives. They are convinced that such programs have the potential to change education and its relevance for students.

The summer institute itself gave me further insight into what a service-learning program should and should not be, as I worked with school teams of classroom teachers and administrators to develop service-learning programs. I observed teams struggle with definitions of service, service-learning, curriculum content, and reflection. I saw their creativity in designing programs and incorporating service into the curriculum. And as I watched the demonstrations that culminated the week's study, I began to appreciate the synergy of combining service and learning.

During the following school year I visited several sites where projects which combine service and reflection were making a marked impact on students, with increased motivation, self-worth, and academic achievement. In Hazelton, Pennsylvania, special-needs youngsters mentor Alzheimer's patients and have formed a social bond through service. Nearby Scranton's program includes both an environmental project reclaiming a once majestic public park, and a partnership with the community hospital. One potential dropout, because of the program, has emerged as an honor student with a college scholarship.

The key, however, to my buying into service-learning was its connection to school restructuring. Traditional school curriculum, instruction, and daily schedules fail to address the needs of many youngsters, so educators are looking for alternative school organizational and curricular models. Community service-learning provides such a model. As a program evaluator for the state Serve and Learn America project, I have seen service-learning act as a framework for curriculum integration and other school reform initiatives. I have also observed how service-learning can make the curriculum relevant, with students becoming the "doers" who plan and take responsibility for their own learning and establish patterns for lifelong learning.

Seeing all of this happen in community service-learning programs convinced me of the positive effects of service-learning and led to my coauthoring some publications with Carolyn Anderson, about how to build successful service-learning programs. My own commitment to community service-learning continues with my Department of Education work and services as conference presenter and consultant. The opportunity for students to engage with the community on service projects has the potential to change not only the lives of individual students, but the character of American society. Administrators cannot afford to ignore this movement.

ISSUES FOR ADMINISTRATORS IN ESTABLISHING SERVICE-LEARNING PROGRAMS

Administrators will find themselves faced with three tasks: (1) helping schools decide if they are ready for service-learning; (2) conceptualizing the types of programs possible; and (3) setting up management procedures to ensure continued success. The unifying thread in all these tasks is generating broad-based support for community service-learning.

Deciding If Schools Are Ready for Service-Learning

Service-learning programs are almost always initiated by "believers" who are usually teachers. Often we assume that service-learning is universally accepted and then only address the "how to" questions in planning. In reality, programs have a much better chance of initial approval and long term survival if administrators pay more attention at the beginning to developing the case for service-learning and to promoting an acceptance of the concept.

Assessing relevant knowledge/assumptions of stakeholders and history of the school or district. Every school and district has a history of knowledge, beliefs, and assumptions; this history provides a beginning foundation for building a service-learning program. As the success of service-learning programs depends on stakeholders' beliefs about what is important in teaching and learning, these beliefs need to be acknowledged. Homage must be paid to "the way we do things around here" or there will be no support given by traditional stakeholders to changing the way of doing things around here. Administrators can identify and involve the school's (unofficial) historian: the person with whom everyone checks facts and dates of past events, as well as the values of the school.

With their broader views across grades and disciplines, administrators can also identify connections the school may already have with the community. Are there existing partnerships? Can a program build on the current support of any service organizations? Are any teachers or administrators involved in any service in the community outside of school?

The interest level of teachers and other administrators is important. If there is little interest, the administrator can provide basic information. Even those who dislike an idea at first sight may come around, once the ideas are understood better. Administrators can encourage the staff to explore community service-learning in the same manner as other school programs, by asking: (1) What is it? and (2) Will it benefit students? They can also find staff members who are willing to share their personal experiences of service in the community. Hearing colleagues talk about service experiences can stimulate interest. Sending staff members to visit successful service-learning programs in your area, or bringing people in from these schools to talk to your staff can also help get a fledgling program off the ground.

Assessing possibilities in the current curriculum and extracurricular program. It is not necessary to reinvent the wheel. Instead, administrators should build on what is already in place. Enthusiasts as well as resisters will be more willing to expand what already works than to design a completely new program. There are few areas in the school's academic program that cannot, in some way, be enhanced by a community service activity.

It is also important to list available extracurricular activities, as many of these can be the basis for community service activities because they already involve a volunteer component. In addition, advisors of extracurricular programs are usually among the first to support community service. Key Club is an obvious extracurricular example, but anything from electronics club to drama club can be adapted to community service, and usually can also serve to connect curriculum and service. Administrators should not overlook opportunities for students to provide service to one another. Peer tutoring, peer mediation, peer mentoring, and peer counseling are all effective forms of student-to-student service-learning that already occur in many high schools.

Determining existing resources and needs. Administrators generally assess needs and then find resources to meet those needs. With service-learning, however, it is sometimes easier to first determine possible resources and then decide what those resources can support. Again, this is a natural role for administrators because of their bird's-eye view of the school, district, and community. Administrators can identify who is most likely to be interested in community service-learning, especially a person who might serve as coordinator. Where is funding likely to come from? How can time be rearranged? When can these resources be brought together? Looking for existing community groups who might want to be involved is an important task during the start-up phase.

In determining community needs, administrators should be sure to include members of the community and the students themselves. Service-learning cannot be imposed; agencies must be full partners. Program partners should look for needs that are authentic (not just constructed for the school), have significance for students, allow for reflection, provide skill and knowledge development, and assure meaningful service opportunities (as opposed to "servitude").

Gaining support of stakeholders and decision makers. Without the support of all stakeholders and decision makers in both the school and the community, a successful community service-learning program is not possible. The key to gaining that support is to involve all stakeholders and decision-makers from the outset. Administrators should let key people know what they are doing, ask them to serve on advisory boards, and keep them informed as to the progress of the program. There are many tasks in implementing a service-learning program, and all stakeholders—faculty, students, other administrators, parents, community leaders—should be represented in each task area. Without the support of each group, objectors may derail the program.

Administrators may focus so much on the needs assessment, program design, and organizational planning steps that they overlook typical misperceptions and concerns. Each of these criticisms must be countered: (1) service-learning is a frill and not *really* worthwhile in an academic institution; (2) volunteering is a good activity, but students shouldn't get credit for it; (3) students should not be required to do volunteer work; (4) the program will be costly to operate and will require more staff; (5) students at this age (or maturity) can't handle this program; (6) finding enough placements will be difficult and time-consuming; (7) some placements may be political and cause us a public relations nightmare; and (8) this program will increase our liability and therefore insurance costs. Failure to take these concerns into account can prevent a program from ever getting off the drawing board. (See Anderson and Witmer, 1994 for more details.)

Conceptualizing Possible Service-Learning Programs

Administrators can help to structure initial conversations about service-learning by providing a framework for discussing program options. Such a framework helps those who will plan the actual program and those who will choose whether or not to fund it. One option for conceptualizing the program is to use Conrad and Hedin's (1987) continuum. Another option is to think of service-learning along two dimensions: (1) whether it is required or optional and (2) whether it is included in the curriculum as a separate course, as part of a course, or as a club or activity (Witmer and Anderson, 1994).

Pros and cons of requiring service-learning. Some schools require service-learning of all students; others require it only as part of selected courses; still others offer it as an optional course or assignment within a class. Administrators need to remain aware that programs required for all students will need more personnel to operate, if there is a serious focus on the learning component and not just a requirement for students to put in their time in volunteer activities. Programs will also require multiple placement opportunities and student choice for placement. Even with the greatest consensus about the value of service-learning, some parents may occasionally object, and schools may need to set up some legitimate alternatives. These options, which we call "academic escape valves," can include research papers on a related issue, community interviews, and collections of articles and commentary on a social issue. If required programs carry credit, students who are not initially inclined to be involved may offer less resistance.

In general, we favor optional programs or required components in elective classes. An advantage of an optional program is that administrators and program coordinators can start small and learn the ropes of managing this kind of alternative program. Another advantage is that all students who participate come with at least some motivation or interest, and can help set up a positive track record, both with students and agencies. Whether or not the program becomes required depends on the culture of the school, the district, and the community. In general, we believe that optional programs work best, especially in a pluralistic society. Well run optional programs will establish a name for themselves, and in time a large percentage of students will avail themselves of the opportunity. Even with optional programs, offering credit of some kind is a good incentive.

Pros and cons of service-learning as a course, an assignment, or a club. The visibility of a separate program is both its strength and its Achilles' heel. On the one hand, a separate course is identifiable; it can be "promoted" and students can identify with it. It also allows easy access to students for reflection and group conversation about the field experiences, important ingredients for community service-learning. Depending on when the program is scheduled and the length of periods, some service work can be done during the class time. On the other hand, new courses are harder to initiate in an era of reduced resources, and existing courses not mandated by the state can be a visible target for budget cuts.

Extracurricular activities and clubs can offer many opportunities for different kinds of service, from individual assistance projects to group activities to community problem solving ventures. The drawback is that, without some planning, most clubs do not include much writing or talking about the experiences, and thus lose the ability to increase the learning dimension. Another service-learning option, outside the curriculum, is the graduation requirement. This option has the same potential drawback, without special planning.

A third option is to make service-learning an assignment within an existing class. The assignment can be required or optional, and can be related to the course content. This option is referred to as curriculum infusion and has several benefits. First, it can be started by one teacher, if a school is unable to generate a broad commitment to the concept. After students have a positive experience in this class, there may be a greater base for expanding beyond one class. Second, students are more likely to reflect on the experiences when they are part of a graded assignment. Third, there is relatively little cost to this approach, which protects it from the budgetary ax.

Other Program Design Considerations

Once the framework is selected there are other design issues which administrators must help to evaluate. These include criteria for acceptable service experiences and constraints and opportunities inherent in the school organization. Administrators must make sure these issues are discussed and decided on.

Identifying conditions that will be acceptable for the service activities. Regardless of the design, administrators will have to make decisions about the purpose of the program, characteristics of an appropriate site, and characteristics of an appropriate task at the site.

A service-learning program will have a longer life if the administrators can articulate its purpose to the school board, particularly the outcomes students should achieve. Another way to strengthen the program is to connect it to the school or district's goals, mission statement, or both. Often a service-learning program may be a major way to address affective and social skills, which may be part of the district's goals and which academic classes may not address. Operating from a purpose and outcomes, administrators can evaluate sites and placement opportunities in terms of how well they will help students achieve these outcomes. As a general rule students should be engaged in activities of a nonroutine nature and should be engaged with people more than paper. More important than the extent of personal contact, however, is that the activity have some visible results.

A related issue is whether or not to seek experiences that cause students to see the connection between the social problem and its causes. This advocacy issue can be connected to political or economic aspects of our society: it will likely surface during reflection time. In fact, wanting to solve the problem is a logical next step for students with service-learning experience.

In finding placements, one option is to focus on service sites that fit a certain topic or theme. This may be particularly appropriate if the model selected was curriculum infusion, where the service should fit the course content outcomes. For example, in a political science class the service might focus on advocacy projects or work with government agencies. In a health class, the service projects might be limited to hospitals, clinics, or nursing homes. Administrators must also raise questions about the type of site. Should students work with existing agencies or can they find and work with individuals in need? We think the agency route is easier to manage and supervise; but districts that require a certain number of hours of service-learning from every student may not be able to locate enough sites and may need to let students find their own place and type of service.

Identifying constraints and opportunities in your current program. Every school and district is different, each with a set of conditions that will restrict community service-learning options, and other conditions that will expand opportunities. Identifying these is an important job for administrators. Age of students served, staff availability, space availability, class size, scheduling, and resources are organizational conditions. Other factors to consider include resources and public relations, management procedures, site selection and cultivation, student-site matching, and planning for long-term success. (See chapters 3 and 8 for further details on many of these aspects.)

Setting Up Management Procedures
to Ensure Continued Success

Service-learning requires more coordination than most school programs, because there are so many components. As with electronics, the more complex the technology, the greater the likelihood that something can go wrong. Anticipating the potential problems and taking precautionary steps is an important role for the administrator. For example, community service programs sometimes falter because schools neglect to build a collegial relationship with an agency before they begin implementation. Administrators can provide the initial contacts, an introductory letter, and if possible can lend institutional credibility by attending the initial meeting.

The administrator must also take into consideration the ethical and moral issues of community service-learning programs. These usually include issues of privacy and conduct. The Family and Student Educational Rights and Privacy Act forbids an institution from releasing student information without consent of the student, and likewise, students must understand that, as guests of the agency in which they serve, they must not reveal any information about the agencies or their clients. Students must also be advised that when faced with a situation of questionable conduct, they must consult with a supervisor or other responsible adult.

Planning for the long-term success of the program. Only programs that are carefully designed, implemented, and nurtured will last beyond a trial stage. Therefore, it is essential to keep records and to submit reports on a regular basis. As much as possible, administrators should try to move the service-learning program into the curriculum so that its budget is viewed as part of the expenditures for instruction. In addition, seeking outside funding through business partnerships and state and federal grants may be helpful. School reform initiatives have opened doors to classrooms beyond the school walls; programs should capitalize on this movement and tie into these projects.

The administrator should become involved beyond the school community by networking, making presentations and sharing information. Most everyone is interested in "what is happening in the local schools," and service-learning is a good human interest story for the press. In short, showcasing the work of students in the program, through board meetings, school assemblies, displays, news articles, and television or radio interviews will help to build community support. If administrators become spokespersons for community service-learning, people will listen!

RECOMMENDATIONS FOR ADMINISTRATORS OF SERVICE-LEARNING PROGRAMS

Your role is crucial to the success of any service-learning program, not just in getting it approved but in running interference. Before the program is planned, your assistance is needed to conceptualize the design and select the components. After it is developed, you must convince the school board and other constituent groups to accept it, and you must find resources to fund it. Once implemented, you need to seek good press for the program and continue to support those who are coordinating it.

1. *Evaluate your school's or district's potential for service-learning.* Schools cannot all develop the same kind of service-learning program, both because of traditions or past experiences, organizational conditions and resources, availability of service opportunities, faculty interest, and values of the community and school board. You can help people who will plan and implement a program to reflect on these influences and use them to construct a viable program.

2. *Evaluate the design options that best fit conditions in your school or district.* You can provide the framework for helping people select the type of service-learning program that will best fit the needs and values of the district. A framework such as the one discussed in this chapter (required versus optional and separate course versus assignment within a class versus an extracurricular club) can focus discussion after planners have completed a needs assessment. Your framework can provide the basis for discussing options.

3. *Specify conditions which make a service-learning activity acceptable for your program.* You can help the planners and implementors by identifying the issues they need to decide in selecting placements and service activities. By doing so you help them anticipate potential problems and understand the strengths and weaknesses of various approaches to service-learning.

4. *Develop management procedures that are clear to everyone and that protect everyone.* Service-learning can be a complex management task, and your assistance in designing procedures to manage and monitor the program, and to work with placement sites can help overcome these potential barriers.

5. *Take the time to plan carefully and to evaluate adequately.* Enthusiasm for and commitment to service-learning is important, but adequate planning and a good evaluation plan can make the enthusiasm and commitment pay off. Spend extra time at the beginning with planning and dialogue. Don't rush; be sure all stakeholders are on board and all procedures are in place before you ask the Board for approval or begin to implement.

6. *Don't overlook or dismiss typical concerns of decision makers.* These concerns are sometimes about values (How can service-learning fit with academic learning? Why should we give credit for volunteering?). They may be about the connection of service-learning to the existing curriculum (Why add a program?). Sometimes they are about potential public relations problems (Will parents support us if we require service of students? Will some placements be controversial?). Sometimes they are just about costs (Will our insurance premium rise? Will we spend more to operate the program?). And sometimes there are worries about practical problems (Will there be enough

placements? Can students handle this kind of program?) You must anticipate *all* these concerns to be successful in establishing a service-learning program.

IN CLOSING

On the one hand, administrators certainly can't develop service-learning programs alone. On the other hand, in some settings these programs won't even get off the ground without administrator guidance and troubleshooting; and programs that do get started without administrators may later run into problems without someone to navigate past potential land mines—functions that administrators are well-equipped to handle. Administrators can play important roles that will guarantee long-term success for service-learning opportunities in any school—by asking the right questions initially, setting forth options and important choices, and developing management procedures.

Chapter 16

School Program Coordinator

Winifred Evers Pardo

MY STORY

A school committed to service-learning must have someone within the school who assumes primary responsibility for organizing and facilitating the program. Having said this, however, I must be quick to add that there is wide latitude concerning the amount of time devoted and the category of the employee filling this position. The service-learning coordinator may be a teacher or guidance counselor (full-time or part-time), a teacher assistant or an administrator. Title matters less than the responsibilities being met and the organizational skills and commitment of the person in the position.

The focus of this chapter will be on the role of a school-based service-learning coordinator. The scope of any given program and, hence the workload, varies greatly from school to school depending on the commitment of faculty and administration to service-learning and the number of ongoing service projects. A program may be schoolwide, either mandated by administration or the result of teachers buying in voluntarily. Or it may begin small, as a grass-roots effort of a small group of staff. In any case, although the extent of the programs may vary, basic similarities exist in the role of service-learning coordinators.

One school's experience encapsulates many of the elements inherent in building a service-learning program from modest beginnings into an extensive schoolwide and districtwide endeavor. In this instance the position of Community Service Coordinator and the addition of other supporting staff grew exponentially with the success of the program. Different models have been successful in other schools. All have seized on opportunities for service-learning and successfully met the challenges.

Community Service-Learning at the
Shoreham-Wading River Middle School

In 1973 there was a dearth of service activity in public elementary and middle or junior high schools, although there was a smattering of programs in public high schools and, perhaps to a slightly greater degree, in private schools. The Shoreham-Wading River Middle School was one of the first schools to become a middle school, grades 6, 7, and 8, and to adopt the then-innovative philosophy of child-centered, experiential learning appropriate for early adolescents. It was also one of the first in the country to initiate community service as an integral part of the curriculum for eleven- to fourteen-year-olds. At first an eighth-grade English/social studies teacher and the principal, discussing a group of disaffected students, hit on the idea of offering them the challenge of "real" work out in the community. They approached me, then a PTO parent, for help. I readily found a nursing home and a day-care center willing to receive volunteers. And so began hurried trips back and forth by the teacher, kids actively engaged and working hard, and the first demonstration of an experiment too good to ignore.

By year two a teaching assistant position was redefined to assume responsibility for coordination and facilitation of a greatly expanded community service program. Since I had organizational and community experience and an interest in the challenge, I applied for and was given the twenty-five-hour-a-week job and the program took off. From the beginning this was intended to be an integral part of the school day, although with only one staff member and one minibus it was, of necessity, only a pull-out program. It was a hectic year indeed, as groups of six or eight students each fanned out into local nursery schools, a nursing home, a regional special education school and the lower grades of the district's own elementary schools. Hundreds of students participated. The impact was immediate, as students, parents, and teachers recognized the importance of the responsibility students were assuming and the relationships they were forming across barriers of age and capability.

In those early stages of the program I had several worries which, fortunately, dissipated rapidly. One was that parents would object to children missing class-time. Another was that agencies might not welcome volunteers so young. A third was the question of how to orient students and have time for evaluation and preparation, when a whole class was not involved in a project. And logistics, of course, needed attention.

The enthusiastic messages children brought home, as well as the fact that teachers, during parent open houses, began early on to present community service as part of the curriculum, led to overwhelming parent acceptance. As coordinator, I made sure that promises were kept with participating agencies. That fact, along with the quality of the relationships formed, quickly converted skeptics into believers. In subsequent years these and many other community agencies have continued to seek out the student volunteers from Shoreham-Wading River.

The issue of integrating site-based service into the curriculum was readily solved in year three, when two seventh-grade team teachers decided that their entire group of 45 students would do a unit on early childhood. I worked very closely with them in planning how to incorporate site-based experiences with preschoolers into their curriculum. Students were expected to plan and lead activities for one hour weekly for ten weeks with three- and four-year-olds, some who came into the school and others at local nursery schools. Both teachers were involved, along with myself and an additional teacher assistant. Each of the four adults supervised one group of seventh-graders, planning with them, discussing their experiences and overseeing their activities with the preschoolers.

The vitality of the "real-life" experience added special meaning to the team's curriculum. Using the "Exploring Childhood" materials that I had secured, students did their reading, language arts, science, social studies, and art as an effective interdisciplinary service-learning unit. In addition, they had practical problems to solve, deadlines to meet, emotions to encounter and responsibilities for their little charges that needed to be faced and met.

The power of the program was such that other teachers quickly took note and approached me about committing their teams and blocks of teaching time to service-learning. Another seventh-grade team, for instance, zeroed in on the elderly, with forty-five students making weekly visits to local nursing homes and health-related facilities. As program coordinator, I made all the arrangements with field-site agencies, handled transportation, and provided classroom back-up including use of filmstrips and library materials about old age, orientation by therapists, dietitians and administrators from the nursing homes, journal-writing, and the like. The students sent articles to local newspapers and finally a book of their writings was published. Regularly, one period per week was devoted to preparation by students of activities for site visits, as well as evaluation of each visit.

After the first two years there was no longer a need for pull-out service-learning projects. The program grew rapidly and voluntarily. Teachers, always working with me as coordinator, eagerly found creative ways to incorporate service into their curricula. A great variety of programs subsequently flourished. (See chapter 10 for further details on some of Shoreham-Wading River's service-learning activities.)

Throughout the rapid expansion of the community-based program, the involvement of teachers remained voluntary. Teachers were assured of the support of the Community Service Coordinator and the growing staff of teacher assistants, and they became aware of the impact that the site-based experience had on students, parents, and the community. In the 1990s, every team in the middle school is, by choice, doing one unit of service-learning during each school year. This means that hundreds of children are serving others in the larger community and also enjoying the privilege of several different experiences in grades 6, 7 and 8 which have major and lasting impact on their own lives.

Obviously this expansion of the service-learning program put increased demands on the person coordinating it. In 1981, my position as Community Service Coordinator became a teaching position. Four teacher assistants were ultimately assigned to the program and four minibuses were allocated primarily for this purpose. The present coordinator, Joanne Urgese, and the service-learning staff members are assigned to specific programs, work closely with the teachers, make contacts and arrangements with the appropriate agencies, plan orientation, transportation, and the gathering of supplies and materials. Each adult (teacher or teacher assistant) assumes responsibility for approximately ten middle school students, discussing and planning with them for their site visit, driving them to the site and overseeing their work there.

The service-learning coordinator has overall responsibility for this complex program and staff, laying out the year's schedule by early September and assuring that all the pieces fit together—teachers, students, agencies, staffing, transportation and the like. It is an exciting position, never boring or routine, and amazingly fulfilling as it offers a unique opportunity to observe the importance of service to young people and the persons whom they serve.

ISSUES FOR SERVICE-LEARNING
SCHOOL PROGRAM COORDINATORS

Obviously Shoreham-Wading River Middle School provides only one pattern for the development of a program that incorporates community service as an integral part of classroom curriculum. Other schools and school districts have moved in the same direction, but in different configurations and utilizing different kinds of leadership. In some instances a building administrator has made the decision that everyone in the school will be involved in some service activity, and has provided the support of a coordinator, supplies, transportation, and so on. In some communities it is a districtwide commitment and schools are provided with the kind of support which that kind of a commitment implies.

The challenges for a service-learning coordinator no doubt vary depending on the source of the initiative. On the one hand if the program begins small, as a grassroots effort initiated by teachers, or even as an optional program suggested by a building principal, it may be more difficult to demonstrate the need for a coordinator, to have time set aside for planning and to secure funds and transportation. On the other hand, a coordinator in this situation readily becomes a teammate to teachers eager to have the program; teachers are genuinely appreciative of the coordinator's assistance. Expansion of the program and also of the position itself then depends on the effectiveness of the coordinator in working with others on the staff and in assuring high-quality programs that have a significant impact on both students and community.

A program that is mandated at the building or district level has the obvious advantage of support in the form of staffing and funding, without teachers having to struggle for time and backing. A coordinator in this position has time and resources and a somewhat different set of challenges. Such a mandate inherently encounters resistance from faculty not interested in change, which in this instance means incorporating community service into their classrooms. The coordinator must be sensitive to feelings, diligent in involving faculty members and building administrators in discussions and decisions, careful to provide training, and creative in helping teachers devise projects that are both exciting and relevant to what goes on in the classroom.

A third pattern that exists in many districts is for community service to be done during afterschool and weekend hours, or even during week-long stints at outdoor education sites or parklands. In this instance the coordinator has the added challenge of encouraging students to offer personal time, competing with the demands of homework, part-time employment, sports, and other social life. The coordinator must make a special effort to provide orientation for students and opportunities for them to discuss problems and successes. He or she must visit students on-site, to be sure that the quality of their work and their experience is first rate.

One might question why it is necessary to have a coordinator for service-learning activities. Budgets are tight and it may be tempting to think that teachers could make the arrangements themselves. Neither argument suffices. If anything of significance is to occur and the program is to grow, the school or school district should be prepared to commit some staff time to supporting and facilitating it. The service-learning coordinator, whether working part-time or full-time, is needed as an enabler, one who oversees the program and attends to details so that other teachers are encouraged and supported. Being realistic, it is just too time-consuming for one classroom teacher or a team of teachers to take care of all the arrangements with agencies, as well as other details, and at the same time plan curricular work that dovetails with the site-based work.

Of critical importance is the coordinator's role as adviser and teammate. Classroom teachers seek help in knowing what opportunities exist "out there" in the community and what materials are available concerning this or that population. They welcome help with arranging for orientation and with creating the rich interdisciplinary curriculum—academics, art, music, physical activity—which can so readily be developed around a community service experience. The coordinator also becomes the focal point for stability and for quality control, in the sense that good models are presented, adequate planning and supervision are assured, and the school's work continues to be welcomed by the agencies being served.

In contemplating the establishment of a service-learning program in one's school or district, the question of funding comes quickly to mind. If it is clearly a priority for the educational program, funds will be allocated for a coordinator's time, just as they are for any other curricular or extracurricular program considered to be of value and therefore included in the budget. It may be a part-time position or, preferably, a full-time one, but in either case the work can be supplemented with secretarial and other logistical support, as well as administrators' time and attention. If service-learning is part of the school's day-time curriculum, it automatically becomes part of the participating teachers' regular teaching-planning responsibility and the availability of students is assured since the program is a part of their regular classes.

The coordinator should expect to be provided with an office, space for storage of curriculum materials and art supplies and for the use of classrooms, as needed, for planning sessions with students. The coordinator should request time, either during the summer or during common prep periods, for meeting with teachers to organize and implement service-learning units. Modest amounts of money are needed for art and craft materials and books. Over time audiovisual and printed curriculum material should be assembled on relevant topics, such as child development, the elderly, handicapping conditions, the environment, and so on.

The school system also needs to provide funds for transporting students to work-sites in the community. Some schools in urban areas are fortunate in having nursing homes or day-care centers close to the school and within walking distance. It may simply be the coordinator's job to have children escorted, unless they are of high school age and able to travel on their own. In some rural or suburban communities the service-learning school may be in close proximity to one of the district's own preschools or elementary schools, and service may be offered without the need for vehicles. Where distances become a problem, it is the coordinator's job to arrange for minibuses—which in some instances the teachers and community service staff drive—or for large school buses.

Once assured of administrative support in the areas of time, space, funds, transportation, and so forth, the coordinator's role is to be the bridge between school and community—to reach outward in search of opportunities for service in the community and to build solid relationships with teachers in the school as they contemplate service-learning. The aim is to seek out community agencies where students can work on a regular basis, establishing relationships over time and avoiding the "one-shot" Christmas-caroling-type programs.

When contacting agencies, the coordinator should be aware that there may be some reluctance to accept volunteers. Past experience with other volunteers who failed to follow through may be at the root of such reluctance. Then again, some agencies may consider it inadvisable to have young children as volunteers. In any event, the coordinator should be careful to commit to specific times and dates, promising to be there without fail. The promise should also be made that students will be well-oriented and that they will come prepared with enough activities to fill the allotted time. Once given a chance, it is incumbent on the coordinator to see that students are there when promised, and that they are well prepared. Students should be supervised by school personnel, especially when they are of elementary or middle school age. For high school students the need for adult supervision is not as great.

Within the school, the coordinator needs to work closely with classroom teachers to develop a yearly master schedule as well as detailed schedules for each unit. These should be committed to writing and distributed to all concerned. There is transportation to arrange (with the accompanying insurance protection and field trip permission forms); materials and supplies to gather; films, speakers, or other forms of orientation to set up; and staff assignments to be made so that an adult supervisor is provided for each subgroup of students working at a field site.

This calls for someone skilled at working with people, capable of "keeping many balls in the air" simultaneously, and who is highly organized. Good intentions alone will not suffice. Details must be carefully worked out and fully communicated. Letters must be written, calls exchanged. Parents, administrators, and other interested parties must be kept informed.

As indicated earlier, a central role for the coordinator is to be a teammate to participating teachers in the area of curriculum, as well as logistics. This may mean arranging for speakers or videos, seeking out curricular supplements, brainstorming for interdisciplinary possibilities for the classroom, receiving students' journals and finding opportunities for them to publish or speak about their work.

The coordinator, his or her assistants, and the classroom teacher(s) each take responsibility for a small group of students as they prepare and carry out their field-site work. In these instances, in addition to preparing and supervising the students, the service-learning staff members evaluate students' work and report in writing to the classroom teacher. The coordinator may also undertake evaluation of the service-learning program itself through use of evaluation forms, solicitation of written comments from agency personnel, clientele, students, teachers and parents, or by doing "before and after" problem-solving exercises.

If the service-learning program is to flourish, the coordinator must earn the trust and respect of building administrators, faculty, and staff. Again, this calls for communication. It may mean inviting the principal to go with students to a nursing home or to observe a group leading a forty-five-minute Head Start class. It may mean inviting nonparticipating teachers to share a skill or to drop in and observe. It may mean reaching out to parents to assist as volunteers or to report on their children's experiences at PTO meetings.

The larger public relations function also belongs to the coordinator. What students do in community service is compelling and is an experience crying out to be told. Students speak eloquently of their work and the new relationships formed. Opportunities should be found for them to speak at other schools and conferences, to community organizations, or to their Board of Education. Slides or videos of the field-site activities are very effective, as is students writing for their school publications or for local newspapers. The message about the power and importance of service needs to be told. It is a means of gaining continuing support for the program within one's own school district and an encouragement to other schools seeking to initiate similar programs.

RECOMMENDATIONS FOR SERVICE-LEARNING PROGRAM COORDINATORS

1. *Assume that all children can be productively involved in community service-learning.* Look for opportunities for children of all ages, at all grade levels, and at all levels of ability to perform community service. They are all capable to different degrees and at different levels of sophistication. Instances abound of otherwise "turned off" students succeeding at service activities, discovering self-esteem in the process.
2. *Integrate service-learning as part of the regular school day.* Site-based work should be integrally connected with academic core subjects, the arts, music, physical education, and so forth. Should the service component occur after school hours, be sure it is done under careful supervision.
3. *Be bold and creative.* Look carefully at your community for interesting service prospects. Tempt your teachers and students with the possibilities. In addition to taking students outside of the school to work, have them teach art or jewelry making or computer skills to community residents who come to the school, or offer story hours for toddlers.
4. *Begin small.* Unless there is a top-down district commitment to service-learning, begin with a modest project, where there can be enthusiasm and where you are able to do it very, very well. "Less" may be better. A program that excels sells itself and other teachers will seek to jump on board.
5. *Plan carefully and be attentive to details.* Be very specific in arrangements with agencies and stick to your commitments. Be there when promised and be sure students are well prepared and well supervised. Write out schedules. Attend to acknowledgments and "thank-yous."

6. *Be attentive to communication and public relations.* It is important that school personnel, parents, and the community be told of the exciting work that the students are performing and its impact on their lives and the lives of those they serve.

7. *Recognize that you are doing something very important.* No matter what is required for service-learning to occur, the experience is crucial to a young person's development and adds to the health and life of the larger community.

IN CLOSING

The service-learning coordinator is at the center of an important and rewarding undertaking. Working cooperatively with diverse personalities in the school community and reaching out to all kinds of interesting people and places outside of the school walls is a continuing challenge. There is no time to be bored. The possibilities for creative programs are as great as the coordinator, the teachers, and the students make them.

Perhaps the best part of the job is the experience shared with students. Working with them and watching them grow in competence and responsibility is reward indeed. Especially thrilling is watching relationships form—one student with a nursing home partner, another reading to a three-year-old, another struggling to make contact with an autistic child. It's all about the stuff of life and the reward is in being part of it.

Chapter 17

Staff Developer

James and Pamela Toole

OUR STORY

"Just how much can you learn from raking leaves for a senior citizen?" The high school teacher asking this question had come to the prep period meeting on service-learning at the urging of his school principal. He was someone with a great deal of classroom experience and highly regarded by the rest of the staff. If the national standards in education are in any danger, it would not be in his classroom. He was exactly the type of strong content-area teacher that we wanted to interest in service-learning.

We could tell by his question, however, that the concept of service-learning made little initial academic sense. Typically, educators have prior knowledge of community service, but not service-learning. Teachers often grow up performing service through Boys or Girls Clubs, YMCA or YWCA, 4-H, Scouting or church youth groups, where the goal is positive youth development. Service has to do with learning character, empathy, and prosocial values; not biology, language arts, or social studies. It is not that this teacher thought service-learning was a bad idea. It is just that his beginning impression was that it did not belong in his already overcrowded curriculum.

We smiled because we had heard his question, and others like it, numerous times before. Since 1991, when the W. K. Kellogg Foundation funded the National Service-Learning Initiative through the National Youth Leadership Council (NYLC), we have been in over thirty-five states and Canada conducting workshops in a great variety of communities and schools. This work has been fueled further by a grant from the DeWitt Wallace/Reader's Digest Foundation to NYLC and five regional partners to establish a chain of thirty-three elementary and middle "Generator Schools" that incorporate service-learning into the main framework of their institutions.

Because of such support from foundations and from the National and Community Service Acts of 1990 and 1993, there is currently an opportunity for educators to investigate and develop model service-learning programs, establish effective pedagogy, and build a solid base of research. If service-learning is to fulfill this potential, we believe that staff development will play a critical role. It is our goal in this chapter to share our own staff development perspective and experiences. As Directors of Professional Development for NYLC and as codirectors of Compass Institute, we will cover: (1) some of the key lessons we have learned; (2) what we see as the outstanding issues; and (3) our recommendations for future directions.

Our own work in youth service staff development started just out of college in the mid-1970s. For fifteen years we worked in a school district in northern California, coordinating students acting as mentors, cross-age health educators, computer tutors, parent educators, group facilitators, peer counselors, new student welcomers, special friends, and in many other roles to improve campus life. This work involved curricular and extracurricular activities as well as an emphasis on both school guidance and classroom instruction. Because our program was initially funded by the National Institute of Mental Health and then a California Department of Education dissemination grant, we began our careers having the opportunity to visit and share with many schools. This broad base of practical service-learning experience has been essential for working with teachers who always want to know whether "you know schools" and whether "you have done this with youth yourselves."

It was this ongoing peer helping and school guidance work (e.g., prevention, early intervention, group counseling) that gave us the expertise we consider most vital to our careers as staff developers. Although there is a great deal of talk about teachers being "coaches" today, Jim received no real training in coaching skills in his teacher preparation program. The paradigm of facilitation belongs historically much more to the area of guidance than classroom instruction. Pamela's degrees in counseling and educational psychology offered a much better preparation. In guidance, one learns to foster other people's thinking, listen reflectively, ask open-ended questions, lead productive group discussions, and develop an attitude of trust in the emergent wisdom of students. It is not hard to transfer these process skills from the content of people's lives (in guidance work) to the pedagogical content in staff development.

Since moving to Minnesota in 1989, our experience has included one- to three-day introductory service-learning workshops, six day summer residential institutes, advanced special interest topics, and ongoing work with groups like the Points of Light youth ambassadors, the National Indian Youth Leadership Council, and the NYLC Generator School staffs. Through the Kellogg National Service-Learning Initiative grant, we were also able in 1991 to write a training of trainers manual that is utilized by our regional partners to reach thousands of teachers.

What are the most significant lessons we have learned from our staff development work? Let's begin with the teacher in our opening paragraph–whose prior knowledge is community service, not service-learning. We learned very quickly the importance of spending sufficient time on key concepts–the differences between such terms as volunteerism, community service, peer helping, community-based learning, and service-learning. For example, when we met with the emerging service-learning leaders in one state, we could see that there was no group consensus about where they would be leading. With any educational innovation, it is a struggle and a prime task for staff development to ensure that everyone starts the project with a common vocabulary, a shared cognitive base, and a set of skills and vision for its impact on youth.

In addition to developing a common foundation, staff developers always face another predictable hurdle when working with adult learners. If teachers are not convinced of the immediate practicality of the workshop content, then they won't have time for it. With service-learning, we found that the best way to capture teachers' attention is to give them the opportunity to perform service themselves. We take teachers into predictable placements such as nursing homes, river projects and homeless shelters, as well as less typical sites such as an AIDS hostel, archeological museums, and a raptor center (where we worked on a project to catalog and replace feathers on injured birds of prey). Wherever possible, we offer workshop participants a selection of several projects that reflect genuine needs, divergent tasks, and diverse cultures.

We have had some very memorable battles with administrators who were initially against including a half-day service project during the workshop. They would tell us that, "Our staff are beyond that. What they need is the 'knowledge' to do service-learning." There is a wonderful irony in these debates. The implicit message is that "we think that learning should involve hands-on education, utilizing the community as a resource, and offering genuine opportunities for responsibility and service, but don't do any of that as part of staff development."

Fortunately, we have never lost one of these debates and all of the administrators, after the fact, have become enthusiastic supporters of teacher service projects. One of our most common projects is to conduct an oral history at a nursing home. One of our teachers interviewed a man who spoke seven languages, had written several books, and even played a song on his guitar. What an educational resource! Equally surprising, however, was the fact that at the end of the interview this senior became tearful and said how much the visit had meant to him. The experience demonstrated the potential synergy between learning and service.

Teacher service projects continually reinforce to us how much the traditional culture and norms of schooling have isolated the thinking and physical presence of teachers from their own communities. Because of this separation, we may underestimate how adventurous service-learning methodology may be for even some experienced teachers. We have always smiled when former Penn Serve Director John Briscoe rightly shares that "We will have real school reform when every teacher has a large rolodex and a phone on his or her desk." Everything in our service-learning pedagogy tells us that if we are to break through teachers' sense of isolation from the community, they will need to get their own feet wet, not hear a lecture about water. They need to experience the sight, touch, taste, and smell of participation in community life. The man who conducted the oral history remarked afterwards that, having done the project himself, he was much more likely to take his students there. We have learned that, for students and teachers alike, context is content.

We find that many teachers are quickly captivated by the idea of integrating service into subject matter disciplines; they respond with interest in the curriculum examples we share. Entering a classroom to face twenty-five to forty young faces every morning, however, makes one very practical. Although teachers get excited, they immediately have a hundred questions about its practice. We call this the "yes, but" stage. The "but" may be pedagogy (How do you have student choice and still cover the district curriculum?), logistics (transportation, liability, scheduling), standardized testing (How will this affect test scores?), leadership ("My principal wouldn't like this."), assessment (How will we measure student performance in field-based experiences?) or subject matter content ("Yeah, but can you do this in ninth-grade algebra?").

The service project helps to foster teacher commitment and also functions as one of the main "textbooks" for our workshops. The experience allows the staff developer to model how service-learning is performed–the pedagogy used before, during, and after a service project. When we introduce the theory surrounding service-learning methodology, teachers then have the prior knowledge of their own personal experience. After a group of rural teachers had served lunch at an urban homeless shelter, for instance, it was not hard to teach about the importance of thoughtful preparation and subsequent reflection for service projects. Their personal experience had already illustrated that reflection is an indispensable tool by which service experiences are turned into learning experiences (Toole and Toole, 1995).

The topic of collaboration also brings its share of staff development challenges. When we ask teachers how many have collaborated with a community agency around their curriculum, we usually see about three hands for every forty people. To give teachers a chance to practice collaborative skills, we have participants either visit community agencies or have agency representatives come to our workshops. In both cases, teachers simulate a first meeting to explore setting up possible student placements. There is often a tangible excitement in the room as these heterogeneous groups share perspectives and possibilities. After a recent experience in one school district, we asked a group of teachers their reactions. One shot back in a surprised voice: "They need us." What she didn't say, but what will become apparent as schools move out into the community, is that schools also need the community as a rich context for authentic instruction, for their strong history of working with youth in informal learning, and for their curricular and other resources.

These are some of the most vital lessons we have learned. Our experiences have also generated a list of key issues that we think anyone coordinating service-learning staff development today must face. In the section that follows, we list and discuss ten such concerns. Each issue is stated in the words that we have heard from teachers or administrators.

ISSUES FOR STAFF DEVELOPERS IN SERVICE-LEARNING PROGRAMS

Issue 1: "Staff in-service trainings are not going to improve education dramatically."

The biggest issues in service-learning staff development have nothing to do with service-learning. They have to do with what we have learned about effective staff development, about how teachers learn new skills, and about how organizations change. Many school district and state-level service-learning initiatives began with one-shot in-service workshops. The real nature of successful staff development, however, is that it includes not only initial training, but an ongoing set of activities that Dennis Sparks (1995) calls "multiple forms of job-embedded learning" (p. 4).

These activities include the use of peer consultants, peer coaching, teacher reflective dialogue, action research, study groups, journals, staff curriculum development, and teacher involvement in developing a clear vision for school improvement. The importance of such "job-embedded learning" is perhaps best exemplified in the area of teacher learning about reflection. Although we use a wide variety of methods to clarify and demonstrate the concept in our beginning workshops, we know that teacher skills will be constrained if they don't have structured opportunities to practice and receive coaching through follow-up activities.

The standard for staff development success becomes not "a successful workshop," but the transformation of teachers' instructional behavior in ways that improve core student outcomes. The question facing the field of service-learning is whether or not it will adopt the staff development paradigms required for authentic teacher growth and success.

Issue 2: "I gave up trying to change this school years ago."

The second biggest issue facing service-learning staff development is the wider organizational context of the schools in which it takes place. As the research of Susan Rosenholtz (1991) shows: "The question of what teaching is, how it is performed, and how it is changed cannot be divorced from the social organization in which it occurs" (p. 205).

Too often, teachers become so frustrated by their school's social organization that they survive by the philosophy of "my kids, my class, this year." They are in the school, but not a part of it. This is consistent with Ann Cook's (1995) observation that Hollywood films such as "Stand and Deliver," "Dead Poets Society," and "To Sir with Love," have all "cast hero teachers as *defiers*, not *definers*, of the institutions in which they work; that is, the teachers gain their reputations in *contradiction* to, rather than in *collaboration* with, the schools in which they teach" (p. 40).

Scholars are increasingly emphasizing that it is the school that must be the focus of educational improvement. Students benefit when every teacher takes a collective responsibility for what happens in the building. Teachers then become like good basketball players who act in ways that make their teammates look better. The best staff development programs will therefore need to find ways to foster and reward collaboration and consensus-building.

To illustrate the importance of social organization, imagine initiating service-learning into the contrasting contexts described by Rosenholtz: "Schools where teachers share common goals, and schools more like organized anarchies; schools where colleagues help one another, and schools of professional isolation; schools where teachers and students learn and grow, and schools where most of them stagnate; schools where teachers believe in themselves, and schools of contagious uncertainty; schools where teachers spark enthusiasm and hope, and schools where they (have) only despair" (p. 1). She labels schools, in the most broad sense, as either "stuck" or "learning" organizations.

We have seen people leave our workshops and receive great organizational support ("our superintendent was in the Peace Corps") or have fellow staff members show no interest whatsoever. Service-learning staff development initiatives must not only face the issue of teaching new skills, but of how to improve the structural, social, and human conditions of the teachers' workplace that will enable instructional initiatives to succeed. Louis and Kruse

(1995) show how deprivatizing teacher practice, increasing teacher reflective dialogue, and developing shared norms, values, and instructional focus can have a large impact on the success of change efforts.

Issue 3: But is service-learning really academic?

A huge and ongoing issue in staff development is that service-learning will not look "academic" enough to some teachers, administrators, and parents. When we asked our preworkshop participants to complete the sentence "I think of Service-Learning primarily as . . ." 48 percent of participants answered "a tool to increase students' personal growth and 38 percent checked "a tool to increase students' sense of social and civic responsibility." Only 25 percent checked "a valuable teaching method that helps students learn," and 10 percent checked "an important tool in school restructuring." We think that *all* of these outcomes are important, and that thoughtful service-learning might be able to succeed simultaneously on multiple levels. But it is the connection to school reform and student academic growth that is most driving the current initiatives and justifying the funding. Staff developers face the challenge of helping others to see the potentially powerful connections between service and learning.

Issue 4: "Service-learning seems like a lot of work!"

Many of the ideas promoted by school reform advocates, including service-learning, can be categorized as "teaching for understanding." Cohen, McLaughlin, and Talbert (1993) commented on the complexity of such approaches: "Teaching for understanding assumes substantial new learning on the teachers' part; it requires change not only in what is taught but also in how it is taught. Learning how to involve students actively in the construction of knowledge, how to move beyond fact-based concepts of knowledge and learner outcomes, and how to fashion new classroom roles and relationships involves more than simply sharpening up teaching skills or teachers' professional knowledge base as conventionally conceived" (p. 2).

Staff developers must address this issue of teaching complexity. We can talk about "teachers as coaches," "the community as a classroom," and "students actively exploring and constructing their own knowledge," but the pedagogical implications are immense. Such transformations require new roles, relationships, skills and attitudes (e.g., adaptations in everything from classroom management to methods of assessment). Additionally, people miss that such methods also require more in-depth knowledge of subject matter. If a teacher knows little about mathematics, he or she will by default follow the textbook verbatim. When teachers open the class to increased student thinking and exploration in service-learning, they will need a deeper and more flexible content base to skillfully guide the process.

There are two telling comments about the complexity of teachers mastering new skills that ring true to us, because of their honesty and realism about what is involved in teachers mastering new skills. The first is Joyce and Showers's (1988) statement that: "To bring a model of teaching of medium complexity under control requires twenty or twenty-five trials in the classroom over a period of about eight or ten weeks" (p. 69). The second is Karen Seashore Louis's observation that one of her favorite findings from her research on school change is that the longer a school is involved in a change effort, the longer the staff thinks it will take before it is completed (Louis and Miles, 1990).

Issue 5: "What are those people in the district office up to now?"

Several years ago, we conducted a workshop where, when the school district superintendent stood to introduce us, we could feel a tangible sense of resentment fill the room. What we learned later was that this district had just been through four years of intensive, top-down change efforts. As Michael Fullan (1991) noted, "If we know one thing about innovation and reform, it is that it cannot be done successfully *to* others" (p. xiv).

This brings up the issue of how districts attempt to implement service-learning. A number of the recent school reform initiatives have emphasized hierarchical control to, in the words of Rosenholtz (1995), "regulate both the content and process of education in the hopes that teacher proof instruction will increase the quality of schooling" (p. 214). Teaching, however, is a non-routine activity that can't be legislated. It will never be replicated or evaluated by a paint-by-number scheme. The issue is whether we have the willingness and ability to instead foster teachers' professionalism and to combine the best of top-down and bottom-up strategies.

Issue 6: "What's the best way to teach?"

Service-learning is part of a larger historical debate about what is the best way to teach and organize curriculum. Should we emphasize teacher-centered or student-centered curriculum, rigor or relevance, coverage or depth, basic skills or problem-solving, academic or practical knowledge, and expository or discovery learning? While there are no easy answers, we observe that teachers consider and weigh the merits of service-learning from within a larger framework of how they define good teaching.

These dichotomies present a problem for staff development because, in our view, many of them are poorly drawn. Teachers may reject service-learning if they think they must choose between teacher and student-centered curriculum, between rigor and relevance, or between basic skills and thinking skills.

Our sense is that all of these factors are important to good teaching. Rigor and relevance are both valid criteria by which we may judge instruction, not opposite ends of a single continuum. Likewise, there is nothing mutually exclusive about academic and vocational knowledge. In the case of teacher-versus student-centered curriculum, there is a legitimate dichotomy, but both are important to good teaching. Different models of teaching are appropriate for different types of outcomes (Joyce, Weil, and Showers, 1992).

The real challenge of teaching is how to balance these factors, not choose between them. If teachers are going to add service-learning to their repertoire, they will need time to explore such questions, define their real meaning, and connect emerging answers to an evolving sense of what good teaching and learning look like.

Issue 7: "What is the purpose of school?"

The debate over implementing service-learning is not only about the "best" way to teach. It also involves a strong values component—what *should* the purposes of education be? Because service-learning encourages schools to utilize community partners to help teach students, for instance, many of its advocates quote the familiar postulate that "It takes a whole village to raise a child." Recently we heard a parent share that "I don't want the village to raise my child!" It reminded us again that education is always a value-laden enter-prise.

Parents in some parts of the country have challenged service-learning programs as "involuntary servitude" (typically when there has been an out-of-school mandatory requirement). Others recognize that service-learning is an essential element of public schooling, given the schools' historic mission of developing active and informed citizens. When schools develop their program rationales, they will need to address local community concerns and beliefs. Since there is always value-based and political dimensions to education, this will also be true for staff development.

Issue 8: "What research is there to show the benefits of service-learning?"

One of the more challenging aspects of service-learning staff develop-ment is that its pedagogy and base of research is just emerging. As a field, service-learning stands where cooperative learning was an educational gener-ation ago when researchers such as Johnson and Johnson (1975), Elizabeth Cohen (1986), and Robert Slaven (1987) started to document how we could effectively organize groups for learning. Since staff development is increasingly relying on research-based models of instruction, service-learning will need to create documented evidence of its effectiveness. (See chapter 2 for a brief review of the research on K–12 service-learning programs.)

Issue 9: "What's the role of the community in our staff development efforts?"

In the early stages of the service-learning movement, we had a picture of thousands of schoolchildren preparing for community-based experiences without anyone telling the community that they were coming. While there were huge national efforts to educate teachers, there were very few inviting the participation of community-based organizations (CBOs) to become equal, informed, willing, and effective partners. Staff development must respond to the twin issues of: (1) How will we address teachers' previous lack of training or experience in community collaborations? and (2) What will be the role of community organizations in our initiatives?

We are consistently struck by the enthusiasm of teachers when they do participate in their communities. We realize how much of the vitality of community life is typically hidden from the people who live there. We have seen what is possible when teachers get involved. After one of our midwestern workshops, four middle school teachers took the initiative to invite their entire faculty to perform ongoing service work. They were surprised that almost everyone chose to participate. The school staff took over preparing and serving meals one afternoon a week at a nearby shelter, something that quickly overflowed into entire families becoming involved on the weekends. It changed not only the relationships among the faculty, but also the school's sense of identity and relationship to its community.

Issue 10: "This will never work in my school because . . ."

Search Institute conducted a follow-up survey and interview with ninety of our past workshop participants between twelve and eighteen months after the training. Educators were asked to rate the barriers they had experienced to implementing service-learning. On a scale from 1 (no barrier to implementation) to 5 (a major barrier), the top-rated six items (listed in rank order along with their mean scores) were: lack of time in an already crowded curriculum/program (3.20); lack of time, personally, to promote service-learning in my organization (2.91); lack of funding (2.73); problems integrating service-learning into curriculum/programming (2.50); bureaucracy/"red tape" within organization (2.24); and lack of support from teachers/staff (2.21).

This list reinforces the concept that staff development needs to concern itself not only with teacher skills, but with the conditions in which those skills will be applied. Time emerged as a central factor. When we showed these results to our friend and staff developer Candace Simpson, she commented that: "An issue I have been preoccupied with is trying to get people to stop talking about a lack of time and start talking about the setting of priorities." Nobody can make more hours in a day, but we can question often unexamined, previously set priorities that stand in our way.

RECOMMENDATIONS FOR STAFF DEVELOPERS IN SERVICE-LEARNING PROGRAMS

What do we see as the most important steps for future service-learning staff development efforts? Here is our list:

1. *Focus staff-development decisions on improving student learning.* Staff development is becoming increasingly results-driven. It is evaluated not by how participants rate a workshop, but on whether and how well teachers utilize an instructionally effective method in their classroom. What ultimately counts is the positive impact on student learning. A persistent focus on student learning will give our efforts a prism through which to pass all of our decisions and through which to evaluate our success.
2. *View teacher adoption as a developmental process.* Since service-learning represents the integration of a good number of complex skills, teacher adoption needs to be viewed as a developmental process. Many teachers' initial efforts will be more honestly labeled as community service rather than service-learning. We have come to believe that this may be a necessary stage of development. The logistics of setting up a community-based project, transporting students, and completing some meaningful service is itself a significant accomplishment. After teachers accomplish this, they will be more ready to refine integrating service within the curriculum and practicing the skills for reflection. We will need to set realistic expectations and support structures for teacher change as a developmental process.
3. *Convert "in-service" activities into staff development programs.* There is a growing emphasis in the service-learning field on deepening practice. This is the right direction. We need to create structures for ongoing support and reflective dialogue for teachers. One of the model national initiatives for this is the National Service-Learning Cooperative's Peer Consultant Network, funded by the W. K. Kellogg Foundation, which involves the development of a cadre of teacher and youth mentors to work with individual schools for up to three years. On the state level, Maryland, Washington, and the Pennsylvania have already cultivated their own highly successful network of fellows or peer advisers. The Kellogg National Service-Learning

Initiative is also noteworthy because it supports whole school collaborative efforts to implement service into the curriculum.

4. *Involve youth in staff-development activities.* If service-learning is to walk its talk—that youth are resources, it will need to involve youth as staff developers themselves. At the 1995 NYLC national conference, for instance, youth with Down's syndrome who had been volunteering with senior citizens led adult teachers in a full day intergenerational project and then conducted their own reflection session. Likewise, Minneapolis's Webster Open School is currently training its young students to help train teachers from other schools. This element has also been part of the design for the national Peer Consultant Initiative, which provides schools with both an adult *and* a youth mentor for three years of program support.

5. *Study and document your practice and successes.* Service-learning needs to create a base of research for its practice similar to what has occurred for cooperative learning. Therefore staff development efforts should be partially research-driven through action research by teachers and through the assistance of local universities. Fortunately, there is a great deal of current research activity by the National Service-Learning Cooperative, the Generator Schools, foundations, and other groups that should rapidly increase our understanding of the educational benefits and the conditions under which these occur.

6. *Connect service-learning to other school reform initiatives.* Service-learning has strong potential links with many existing reform efforts, including school-to-work transition, citizenship education, character education, critical thinking, authentic instruction, problem-based learning, and performance-based assessment. Unfortunately, too many school districts still approach change initiatives in a piecemeal manner, further confusing teachers and dissipating energy.

Before beginning any staff development activity, we need to investigate each school or state's local needs, teacher concerns, previous staff development efforts, and current mission. Service-learning can then be presented in terms of how it fits with and builds on preexisting district momentum. When working with Kentucky educators, for instance, we worked hard to connect everything in our workshops to the various components of KERA (the Kentucky Education Reform Act). We have been able to make these connections because for the past five years we have received funding through Compass Institute to deepen our understanding of the whole stream of school-improvement initiatives.

7. *Connect service-learning to each school's unique culture and values.* School reform advocates increasingly point out that we already have effective educational models and that we must now emphasize replication or "scaling up." Building a good school, however, will never be like purchasing a fran-

chise from McDonald's. The architects of good schools are the teachers and parents and children who inhabit them, and the plans will need to stay flexible and open to local change throughout the building process. For this reason, we think that the three most important rules for staff development are: (1) know your audience; (2) know your audience; and (3) know your audience! We gather background information about the unique culture, values, and issues of a school, and use these in building an agenda and setting a tone for the workshop.

8. *Address issues of teachers' workplace: build professional community.* Service-learning staff development efforts are likely to meet only limited success unless they simultaneously try to foster increased professional community. We have both the time and a wonderful forum within which teachers can experience the kinds of professional relationships that we want to see replicated within their building. We have always consciously built our agendas not only around service-learning content, but around our goal of positively affecting the relationships of those who attend. This includes both opportunities for serious dialogue and for having fun and enjoying one another.

9. *Foster greater teacher participation in and connection to community life.* It makes great sense to us that school policies in the not too distant past required teachers to live in the districts where they taught. We must invent new ways to help teachers overcome their isolation from their students' neighborhoods. Two strategies are to include community members within our workshops *and* to perform collaborative community work ourselves. The benefits of these strategies include: (1) demonstrating the power of service-learning to teachers; (2) increasing teacher's knowledge of the neighborhoods where their school children grow up; (3) offering cross-training with community-based organizations who work with the same youth in afterschool hours; (4) increasing knowledge about community resources and networking; and (5) more fully integrating teachers into community membership (Toole, Toole, Gomez, and Allam, 1992).

IN CLOSING

Many aspects of conducting staff development activities nationally over the past four years have been fatiguing and not that pleasant. Going to the airport is not the joy it once was. What has been redeeming is the opportunity to work directly with teachers and other youth workers. If we started such work because we believed that service-learning could improve classroom practice, we have continued because of the intelligence, commitment, creativity, and basic goodness that we consistently observe from teachers, *and*, the wonderful ways that they transform the workshop content into programs that fit their schools and youth.

As we are finishing writing this chapter, we heard from a Minneapolis teacher that her primary-age students read books to blind senior citizens for four successive weeks. She shared that her poorest readers practiced their stories "about forty times," repeatedly asking their classmates to listen to them rehearse. One boy who was still a prereader memorized his stories. At the convalescent home, her sometimes difficult students were model citizens. As she talked, we felt a sense of joy about her students' connection both to the real world of senior citizens and to the printed word. Such stories reinforce our desire to both deliver and advocate for the quality staff-development programs that will be required for service-learning to become an accepted and effective model of instruction.

Chapter 18

Community Agency Member

David Kelly-Hedrick

MY STORY

I was hired because of young people and owe my livelihood to their wanting to give of themselves in the community. Youth clamored for more volunteer and service opportunities, ways to get involved and make some positive changes. Fortunately, the city and school district of Bellevue, Washington, had a program to facilitate this want. Bellevue Youth Link is a community agency that exists to guide young people's ideas and initiatives into successful realities. Examples include its Safe Rides home program, Get Real television show, and a skateboard park. A Youth Link task force of youth and adults selected the Youth Volunteer Corps (YVC) program, for which I am currently the director, as an answer to the wish for more youth involvement in the community.

The mission of the Youth Volunteer Corps (YVC) is to increase service opportunities for groups of middle and high school youth. We organize and lead service projects on weekends, after school, and in the evenings. Our major effort is an intensive summer component where youth volunteer on a two- or four-week project based at a local agency. The YVC program was conceived of and started by David Battey in Kansas City in 1986. As a model program, he received a Kellogg Foundation grant to assist in replicating it in other sites. Currently there are YVC programs in over forty cities in the United States and Canada. There is a set of national program standards and operating policies, yet each local YVC has a wide range of flexibility in how it sets up operations. Here in King County, Washington, the YVC is sponsored by seven local nonprofit agencies and organizations. The lead and fiscal agent is the Puget Sound Council of Camp Fire; the others include the Seattle Youth Involvement Network, Bellevue Youth Link, the Bellevue Public School District, the Seattle Public School District, United Way of King County, and the Bellevue Boys and Girls Club.

Each sponsor provides us with some type of financial support or in-kind resources. For example, the school district gives us contacts and access to the schools, while the staff at the Eastside United Way office provides training in volunteer management and assistance with identifying project sites. We generate financial support from a variety of sources including: local foundations and corporations, community grants from United Way, Youth Link, local service clubs, and most recently, through the Corporation for National and Community Service.

The collaboration is not without its challenges. With smaller stakes in the program, a few of the sponsoring agencies have played minimal roles in the program, and it is not always easy to balance the needs and views of all the sponsoring agencies. We have to be careful applying for local funds, especially when the sponsoring agencies are in competition with each other. Overall, however, our collaboration has worked well and the sponsors share a good deal of success for the program.

In the summer, our projects run Monday through Friday, four to eight hours a day, and are conducted by teams of eight to ten youth volunteers led by a college-aged trained Team Leader. Our teams have cleared trails, served the homeless, tutored refugees, worked in the library stacks, assisted at summer camps, aided youth with disabilities, conducted recycling outreach, AIDS education, and a host of other projects. Last summer 268 youth volunteers served on 31 projects and contributed over 10,000 hours of service to the community. This summer those numbers will double.

Although our program has no formal academic goals, we seek to infuse learning into the service projects. The Youth Volunteer Corps includes reflection as a critical and required component on all service experiences. Taking some time to process the experience, to consider the ramifications to self, to clients, to community, and to the world-at-large not only enriches the service but fosters learning and connectedness. Because we draw together a diverse group of youth, from different schools and grades and backgrounds, we find icebreakers and team-building activities to be valuable in forming cohesive groups. The summer teams continue to share initiative and trust games throughout the course of their project as we seek to build on the unity and power of the group's service work.

Journals and group meetings are two standard means for reflection, but YVC projects also include other creative ways of involving students in reflective learning, such as writing news releases and group letters, performing skits for other teams, creating scrapbooks, engaging in wind-down conversations in the van on the way home, participating in one-on-one check-ins between team leaders and youth volunteers, and making presentations to agency staff, boards of directors, Kiwanis clubs, and other community groups.

We encourage and work with local agencies to be partners in this reflection process—to help us guide volunteers through the "What?," "So what?," and "Now what?" of a project. Agency members provide the orientation and training for our groups, and we seek to collaboratively design projects which allow room for youth to make significant choices and decisions as they serve. Choices may be as simple as which cleaning tasks to complete at a shelter or as complicated as the plans for researching and writing a resource guide.

The Education Director at the Sharehouse, an organization that serves agencies with homeless clients, organized an effective summer project, calling it "Homelessness and Youth." The two week project commenced on a Monday night with a pizza dinner shared between the team of youth volunteers and a selected group of teens who have been homeless and are willing to share their stories with others. The project had two objectives: (1) to expose youth volunteers to the many facets of the homelessness problem; and (2) to help local agencies serving homeless individuals doing work such as serving meals and repairing or cleaning shelters. It is a valuable meeting which connects the issue of homelessness to the people living the reality of street life. The team of volunteers then hears about the range of service activities they can perform from the Education Director, and they choose and plan their course of action.

During the school year, the YVC serves as a resource for teachers doing service-learning projects. Our AmeriCorps staff members and I act as intermediaries with local agencies, make contacts and logistical arrangements, conduct some of that midday phone calling that can be impossible during a teacher's schedule, and assist with challenges such as transportation. For instance, Camp Fire and the Boys and Girls Club allow their fifteen-passenger vans to be used for school service projects. We will also do in-service trainings or specialized work with a team of teachers, administrators, and parents.

While our primary focus is coordinating YVC projects, we recognize the need for a local clearinghouse and we have tried to fill in as best as possible. Agencies and organizations now regularly contact us with project ideas, and knowing many of the schools and teachers involved in service-learning, we can make the valuable connections between interested people that can be a critical step in seeing a promising idea come to fruition. Unfortunately, we are not organized adequately to handle all the requests either from agencies wanting youth volunteers for projects or from teachers and classes needing support.

Three years ago we received a Targeted Support Grant from United Way of King County for the Katahdin Project. Katahdin is an Ojibwa word that can be loosely translated to mean, "the act of revealing that which has been held hidden." Our Katahdin Project is a concerted effort to address the needs and interests of at-risk students at Odle Middle School. The grant covers support for a part-time mental health therapist, curriculum resources, and the YVC to provide service-learning projects. Our piece of the project has included planning weekly projects with a class of twelve students. As a community agency we have worked through a number of challenges such as transportation and planning logistics as well as helping agencies interested in working with at-risk youth work through their resistance and fear. Once out on projects, the majority of these middle school youth have excelled at the opportunities for giving and serving. They have packed lunches for the homeless, cut invasive blackberry bushes in the park, and are currently working to build a challenge course at their school. There are many more at-risk young people out there who could benefit greatly from the experience of service, and we would like to improve our work of recruiting and retaining such volunteers.

Most recently, we received eight AmeriCorps positions through a grant from the Corporation for National and Community Service to the Youth Volunteer Corps of America. We placed five of these people in local middle and high schools as full-time service coordinators. They serve as wonderful instigators, organizers, and leaders of service projects with the students. With training and after a certain level of confidence has developed, they are also inspiring and guiding more teachers into the realm of service-learning.

These staff additions have significantly increased our capacity to offer volunteer opportunities to young people. Plain and simple, they are doing amazing things. AmeriCorps participant Mark Thomason regularly visits the "crash," or smokers area just off the high school campus, and there he has recruited volunteers to help deliver meals to homebound AIDS patients through the Chicken Soup Brigade. Julia Sanders hosts a group of students from Washington Middle School every Monday afternoon to plan crime prevention projects in their neighborhood. Teresa Nero recruited middle school volunteers to "Walk the Plank," or carry six-foot planks two miles up a trail on Mount Si for an elevated boardwalk over a soggy section of land.

AmeriCorps has allowed our program to grow from serving just the city of Bellevue to reaching out to youth in Seattle and greater King County. Through this growth, the YVC has sought to stay true to the ideal of Youth Link with youth involvement at all steps of the program. Our Advisory Council is composed of half youth and half adults; youth serve on all the committees. A few months ago I had the great privilege of hiring as an AmeriCorps member one of the same youth who was on the original Youth Link task force and panel. To me, the way such things come full circle is a reminder of the many interconnected lessons which, during the course of service and reflection, rise to the surface for both our benefit and our wonder.

ISSUES FOR COMMUNITY AGENCY MEMBERS
WORKING WITH SERVICE-LEARNING PROGRAMS

At the Youth Volunteer Corps, we straddle the fence between being a community agency and working with youth groups and schools to set up service projects with other community agencies. We are still learning many of the issues and challenges that these agencies encounter through such partnerships and seeking to develop effective strategies for making collaboration successful.

Agency staff often feel that teachers and school officials do not take the time or effort to fully understand the mission and work of the nonprofit agency. Problems arise when assumptions are made as to what an agency does and/or how a group of youth volunteers can work effectively at that agency. Part of this difficulty may lie in what one researcher has called the "culture clash" between the education and nonprofit worlds. In a recent paper entitled "Community Agency and School Collaboration: Going in with Your Eyes Open," Mark Batenburg (1995) interviewed a number of agency representatives to highlight their common problems and recommendations in working with school partners. This "culture clash" exists because schools and agencies tend to be set up under different philosophies and working structures. Batenburg noted that a school is often organized as a rigid and "highly bureaucratized system," whereas community agencies, originating through grassroots or community efforts, are more democratic organizations. "Things tend to be done by consensus rather than by fiat from above. . . . Action is taken only after *lots* of talking with everyone imaginable. Agencies live to find solutions to problems, so they tend to be highly flexible and creative. They tend to say 'Yes' first and then figure out how later. Since most agencies are understaffed and underfunded, there is not enough fat to produce a bureaucracy" (Battenburg, 1995, p. 3).

In addition, every agency has a different working environment where volunteers are viewed, and valued, in a manner that may be radically different from another agency. The general policy toward volunteers is often set by the Board of Directors and/or the executive director in a formal or informal manner, and it falls on the shoulders of the volunteer coordinator to implement strategies under this policy. An infusion of new youth volunteers could disrupt the working environment, and tension might arise between staff, board of directors, clients, and other volunteers. Locally, a science-center volunteer coordinator noticed growing animosity between long-time senior volunteers and a batch of youth volunteers she was recruiting from the high schools. It could have gotten out of hand if she had not pulled together both groups for a pizza party and role-playing session where they acted out scenarios of both tension and resolution.

A similar challenge faced a volunteer coordinator of a domestic violence shelter and myself when we wanted to do a project together. The shelter needed storage shelving for their basement, and I knew of some classes that would be interested in building them. The problem was that the location of the shelter was kept confidential for the safety of the clients. Instead of abandoning the project, we explored how the shelves could be built at school and then transferred by staff and a small number of students who would clear the confidentiality process to the shelter. Issues of confidentiality such as this are often of concern to agency staff members in working with youth volunteers. What if one of the students is a current or former client of the agency? What if a student recognizes the name of a family from their school on a chart or document they weren't supposed to see? Justifiably, agency staff become worried when school staff are not sensitive or understanding of this issue.

Probably the most common issue that frustrates agency personnel (and many teachers) is that of logistics and the often inflexible nature of a school schedule. A teacher will meet with the volunteer coordinator and both get excited over project possibilities only to find a roadblock when it is realized that students can only visit at a certain time during the day and/or for too short a duration to accomplish much of anything. Our Katahdin class, for example, was severely limited because we only had one to two hours very early on Thursday mornings. Another frustrating occurrence is the class that becomes inconsistent with its regularly scheduled visits to an agency.

Finally, I have noticed a fundamental issue creeping up more and more over the past years in agency-school relations. Agency staff sometimes wonder if the students are really "volunteering" of their own free will. Do students really want to be at the agency? Is the issue that the agency works on of real concern to these students, and have they done any background research or discussing? Is it the students' project or the teacher's project or simply one being chosen because of easier logistics? A local food bank now refuses to work with school classes because its volunteer coordinator is so worried that a handful of unruly students will be too difficult to handle. Her first question to a teacher who calls is "How are you going to deal with the disruptive students?" She assumes there will be problems. Also related to this issue is the growing number of schools and districts that are imposing a community service hour requirement for their students but *without* providing any staff or guided support to make it happen successfully. Some volunteer coordinators fear an onslaught of students knocking on their doors and jamming up their phone lines wanting to get this requirement completed as quickly as possible. This concern might make them even more hesitant to embark on a legitimate and well-coordinated service-learning project.

Nearly every agency I approach is willing to at least talk about the possibility of how youth volunteers could support the mission and service of their agencies, but they have real and serious concerns that need to be fully addressed before any project can get underway. Most volunteer coordinators recognize the great value that youth and school classes can bring to their agency. They want to say "yes," and they want to make it happen successfully.

RECOMMENDATIONS FOR
COMMUNITY AGENCY MEMBERS WORKING
WITH SERVICE-LEARNING PROGRAMS

1. *Help teachers and students learn about and understand the nonprofit world.*
   Encourage them to make learning about nonprofit culture part of the curriculum before embarking on the project. How do nonprofit agencies origi-
   nate and what is their history? How does the nonprofit world operate differently from schools or businesses? How does the particular agency fit into the
   larger fabric of the community? Community mapping exercises, class presentations, and other hands-on research can assist students with this discovery.

2. *Share the mission and services of your agency.* Batenburg (1995) cites the
   three primary purposes of a community agency as: (1) direct provision of
   service to their clients; (2) education and outreach in their field of expertise;
   and (3) generating friends and resources. Involve educators in brainstorming
   with agency staff how young people can help them meet their mission and
   serve these purposes. Educators need to be responsive to the needs of the
   agency and its clients. If issues of confidentiality make direct provision of
   service impossible for youth volunteers, be willing to explore ways to have
   youth contribute to education and outreach.

3. *Communicate up-front about logistical challenges and be ready to compromise.* Open communication will be the best solution to any problem. Be
   willing and flexible to work under changing conditions and respond to the
   changing needs of the school. Help educators remember that the agency has
   to respond as best it can to the needs and interest of the clients. Political pressures, funding time lines, special events, and other activities going on with
   the agency may provoke tension and hesitancy on an agency's part. Try to
   respect and be aware of such pressures within your own agency and not
   take it personally if an agency staff member is not immediately gung-ho
   for a partnership.

4. *Make sure students really support the project.* How have the students bought
   into the project? Do they feel a sense of ownership? Most agencies are willing to do class presentations, share literature, or accept one or two students on
   a research visit to the agency all to foster class support for the project. Help
   educators take time to prepare and allow interest in the project to develop in
   the minds of students. For more independent projects, provide guidance and
   support for school staff and students. Offer to help with building in reflection
   and evaluation components for effective program improvement.

5. *Know your agency's and the school's resources and limitations ahead of
   time.* Ask school program leaders up front what resources they have to support the project. What is the school policy regarding field trips and volun-

teering? What kind of insurance does the school provide? What about transportation? Is their any kind of budget for the project? How long before those permission slips can realistically be returned? An agency staff member will be much happier working with a school program if questions such as these can be answered in the first meeting. Information about available resources in both the community agency and the school can be critical in establishing the boundaries and structure of the project to be undertaken.

IN CLOSING

Community agency members can be valuable collaborators in school-based service-learning programs. Both community agencies and school personnel have unique areas of expertise to offer the collaboration. In working together, community agency members can provide valuable opportunities for youth civic service. At the same time, the schools can assist agencies in meeting the needs of their clients and the community. If they listen to each other and learn about the needs and values of each organization, they can develop projects that meet important community needs and offer learning potential for students.

Chapter 19

Parent

John G. Shepard

MY STORY

This chapter describes my experiences helping to develop service-learning programs at St. Anthony Park Elementary School. Before I begin my story, however, I must admit that the chapter omits something important. It makes insufficient mention of the dedication and hard work put forth by the teachers and staff at the school throughout this endeavor. Despite the fact they enthusiastically bore the lion's share of the work required to infuse service-learning into the school's curriculum and culture, these key players have largely been left out of this story because the requirement of this chapter called for a focus on my role as a parent advocate. This chapter, then, is dedicated to the excellent teachers and staff at St. Anthony Park School.

It was late September, 1991, when I picked up the phone to call Dr. Hope Lee, the principal of my daughter's public elementary school. Just a few weeks had passed since Anna, my eldest child, had begun morning kindergarten. I was eager to alert her principal to a tremendous opportunity I had just learned of. Our school had a chance to apply for a three-year grant from the National Youth Leadership Council. If we were funded, St. Anthony Park Elementary would receive eleven thousand dollars, training, and technical assistance to support it in becoming one of the first nationally recognized model schools for service-learning—a Generator School.

In retrospect, I suppose the fact that I hadn't actually met Dr. Lee yet—that I knew nothing of her priorities, commitments, concerns, and interests—was not the most auspicious way to begin the kind of venture I had in mind. But I was enthusiastic. In my mind, service-learning held such obvious promise, embraced such core American values—service to others, democracy in action, improving community life while enhancing education—that I couldn't imagine why someone—*anyone*—wouldn't be as captivated by the idea as I was.

I introduced myself to Dr. Lee, briefly explained my mission, and tried to describe service-learning and its numerous redemptive qualities in a couple of breathless sentences. Just as succinctly she said that she and her staff had established their curriculum and training priorities for the year. She suggested that I see if one of St. Paul's magnet schools—elementary schools dedicated to special curricular themes or educational methodologies—might be interested in my idea. Almost before it had begun, it seemed, the conversation was over.

My subsequent experiences with Dr. Lee have only suggested that she is a competent, committed principal. Who knows what kind of crazy day she might have been having when she picked up her phone to find a zealot on the other end proposing that her students be empowered to transform the school, enhance the community, and become models for the rest of humanity. I could only conclude that I had a thing or two to learn about generating the kind of support I needed to realize my intentions.

By the time Anna entered first grade Dr. Lee had moved on; St. Anthony Park had a new principal, Tom Foster, and I had reconsidered my strategy. Midway through the year I was having a conversation with Lisa Griffin, the school's community education representative and volunteer coordinator. I mentioned that I had worked at the National Youth Leadership Council and had some experience developing and leading service-learning programs.

It turned out that service-learning was beginning to emerge as a topic of note in community education and that it had caught Lisa's attention. I tentatively asked if she thought any of the teachers at St. Anthony Park might be interested if I were to lead an interdisciplinary service-learning project on stream ecology and stewardship. She wanted to hear more. Encouraged, I explained that I was in the process of writing a book and was going to develop a middle-school curriculum on the subject. I said I would welcome the chance to work with a group of older elementary students to try out some of my ideas. She thought the project might fit in the fourth-grade curriculum and said she would see if the teachers were interested in offering it as one of the school's many enrichment programs.

The fourth-grade team, whom I met a couple of weeks later, were receptive to the idea. We decided to assemble our "Stream Team" from all three of their classes and decided that I would run the project over a six-week period from early May through the end of school in June. Our plans included a one-session introduction to the project, in which I would give a presentation to all three classes on the significance of rivers during the fur-trade era in Minnesota (a topic of interest to me that blended with the fourth-grade local history unit). The next week I would meet with my group of ten students at school for fifty minutes to orient them to stream ecology and plan for the three-hour field investigations of Rice Creek scheduled for each of the following two weeks. Week five was to be dedicated to reviewing our field data, reflecting on our experiences at Rice Creek, and preparing presentations that the students would give to their classmates for our final meeting—a fourth-grade assembly the last week of school.

My previous experience directing an environmental education center and leading service-learning programs at the National Youth Leadership Council equipped me to design the project, figure out logistics and teaching supplies, and lead most of the sessions. But I had no training in aquatic biology and knew that the heart of the field experience—collecting and identifying aquatic insects—would be weak if I tried to lead these sessions alone. Determined to find some qualified help, I made a few calls to several University of Minnesota environmental science departments until I connected with an aquatic biologist who was happy to join us on our first visit to Rice Creek at no charge. Another parent and one of the fourth-grade teachers offered to provide additional supervision for our outings.

During the two months I had to prepare for the project I learned that a middle school near the banks of Rice Creek was engaged in a similar project to mine. One afternoon I visited with the three teachers at Fridley Middle School who were in the process of planning several outings on the creek with their students. The curriculum ideas and resources they shared proved helpful. These included some excellent watershed maps available free of charge from an agency I'd never heard of called the Rice Creek Watershed District.

Maps in hand, I made a scouting trip to locate two good sites for our field experiences. These were to involve collecting water samples and assessing the diversity of aquatic insects found in them as indicators of water quality. I needed to find easily accessible places along the creek that would be safe for wading—preferably in different enough areas so that land use activities might result in significantly varied results. I found a site near the headwaters where the creek drained from a large lake. The other site, a city park at the confluence of Rice Creek and the Mississippi River, happened to include a historic building that had served as a tavern to soldiers and fur traders in the mid-1800s.

From start to finish, the Stream Team approached their work with ample enthusiasm. It was a diverse group of students—some excelled academically, some didn't; the school's primary ethnic groups were well represented; and there were equal numbers of boys and girls. We had lots of fun. And, as their final presentations to their classmates revealed, we all learned valuable lessons: that people's day-to-day activities can have profound environmental impacts, that the web of life includes some wonderfully bizarre creatures beneath the placid waters of a stream, that learning can be an adventure, that each of us has something valuable to give.

The fourth-grade teachers, Principal Tom Foster (who attended our final assembly), and Lisa Griffin liked what they saw. In fact, they were enough impressed by the work of the Stream Team that when I mentioned that the Generator School project was still accepting applications they wanted to learn more. Things moved quickly after that. Service-learning struck a strong chord with Tom Foster's personal values. Though he expressed some initial concern that the faculty might be leery of what could be perceived as yet another curriculum add-on, as he learned more he concluded that service-learning and the Generator School program were a good fit for St. Anthony Park.

The fourth-grade team formed a key nucleus of support for the project among the staff, with teacher Fran Fuerstneau offering to serve as the project leader. I gave a presentation about service-learning and the Generator School Project to the school's active parent teacher organization, which was presided over by none other than Lisa Griffin. With the PTO's blessing and a green light from Tom Foster; Lisa, Fran, a few other teachers and I set about planning how we would develop our participation in the Generator School Project.

I offered to draft the proposal, figuring that my previous experience authoring such documents and working at NYLC would help our chances of winning the grant. Through the give-and-take of the writing and review process we began to shape a plan that focused initially on providing service-learning training experiences for the staff. I offered to lead for a group of teachers a half-day hands-on orientation to the Stream Team project that I had conducted with the fourth grade students. After a brief introduction to the project in the classroom, we were to spend the morning wading about Rice Creek in search of hellgrammites, caddis fly larvae, and others of their kind.

Once a sufficient number of teachers had been oriented to service-learning, we hoped to launch one or two schoolwide projects that would be visible within and outside the school community. The third year of the project required that we share our experiences with other schools.

My daughter Anna, now a fourth grader, came home from school the other day beaming with pride at having been nominated by her classmates as one of the school's peer mediators for the 1995–1996 school year. Next week Anna and about fifty other fourth-, fifth-, and sixth-graders will receive two days of communication skills training to prepare them for helping younger students resolve playground conflicts. In this, our third year as a Generator School, the peer mediation program stands out as one of several milestones in our growth as a school community in which service and learning are both recognized as core elements of our mission.

The peer mediation project emerged in part from a districtwide commitment to reduce school violence and teach peaceful conflict resolution. It has found fertile soil at St. Anthony Park. Our service-learning perspective supported the staff in using conflict resolution training to empower students to become servant-leaders among their peers. Tom Foster reports that since peer mediators started patrolling the playground a year ago, disruptive conflicts at recess have been reduced from a daily problem to a rare occurrence.

St. Anthony Park is now a Peace Site, too. This project was started last year by a group of teachers who were among the first to attend National Youth Leadership Council training sessions in service-learning. They obtained a grant to develop a peace forest that now crowns what was a play-worn hilltop in front of the school. Students helped plan the forest and the entire student body spent a glorious day last spring preparing the soil, planting trees and shrubs, and spreading mulch.

To augment this service with learning, teams of parent volunteers spent the day conducting hands-on environmental education activities with students waiting their turns to work with shovels and spades. I volunteered to design these activities and orient the other parent volunteers. The activities helped the students understand the ecological importance of the trees and shrubs they were planting.

Other signs of being a Generator School are less obvious, but just as significant. Two days of in-service training concerning service-learning for the entire staff and additional intensive training experiences for more than a half-dozen teachers have resulted in the birth of several smaller initiatives. Classes have expanded their occasional visits to a nearby nursing home to include regular contact and cross-age activities that are integrated into the curriculum. Peer tutoring between grade levels in reading has been expanded and tutoring has evolved as a teaching strategy in the new computer lab. Also, a partnership is being established with a Twin Cities suburban school that has also developed a peace forest so that students and teachers from both schools can share and learn from their experiences.

With some regret, I've not had the opportunity to be as intimately involved with these recent developments. The year after we became a Generator School I was elected to succeed Lisa Griffin as president of the St. Anthony Park School Association. The responsibilities of that office have kept me busy—but not enough to obscure my joy at seeing the seeds of service-learning grow. Now that the staff have taken hold of the notion of service-learning and are developing their own projects, I've been able to help keep the concept of service-learning alive among parents and in the community at large.

The school has an active enrichment program that brings parents and other adults into the classroom to augment the standard curriculum. I've begun exploring with the school's enrichment coordinator, who has received training in service-learning, how to infuse service elements into enrichment activities that have traditionally had an academic-only focus. She would like to introduce two new service-learning projects. One would involve students writing and performing a play concerning homelessness—a project that was initiated by a student's grandmother who works in a shelter for battered women. The second project would have a winter ecology or environmental education focus.

In searching for qualified adult leaders for these projects I got on the phone once again. After only a few calls, I found a receptive response from nearby Hamline University. The head of the theater department and the director of the college's environmental education training program both thought students in their programs would be interested in leading these activities as independent study projects.

ISSUES FOR PARENTS WORKING ON SERVICE-LEARNING PROJECTS

For community-based service-learning programs to succeed, strong bridges must be built between the school and the community. Parents, as experienced, well-connected community members, can provide invaluable assistance with this process. They can offer adult leadership and logistical assistance as teachers plan service-learning activities in the community or at school. Parents also can be effective advocates and supporters for service-learning by working with teachers, school administrators, and school districts through parent-teacher organizations. This part of the chapter will explore these three areas of parental participation.

Parents as Community Resources

Browse through a contemporary social studies textbook and you'll see distillations of the social institutions and issues many parents work with every day. In science classes students replicate research methods and explore the kinds of questions addressed by adult scientists.

In any school there are parents with enough diverse life skills, networks of contacts, and work experiences that if teachers could tap their talents and connections for service-learning projects the education of every student would be profoundly enhanced. Perhaps the only obstacles to making the most of such opportunities is that teachers are unlikely to know what resources await them and parents don't know they have a role to play.

Parents can start by assessing themselves as service-learning resources. Then they can discuss with teachers how these resources might apply to service-learning projects under consideration. Parents can consider the following questions to begin the assessment process:

• What social, environmental, economic, and community issues are you concerned about in your work and personal life? (If service-learning projects are under way in your school, also consider the issues addressed by these projects.) What resources would young people need to be empowered to address these issues? How might you help provide these resources to students in your school?

- To answer the previous question, parents can list organizations they belong to that address the issues identified above. Consider how students could participate in the work these groups do. If young people aren't currently involved, look for areas where they might be able to contribute.
- Parents can list the people they know who share an interest in these issues. Consider how these contacts and the organizations they work with might be supported by students providing assistance through service-learning projects.
- If the places parents work or community organizations (nonprofit, fraternal, or neighborhood organizations) they belong to address issues identified above, parents can explore with their colleagues and supervisors how students could become involved. Look for areas where current resources are insufficient to complete needed work or where student participation could free staff to address other priority concerns.
- Parents can identify skills, interests, and hobbies that could be useful for students in service-learning projects (e.g., communications skills, artistic abilities, athletic skills).

Providing Support to Teachers

Teachers who decide to incorporate service-learning activities in their classes may need support from sources they've never considered before. Teachers must find time and resources to plan service-learning activities that don't easily fit in the schedule and are above and beyond traditional job descriptions. While it's important for parents to remember that teachers are rightfully in charge of educating their students, parents may well be able to provide valuable assistance.

- Parents can let teachers know they're available and interested in helping with service-learning projects. As parents learn about plans they should listen for areas where teachers may benefit from help. Sometimes teachers may not be aware that they could be assisted with a particular task and they may not know of parents' skills. At the same time, it's important to allow teachers plenty of room to decline help in areas they'd rather manage themselves.
- Parents can help with logistical arrangements during the planning phase of the project. This could entail anything from preparing information forms to be sent home to all students to soliciting adult volunteers or older students to serve as leaders on outings. Teachers may also need help arranging for transportation and obtaining special supplies.
- Parents can serve as adult leaders on service-learning activities in the community or in school. This might include driving students to service sites.

Teachers and students may appreciate having concerned adults present in ratios that allow for closer contact than is usually the case.
• Parents can provide assistance documenting service-learning activities through photography, videography, or audio recording. Such records can be useful for students during reflection periods and for sharing service-learning projects with larger audiences—other students and classes at school, parents, and the media.

Parents as Service-Learning Advocates

Often, interest in service-learning begins with a spark generated by one or two interested teachers or by a principal. For the spark to grow, schools must make a significant commitment of time and resources. If teachers are unable to spread their enthusiasm to their colleagues or if administrators can't excite their staff, the spark may sputter out.

Parents, working in partnership with interested faculty and administrators, can be powerful advocates in fanning the flame. The structure provided by parent-teacher organizations (PTOs) gives parents a powerful, united voice in support of service-learning. Following are suggestions of how interested parents can advocate for service-learning within and outside of PTOs.

• If there is no movement to develop service-learning programs, parents can propose a special PTO presentation by teachers from other schools leading successful service-learning programs or from professionals in the field. They can invite the principal and key faculty to the meeting.
• If faculty or the principal have initiated a service-learning project, parents can arrange for those teachers to share their experiences with the PTO.
• Parents can organize a service-learning PTO committee. This group can meet with faculty and administrators to participate in program planning, offer logistical assistance to teachers, and help teachers make connections with community organizations. This committee can also help raise funds for service-learning programs.
• Parents should develop good working relationships with principals and teachers interested in service-learning. Parents should learn about their interests and priorities and explore ways to help develop service-learning programs that build on existing commitments and school strengths.

RECOMMENDATIONS FOR PARENTS WORKING ON SERVICE-LEARNING PROJECTS

Due to the fact that service-learning often engages students directly in community life, there are ample opportunity for parents to participate. As they do so, parents may want to keep the following recommendations in mind.

1. *Build strong partnerships with teachers and administrators.* Most teachers and principals welcome support offered by perceived allies. Remember that service-learning can be demanding for school staff and will be embraced more readily if sympathetic support is offered from resources in the community.
2. *Be persistent.* While service-learning can readily complement many educational initiatives and directives (e.g., multiculturalism, outcome based education), instituting change in institutions takes time. Work to build and expand networks of support on the faculty and among parents.
3. *Set realistic goals.* A service-learning initiative will grow in a school by building a strong track record. It's better to begin small and accumulate a series of demonstrable successes than to tackle an overly ambitious project that flounders at the start.
4. *Participate in service-learning training.* Training opportunities in service-learning for faculty can often be attended by parents as well. This is a good way to build relationships with faculty members, deepen your understanding of service-learning, and broaden the kind of assistance you can offer.

IN CLOSING

Parents can be valuable partners in school-based service-learning programs at all levels. The skills, expertise, community connections, and time that parents can devote to service-learning activities will benefit both busy teachers and their students. By offering adult leadership, logistical assistance, and support for service-learning; parents can be key players in working with school personnel to create a culture of service in the school community.

Chapter 20

Statewide Service-Learning Coordinator

Cynthia Parsons

MY STORY

I was a classroom teacher for some fourteen years, the education editor of *The Christian Science Monitor* for another fourteen years, a syndicated columnist for three years, and continue to do some guest lecturing in education at colleges and universities. Today I run a statewide initiative encouraging all Vermont schools to engage all students in service-learning. In many ways, the teaching and writing in those first thirty-plus years were preparation for SerVermont. Begun in 1986, SerVermont is a nonprofit grantmaking organization whose purpose is to encourage all students in Vermont to do community service integrated with academic study.

I grew up on a farm, which means I learned early what it means to help your neighbor, and how what you do for the community is reciprocated in what your community does for you. I volunteered to work with the Red Cross during World War II, knitted mittens and caps for American soldiers, and shared what we grew in our truck garden with those who needed food. I did volunteer work as a Girl Scout and in my 4-H livestock project. Unfortunately little of what I did as a community volunteer was honored by my schools, or seen as vital practice of academic skills.

I am truly puzzled. I don't understand why service to the community isn't part and parcel of every school experience throughout the United States. Schools have two distinct tasks: first, to teach every pupil to be literate in the arts, humanities, and sciences; and second, to prepare every pupil for involvement in participatory and representative democracy. We must prepare students in the U.S. for citizenship in a democracy, which is based on the following premises: when the followers lead, the leaders will follow; the citizen is governor; the elected serve the electorate; and the community is managed by its members in cooperation not competition.

Research has shown that one of the best ways to learn to be literate is by helping another to achieve the same goal. Reading aloud to a senior citizen or a preschooler (a service to both) is a learning experience for the oral reader. One can't learn to sing without singing; to read without reading; to write without writing; or to numerate without numerating.

Given the central role of experience in learning, it is a mystery to me that every public and private school throughout the United States doesn't guarantee every pupil a service-learning opportunity right across the curriculum. A further mystery is why state authorities allow their public schools to teach autocracy instead of democracy and why they don't expect every elected official in every village, town, city, county, as well as at the state level to provide service-learning experiences for every pupil.

In 1985, I received a grant from the Edwin Gould Foundation for Children in New York to explore why the United States did not have a national service program for youth aged seventeen-plus. I concluded that public schools' exclusion of service experiences was the major reason seventeen-year-olds were not occupying their developmental thoughts with ways to serve their country and their communities. Bolstered by this realization, I began talking with then Governor Madeleine Kunin and Vermont's Commissioner of Education. When I got their endorsement, I visited every one of the sixty-seven public academic high schools in Vermont to ask why they did not have their students involved in community service. As I listened to them, I tried to think of ways to overcome their concerns and objections. Their concerns and my responses to them formed the foundation of SerVemont.

When I began SerVermont in 1986, three events signaled what was to become success in service-learning statewide. First, the governor (then Madeleine M. Kunin; now U.S. Deputy Secretary of Education) announced SerVermont in her State of the State address (and privately saw to it that no effort would be made to make student volunteering "mandatory," or to consider giving grade points to non-school-related service activities). Second, the Commissioner of Education coauthored with Governor Kunin a letter sent to every secondary school explaining that I, as the coordinator of a private grantmaking organization, would be contacting them with an offer to help them financially and with training and technical assistance to provide opportunities for students to integrate community service with the curriculum. Third, I developed a simple procedure by which school districts could apply for funds to support their service-learning activities.

These three events, described further below, were very important to SerVermont's success. Governor Kunin, the first woman and one of a handful of Democrats to be elected governor of Vermont, had made education a priority while serving as Lieutenant Governor and as a candidate for the Governorship. If I couldn't get her to welcome service-learning as a positive and important part of the life of each Vermont student, I was sure SerVermont wouldn't get very far. I could imagine the difficulty I would have with my efforts if she talked it down during speeches to teachers, school administrators, and workers in the department of education.

I talked with candidate Kunin, and after her election with Governor Kunin. I talked with her education officer and legal adviser. I talked about the need for a national service opportunity for all youth aged eighteen-plus. I talked about what a difference it would make for many students to be engaged in ser- vice-learning with college youth emphasizing over and over that learning by doing was not something that should be reserved for out-of-school experi- ences. I cited my own experiences and anecdotal evidence I found in Vermont and learned that her own children had done community service while in high school. I also emphasized how important it would be if she and the commis- sioner of education were to tell all the school authorities how much they sup- ported student community service.

All of this took longer than I thought it would. I must not have gone about my explanations in such a way as to make the governor politically com- fortable. But as we talked and as her executive aides asked strategic questions, I understood better how much she did not want to make service a mandate or, as Ernest Boyer had recommended, make it a Carnegie unit credit course. (He since has withdrawn that suggestion; believing, rather, that service should not be separate from regular academic coursework.)

Once I was assured of the governor's backing—having invited the com- missioner of education and his key staff to sit in on many of the discussions— I knew that it was then necessary to let every school principal understand these state officials' interest in service-learning. After sending out letters cosigned by the governor and commissioner, I wrote press releases for all Vermont dailies and weeklies, citing the letter and SerVermont's offering of minigrants to defray out-of-pocket expenses for student community service projects. These news items, along with the Governor's inclusion of SerVermont in her State of the State address, laid the ground work for service-learning throughout all of Vermont's schools—particularly its secondary schools.

Because most state-initiated grant programs required elaborate proposals, I was determined to make SerVermont's grant application process as simple as possible. First, I targeted a community need. Then I prepared a one-page flyer describing the need and how student community service might help to alleviate that need. I delivered as many copies as there were teachers to a set of high schools, urging whoever accepted them to duplicate and provide the flyers to as many students as possible

The first competition for SerVermont minigrants asked for suggestions of how students might help the elders in their community. The application was a brief letter explaining: (1) who the students would serve; (2) what they would do; and (3) the amount needed (up to $200) to defray out-of-pocket expenses. If the letter was written by a school official, it had to be cosigned by at least one student and a representative of the elderly population to be served. If the letter was written by a student, it had to be cosigned by a teacher and an elder.

We estimated that about 10 percent of the sixty-seven secondary schools throughout the state of Vermont had at least one service-learning type program in place in 1986, and within four years some 90 percent of the schools were involved in service-learning. One example is a program called Project Graduation. A couple of high schools were thinking of holding alcohol-and drug-free senior parties at graduation time. SerVermont offered two hundred dollar challenge grants calling on high school seniors to use the SerVermont minigrant to gain another two hundred dollars. The following year SerVermont said it would provide one hundred dollar grants to any senior class interested in a Project Graduation party to help them to get organized. By 1990, all schools held such parties, and except in very rare instances where parent groups are the main organizers, all the work is done by the students in cooperation with parents, college students, and community leaders.

As the SerVermont initiative grew, we garnered more collaborators. Project Graduation was supported by an office in the Department of Education, and we cooperated with them to get the word out about SerVermont grants. A good many Vermont colleges had organizations in place to support alcohol-free events, and we connected them up to assist the high school seniors. A graduate student taking the University of Vermont's course in service-learning chose SerVermont as the organization in which to intern. She visited selected schools, talked with students, helped design the minigrant announcements, organized regional workshops in service-learning for teachers throughout the state, and visited many of the programs to provide technical assistance. Collaboration—between state officials, public schools, community members, and students—has been, and continues to be, integral to our efforts to involve all Vermont students in service-learning.

ISSUES FOR INDIVIDUALS WORKING AT THE STATE LEVEL ON SERVICE-LEARNING PROGRAMS

My early conversations with principals of Vermont high schools not organized for student community service provided me with the following strong argument: Studying *about* democracy was school business, and there was little enough time as it was for school-based coursework, the reading of history and social studies textbooks, and preparation for standardized tests. One strong barrier to the inclusion of service in the school agenda was the fact that many a rural high school was placed physically out of reach of a local community (up on a hill or in the middle of a field), and that regional high schools drew students from several communities. But the widest gap between experiential service-learning and seat work came from the teaching staff and administrators. They had not done any service-learning while in school, nor had their undergraduate studies in teacher education included lessons in how to manage service-learning or why it was important to support both lessons in democracy as well as lessons in patience, kindness, thoughtfulness, gratitude, and so forth.

Another barrier to service-learning at the state level deals with mandates for youth service. State departments of education are in the regulatory business, and all local schools are constantly having to deal with state-level mandates that impinge on time and budget—the very backbone of public schooling. The regulations pour forth, they often become contradictory as one chief state education officer is replaced by the next, and student service often becomes a "throwaway" line in the regulatory package. Generally state-level references to student community service aren't so much service integrated with academic coursework, but more often service disconnected with school work; service, in fact, which must be done in a non-school-related environment no matter how much the service work supports the academics.

This kind of non-service-learning thinking is epitomized by the mandated seventy-five to one hundred hours of community service to be done by high school students in some of our nation's schools. It is not unheard of to require that the service be done outside a school setting (out with any peer tutoring!). Frequently, no reports of any type are provided to a classroom or subject-matter teacher. Nor is there any report submitted by the appropriate service organization (except for the number of hours) to the school authorities.

The correlation of schooling and timing has caused many a state to set minutes and hours as *standards* for learning, and this, of course, has permeated state-level thinking about student community service. Will a State Department of Education allow a high school to require that every senior do "ten" or "twelve" of "so-many" hours of community service as a graduation requirement? Yes, some will, reinforcing the notion that the quality of the service is in the hours of performance, and not in the service provided. Hence, the twelfth-grader who visits a resident of a nursing home an hour a week for ten hours is doing no more than he or she would have done as a fourth-, seventh-, or ninth-grader. If that twelfth-grader is not writing about that experience, reading about the needs of such patients, doing research on the physical and mental needs facing nursing-home supervisors, using the encounters to make oral history tapes, and so forth, then critics of community service in the schools are correct: That type of "service" is time away from academic study, and not time well spent integrating the service and the learning.

Another state-level barrier to widespread use of service-learning throughout the schools is the limited value placed on experiential learning. If school officials—as poorly trained in learning theory as graduate and undergraduate students in teacher education—truly believe that experiential learning is inferior to in-school seat work, then they will not make the necessary adjustments to a didactic syllabus to provide these experiences for all students.

In fact, what most school officials believe, and many state education department employees reinforce, is that a school system should be judged by what percent of its graduates go on to postsecondary schooling, particularly to four-year liberal-arts colleges. Until the most selective colleges began asking on their enrollment applications about the service-learning done by applicants, few high school counselors encouraged, much less suggested, that the school provide service-learning activities for the college bound.

Then, too, there is the strong emphasis at the state level for schools to score well on standardized state-level as well as national tests. Most state-level tests are based on material provided in seat-work assignments (text reading and response; workbook sheets; material provided by the publisher of the academic material of a quick-response nature), and not on exploration and problem solving. This test-score mentality resists providing any learning experiences that aren't supporting answers to types of questions that can be scored electronically.

Granted, some state departments are venturing into the world of "alternative assessment." Those states, for example that are experimenting with portfolio assessment as an alternative to number and letter grades are busy trying to make a correlation between portfolios and multiple-choice test questions; that is, can a portfolio's contents be "reduced" to a letter grade? If not, then better to keep the grading system, and have portfolios as an "extra."

Vermont is not alone in countering these service-learning challenges with specific programs. In-service teacher education programs, encouraged by the Department of Education, offer courses in service-learning that often involve some hands-on experiences. Departments of education in most states have designated someone to be the authority on service-learning; someone who helps to funnel federal funds given to the state for service-learning projects to get to interested districts. These state officials use some of the funds to provide training, technical assistance, documentation, and even evaluation.

What many school officials seem to need are specific examples of service-learning projects and programs. Vermont, at least once a year, offers a statewide conference where service-learning practitioners share experiences, often with students doing much of the presentation. In larger states, such as Massachusetts, Colorado, California, Minnesota, and Pennsylvania, regional meetings are held for similar purposes.

In addition to SerVermont, a private initiative supporting service-learning, Vermont now has a state level office dealing only with school-level service-learning; another office dealing with youth and adult service involving service-learning; and a statewide commission made up of representatives from volunteer-using organizations throughout the state. Several of the state's colleges offer courses on service-learning for undergraduates as well as graduate students and SerVermont's original booklet citing ways to do service-learning, published by Corwin Press under the title *Serving to Learn, Learning to Serve* (Parsons, 1995) is now available to a wider audience.

RECOMMENDATIONS FOR INDIVIDUALS WORKING AT THE STATE LEVEL ON SERVICE-LEARNING PROGRAMS

1. *Encourage every supervisor in every department of state government to recognize that service-learning is essential to developing wise U.S. citizens, and that they can play a part in this achievement through participation in school-level service-learning programs.* Public school students throughout the state can carry out service-learning experiences supervised, in part, by state employees in transportation, human services, parks and recreation, education, library system, health care, and so on.

2. *Encourage the State Department of Education to advocate that every public school pupil should annually be involved in peer tutoring.* One key standard for certification of any state school using public funds should be the degree to which peer tutoring takes place, providing students with learning problems more peer tutoring time than those students who are high achievers. Research has shown consistent academic and personal benefits for both tutors and tutees (Conrad and Hedin, 1991).

3. *Encourage every state employee as far as possible to cosupervise (with a school official) a period of internship in service-learning for students in grades seven through twelve.* From the litter-picker-upper in the transportation department to the commissioner level, every single publicly funded employee should be encouraged to assist in providing an age-appropriate service-learning activity for a public school student. Combining these thousands of opportunities with those provided by the independent sector, every secondary-level student should be able to graduate from the twelfth grade with at least six service-learning internship experiences on his or her cumulative record.

4. *Assist the State Department of Education in cohosting periodic (at least twice a year) regional service-learning fairs.* For each fair, invite an independent cosponsor, such as the United Way or the Red Cross. Let each fair celebrate a theme, such as the improvement and expansion of day-care programs, and ensure that service-learning groups are invited to display how what they have done individually and in groups has met the stated need.

All internships cosupervised by a state employee that have worked on the theme should be encouraged to participate in the fair, and those who have not, should be allowed to attend the fair to gather ideas for how to do service-learning projects to meet this specific need in the future.

5. *Help each major department of state government (executive, legislative, judiciary) hold annual regional "town meetings" at which public school students involved in community-improvement service-learning projects propose resolutions, participate in the parliamentary debate on the resolutions, and present new resolutions to the proper authorities for serious consideration.* As budgets are finalized for each department, funding for these "town meetings" will need to be included. Student groups, as part of their service-learning activities, can be given the task to organize the meetings. Through the meetings, serious statewide issues will be aired through participatory democracy, and the upcoming voters in the state will be prepared, when their time comes, to exercise their right to vote with knowledge and expertise.

IN CLOSING

What if these five recommendations were to be embraced by our fifty states? Would our democracy be more vibrant? Would our school students receive better civics instruction? Would our students be more conscientious about developing their literacy skills? Would collaboration between the private and public sectors of our economy enhance our communities? State-level efforts for service learning, in concert with individuals in schools, towns, and cities throughout the state, hold great promise for both community improvement and student learning.

Part 4

The Future of Service-Learning

The last part of this book examines the many challenges that must be faced to ensure success for service-learning over the long term in our nation's public schools. Chapter 21 focuses on challenges within three spheres: the public school system, service-learning programs, and the national service-learning movement. In chapter 22, models and options for service-learning in preservice teacher education are presented. Finally, the concluding chapter highlights both the promise and the potential for service-learning as an essential aspect of civic education.

The energy of youth warms the hearts of senior citizens.
Photo Credit: Kevin Eans

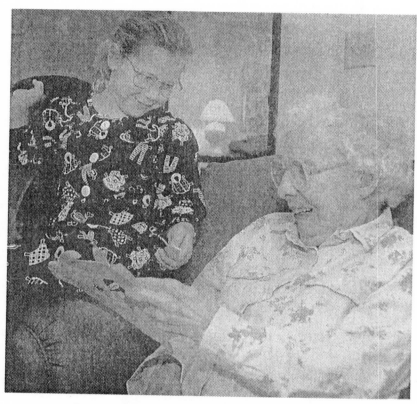

Integenerational projects bring joy to youth and seniors.
Photo Credit: Kevin Eans

Chapter 21

Challenges to Effective Practice

Rahima C. Wade

If service-learning is to thrive in public schools of the twenty-first century, there are many challenges that must be met. Most service-learning program leaders are "doers" focused on "getting things done," yet the value of educators' reflections on the practice of service-learning programs is no less critical than the role of student reflection on service activities. While many educators may be convinced of the value of service-learning through their contacts with student and community participants, a healthy dose of critical reflection and analysis is essential to producing and sustaining quality programs.

Service-learning advocates, by and large, have not devoted much effort to critiquing either the practice of service-learning in schools or the national service-learning movement as a whole. In general, service-learning practitioners engage more in cheerleading for their programs than in introspecting about their shortcomings. While there are perhaps some legitimate reasons for neglecting the latter—such as the fear that opponents might use such critiques to undermine the movement—critical reflection is essential to improvement. The ideas in this chapter are offered in the spirit expressed by Purpel (1995) in his statement: "The best criticism ought not to disarm and neutralize but instead should serve to rearm and energize" (p. 4).

The challenges to service-learning exist on many levels from the personal to the planetary and from the psychological to the political. In this chapter, I discuss some of the difficult challenges that face service-learning practitioners within three contexts: the structure of public schooling in the United States, the school-based service-learning program, and the national service-learning movement. Although these three spheres overlap and influence each other, they offer convenient demarcations for a discussion of problems and challenges that must be met with creativity and persistence if service-learning is to resist joining the realm of fads on the distant educational horizon.

PUBLIC SCHOOLING IN THE UNITED STATES

Many aspects of the current structure of public schools in the United States pose significant challenges to the practice of service-learning. Perhaps most pervasive and potentially daunting, is the value public schools place on individual success over collective well-being. As public institutions, schools mirror society. Thus, the trend toward individualism so prevalent in our nation is predominant in our schools as well. The norm in public school classrooms at all grade levels is individual work (e.g., seat work, homework, tests, essays). Frequently communication and collaboration among students is discouraged; indeed, these types of behaviors may be labeled "cheating." Elementary students, in particular, are often admonished to "keep your eyes, hands, and feet to yourself." High schools are typically characterized by fifty-minute, single-subject classes in which students are lectured and individually tested on the course material. Bricker (1989) noted the potentially damaging effects of the subtle messages students receive about citizenship when these types of guidelines and structures are operant.

> I am worried about the cumulative impact that ignoring others has upon the civic imagination of young people. I do not want young people to believe that to be a good citizen one must simply stay within one's own morally protected space—that space described by the idea of possession—and never to serve with others or join with others. A society in which citizens always stand at a distance from each other because they fear that joining might violate someone's right of possession would not be a decent society. Yet I have reason to believe that is precisely how students perceive citizenship in our nation's classrooms. (p. 3)

The focus on individualism goes beyond the students. While many exceptions can be found, schools do not generally encourage collaboration among teachers or between school and community. Given the central role of collaboration to effective service-learning programs, teachers may find themselves treading rough waters as they attempt to collaborate with others in and outside of the school walls. The public school structure makes this difficult; most teachers do not have telephones in their classrooms, nor do they have many minutes in the school day to make or receive phone calls. While some schools encourage shared planning time or team teaching, most often teachers are not provided with long lunch hours or congruent planning periods. Thus, teachers of service-learning must make a concerted effort to collaborate with others on project activities. Establishing support systems that make use of service-learning coordinators, teacher mentors, or peer consultants can assist in building a climate of collaboration in the school.

Another challenge mentioned frequently by teachers as a major barrier to implementing service-learning in their classrooms is time. Teachers need considerable time for planning service-learning activities that are site specific. This task involves collaboration with others, creative thinking about how to tie service to the curriculum, and making logistical arrangements for funding, transportation, student supervision, and so forth. Many teachers note that even if they had the time to do all of these tasks, they would still have difficulty finding time to fit service-learning projects into the school day, given all of the other demands in an increasingly overcrowded curriculum. Teachers who are not skilled in blending service with academics may view service-learning as valuable, but nonetheless a time consuming "add-on."

School systems that expect teachers to engage in service-learning over the long term need to take the time problem seriously; many creative options exist for scheduling, staffing, and other supports that can make the difference for busy teachers. For example, in our collaborative university/public school service-learning program, we provide teacher education student assistance, use of service-learning resource "kits" on themes of interest (e.g., intergenerational, environmental, and so on), and paid planning time at school site workshops. While there will always be challenges in regard to time, these supports help many teachers continue to implement service-learning without "burning out."

A perhaps more subtle yet central challenge to service-learning in public schools is the pervasive notion of "learning" as the memorization of factual information. Teachers who believe that their primary or only role is to present information to students and have them answer questions in a textbook or take a test to determine how much of the material has been retained are unlikely to take the time and effort to implement service-learning activities in their classrooms.

Service-learning projects focus on more than fact retention; they provide students with the opportunities to develop knowledge, skills, and attitudes than can be applied to real-life situations. Community activities such as service-learning bring students in contact with a wide variety of people and tasks, and thus, provide opportunities for personal and social development as well. Teachers who choose to include service in their curricula value these outcomes in addition to their students' academic development (Wade, 1995a). Those who believe that the sole purpose of school is fact acquisition may think that service-learning is unnecessary, inappropriate, or a waste of time.

All of these challenges—individualistic values, time, and learning as fact acquisition—can combine to produce a climate unsupportive of service-learning. In a tongue-in-cheek article on the demise of service-learning as an educational movement supposedly written in 2010, Hill (1994) assessed the reasons why service-learning stayed on the periphery of mainstream education.

The models that were developed and publicized stressed a level of talent, time commitment, and professional risk that enticed only the most self-confident and dedicated. Most teachers, faced with persistent problems of large class size, disruptive student behavior, and accelerating public criticism, never opted to experiment with service-learning. (p. 2)

If this fate is to fall short of reality, service-learning advocates will need to respond with creativity and persistence to the challenges posed by the public school system. Connecting service-learning with compatible educational reform movements and seeking alternative approaches to fund, staff, and schedule community-based activities will help teachers envision the contributions service-learning can make to their students, schools, and communities.

SCHOOL-BASED SERVICE-LEARNING PROGRAMS

Most of this book has focused on the examination of public school service-learning programs. Challenges exist in virtually every aspect of service-learning discussed in Part 1 of this book. While these challenges are related to many of the issues discussed above, they can also be present in schools where there are supportive and collaborative structures in place. Five of the most challenging aspects will be discussed here: logistics, service, reflection, curriculum integration, and evaluation.

Logistics

Most educational strategies, once learned, can be implemented within the classroom setting using typical school resources. Cooperative learning and whole language, for example, are relatively easy to integrate in a classroom setting. Service-learning, on the other hand, can be a logistical nightmare. Funds, transportation, scheduling, volunteer help, supplies: all these and more can face a teacher who attempts to establish a service-learning experience for her class. Program planners need to acknowledge the time and effort required to deal with logistics and plan accordingly. Considerable support is needed for teachers, and school coordinators or community members can be of much assistance in handling many of the logistical challenges mentioned here.

In programs where teachers are expected to take on these tasks, appropriate release time or additional financial remuneration may work. Staff developers, program leaders, and others who introduce teachers to service-learning should be realistic about the time needed for logistics and encourage teachers to start with small, manageable projects.

Service

Many troubling questions exist about the practice and value of service in school-based programs. In chapter 4, I raised issues surrounding the differences between service and charity. Too many service-learning projects focus on fund raising, collections, or other indirect activities that alleviate guilt but do little to build the solidarity and communal relationship characteristic of service as defined in this book. Even when students interact with members of the community, service is often expressed as "do-gooding." Barber (1993) maintained that the focus of service-learning should be on citizenship, not charity.

> If education is aimed at creating citizens, then it will be important to let the young see that service is not just about altruism or charity; or a matter of those who are well-off helping those who are not. It is serving the public interest, which is the same thing as serving enlightened self-interest. Young people serve themselves as members of the community by serving a public good that is also their own. (p. 256)

Sigmon (1995) noted the lack of this shared sense of community in the way that educators often talk about "using" the community and its agencies for students to gain experience, explore a career path, test a theory in practice, or do something for someone in need. He suggested that program leaders focus on expanding this limited relationship and "slow down, even curtail some of our direct service work, and examine what we are doing, by going into communities and organizations to 'sit down, be quiet, and pay attention'" (Sigmon, 1995, p. 31). Through this process, Sigmon maintained that educators will "begin to hear of creative ways we can relate in mutual serving and learning across the boundaries of gender, race, age, credentials, economic status, national origin, faith, and educational attainment" (p. 31).

Indeed, the many barriers to equality that presently exist among people of different creeds and cultures in our society cannot be ignored in the design and conduct of service-learning programs. Purpel (1995) noted the potential for miscommunication, cultural misunderstanding, and even bewilderment in projects where dominant culture students are serving marginalized members of society. He also asserted the possibility of service fostering

> a sense of arrogance and condescension on the part of those who presume to know and act to intervene for what is best for other people . . . Lurking in the background of such relationships is the very real possibility of enhanced resentment, guilt, humiliation, and alienation for all involved which can culminate in the pain of embittered polarization. (Purpel, 1995, p. 2)

Cruz (1990) posited that "in the context of conflicting interests and historical dominance of one racial or gender group over another, it is possible that 'service,' in and of itself, can have racist or sexist outcomes despite good intentions" (p. 322). Indeed, Hondagneu-Sotelo and Raskoff (1994) found that their college sociology students, following service with multicultural school populations, had a "tendency to reach unwarranted, often racist conclusions based on selective perceptions" (p. 250). Thus, while service-learning might empower student learners, it does not always promote the common good if it reinforces a sense of inferiority among those served or superiority and prejudice among those who do the serving (Cruz, 1990).

There are no easy answers for how to structure service-learning experiences between individuals from different cultures or socioeconomic levels. Sigmon suggested listening to those whose voices have traditionally been marginalized. Cruz asserted that it might be best to focus on the learning that can be shared between people, rather than on "service," persay. In chapter 4, I promote engaging in service activities where the boundaries between server and served become blurred through mutual goal-setting and collaboration. While none of these ideas are a panacea for the problems discussed here, they may all offer some potential for service-learning practice that fosters more equitable relationships and empowers all those involved.

Another equally challenging concern is the efficacy of service. Whether or not service activities will actually have a long-term impact on social and environmental problems remains a question. A number of educators have noted that service-learning activities, in and of themselves, are unlikely to change the deeply structured inequities in our society (Gorham, 1992; Leeds, 1994; Purpel, 1995). Purpel (1995) pointed out that "relatively modest successes can actually exacerbate problems through the process of co-optation in which amelioration serves to prop up the very structures that created the problems in the first place" (p. 3). Gorham (1992) underscored this view and asserted the importance of advocacy activities in service-learning programs. He noted that "conserving nature involves fighting corporate polluters as much as it does planting trees. Making homes energy efficient means lobbying against utility rate increases as much as it does weatherstripping houses" (p. 118).

Recognizing these limitations, Leeds (1994) promoted taking a realistic view as to how much service projects can accomplish.

> Grandiosity is the enemy of a well-thought-out, inevitably small-scale attempt to make some impact on several overwhelming social problems. Overselling a good idea can lead to disappointment with modest results. It also creates another short-run hope (and hype) for "solutions" which distracts from the needed serious intractable social problems. At its best,

service will demonstrate not only how much students and others might do, but *how much more* needs to be done and thought about. (p. 16)

Thus, service-learning practitioners need to imbue their work with a sense or reality and humility. While service-learning projects may be unlikely to change the world, they can help. "Problems surely can and should be ameliorated, suffering and pain reduced, justice and equity increased, peace furthered, violence lessened, meaning strengthened" (Purpel, 1995, p. 12). Service-learning programs may not rid society of its ills, yet the limited gains they can accomplish can be heartening. Further, students can reflect on their service experiences, considering the underlying root causes for the problems they are addressing; and develop ideas as well as actual activities for advocacy efforts aimed at altering larger structural concerns.

Reflection

The reflection component is a critical aspect of service-learning programs. Indeed, in a metaanalysis of research studies on community service and service-learning, Conrad and Hedin (1982) found that reflection was the single most necessary element in a service program leading to student learning. Reflection, however, is not typically a central focus in public schooling. While we know that students learn by constructing meaning from their experience (Brooks and Brooks, 1993; Prawat, 1992), schools seldom provide the direct experience and subsequent reflection that learning requires. In general, schools are more concerned with having students memorize facts and develop skills in reading, writing, and mathematics. The notion that important information lies in students' experience and processing of that experience, rather than only in external authorities or textbooks, is an alien idea in many school settings.

Because reflection is not a predominant type of thinking emphasized in most schools, teachers are generally not skilled in facilitating reflective thinking and students are not skilled in practicing it. Thus, the influence of the culture on the individuals within it, both teachers and students, works against the practice of reflection. This is a challenge even for schools that embrace service-learning and the role of reflection in learning from service. Adding the time consideration discussed above to the lack of skill in leading reflection sessions leads to many service-learning teachers not spending the time on reflection that is needed to enhance students' learning from service.

Specific strategies for leading reflection activities can be found in the service-learning literature (see chapter 6), yet little research has been conducted that focuses explicitly on the effectiveness of these strategies. Nor is there an explicit focus in the literature on how to move students beyond simply recounting what they have experienced and their related feelings to making significant connections between their service activities and their beliefs, values, future careers, and lifestyles. Clearly, much work remains to be done in carefully evaluating the benefits of different types of reflection strategies.

Curriculum Integration

Service projects are often carried out in public schools; much less often are they integrated in the curriculum so that students learn academic skills and content through their service activities. For example, elementary schools may conduct canned food drives but usually do not connect this activity with math skills and nutrition education. In high schools, service is typically relegated to club activities or as a requirement for graduation in which students must complete a specified number of hours on their own time outside of school. The Tooles note in chapter 17 on staff development that for many teachers just starting to implement service-learning, it is challenging enough to set up and carry out a service activity unrelated to the curriculum.

Yet if service-learning is to secure a central position within the public school system, it must be tied to the academic agenda. Labeling a program community service-learning necessitates the inclusion of both structured opportunities for reflection and connections to academic skills or content. Kinsley notes in chapter 9 that one of the most challenging tasks for the field is to move beyond the perception of service-learning as an extracurricular activity to viewing it as a useful teaching process. Citing the positive influences on student motivation and achievement when service is integrated in the curriculum, supporters maintain that service-learning is a viable teaching strategy for academic growth.

Connecting service activities to academic objectives requires time and creativity on the part of the teacher. Often I have worked with teachers who have not seen the potential connections between a community project and their academic goals. While program leaders can provide numerous examples of such connections, the site specific nature of service-learning activities necessitates that teachers develop these connections. Again, collaboration within the school between teachers and mentors, peer consultants, or a service-learning coordinator can greatly enhance the connections formulated between service and the academic curriculum.

The service-curriculum connection is vital not only to effective practice but also to the longevity of service-learning in public schooling. Currently, a debate is raging in the United States about the legitimacy of requiring community service for high school graduation. Critics question the constitutionality of "enforced slavery" and argue that it will take time away from students' academic studies, jobs, or families. Some opponents even argue that mandating voluntarism will, in the long run, undermine students' caring and initiative to help others.

To understand the roots of this critique we need to look at some of the other required aspects of schooling: reading, writing, mathematics, science, and social studies. Why is it that service opponents do not also target these requirements as time consuming and unconstitutional? The difference, as I see it, is that these subjects are deemed useful and valuable learning whereas service is seen as unrelated to academic learning. By connecting service with the academic curriculum, and where possible including the service activity within the school day, teachers can help critics see that service-learning is a teaching technique that reaches many students who have not responded to traditional modes of instruction and a method that can provide all students with a motivational and relevant means for learning.

Elsewhere I have advocated that educators avoid the use of the word "volunteer" in relation to service-learning programs (Wade, 1994). Community participation in a democratic society is not simply an option; it is both a right and a responsibility. It is the schools' obligation to develop students who have the skills, knowledge, and attitudes not only to be successful in their careers, but also to participate as informed and active members of their communities.

Evaluation

The future of service-learning rests in part on educators' abilities to demonstrate its effectiveness. Evaluation, therefore, serves first and foremost to assess the outcomes of the service-learning program for students, schools, and communities. Evaluation also provides important information for making program modifications. Often the information gathered in evaluations can be used to justify the continuation of the program, to bolster fund-raising efforts, or to garner support for the program from administrators or stakeholders. For all of these reasons, evaluation should be a carefully planned, central component of every service-learning program.

The challenges to planning and conducting sound evaluations are many. In chapter 1, I briefly summarized many of the difficulties; further explanation is provided here. First, the term "service-learning" can encompass many different types of programs with a wide variety of purposes and outcomes. How can the outcomes of third graders reading to Head Start preschoolers and high school seniors conducting a voter registration drive be compared with each other? Even within one of these programs, it is likely that student participants will have very different experiences, learn different skills, realize different understandings, and develop different attitudes toward themselves, others, and the act of making a difference. Because service-learning is experiential education usually involving people, places, and tasks new to student participants, the full range of potential outcomes is difficult to anticipate.

While this aspect of evaluating service-learning programs would be challenging enough by itself, there are further complications associated with the desired outcomes identified by the service-learning program. Some service-learning programs focus on assessing outcomes that service activities do not support. For example, if the program involving third-graders reading to preschoolers identified political efficacy as one of the desired program outcomes, the program is probably barking up the wrong tree. Second, many service-learning programs have identified outcomes associated with broad and stable personality characteristics that do not change quickly (e.g., self-esteem, social responsibility, empathy). Given that many service-learning experiences are of relatively short duration, it is unlikely that students in the program will demonstrate significant gains on these criteria.

These problems with identifying appropriate outcomes, coupled with three other factors—the lack of appropriate evaluation instruments, the lack of time for conducting evaluations, and the lack of expertise in evaluating educational programs—make conducting sound evaluations of service-learning programs extremely problematic. While program leaders can conduct evaluations of their programs without outside assistance; collaboration with others, especially those skilled in research and evaluation, is likely to facilitate the process.

Many service-learning advocates are looking for ways to entice higher education faculty's interest in the field. Requesting faculty's assistance with program evaluation may be a suitable means for doing so if faculty rewards involve such collaboration and if the possibility exists for the faculty member to author or coauthor an article on the program evaluation for publication in a professional journal. If such assistance is not available, program leaders must think carefully about how to evaluate program outcomes.

Considering the purpose for the evaluation, the needed information to accomplish this purpose, and the audience for the evaluation (i.e., Who will use the information gathered?) are important beginning steps. Early planning with careful attention to matching program activities with potential outcomes and appropriate means for assessment is essential. In general, those new to evaluation should start with a small and simple effort focused on one or two key outcomes. An alternate strategy would be to employ the documentation strategies described in chapter 7, and then complete a case study of the program during a break in the program or over the summer. Clearly, published guidelines for evaluating service-learning programs are greatly needed for the improvement of practice and the longevity of the service-learning movement.

THE NATIONAL SERVICE-LEARNING MOVEMENT

Service has a long legacy in American history; its practice is rooted in many cultures, communities, and grassroots movements for change. Service-learning as a teaching method is a much newer phenomenon. While schools have always included opportunities for students to serve the school and larger community, the idea of making this activity a focus for learning academic skills and content is an idea that has taken off only in the last twenty years. Since 1990, K–12 service-learning programs have been supported by government legislation and funding. Most states have received federal funds to administer K–12 service-learning programs and a number of private foundations have supported the development of service-learning programs as well.

The funding and associated publicity for service-learning activities have spawned numerous initiatives and networks in communities, states, and nations. At present, the growth of service-learning programs is on the upswing. More teacher education programs are including service-learning in their courses; more high schools are requiring service or service-learning for graduation; more teachers are attending staff development workshops, regional meetings, and national conferences to learn about this exciting teaching strategy. National reports calling for youth service are echoed by growing numbers of professional education organizations promoting service-learning. Books, curriculum guides, and thematic issues of journals on service-learning are supporting the interest among educators.

It is impossible to predict how the service-learning movement will change. The history of education is littered with fads that sparkled briefly and then faded away. One can also point to examples, however, of educational strategies such as whole language and cooperative learning, that not too many years ago were thought of as "innovative," and now appear to be common educational practice in many communities across the nation.

While the future of service-learning cannot be predicted, there are some issues that can be identified that pose significant challenges to the service-learning movement. First, given the surge of interest generated by federal funding for service-learning programs, one concern is what will happen to the movement if funds are cut. As with most types of hands-on learning—take science labs, for example—service-learning activities often require funds for equipment and supplies. Some of these materials, such as paint for houses or trees to plant in parks, are not typically provided by schools. Additionally, when service happens at community sites, funds may be needed for transportation. Third, many programs need funds for support staff or a service-learning coordinator to handle all of the logistics associated with student service projects. These needs can be contrasted with strategies like cooperative learning or whole language, in which funds are required for teacher training but practice is implemented in the classroom setting with minimal or typical school supplies.

These issues point to the fact that ongoing funding, beyond initial teacher training and start-up costs, is necessary for most service-learning programs. For example, the collaborative university/public school service-learning program that I coordinate requires about eight thousand dollars a year for teacher training, project supplies, and transportation for about fifty teachers' projects. While this is not an enormous amount of funds, it is a sum that must be generated each year. Fortunately, there are many potential avenues for seeking funding. Given the current broad base of support for service-learning activities, funds may be garnered from federal, state, private, community, university, and/or school district resources. Thus, while federal funds have given a tremendous boost to the service-learning movement, there are other sources of support for programs.

Perhaps the more critical factor, then, in sustaining the service-learning movement over the long term rests with the viability of service-learning as a demonstrated and successful teaching strategy. Sound research on the outcomes of service-learning for both students and communities must be generated to support the promising findings thus far and the substantial anecdotal evidence supporting service-learning. Finding ways to make service-learning work for teachers and students within the structure of U.S. public schools is also essential as is addressing the challenges to effective practice within service-learning programs. Service-learning programs will have to both fit within existing public school structures and, at the same time, attempt to transform them. Schools that have adopted a more student-centered, authentic approach to learning with flexible scheduling and collaborative work structures will undoubtedly have an easier time adopting service-learning. More traditional schools will be challenged to adapt service-learning practice to fit the school structure, make changes to support service-learning practice, or both. Programs in these two kinds of schools will benefit from employing new teachers who have been trained in service-learning methods as part of their preservice teacher preparation programs.

IN CLOSING.

There are no easy answers to the question of how to ensure the future of service-learning in our democratic society. While many challenges remain to effective practice in schools and the future of the service-learning movement as a whole can only be guessed at, service-learning advocates must move ahead, one day at a time, to develop and sustain quality programs. Service-learning practitioners must bridge the inherent dualities in this work: to act and reflect, to be decisive and contemplative, to adapt service-learning to fit the school structure and attempt to change the institution of public schooling, to deal with immediate community needs and work for long-term structural changes in society.

This work will take much time and energy from many people in the coming years. There are problems to face in the present; success in the future is not guaranteed. Yet despite the many shortcomings of service-learning practice in schools, advocates are heartened by the potential of service in the public school curriculum. Purpel (1995) concluded his critique of service-learning with the following affirmation.

> Humanity's greatest achievements would seem to be its persistence in its aspiration for goodness in the face of the incredible pressures for mere survival and self-enhancement. The arrival of the service-learning movement signals that this impulse has been re-energized with fresh urgency and hope. (p. 12)

Chapter 22

Service-Learning in Preservice Teacher Education

Rahima C. Wade

Given the central role of the teacher in school-based service-learning programs, the future of service-learning depends in part on how teachers are trained in this teaching method. Service-learning programs in elementary and secondary schools will be greatly enhanced if new teachers come into their full-time positions with training and experience in service-learning. This chapter focuses on the rationales and options for infusing service-learning in college and university preservice teacher education programs. Examples are provided of programs around the country that are integrating service-learning in their practica and course offerings. In this chapter, I will also address the importance of establishing links between preservice teacher education and the K–12 educational system.

RATIONALES FOR SERVICE-LEARNING IN TEACHER EDUCATION

Several rationales have been offered for including service-learning in preservice teacher education (Allam and Zerkin, 1993; Anderson and Guest, 1995; Root, 1994; Root, Moon, and Kromer, 1995; Sullivan, 1991). One rationale promotes service-learning as an effective component of a reflective teacher education program. Sullivan (1991) noted that placements in unfamiliar settings in the community can encourage teacher education students to question prevailing policies, examine their assumptions about classroom practice, and begin to develop habits of personal reflection. Given preservice teachers' tendency to rely unquestioningly on the methods provided by their cooperating teachers, service-learning can help students to establish habits of critical inquiry concerning educational practices. Allam and Zerkin (1993) asserted that through reflection on their own learning, preservice teachers "gain experience in working with their colleagues to research issues, make decisions, and solve problems—skills they will need as collaborative decision makers to promote a caring, equitable, and challenging school environment for all children" (p. 12). Research has shown that reflection is a critical component in helping students learn from their experience (Conrad and Hedin, 1991; Serow, 1991); thus, experience coupled with reflection can greatly strengthen teacher education programs that aim to develop reflective teachers.

A second rationale centers on the consistency between service-learning and other educational reforms. Root (1994) noted three characteristics of service-learning activities that lend themselves to the more purposeful, connected, and relevant learning advocated by educational reformers:

> (1) Service learning can be a context for "authentic" or performance-based assessment of skills; (2) community needs and proposed actions can supply "themes" for integrated teaching units; and (3) service activities in which students identify community problems and potential solutions can engage cooperation and higher order thinking skills. (p. 94)

Through the use of service-learning as pedagogy in the public school classroom, teacher education students have the opportunity to develop a democratic classroom in which their roles shift to coach or facilitator and students engage in cooperative learning, shared decision making, problem-solving, and class discussions. Both preservice teachers and their students can document their learning through authentic assessment strategies such as portfolios and exhibitions. Thus, service-learning can serve as an umbrella under which many other educational reforms can be actualized within a meaningful and practical context.

A third rationale for service-learning in teacher education is concerned with the needs of students in our multicultural society and the promise for establishing a climate of care in schools (Noddings, 1992; Chaskin and Rauner, 1995). Root (1994) noted that there is a growing recognition among educators that schools cannot address children's cognitive needs in isolation from the difficult circumstances of their lives. High divorce rates, substance abuse, teen pregnancy, violent crime, and declining academic achievement are among the many indicators of youth in trouble in our society (National Center for Education Statistics, 1993). An important element of multicultural education is empowering students with the knowledge and skills to make changes in their own lives and in their communities (Sleeter and Grant, 1987). Working with adults, students can begin to address the issues that beset them and develop skills and strategies for continuing to work for community improvement.

Whether due to social problems, diverse linguistic backgrounds, or a variety of different learning styles; teachers in the 1990s are challenged to find effective means for engaging all youth in the learning process. Teachers, therefore, must be concerned with their students' well-being as a whole, not just their academic growth. In a learner-centered classroom, teachers can employ service-learning as one effective means for motivating students to learn through meaningful involvement in their schools and communities. Root (1994) asserted that "participation in service-learning experiences which are focused on the needs of children may prepare prospective teachers to participate in a learner-centered educational system and in ways that reflect a caring ethic" (p. 96). Service-learning experiences can contribute to: developing student-sensitive curricula and instructional tools, establishing caring relationships with students, and enabling prospective teachers to act as advocates for youth in partnership with youth service providers (Root, 1994).

A fourth rationale, directly related to the third, posits that through service-learning, teacher education students can begin to envision themselves in a variety of roles in the classroom. No longer can teachers function simply as instructors of academic subject matter; increasingly teachers must be counselors, community liaisons, scholars, and moral leaders for their students. Through service-learning, prospective teachers can learn to use community resources and youth-serving systems, as well as gain a better understanding of the home and community environments influencing children's lives (Allam and Zerkin, 1993).

In the 1990s, the trend in school-community collaboration is increasing. Community professionals are setting up shop inside or near the schools, providing counseling, medical, dental, and other human services to both youth and their families (Lawson, 1994; Pennekamp, 1992). As the barriers separating public schools and youth social services begin to disappear, service-learning-trained teachers can be instrumental in helping to bring needed social services to students and their families (Wade and Anderson, in press). An Alma College teacher education student asserted that her service-learning involvement "helped me to see ways that a teacher could get help for a student outside of the classroom. It also showed me how I could become involved with the community and with children other than as a teacher" (Root, 1994, p. 97).

In summary, service-learning can provide future teachers with opportunities to practice reflection; to improve their repertoire of instructional strategies; to develop a student-centered, caring approach to teaching; and to extend their visions of themselves as teachers to include other needed roles. Given the realities of childrens' lives in our multicultural democratic society, service-learning has the potential to become a valuable component of teacher-training programs nationwide.

OPTIONS FOR INFUSING SERVICE-LEARNING IN TEACHER EDUCATION

Colleges and universities across the nation are experimenting with varying approaches to involving teacher education students in service-learning. Future teachers are getting involved in direct service to their communities as well as learning how to conduct service-learning activities with students in K–12 school settings. Some preservice teachers complete service-learning activities as part of their regular coursework or practicum placements; others participate in specially designed elective courses or internships. Following a discussion of different infusion options are descriptions of some current promising practices in service-learning in U.S. university and college teacher education programs.

Options in the Regular Program

Often the easiest way to infuse service-learning in a teacher education program is to offer a service-learning experience in conjunction with an existing course or practicum. Course and field experience possibilities include the following:

- *Foundations or "Methods of Teaching" course.* The foundations of education course or a general introduction to teaching methods may be among the first courses teacher education students take in a program. Students can be introduced to service-learning in the course within the context of the teacher's role in the school and community in our democratic multicultural society. Professors can also introduce service-learning in conjunction with the original sociocivic mission of public schooling and connect service-learning with contemporary reform efforts.
- *Human development, human relations, or multicultural education courses.* Many programs require students to take courses under one of these titles. Structuring opportunities for preservice teachers to work directly with diverse youth in the schools or the community may be one of the most effective means for helping students accomplish the objectives in these courses.
- *Subject area methods course.* Subject area methods courses can include service-learning activities specifically related to course content. Social studies, with its professed goal of creating active and informed citizens, is one obvious subject in which to include service-learning. Science methods might involve teacher education students in environmental improvement projects. As part of math or reading methods, preservice teachers could tutor K–12 students. Music, art, or physical education methods students could work with the elderly, children with special needs, or other populations to enhance their

enjoyment and skill development in these areas. (For further ideas on infusing service learning in specific subject areas, see chapter 6.)

• *Practicum placements.* Teacher education programs generally require pre-service teachers to complete at least one practicum in a public school setting prior to student teaching. These placements can be opportunities to engage in service-learning activities with K–12 students, such as tutoring or afterschool programs, or assisting K–12 students as they complete service-learning activities in their curriculum.

• *Student teaching.* A number of teacher education programs have been able to utilize the student teaching experience as a way to develop preservice teachers' knowledge of service-learning as pedagogy. In some programs, university professors and supervisors assist student teachers with designing projects that fit the curriculum objectives in their placements. In school districts with established service-learning programs, student teachers learn as they assist their cooperating teachers with projects.

New Courses and Internships

Some programs choose to develop special required or elective opportunities that focus exclusively on service-learning. Elective courses or internships generally include fewer teacher education students than a required component, yet an advantage is that the students who do enroll are already service-minded. Following are a few options for special experiences that can be added to a teacher education program:

• *Independent study.* Future teachers can sign up for independent study credit for completing service activities in K–12 schools or community agencies. Varying numbers of credits can be awarded depending on the hours students spend serving others. Professors supervising independent study students should be sure to include occasional seminars, individual meetings, or writing assignments so that teacher education students include a reflection component in their activities.

• *Community or school-based internship.* Students enrolled in an internship should complete service activities in a school or community agency and also attend a weekly seminar to reflect on their service activities. As with an independent study, credits could vary depending on the hours students devote to the project.

• *Service-learning course.* Some teacher education programs offer a course specifically in service-learning or service leadership. The advantage to this approach is having more time to devote to the study and practice of service-learning than would be possible when infusing service-learning in an existing course. Service-learning courses can afford students the opportunity to study experiential education theory and essentials elements for quality service-learning programs. Such courses should also include a field component where students are actually involved serving others. Professors teaching separate courses on service-learning would be wise to create links wherever possible with other courses in the teacher education program so that preservice teachers realize the possible connections between service-learning and the subjects they will be teaching in the future.

Service-Learning Participant or Teacher?

One question teacher educators should consider carefully is whether they want teacher education students to participate in service activities themselves, to develop skills using service-learning as a teaching technique in the public school classroom, or both. A recent study by George et al. (1995) revealed that teacher education students who participate in service-learning projects in the community tend, on the whole, not to employ service-learning in their first year of teaching. My own work tends to support the notion that teacher education students need both experience serving others and practice in guiding students through service-learning activities to develop commitment to and expertise in service-learning.

Clearly, there are different skills and benefits associated with both kinds of experiences. Through providing service and reflecting on their contributions, prospective teachers have the opportunity to learn about the frustrations and rewards involved in making a difference. Through assisting with K–12 service-learning projects, they develop skills in managing the classroom, connecting with the community, supervising students at field sites, and involving students in discussion, decision making, and problem solving. While the best approach is probably to provide a variety of experiences including coursework on service-learning and both types of direct involvement described above, teacher educators may not have the time, energy, or opportunity in their programs to do all three of these. If time allowed for only one option (I currently do them all), I would choose involving future teachers in assisting K–12 students with service-learning projects. Although research on the effects of these approaches is still in the preliminary stages, it appears that direct experience with service-learning as pedagogy may be necessary for teacher education students to have the knowledge and expertise to implement service-learning in their first few years of classroom teaching (George, Hunt, Nixon, Ortiz, and Anderson, 1995; Wade, 1995c).

Decisions for Structuring Service-Learning Experiences

Let's imagine that a professor has chosen to include a service-learning experience in his or her subject matter methods course. There are still many decisions to be made. Will the project have a particular focus in connection with the objectives of the course? Will the project be required, extra credit, an option for an "A" in the course? Will all classmates participate in the same project or will they choose individual placements in the community? Will project activities be coordinated with a specific community agency or K–12 service-learning program? What types of transportation, scheduling, or liability issues will need to be addressed? How will reflection and learning from service be enhanced through in-class activities or homework assignments? The options for and intricacies of setting up service-learning experiences in teacher education programs are enough to deter all but the most committed teacher educators.

Admittedly, the coordination of most service-learning activities in preservice teacher education does take time; however, effective projects can be structured with minimal effort as well. For example, during my first few years working in teacher education, I simply instructed my students to "do something to make a difference." I did not provide them with examples, but rather asked them to think about the community around them and consider what bothered, interested, challenged, or intrigued them. The "Making a Difference" projects were ungraded and no hourly requirement was specified. The preservice teachers were required to submit a two-page reflection paper detailing what they had done and what they learned from the experience at the end of the semester. (See Wade, 1991; 1993 for further information on this project.)

While a few teacher education students gave minimal attention to this assignment, I was amazed that most struggled with what to choose and eventually found something that was both meaningful for them personally and a valuable contribution to the community. Projects ranged from reconciling with an estranged father to working at the polls on election day. Teacher education students raked leaves for the elderly, organized recycling projects, assembled food baskets, read for blind students, worked with the mentally ill, and participated in fund-raising walks. For professors just starting out with service-learning in communities with many options for student involvement, I would recommend the "Making a Difference" project. The project requires minimal effort on the part of the professor and community connections will be made that can be strengthened and developed later on. If I were to take this approach again now, I would develop a stronger reflection component and integrate more information about service-learning in the course itself. I would also require that the project involve spending at least fifteen contact hours with youth of the grade-levels teacher education students are being certified to teach.

I have experimented with many other approaches to service-learning as well; most have been more time consuming than the option described above. I have involved all students in my courses with one project that involved collaboration with two community agencies. During the 1995–1996 school year, students in my methods course have the option to participate in one of four existing projects, all involving elementary children, or choose their own project within certain guidelines (i.e., must involve children in need, 15 hours of service). Over time I have learned about the importance of connecting the service experiences with my course objectives and encouraging frequent and varied forms of reflection (Wade and Yarbrough, 1996). I have also learned from the efforts of my colleagues in other teacher education programs as they have tried out different approaches to service-learning for preservice teachers. Following are descriptions of some current promising practices in service-learning in teacher education programs in the United States. These descriptions are divided into two categories: comprehensive programs and single courses or internships.

COMPREHENSIVE PROGRAMS

A comprehensive program in service-learning is defined here as one that includes more than a single course or internship focused on service-learning. Service-learning experiences are tied to the overall goals of the teacher education program and usually include courses or field experiences that take place over more than one semester. Four programs—at the University of Iowa, Seattle University, Providence College, and Clark Atlanta University—are described here.

University of Iowa

Service-learning is integrated in four phases of the elementary teacher education program at the University of Iowa. First, the concept of service-learning is introduced in the Foundations of Education course, one of the first courses elementary education majors take. Service-learning is discussed in relation to the sociocivic function of public schooling and is presented as a teaching method consistent with other current educational reforms.

In one of two methods blocks, teacher education students participate in a service-learning project as part of the requirements for the social studies methods course. In this project, they are participants providing service and reflecting on their learning in relation to serving. They have a choice of participating in the intergenerational YES! (Youth and Elderly in Service) project, tutoring in an afterschool program for low-income children, working with children from single parent families in Big Brothers/Big Sisters' GAP (Group Activity Program), coordinating an evening child-care program for bilingual children whose parents are attending English tutoring lessons, or conducting Traveling Trunks presentations with school groups for the local Heritage Museum. The preservice teachers can also arrange their own placements in the community as long as their project involves at least fifteen hours of contact with children in need at a site where they have not been involved before. These stipulations have been established because in the past some students have wanted to count working at an afterschool program or volunteer work in which they are currently engaged. The service-learning project is thus designed to give them a new experience on which to reflect.

Course readings, assignments, and class discussions help teacher education students reflect on their service experiences. In particular, the preservice teachers are encouraged to connect their community experience with their emerging role as a teacher, their understanding of issues effecting children's lives, and their knowledge of available community services for youth. In a final project for the course, students create a photo essay, journal, or portfolio to share what they have learned from their experience working with children in need.

Concurrent with their participation in the community through the social studies methods course, teacher education students complete a one-credit practicum in the University of Iowa/Iowa City School District Collaborative Service-Learning Program. They assist teachers as they plan and carry out service-learning projects with kindergartners through eighth-graders. In this experience, the future teachers learn how to design and conduct service-learning activities with a classroom of children. Each teacher education student is required to complete five tasks in the practicum: observation, bulletin board display on the service theme, whole class lesson integrating academic skills and content with the service theme, reflection activity, and participation in the service activity with the children. Research on the practicum and service-learning project in the methods course have revealed the following student outcomes: increased self-esteem, self-knowledge, and self-efficacy; personal enjoyment of service; development of new teaching skills; increased knowledge of and respect for others; increased knowledge of and commitment to service; increased creative thinking and problem solving skills; increased reflective thinking ability; increased responsibility and time-management skills; and enhanced understanding of the challenges and benefits of service-learning as a teaching strategy (Wade, 1995c).

Finally, student teachers have the option to complete a service-learning project during their student teaching experience. Approximately one-third of the student teachers take advantage of this opportunity. In some cases, the cooperating teacher has had no experience with service-learning and thus is willing to let the student teacher plan and conduct the project on his or her own. In other cases, the cooperating and student teachers work together as a team to plan and carry out the project.

All of these activities require funding for training, project supplies, transportation, supervision, and curriculum materials. The service-learning activities have been generously supported by local community agencies, the University of Iowa and the Iowa City School District, as well as by grants from the Fund for the Improvement of Postsecondary Education (FIPSE) and the Corporation for National Service. (Further descriptions and research on the service-learning activities at the University of Iowa are available in Wade, 1995a, 1995b; Wade and Anderson, in press; and Wade and Yarbrough, 1996).

Seattle University

Seattle University attempts to establish an ethos of community service and a commitment to service-learning among the graduates of its Masters in Teaching (MIT) program. As a Jesuit institution, the teacher education program is founded on a tradition of commitment to the liberation of the human community from oppression and a vision of the human being as someone who relates to others in community through knowledge, love, and service (Anderson & Guest, 1995).

The service component of the program includes classroom instruction during the first quarter of the MIT program and a special two-credit course titled "Service Leadership." The overarching goal of the course is "to encourage new teachers to incorporate societal needs and community service into the K–12 school day so that *their* future students learn academics while meeting community needs" (Guest and Anderson, 1994, p. 34). In preparation for the course, students receive extensive information about the theory, research, and practice of service-learning. The principal activity in the Service Leadership course is a field placement. Teacher education students can choose between a placement in a K–12 school setting (most choose this option) where they assist teachers and students in designing and carrying out service-learning projects or a service experience with a community agency.

In school settings, MIT students have helped create a Hispanic Community Center in a middle school, organized cross age and peer tutoring projects, coordinated a project to restore an urban stream, and raised funds to benefit a homeless shelter. Examples of community agency placements include: social service agencies (e.g., homeless shelters, food banks), cross-cultural settings (e.g., a rural health center in Paraguay, teaching English in a remote Mexican village), group programs for children (e.g., a camp for children with cancer and their siblings, an environmental issues club), and local health care settings (e.g., a halfway house, a program for children with HIV/AIDS, a prenatal education program).

The course also has a strong reflection component. In addition to frequent journaling and discussion, the culminating activity for the course is the Service Leadership Conference, where MIT students present to their peers the knowledge and insights they have gained from their placements in the schools or community agencies. The conference follows a professional format including keynote speakers and individual sessions on relevant topics. School district and community personnel are invited to attend and often join with the MIT students in presenting their projects. Following the conference, students share journal entries and participate in small- and large-group activities addressing:

> insights gained as a result of their service experiences and conference presentations; policy dimensions and ethical issues these experiences bring to the forefront; possibilities and procedures for creating collaborative partnerships among schools, businesses, and youth serving agencies; and questions regarding the role of the schools and teachers in relation to societal issues raised by participation in these community service-learning settings. (Anderson and Guest, 1995, p. 20)

These four topics then serve as the focus for a final paper each MIT student writes to express personal reflections on his or her experiences. Following the course, the preservice teachers have the option to plan and conduct a service-learning project during their student teaching experience. (For further information about Seattle University's service-learning activities, particularly in regards to assessment and research, see Anderson and Guest, 1994, 1995.)

Providence College

The Providence College program is a partnership between faculty in the school of education, staff from the Feinstein Institute for Public Service on campus, teachers and administrators from the two participating elementary schools (Camden Avenue Elementary School in Providence and Baldwin Elementary School in Pawtucket), as well as a few parents and community members. A team at each school, with representatives from each of these groups, works together to plan service-learning activities that will be meaningful learning experiences for both elementary students and Providence College teacher education students. Through a Corporation for National Service grant, the program provides funding for: training in service-learning, project supplies and transportation, substitutes for collaborative work sessions and conference attendance, and graduate and undergraduate student assistance with projects.

Initially, the program targeted math and science methods courses as a place to infuse service-learning in the undergraduate curriculum. During the 1995–1996 school year, service-learning has been integrated in reading methods and social studies and language arts methods courses as well. Gradually, the numbers of teacher education students and public school classrooms will be increased, based on teacher and student interest. Undergraduate students work with the elementary teachers and students to carry out service-learning projects in the local community. Over time, the school service-learning teams described above continue to take on more of the planning and implementation functions in the two schools and work toward involving more of the teachers and schoolchildren in the program.

While the program does not involve all teacher education students, it does provide those who participate with extensive training and support. College student participants go through an application and review process to be selected for the program, and when accepted, take courses in the Feinstein Institute for a minor in Public and Community Service Studies. In the fall semester, teacher education students receive training and support from the Feinstein Institute staff and student "Service Corps" members to develop skills in conflict resolution, reflection, and working with diverse urban communities. The new college student recruits are also mentored by the elementary education students who began in the first year (1994–1995) of the project.

Clark Atlanta University

The service-learning activities at CAU's School of Education are part of a larger campuswide initiative, Culture of Service. The overall aim of the initiative, launched in 1992, is "to strengthen and enhance an institutional culture where community service is linked intrinsically to academic work" (Clark Atlanta University, 1994, p. 1). One of the Culture of Service objectives relates specifically to the teacher education program: "to promote the adoption of service-learning in public school education by developing a model program for integrating service learning into teacher preparation and by promoting and disseminating knowledge of service-learning through community and statewide forums" (Clark Atlanta University, 1994, p. 1).

In February, 1992, the School of Education faculty adopted the following "Policy on Service-Learning" to guide program development.

> Community Service Learning is an educational process which involves young people in their own learning as they give valuable service to their communities. In the School of Education at Clark Atlanta University, teachers, prospective teachers and related educational personnel are imbued with the principles of community service and are trained in the skills necessary to develop, supervise, and organize community service activities for students of all ages. Service learning is integrated into the teacher education curriculum at all levels and provides opportunities for both experiential learning, individual reflection and organized group discussion. (Clark Atlanta University, 1992, p. 1)

Service-learning experiences in the School of Education comprise the following sequence. As part of a freshman orientation to community service and service-learning, college students complete service activities at a wide variety of sites in the community. They contribute thirty hours of service plus complete field journals and reports. In the Foundations of Education course, teacher education students complete service-learning activities in schools and other youth-serving agencies. Their service experiences form the basis for developing understanding about youth development and educational issues. Teacher education students engage in a unit of systematic study on service learning in their certification level methods course (early childhood, elementary/middle grades, or high school). The emphasis in the units is on the role of the teacher in developing, supervising, and organizing learning activities that include a service component. Finally, as part of the student teaching experiences, student teachers may design and carry out a service-learning project under the direction of the cooperating teacher.

A unique aspect of the program at Clark Atlanta University is a service-learning experience for graduate education students in which they develop a mentor relationship with a high school student who is completing service activities as part of a graduation requirement in the Atlanta Public Schools. Along with the process of supporting the high school student, each graduate student conducts a case study of the program with a specific focus on the involvement of his or her high school student. General questions to be addressed in the case study include: How is the program managed? What do students do? What do they learn? How effective is the program in accomplishing its objectives? What is the impact on school and community? Graduate students present their case studies in written reports that follow a typical sequence for sections included in professional journal research articles.

SINGLE COURSES OR INTERNSHIPS

Most service-learning activities in teacher education programs begin with an experience tied to a single course or internship. When supervisory responsibilities fall to one professor and there is not a widespread commitment among the faculty to service-learning, the single course or internship may be the best option with which to begin. Single service-learning experiences may provide the foundation for garnering greater faculty and community support and expanding to a more comprehensive program in the future. Three single course/internship experiences are described here from the University of Houston; Queens College in Manhattan; and Keene State College in Keene, New Hampshire.

University of Houston

While no longer in existence due to changes in program structure and state requirements, the University of Houston's inclusion of service-learning in a four-credit introductory "Learning to Teach" course provides a model for service-learning inclusion in inner-city teacher education programs. The community experience was chosen by over 80 percent of the course's 250 students each semester. Because the teacher educators at Houston hope that their future teachers will see teaching linked with the improvement of our multicultural society, the service activity involved twenty hours of volunteer work with a culture with which the teacher education students were unfamiliar. Goals of the program supported through the service-learning project included: understanding the relationships among the dominant culture ideology, the disaffection among people of color, and the disenfranchisement of those for whom poverty is a way of life.

Working with the University's volunteer program, students were placed in Chicano family centers, YMCA afterschool programs, community health centers, homeless shelters, and other agencies meeting critical community needs. Students reflected on their learning through both in-class discussions and the writing of a final report, in which they explored the connections between the social problems they witnessed and current and potential practices in public schools. These reflections were enhanced by forty-five hours of observations in the schools completed concurrently with the service-learning activities. Houston teacher education students realized new connections between teaching and social services as a result of the service-learning project. For example, a student who volunteered in a shelter for battered women and their children noted that "so many schools stress academics without considering the children's personal situations" (Tellez and Hlebowitsh, 1993, p. 89).

Queens College, Manhattan

In 1989, Professors Salz, Trubowitz, and Harris began the Big Buddy Program, a project aimed at ameliorating the devastating effects of homelessness on children. In the Big Buddy Program, a college student is paired with a child living in one of the city's homeless shelters. Each Saturday, the pair spend the day sharing a variety of educational, cultural, and recreational activities. Queens College students might take the children on subways or buses to other parts of the city to tour museums, view performing arts or sports events, walk through a zoo, or eat lunch and play frisbie in a park. The year-long program seeks to address both the affective and cognitive needs of the children by providing them with a mentor who serves as a friend, confidante, and role model (Salz and Trubowitz, 1992).

The program is a true partnership model. Originally developed by both community members and School of Education faculty, both groups share responsibility for organization and supervision of the program. Queens College students attend biweekly seminars and keep weekly journals to reflect on the impact of the experience on the children and themselves. About forty Queens College students a year, including noneducation majors, participate in the six-credit elective course offered through the School of Education. Some of the Big Buddies attribute new meaning in life or important changes in themselves to their experience. One college student shared, "I've gained a lot of patience, understanding, and compassion. Carlos [the child] has made me into a different person" (Salz and Trubowitz, 1992, p. 554).

Keene State College, Keene, New Hampshire

The teacher education program at Keene State College (KSC) initiated a service-learning experience in conjunction with the general education methods course during the fall of 1994. Teacher education students were offered the option to serve students in an elementary school or a middle school in the areas of mentoring and literacy. About seventeen teacher education students chose the service-learning option, completing two hours a week of service at one of the two school sites. They helped the younger students with a variety of literacy activities including tutoring at an afterschool homework club and assisting with putting journal entries on the computer.

The volunteer coordinator at Franklin elementary school, Nancy Gilliard, was particularly instrumental in making the project work.

> My role as school coordinator has been critical in making a meaningful connection in the community while being sensitive to the needs of our school. Some of my responsibilities include communicating with our staff potential community service-learning ideas, possibilities, planning with KSC faculty, identifying college students, screening, orientation, placement, and evaluation in the school. (N. Gilliard, personal communication, June 22, 1995)

Gilliard also noted the importance of the contributions made to the program by the KSC coordinator, Don Hayes, as well as an Americorps employee, some dedicated teachers, and the school principal. Next steps in the collaboration include developing: plans for evaluating and sustaining the program; procedures for effective communication between the school-college partnership and placement of college students in the schools. At least two other Keene elementary schools have now asked to be included; the program will expand to include these schools and at least fifty additional college students in the fall of 1995 (D. Hayes, personnel communication, June 8, 1995).

BRIDGING THE GAPS: LINKING CAMPUS, COMMUNITY, AND K–12 EDUCATIONAL SYSTEMS

Preservice teacher education programs will be most effective in designing positive service-learning experiences for their students if they engage in meaningful collaboration with both community agencies and the K–12 education system. These links not only model the importance of collaboration in service-learning; they also build bridges that can be beneficial for all involved. Many of the programs described in this chapter illustrate how collaboration outside of the college setting is essential for quality service-learning program development. A further description of our efforts in Iowa is provided here as just one example of how interagency collaboration can begin to build a statewide infrastructure for service-learning.

Many of Iowa's teacher education program graduates obtain their first teaching jobs within the state. Our statewide efforts are based on the premise that these first-year teachers will be more likely to implement service-learning in their classrooms if they work in school districts where they are encouraged and supported in being involved in service-learning. Toward that end, we work closely with the State Department of Education, the regional Area Educational Agencies (AEAs), and Iowa school districts involved with and interested in implementing service-learning. We also take specific measures with our graduates to connect them with these educational agencies.

Joining forces with the K–12 Learn and Serve Coordinator at the Iowa Department of Education has been an essential step in building a statewide service-learning movement. Joe Herrity and I, with assistance from graduate students in the College of Education, have coordinated grant activities together, cosponsored workshops and trainings, conducted a survey of all Iowa school districts in regard to their community service and service-learning activities, and worked to support K–12 ComServe grant recipients as they implement service-learning programs in their schools. We find that our efforts have been mutually supportive in getting the word out about events and opportunities surrounding service-learning in the state. We touch base frequently by phone and meet in person at least three or four times a year.

Currently, our collaboration is focused on bringing together consultants from the Area Educational Agencies and Iowa school districts. During the spring 1995, we jointly sponsored a training for school district service-learning coordinators and AEA consultants. The coordinators attended a week-long training, culminating in presenting much of what they had learned during the first three days to the AEA consultants who joined us on Thursday and Friday. The AEAs have each been given planning grants to sponsor service-learning trainings and program development in their respective regions; the service-learning coordinators are required to present an in-service session in their region during the fall following the training they attended. Thus, collaboration is beneficial for both of these groups as they work together. Resource materials, curricula, videos, overheads, and handouts provided to both groups enhance their efforts.

We also make efforts to connect our teacher education graduates with the districts and AEA consultants involved with service-learning. Student teachers who complete service-learning projects are provided with a list of Iowa districts interested in hiring service-learning teachers. I encourage all of the students who complete service-learning activities through our program to talk about service-learning at their interviews and to include photos and journal entries from their service-learning activities in their interview portfolios. Some of our graduates have returned to tell me that interviewers have been very interested in their service-learning experience; a few have felt that this experience is what led to a job offer. It is to be hoped that these graduates will find a supportive climate in their teaching positions that will encourage them to include service-learning in their curriculum. Research efforts in the next few years will attempt to find out when, how, and why beginning teachers who graduated from our program do or do not implement service-learning in their classrooms.

IN CLOSING

If service-learning is to become commonplace practice in the nation's K–12 schools, preservice teacher education programs must give future teachers experience in and information about quality service-learning. There are many rationales for infusing service-learning in teacher education in a democratic, multicultural society. Given the variety of program options, teacher educators can build on the experiences of others and explore the best fit for the time they have to invest and the particular needs of their programs and communities. Linking these efforts on campus with community agencies and the K–12 educational stream will benefit all those involved and begin to build supportive infrastructures for service-learning in our states and communities.

Chapter 23

Service-Learning in a Democratic Society: Conclusion

Rahima C. Wade

The authors of this book have addressed the promise, the practice, and the problems of service-learning in our nation's public schools. Throughout, the focus has been on recognizing the potential contributions that service-learning can make to students, schools, and communities, yet, at the same time, acknowledging that there are significant challenges to be addressed if this potential is to be realized. While many programs are only shadows of what they could be, there are also many quality service-learning programs in our nation's schools. From coast to coast, from small town to inner city, one can point to numerous examples of projects that are making significant contributions to local communities and enhancing students' learning and social development.

These exemplary practices in our nation's schools, many of which are described in this book, can serve to bolster our energy and commitment to creating high-quality service-learning programs throughout the nation. At present, there are too many programs that do not meet the standards of quality set forth in this book: programs that do not include reflection, have no evaluation component, are not integrated with curricular objectives, or do not include meaningful and challenging service activities. Much work remains to be done to promote quality practice and to document the effects of such practice through research and evaluation.

The journey to quality service-learning can be likened to a long hike up a high mountain. We must plan carefully before we set out, bring appropriate provisions, schedule time for rejuvenating breaks along the way, and anticipate the problems that may confront us, both within and outside of ourselves. In short, we must be realistic about both our eventual goal and what it will take to get there from here.

Part of that realism in our service-learning work is remembering that the nation's schools, as public institutions, are a reflection of society. As such, they often mirror the individualistic, "get ahead" mentality so prevalent in our culture. Yes, we can find many examples of people reaching out to each other and placing the common good before individual success. Yet it is just as easy to identify the many ways our society fosters individual gain and the resultant inequity and injustice. We are a culture of paradox, and our schools reflect the dualistic nature of our national community.

While service-learning is unlikely to resolve this dilemma, it has the potential to make a contribution toward justice and equality. It is difficult to base a service-learning project on competition or individual success. Service-learning projects are team efforts, involving collaborators both within and outside of schools. Service-learning, by its very nature, brings people together in pusuit of a common cause, a shared goal. The practice of service-learning, then, can have a transformative effect on the individualistic values of schools and communities, and on the values of the people within them.

This change is unlikely to happen, however, unless program leaders engage students in examining the beliefs underlying individualism: that there just isn't enough to go around, that some must win while others lose, that personal fulfillment lies only in individual wealth. Service-learning can help young people realize at an early age that there is another way. When everyone shares there can be more than enough to go around, we can all "win," and we can realize more fulfillment in community connections than we ever could on our own. As public school students graduate and enter colleges and careers of their choosing, they will hopefully take these values with them and put community-mindedness into practice in government, business, and industry, as well as in human services.

Educators must not forget that while our schools mirror society, they also serve as agents of cultural change. The transformative element of schools, however, must be put into perspective. Schools are unlikely to make significant changes toward justice and equality without commensurate efforts in the other political, economic, and social spheres of our democracy. Shifting the balance away from privatism and toward community-mindedness requires that we address the root causes of greed and narcissism and the political, social, environmental, and economic issues that plague our society.

At present, there are too few service-learning programs that address the larger structural issues that create needs for service in the first place. Students who engage in advocacy projects are the most likely to examine the political, social, or economic problems and related policy issues that contribute to community needs. However, even those students who are engaged in one-to-one direct service with individuals or indirect service projects benefiting community agencies should be encouraged to consider the "big picture" in terms of actions that might contribute to a better society for all. Students need to be encouraged to connect their direct or indirect service with other civic acts such as voting on referenda and public policy issues, electing officials who support social justice and environmental improvement, attending and participating in community meetings, and writing letters to public officials and policy makers.

Through this more comprehensive approach to service-learning, students can become aware of and in some cases begin to experience a wider range of civic behaviors beyond those one might label "service." Thus, students graduating from such civic education programs will have in-depth skills and knowledge of societal issues and they will understand service as an essential act among many performed by an engaged citizen in a democracy.

We have no guarantees of this outcome, of course, but it is possible; we can hope. And for those of us committed to contributing to the creation of a just and equitable society through public education, service-learning may be our best bet in an uncertain world. Who knows what the society of the United States will look like in the future? As a nation, we can't go back in time to the colonial villages or small farms of the past. We are unlikely to dismantle our multileveled school systems and return to the one room schoolhouse communities of the past.

Instead, we are called on to forge a new vision of what community-mindedness might look like in an increasingly diverse society with limited resources and dissimilar values. We must seek out creative means for involving citizens in public life, for finding common goals we can all work toward, for obtaining the necessary resources to make our plans a reality. We must find ways to support a vibrant democracy and, at the same time, to question its inequitable practices. We must work on these goals both in our communities and in our schools.

Faced with the complexities of our faltering democracy—the myriad social and environmental problems in our society, and the relatively ineffectual nature of current civic education practices in public schools; these goals are both urgent and unavoidable. Committed educators must not be daunted by the enormity of the challenge, but rather, they must plan thoughtfully for the uphill journey ahead. With hope, persistence, and creativity in our sack of provisions, as well as plans for stopping and appreciating small successes along the way, we just may be able to get there after all.

Appendix: Resources for K–12 Community Service-Learning Programs

Jean McMenimen

BOOKS AND REPORTS

Alliance for Service-Learning in Education Reform. *Standards of quality for school-based service-learning*, 1993.

Bellah, R. N., R. Madsen, W. Sullivan, A. Swidler, and S. Tipton. *Habits of the heart: Individualism and commitment in American life.* New York: Harper & Row, 1986.

Bernard, B. *Youth service: From youth as problems to youth as resources.* Prevention Resource Center, Inc., 1989.

Cairn, R. W. and S. Cairn. *Collaborators: Schools and communities working together for youth service.* Roseville, MN: National Youth Leadership Council, 1991.

Carnegie Council on Adolescent Development. *Turning points: Preparing American youth for the twenty-first century.* Washington, DC: Task Force on Education of Young Adolescents, 1989.

Coalition for National Service. *National service: An action agenda for the 1990's.* Washington, DC: National Service Secretariat, 1988.

Coles, R. *A call of service: A witness to idealism.* New York: Houghton Mifflin, 1993.

Commission on National and Community Service. *Serve America.* A newsletter on issues concerning national service.

Conrad, D. and D. Hedin. *High school community service: A review of research and programs.* National Center on Effective Secondary Schools, U.S. Department of Education, Office of Educational Research and Improvement; Wisconsin Center for Education Research, School of Education, University of Wisconsin-Madison, 1989.

Conrad, D. and D. Hedin. *Instruments and scoring guide of the experiential education evaluation project.* Report for the Center for Youth Development and Research, 1981, September.

Conrad, D. and D. Hedin. *Youth service: A guidebook for developing and operating effective programs.* Washington, DC: Independent Sector, 1987.

Council of Chief State School Officers Service Learning Project. *Federal funding guide for K–12 service learning.* Washington, DC: Author, 1993.

Council of Chief State School Officers. *Learning by doing.* Washington, DC: Council of Chief State School Officers, 1989.

Crowner, D. "*The effects of service learning on student participants.*" Paper presented at The National Society for Experiential Education in Newport, RI, 1992, November.

Cunningham, C. *School sanctioned youth community service.* Washington, DC: Council of Chief State School Officers, 1989, July.

Dluhy, M. J. *Building coalitions in the human services.* Newbury Park, CA: Sage Publications, 1990.

Duckenfield, M. and L. Swanson. *Service learning: Meeting the needs of youth at risk. A dropout prevention research report.* Clemson, SC: National Dropout Prevention Center, 1992, June.

Eberly, Donald J., ed. *National Youth Service: A democratic institution for the twenty-first century.* Washington, DC: National Service Secretariat, 1991.

Ehrlich, T. "Community service: A learning tool." *Serve! America: The Newsletter of the Commission on National and Community Service* 2 (1993): 8.

Fertman, C. I., I. Buchen, J. Long, and L. White. *Service-learning reflections: Update of service-learning in Pennsylvania.* Pittsburg, PA: Pennsylvania Service-Learning Resource and Evaluation Network, 1994.

Fertman, C. *Service learning for all students. Fastback 375.* Bloomington, IN: Phi Delta Kappa Educational Foundation, 1994.

Giles, D. E., E. P. Honnet, and S. Migliore, eds. *Research agenda for combining service and learning in the 1990's.* Raleigh, NC: National Society for Experiential Education, 1991.

Gomez, B., J. Kielsmeier, C. Kinsley, K. McPherson, and C. Parsons. *Service-learning advances school improvement.* A position paper from the National Service-Learning Initiative. 1990.

Harrington, D. and J. Schine. *Connections: Service learning in the middle grades.* New York: Center for Advanced Study in Education/CASE, The Graduate School and University, 1989.

Harrison, C. H. *Student service: The new Carnegie unit.* Princeton, NJ: The Carnegie Foundation for the Advancement of Teaching, 1987.

Honnet, E. P. and S. J. Poulsen. *Principles of good practice for combining service and learning.* Wingspread Special Report, 1989, October.

Jones, B. L. and R. Maloy. *Partnerships for improving schools.* New York: Greenwood Press, 1988.

Kendall, J. C. and Associates. *Combining service and learning: A resource book for community and public service.* Vol. I. Raleigh, NC: National Society for Internships and Experiential Education, 1990a.

Kendall, J. C. and Associates. *Combining service and learning: A resource book for community and public service.* Vol. II. Raleigh, NC: National Society for Internships and Experiential Education, 1990b.

Kendall, J. C., J. S. Duley, T. C. Little, J. S. Permaul, and S. Rubin. *Strengthening experiential education within your institution.* Raleigh, NC: National Society for Internships and Experiential Education, 1986.

Kinsley, C., ed. *Community service learning sourcebook.* Springfield, MA: Springfield Public Schools, 1988, September.

Lewis, A. *Facts and Faith: A status report on youth service.* Washington, DC: Youth and America's Future. The William T. Grant Foundation Commission on Work, Family, and Citizenship, 1988.

Luce, J. (1988). *Combining service and learning: A resource book for community and public service.* Vol. III. Raleigh, NC: National Society for Internships and Experiential Education, 1988.

Maryland Student Service Alliance. *Maryland's best practices: An improvement guide for school-based service-learning.* Baltimore, MD: Maryland Department of Education, 1995, May.

McPherson, K. *Enriching learning through service.* Vancouver, WA: Project Service Leadership, 1989a.

McPherson, K. *Learning through service.* Seattle, WA: Safeco Insurance Company, 1989b.

Minnesota Office on Volunteer Services. *The power and potential of youth in service to communities.* St. Paul, MN: Department of Administration, 1993.

Minnesota State Department of Education. *Model learner outcomes for youth community service.* St. Paul, MN: 1992.

National Center for Service Learning in Early Adolescence. *Connections: Service learning in the middle grades.* New York: Author, 1991a.

National Center for Service Learning in Early Adolescence. *Reflection: The key to service learning.* New York: Author, 1991b.

National School Volunteer Program, Inc. *School volunteer programs: Everything you need to know to start or improve your program.* Alexandria, VA: 1981.

Newmann, F. M. and R. A. Rutter. *The effects of high school community service programs on students' social development.* Madison, WI: Wisconsin Center for Education Research, University of Wisconsin, 1983.

Parsons, C. *Removing barriers: Service learning in rural areas.* Washington, DC: Council of Chief State School Officers, Resource Center on Educational Equity, 1993.

Rolzinski, C. A. *The adventure of adolescence: Middle school students and community service.* Washington, DC: Youth Service America, 1990.

Sagawa, S. and S. Halperin. *Visions of service: The future of the national and community service act.* Washington, DC: National Women's Law Center and American Youth Policy Forum, 1993.

Schine, J. *Young adolescents and community service.* Washington, DC: The Carnegie Council on Adolescent Development, 1989.

Shields, K. *In the tiger's mouth: An empowerment guide for social action.* Philadelphia, PA: New Society Publishers, 1994.

Silcox, H. C. *A how to guide to reflection.* Holland, PA: Brighton Press Inc., 1993.

W. T. Grant Foundation Commission on Work, Family and Citizenship. *Pathways to success for America's youth and young families.* Washington, DC: Commission, 1988b.

W. T. Grant Foundation Commission on Work, Family, and Citizenship. *States and communities on the move: Policy initiatives to build a world-class workforce.* Washington, DC: Commission, 1991.

W. T. Grant Foundation Commission on Work, Family, and Citizenship. *The forgotten half: Non-college youth in America.* Washington, DC: Commission, 1988a.

COMMUNITY ACTION BOOKS

Adams, P. and J. Marzollo. *The helping hands handbook.* New York: Random Books Young Readers, 1992.

Bellamy, D. *How green are you?* New York: Clarkson N. Potter, Inc, 1991.

Berger, M. *Can Kids save the earth?* New York: Newbridge Comms, 1994.

Berry, J. *Every kid's guide to saving the earth.* Nashville, TN: Hambleton-Hill, 1993.

Dee, C., ed. *Kid heroes of the environment.* Berkeley, CA: EarthWorks Press, Inc, 1991.

Elkington, J., D. Hill, and J. Makower. *Going green: A kid's handbook to saving the planet.* Willard, OH: R. R. Donnelley & Sons Company, 1990.

Fiffer, S. and S. S. Fiffer. *Fifty ways to help your community: A handbook for change.* New York: Main Street Books, 1994.

Fleming, R. *Rescuing a neighborhood: The Bedford-Stuyvesant volunteer ambulance corps.* New York: Walker and Company, 1995.

Gilbert, S. *Lend a hand: The how, where and why of volunteering.* New York: Morrow Junior Books, 1988.

Goodman, A. *The big help book: 365 ways you can make a difference by volunteering.* New York: Pocket Books, 1994.

Greene, C. *Caring for our people.* Hillside, NJ: Enslow Publishers, Inc, 1991.

Hanmer, T. *Taking a stand against sexism and sex discrimination.* New York: Franklin Watts, 1990.

Hatkoff, A. and K. Klopp. *How to save the children.* New York: Fireside Books, 1992.

Hollender, J. *How to make the world a better place: A guide to doing good.* Quill-Morrow, 1990.

Hoose, P. *It's our world, too! Stories of young people who are making a difference.* Dubuque, IA: Little, Brown, 1993.

Hurwitz, S. *Working together against homelessness.* New York: The Rosen Publishing Group, Inc., 1994.

Isaac, K. *Civics for democracy: A journey for teachers and students.* Washington, DC: Center for Study of Responsive Law and Essential Information, 1989.

Javna, J. *Fifty simple things kids can do to save the earth.* Kansas City, KS: Andrews and McMeel, 1990.

Kroloff, C. A. *Fifty-four ways you can help the homeless.* Southport, CT & West Orange, NJ: Hugh Lauter Leven Assoc. Inc. & Behrman House, Inc., 1993.

Kronenwetter, M. *Taking a stand against human rights abuses.* New York: Franklin Watts, 1990.

Langone, J. *Our endangered earth: What we can do to save it.* Boston, MA: Little, Brown and Company, 1992.

Logan, S. *The kids can help book.* New York: Perigree Books, 1992.

McKissack, P. and F. McKissack. *Taking a stand against racism and racial discrimination.* New York: Franklin Watts, 1990.

Meltzer, M. *Who cares? Millions do*. New York: Walker & Co, 1994.

Newkirk, I. *Save the animals! 101 easy things you can do*. New York: Warner Books, Inc, 1990.

Newton, D. E. *Taking a stand against environmental pollution*. New York: Franklin Watts, 1990.

Plattner, S. S. *Connecting with my community*. Carthage, IL: Fearon Teach Aids, 1991.

Salzman, M. and T. Reisgies. *One hundred fifty ways teens can make a difference*. Princeton, NJ: Petersons Guides, 1991.

Thro, E. *Taking a stand against nuclear war*. New York: Franklin Watts, 1990.

CURRICULUM GUIDES

Buchen, I. and C. Fertman. *Creating a culture of service: Effective service learning*. Warminster, PA: Mar*co Products, Inc., 1994.

Cairn, R. and J. Kielsmeier. *Growing hope: A sourcebook on integrating youth service into the school curriculum*. National Youth Leadership Council, 1991, April.

Cairn, R. and T. L. Coble. *Learning by giving: K–8 service-learning. Curriculum guide*. Minneapolis, MN: National Youth Leadership Council, 1993.

Florida Department of Education. *Learning by serving*. Tallahassee, FL: Author, 1992.

Hammond, M. and R. Collins. *One world one earth. Educating children for social responsibility*. Philadelphia, PA: New Society Publishers, 1993.

Hatkoff, A. and K. Klopp. *How to save the children*. New York: Fireside Books, 1992.

J.F.K. Library Foundation. *We can make a difference!: Creating citizen leaders though community service*. Boston: J.F.K. Library Foundation, 1994.

Kinsley, C., ed. *Whole learning through service: A guide for integrating service into the curriculum K–8*. Springfield, MA: Community Service Learning Center, 1991.

Lewis, B. A. *A teacher's guide to kids with courage*. Minneapolis, MN: Free Spirit Publishing, Inc., 1992b.

Lewis, B. A. *Kids with courage*. Minneapolis, MN: Free Spirit Publishing, Inc., 1992a.

Lewis, B. A. *The kid's guide to social action: How to solve the social problems you choose and turn creative thinking into positive action*. Minneapolis, MN: Free Spirit Publishing, Inc, 1991.

Lewis, B. A. *The kids guide to service-projects*. Minneapolis, MN: Free Spirit Publishing, Inc, 1995.

Lions-Quest International. *Skills for growing.* Granville, OH: Quest International, 1990.

Maryland Student Service Alliance. *High school service-learning guide.* Baltimore, MD: Maryland State Department of Education, 1993.

Maryland Student Service Alliance. *The courage to care. The strength to serve. Draft instructional framework in service-learning for elementary schools.* Baltimore, MD: Maryland State Department of Education, 1991b.

Maryland Student Service Alliance. *The courage to care. The strength to serve. Draft instructional framework in service-learning for middle schools.* Baltimore, MD: Maryland State Department of Education, 1991a.

Melcher, J. *Caring is the key: Building a school-based intergenerational service program.* Harrisburg, PA: PennSERVE, 1991.

National Youth Leadership Council. *Route to reform: K–8 service-learning curriculum ideas.* St. Paul, MN: National Youth Leadership Council, 1994, September.

Novelli, J. and B. Chayet. *The kids care book: Fifty class projects that help kids help others.* New York: Scholastic Professional Books, 1991.

Parsons, C. *Service learning from A to Z.* Chester, VT: Vermont Schoolhouse Press, 1991.

Pennsylvania Institute for Environmental and Community Service Learning. *Service learning detective series.* Holland, PA: Author, 1992.

Pennsylvania Institute for Environmental and Community Service Learning. *Service learning portfolio.* Holland, PA: Author, 1992.

Pennsylvania Institute for Environmental and Community Service Learning. *The high school project requirement in Pennsylvania: An opportunity for experiential service learning.* Holland, PA: Author, 1992.

Project Service Leadership. *Doing right for yourself and others. A student's guide to today's heroes.* Tacoma, WA: Hitachi Foundation, no date.

South Carolina Department of Education. *Serving to learn high school.* Columbia SC: South Carolina Department of Education, 1994a.

South Carolina Department of Education. *Serving to learn K–8.* Columbia, SC: Department of Education, 1994b.

Springfield Public Schools. *Whole learning through service: A guide for integrating service into the curriculum K–8.* Springfield, MA: Community Service Learning, 1991.

Stephens, L. S. *The complete guide to learning through community service grades K–9.* Des Moines, IA: Allyn & Bacon, 1995.

Thomas Jefferson Forum. *Coordinator handbook: A comprehensive guide for developing high school-based community-service programs*. Medford, MA: Author, 1991.

JOURNAL ARTICLES

Adams, L. B. "How one school builds self-esteem in students and serves its community." *Middle School Journal* 24 (1993, May): 53–55

Allen, J. A. "Eureka A Yurt: Integrating Mathematics, Cooperative Learning, and Community Service." *Journal of Experiential Education* 14 (1991): 39–44.

Anderson, V., C. Kinsley, P. Negroni, and C. Price. "Community Service Learning and School Improvements in Springfield, Massachusetts." *Phi Delta Kappan* 72 (1991, June): 761–764.

Barber, B. "Public Talk and Civic Action: Education for Participation in a Strong Democracy." *Social Education* 53 (1989): 355–56, 370.

Benard, B. "Youth Service: From Youth as Problems to Youth as Resources." *Prevention Forum* (1990, January): 6–14.

Benjamin, S. "An Ideascape for Education: What Futurists Recommend." *Educational Leadership* 47 (1989, September): 8–14.

Berry, H. "Service-Learning in International/Intercultural Settings." *Experiential Education* (1988): 13.

Boyce, K. and R. Cairn. "Orientation and Training." *The Generator* 11 (1991): 6.

Boyer, E.L. "Civic Education for Responsible Citizens." *Educational Leadership* 48 (1990): 4–7.

Boyte, H.C. "Community Service and Civic Education." *Phi Delta Kappan* 72 (1991, June): 765–767.

Briscoe, J. "Citizenship, Service, and School Reform in Pennsylvania." *Phi Delta Kappan* 72 (1991): 758–60.

Calabrese, R. L. and H. Shumer. "The Effects of Service Activities on Adolescent Alienation." *Adolescence* 21 (1986): 675–87.

Caldwell, J. "Community Service Learning in Springfield, Massachusetts." *Equity and Choice* 5 (1989, March): 54–59.

Clark, T. "Youth Community Service." *Social Education* 53 (1989): 367.

Conrad, D. and D. Hedin. "The Impact of Experiential Education on Adolescent Development." *Child and Youth Services* 4 (1982): 57–76.

Conrad, D. and D. Hedin. "School-Based Community Service: What We Know from Research and Theory." *Phi Delta Kappan* 72 (1991): 743–49.

Earle, J. "Helping Youth to Serve: Issues for State Policy Makers. The State Board Connection." *Issues in Brief* 9 (1989, September): 1–8.

Eberly, D.J. "National Youth Service: A Developing Institution." *NASSP Bulletin* 77 (1993, February): 50–57.

Ediger, M., B.S. Hamilton, and W. Hanna. "Community Service Promotes Student Awareness." *Schools in the Middle: Theory into Practice* (1993, September): 24–26.

Furco, A. Building self-esteem and self-knowledge through school-based community service programs. Paper presented at the University of California at Berkeley (1991, December).

Giles, D. "Dewey's Theory of Experience: Implications for Service-Learning." *Journal of Cooperative Education* 27 (1991): 87–90.

Hall, M. "Gadugi: A Model of Service-Learning for Native American Communities." *Phi Delta Kappan* 72 (1991): 754–57.

Hamilton, S. and R. Zeldin. "Learning Civics in the Community." *Curriculum Inquiry* 17 (1987): 407–20.

Hamilton, S. F. and L. M. Fenzel. "The Impact of Volunteer Experience on Adolescent Social Development: Evidence of Program Effects." *Journal of Adolescent Research* 3 (1988): 65–80.

Harrington, D. "Reaching Beyond the Self: Service Learning for Middle Schoolers." *American Educator: The Professional Journal of the American Federation of Teachers* 16 (1992, Summer): 36–43.

Hedin, D. "Students as Teachers: A Tool for Improving School Climate and Productivity." *Social Policy* 17 (1987): 42–47.

Hedin, D. "The Power of Community Service in Caring for America's Children." *Proceedings of the Academy of Political Science* 37 (1989): 201–13.

Hoffman, C. "The Center for Creative Retirement." *Appalachia* 27 (1994, Summer): 40–44.

Kaye, C.B. "Learning Through Caring: Students Serve Their Communities." *Teaching Tolerance* 2 (1993, Spring): 13.

Kennedy, E. "National Service and Education for Citizenship." *Phi Delta Kappan,* 72 (1991, June): 771–73.

Kiner, R. "Community Service: A Middle School Success Story." *Clearing House* 66 (1993, Jan.–Feb.): 139–40.

Kinsley, L.C. "Creating New Structures-Community Service Learning." *Community Education Journal* 18 (1990, Fall): 2–4.

Kohn, A. "Caring Kids." *Phi Delta Kappan* 72 (1991): 496–506.

Langton, S. and F. Miller. "Youth Community Service." *Equity & Choice* (1988, Spring): 25–33.

Lewis, B.A. "Cleanup Crusade: Citizenship in Action." *Social Education* 54 (1990): 238–40.

Lieberman, A. "Expanding the Leadership Team." *Educational Leadership* 45 (1988, February): 4–7.

Markus, G., J. Howard, and D. King. "Integrating Community Service and Classroom Instruction Enhances Learning: Results from an Experiment." *Educational Evaluation and Policy Analysis* 15 (1993): 410–19.

McPherson, K. "Project Service Leadership: School Service Projects in Washington State." *Phi Delta Kappan* 72 (1991): 750–53.

McPherson, K. and M. K. Nebgen. "Setting the Agenda: School Reform and Community Service." *Network* 2 (1991): 1–4.

Nathan, J. and J. Kielsmeier. "The Sleeping Giant of School Reform." *Phi Delta Kappan* 72 (1991, June): 739–42.

Nebgen, M. K. and K. McPherson. "Enriching Learning Through Service: A Tale of Three Districts." *Educational Leadership* 48 (1990, November): 90–92.

Newmann, F. "Reflective Civic Participation." *Social Education* 53 (1989): 357–60.

Newmann, F. and R. Rutter. "A Profile of High School Community Service Programs." *Educational Leadership* 43 (1986): 65–71.

O'Brien, E. "Outside the Classroom: Students as Employees, Volunteers, and Interns." *Research Briefs. American Council on Education* 4 (1993): 1–12.

Parsons, C. "SerVermont: The Little Initiative That Could." *Phi Delta Kappan* 72 (1991): 768–70.

Patchin, S.H. "Community Service for Five-Year-Olds (and Laughing All the Way)." *Young Children* 49 (1994, January): 20–21.

Ruggenberg, J. "Community Service Learning: A Vital Component of Secondary School Education." *Moral Education Forum* 18 (1993, Fall): 13–19.

Sandler, L., J. Vandegrift, and C. VerBrugghen. "From Desert to Garden: Reconnecting Disconnected Youth." *Educational Leadership* 52 (1995, May): 14–16.

Shaheen, J.C. "Participatory Citizenship in the Elementary Grades." *Social Education* 53 (1989, October): 361–63.

Shalaway, L. "Learning from Community Service." *Instructor* (1991, March): 98.

Sherraden, M. *Youth Participation in America. National Youth Service: A Democratic Institution for the Twenty-first Century.* Washington, DC: National Service Secretariat. (1991).

Silcox, H. "School-Based Community Service Programs—An Imperative for Effective Schools." *NAASP Bulletin* 77 (1993): 58–62.

Silcox, H. "Experiential Environmental Education in Russia: A Study in Community Service Learning." *Phi Delta Kappan* 74 (1993, May): 706–09.

Thomas, G.R. "Commitment and Action: New Directions in Citizenship Education Research." *The History and Social Science Teacher* 19 (1984): 238–39.

Thompson, S. "The Community as Classroom." *Educational Leadership* 52 (1995, May): 17–20.

Wade, R. "Social Action: Expanding the Role of Citizenship in the Social Studies Curriculum." *Inquiry in Social Studies: Curriculum, Research, and Instruction* 29 (1993): 2–18.

Wade, R. "Community Service-Learning: Commitment through Active Citizenship." *Social Studies and the Young Learner* 6 (1994, January–February): 1–4.

Wigginton, E. "Foxfire Grows Up." *Harvard Educational Review* 59 (1989): 24–31.

Williams, R. "The Impact of Field Education on Student Development: Research Findings." *Journal of Cooperative Education* 27 (1991): 29–45.

Willis, S. "Learning Through Service." *Association for Supervision and Curriculum Development Update* (1993, August): 1–8.

Willison, S. "When Students Volunteer to Feed the Hungry: Some Considerations for Educators." *Social Studies* 85 (1994, March–April): 88–90.

VIDEOS

All the Difference: Youth Service in Minnesota. Available from Pennsylvania Institute for Environmental and Community Service-Learning. 1995.

Citizen Stories: Democracy and Responsibility in American Life. Available from Close Up Foundation. 1991.

The Courage to Care. The Strength to Serve. Available from Maryland Student Service Alliance. 1994, Revised.

PhilaDEAFia. Available from Pennsylvania Institute for Environmental and Community Service-Learning. 1995.

Route to Reform: Service-Learning and School Improvement. Available from National Youth Leadership Council. 1994.

School Connection to the Real World: Service-Learning. Available from Pennsylvania Institute for Environmental and Community Service-Learning. 1995.

Service Learning: Connecting Youth and Community. Available from Colorado State University, Office of Community Services, 1995.

Service-Learning: Transforming Education. Available from Linking San Francisco. 1995.

We Kids Can! The B.A.T. Club. Available from Silver Burdett & Ginn. 1991.

ORGANIZATIONS

Alliance for Service Learning in
  Educational Reform
One Massachusetts Avenue NW, Suite 700
Washington, DC 20001
202-336-7026

The Association for Experiential Education
University of Colorado
Box 249
Boulder, CO 80309
303-492-1547

Close Up Foundation
44 Canal Center Plaza
Alexandria, VA 22314-9836
703-706-3300

Community Service Learning Center
333 Bridge Street
Suite 8
Springfield, MA 01108
413-734-6857

Constitutional Rights Foundation
601 S. Kingsley Drive
Los Angeles, CA 90005
213-487-5590

Corporation For National and
  Community Service
1201 New York Avenue, NW
Washington, DC 20525
202-606-5000

Council of Chief State School Officers
One Massachusetts Avenue, NW, Suite 700
Washington, DC 20001
202-336-7026

Independent Sector
1828 L Street
Washington, DC 20036
202-223-8100

Institute for Democracy in Education
College of Education
Ohio University
313 McCracken Hall
Athens, OH 45701-2979
614-593-4531

Iowa Service Learning Partnership
N291 Lindquist Center
University of Iowa
Iowa City, IA 52242
319-384-0547

Maryland Student Service Alliance
200 W. Baltimore Street, Room 407
Baltimore, MD 21201
410-767-0356

Michigan K–12 Service Learning Center
Michigan State University
Erickson Hall, Suite 253
East Lansing, MI 48824
517-432-2940

National Dropout Prevention Center
Clemson University
Clemson, SC 29634
803-656-2599

National Helpers Network, Inc.
(formerly National Center for Service-
Learning in Early Adolescence)
245 5th Avenue, Suite 1705
New York, NY 10016-8728
212-679-2482

National Indian Youth Leadership
Project
McClellan Hall
650 Vanderbosch Parkway
Gallup, NM 87301
505-722-9176

National Society for Experiential
Education
3509 Haworth Drive, Suite 207
Raleigh, NC 27609
919-787-3263

National Youth Leadership Council
1910 West County Road B
St. Paul, MN 55113-1337
612-631-3672

PennSERVE
The Governor's Office of Citizen
Service
333 Market Street, 10th Floor
Harrisburg, PA 17126
717-787-1971

Pennsylvania Institute for Environmental
and Community Service Learning
Harry Silcox, Director
Philadelphia College of Textiles and
Science
Henry Avenue and School House Lane
Philadelphia, PA 19144
215-951-0343

Pennsylvania Service-Learning Resource
and Evaluation Network
School of Education
University of Pittsburgh
5D21 Forbes Quadrangle
Pittsburgh, PA 15260
412-648-7196

Points of Light Foundation
736 Jackson Place
Washington, DC 20503
202-223-9186

Project Service Leadership
12703 NW 20th Avenue
Vancouver, WA 98685
206-576-5070

Quest International
537 Jones Road
P.O. Box 566
Granville, OH 43023-0566
614-522-6400

StarServe Program
701 Santa Monica Boulevard
Suite 220
Santa Monica, CA 90401
213-452-STAR

Thomas Jefferson Forum
Lincoln Filene Center
Tufts University
Medford, MA 02155
617-627-3858

Youth Service America
1319 F Street NW, Suite 900
Washington, DC 20004
202-783-8855

Youth Volunteer Corps of America
6310 Lamar Avenue, Suite 125
Overland Park, KS 66202-4247
913 432-9822

Available from the University of Iowa
Service-Learning Department

Joining Hands:
Community Service-Learning Resource Kits

For Kindergarten through Eighth Grade
Service-Learning Programs

The Joining Hands Kits provide busy classroom teachers with hundreds of ideas for planning and conducting service-learning projects. The kits cover two levels, primary (kindergarten through third grade) and intermediate (fourth through eighth grades), for each of six current themes: animals, environmental, health/safety, intergenerational, poverty/hunger, and school community. Endorsed by teachers, students, and the Corporation for National Service, each kit includes all of the following:

• a resource binder with color-coded sections on service-learning basics, service project ideas, reflection questions, curriculum connections, annotated selected children's literature list, literature activities (for the two children's literature selections included in the kit), annotated list of resource books, and a list of national agencies and organizations.
• two children's literature books
• two resource books
• one zippered canvas bag to hold all the kit materials

For further information about the kits or to receive a brochure listing all of the kits' contents, call toll free 1-800-369-IOWA or write to:

The University of Iowa, Service-Learning Dept.
215 Seashore Hall Center
Iowa City, Iowa, 52242-1402

References

A Matter of Time: Risk and Opportunity in the Nonschool Hours. New York: Carnegie Council on Adolescent Development, 1992.

Albert, G, ed. *Service-learning reader: Reflections and perspectives on service.* Raleigh, NC: National Society for Experiential Education, 1994.

Allam, C. and B. Zerkin. "The case for integrating service-learning into teacher preparation programs." *Generator* 13 (1993, Spring): 11–13.

Alliance for Service-Learning in Education Reform. *Standards of quality for school-based service-learning.* Chester, VT: Author, 1993.

Alt, M. N. and E. A. Medrich. *Student outcomes from participation in community service.* Prepared for the U.S. Department of Education, Office of Research. MPR Associates, Berkeley, 1994, June.

Anderson, C. S. and J. T. Witmer. "Addressing school board and administrative concerns about service-learning." *Democracy & Education* 9 (1994): 33–37.

Anderson, J. and K. Guest. "Service-learning in teacher education at Seattle University." Pp. 139–48 in *Building community: Service learning in the academic disciplines,* ed. R. J. Kraft and M. Swadener. Denver: Colorado Campus Compact, 1994.

Anderson, J. and K. Guest. "Linking campus and community: Service leadership in teacher education at Seattle University." Pp. 11–30 in *Integrating service learning into teacher education: Why and how?*, ed. B. Gomez. Washington, D.C.: Council of Chief State School Officers, 1995.

Anderson, V., C. Kinsley, P. Negroni, and C. Price. "Community service learning and school improvement in Springfield, Massachusetts." *Phi Delta Kappan* (1991, June): 761–64.

Arendt, H. "The crisis in education." In *Between past and future: Eight exercises in political thought*. New York: Viking/Penguin, 1961.

Atwell, N. *In the middle: Writing, reading, and learning with adolescents*. Portsmouth, NH: Boynton/Cook Heinemann, 1987.

Ball, D. and S. Rundquist. "Collaboration as a context for joining teacher learning with learning about teaching." In *Teaching for understanding*, eds. D. Cohen, M. W. McLaughlin, and J. Talbert. San Francisco: Jossey-Bass, 1993.

Barber, B. *Strong democracy: Participatory politics for a new age*. Berkeley: University of California Press, 1984.

Barber, B. R. *An aristocracy of everyone: The politics of education and the future of democracy*. New York: Ballatine Books, 1992.

Batenburg, M. P. *Community agency and school collaboration: Going in with your eyes open*. Paper presented at the Annual Meeting of the American Educational Research Association, San Francisco, 1995, April 4–8.

Battistoni, R. M. *Public schooling and the education of democratic citizens*. Jackson: University Press of Mississippi, 1985.

Beck, P. and M. K. Jennings. "Pathways to participation." *American Political Science Review* 76 (1982).

Beister, T. W., K. Kershner, and M. W. Blair. *Evaluation of cumulative effects of RBS career education*. Paper presented at the Annual Meeting of the American Education Research Association in Toronto, 1978, March.

Bellah, R. N., R. Madsen, W. M. Sullivan, A. Swidler, and S. M. Tipton. *Habits of the heart*. Berkeley and Los Angeles: University of California Press, 1985.

Bellah, R. N., R. Madsen, W. M. Sullivan, A. Swidler, and S. M. Tipton. *The good society*. New York: Knopf, 1992.

Beninga, J. S., ed. *Moral, character, and civic education*. New York: Teachers College Press, 1991.

Benjamin, S. "An Ideascape for Education: What Futurists Recommend." *Educational Leadership* (1989, September): 8–14.

Bernard, B. *Youth service: From youth as problems to youth as resources*. Prevention Resource Center, Inc., 1989.

Blyth, D. and R. Saito. *1992–1993 National service-learning initiative*. Minneapolis: Search Institute, 1993.

Bobo, K., J. Kendall, and S. Max. *Organizing for social change: A handbook for activists in the 1990's*. Washington, DC: Seven Locks Press, 1991.

Bowles, S. and H. Gintis. *Schooling in capitalist America*. New York: Basic Books, 1972.

Boyer, E. *High school: A report on secondary education in America*. New York: Harper & Row, 1983.

Bricker, D. C. *Classroom life as civic education: Individual achievement and student cooperation in schools*. New York: Teachers College Press, 1989.

Brill, C. L. "The effects of participation in service-learning on adolescents with disabilities." *Journal of Adolescence* 17 (1994, August): 369–80.

Briscoe, J. "Citizenship, Service, and School Reform in Pennsylvania." *Phi Delta Kappan* 72 (1991): 758–60.

Brooks, J. G. and M. Brooks. *In search of understanding: The case for constructivist classrooms*. Alexandria, VA: Association for Supervision and Curriculum, 1993.

Bruce, S. "Service learning elective: Paoli Junior-Senior High School." *The Clearinghouse database*, New York: National Helpers Network, Inc., 1994.

Buchen, I. H. and C. I. Fertman. "Parents as partners in service-learning." Book IV in *Creating a culture of service: Effective service-learning*, Warminster, PA: Mar*co Products Inc., 1994.

Buckley, W. F., Jr. *Gratitude: Reflections on what we owe to our country*. New York: Random House, 1990.

Burtt, S. "The politics of virtue today: A critique and a proposal." *The American Political Science Review* 87 (1993, June): 360–68.

Button, C. "The development of experimental curriculum to effect the political socializations of anglo, black and Mexican-American adolescents" (Ph.D. dissertation, University of Texas, 1973).

Cairn, R. W. *Learning by giving: K–8 service-learning curriculum guide*. St. Paul, MN: National Youth Leadership Council, 1993.

Cairn, R. W. and J. Kielsmeier. *Growing hope: A sourcebook on integrating youth service into the school curriculum*. Roseville, MN: National Youth Leadership Council, 1991.

Carnegie Council on Adolescent Development. *Turning points: Preparing American youth for the twenty-first century*. Washington DC: author, 1989.

Caskey, F. "A Rationale for service-learning: Outcomes for students, school and community." Pp. 18–35 in *Growing hope: A sourcebook on integrating youth service into the school curriculum*, eds. R. W. Cairn and J. C. Kielsmeier. Roseville, MN: National Youth Leadership Council.

Cawelti, G. *High school restructuring: A national study*. Arlington, VA: Educational Research Service, 1994.

Center for Civic Education. *National standards for civics and government.* Calabasas, CA: Author, 1994.

Central Susquehanna Intermediate Unit Information Services. *News Notes.* 1995, Winter.

Chaskin, R. J. and D. M. Rauner. "Youth and caring: An introduction." *Phi Delta Kappan* 76 (1995): 667–74.

Chaskin, R. J., D. M. Rauner, and Guest Editors. "A Kappan Special Section on Youth and Caring." *Phi Delta Kappan* 76 (1995, May): 665–719.

Clark Atlanta University. *Policy on service-learning.* Atlanta, GA: School of Education, Clark Atlanta University, 1992.

Clark Atlanta University. *Culture of service: An overview.* Atlanta, GA: author, 1994.

Clark, T. "Youth Community Service." *Social Education* 53 (1989): 367.

Cohen, D., M. W. McLaughlin, and J. Talbert, eds. *Teaching for understanding.* San Francisco: Jossey-Bass, 1993.

Cohen, E. *Designing groupwork: Strategies for the heterogeneous classroom.* New York: Teacher's College, 1986.

Cohen, P. A., J. A. Kulik, and C-L. C. Kulik. "Educational outcomes of tutoring: A meta-analysis of findings." *American Educational Research Journal* (1982): 237–48.

Cohn, M. and R. Kottkamp. *Teachers: The missing voice in education.* Albany, NY: State University of New York Press, 1993.

Coles, R. "Community service work." *Liberal Education* 74 (1988): 11–13.

Conrad, D. "School-community participation for social studies." Pp. 540–48 in *Handbook of research on social studies teaching and learning,* ed. J. P. Shaver. New York: MacMillan, 1991.

Conrad, D. and D. Hedin. "Citizenship education through participation." In *Education for responsible citizenship: The report of the national task force on citizenship education.* New York: McGraw-Hill, 1977.

Conrad, D. "Are experiential learning programs effective?" *NASSP Bulletin* 62 (1978, November): 102–107.

Conrad, D. and D. Hedin. *National assessment of experiential education: A final report.* St. Paul, MN: University of Minnesota, Center for Youth Development and Research, 1981.

Conrad, D. and D. Hedin. *Youth service: A guidebook for developing and operating effective programs.* Washington, DC: Independent Sector, 1987.

Conrad, D. and D. Hedin. *High school community service: A review of research and programs.* Washington, DC: Office of Educational Research and Improvement, 1989. ERIC ED 313 569.

Conrad, D. and D. Hedin. "School-based community service: What we know from research and theory." *Phi Delta Kappan* 72 (1991): 754–57.

Constitutional Rights Foundation. *Active citizenship today handbook.* Los Angeles: Author, 1995.

Cook, A. "Teachers as team players: Or, how many heroes does it take to change a school?" *Education Week* XIV (1995, March 8): 30, 40.

Corbett, F. C. "The community involvement program: Social service as a factor in adolescent moral and psychological development." Ph.D. dissertation, University of Toronto, 1977.

Corporation for National Service. *National service resource guide: Strategies for building a diversified funding base.* Washington, DC: Author, 1985.

Council of Chief State School Officers. *Learning by doing.* Washington, DC: Author, 1989.

Council of Chief State School Officers. *Service-learning planning and resource guide.* Washington, DC: Author, 1993.

Croly, H. *The promise of American life.* Cambridge: Harvard University Press, Belknap Press, 1965/1909.

Cruz, N. "A challenge to the notion of service." Pp. 321–23 in *Combining service and learning: A resource book for community and public service. Volume 1.* Raleigh, NC: National Society for Experiential Education, 1990.

Dass, R. and M. Bush. *Compassion in action: Setting out on the path of service.* New York: Crown, 1992.

Dass, R. and P. Gorman. *How can I help?* New York: Alfred Knopf, 1985.

Dauber, S. L. and J. L. Epstein. "Parent attitudes and practices of involvement in inner-city elementary middle schools." Pp. 53–71 in *Families and schools in a pluralistic society,* ed. N. F. Chavkin. Albany: State University of New York Press, 1993.

Dewey, J. *Democracy and education.* New York: Free Press, 1916/1966.

Doob, H. S. *Research Brief: Summary of Research on Middle Schools.* Reston, VA: Educational Research Service, 1975.

Dreyfuss, S. "Student watershed research project—Saturday Academy, Oregon Graduate Institute." *The Clearinghouse database,* New York: National Helpers Network, Inc., 1993.

Dryfoos, J. G. *Adolescents at risk: Prevalence and prevention.* New York: Oxford University Press, 1990.

Dunlap, N. C., S. F. Drew, and K. Gibson. *Serving to learn: K–8 manual.* Columbia, SC: South Carolina Department of Education, 1994.

Dunn, J. Reviews of "Strong democracy," "A preface to economic democracy," and "Retrieving democracy: In search of Civic Equality." *Political Quarterly* 57 (1986, July/Sept): 329–33.

Education Commission of the States. *The next stage of reform.* Washington, DC: Author, 1985.

Eisenberg, N. and P. H. Mussen. *The roots of prosocial behavior.* Cambridge: Cambridge University Press, 1989.

Engle, S. H. and A. S. Ochoa. *Education for democratic citizenship: Decision making in the social studies.* New York and London: Teachers College Press, 1988.

Espinoza, R. "Working parents, employers, and schools." *Educational Horizons* 66 (1988, Winter): 62–65.

Feiman-Nemser, S. and R.E. Floden. "The cultures of teaching." Pp. 505–26 in *Handbook of research on teaching*, ed. M. C. Wittrock. New York: MacMillan, 1986.

Feldman, S. and G. Elliott. *At the threshold: The developing adolescent.* Cambridge: Harvard University Press, 1990.

Ferguson, P. "Impacts on social and political participation." Pp. 385–99 in *Handbook of research on social studies teaching and learning*, ed. J. P. Shaver. New York: Macmillan, 1991.

Fertman, C. I. *Service-learning for all students: Fastback 375.* Bloomington, IN: Phi Delta Kappa, 1994.

Fisher, R. and W. Ury. *Getting to yes: Negotiating agreements without giving in.* Boston: Houghton Mifflin, 1981.

Flanagan, J. *The grass roots fund-raising book: How to raise money in your community.* Chicago: Contemporary Books, Inc., 1982.

Fleisher, P. *Changing our world: A handbook for young activists.* Tucson, AZ: Zephyr Press, 1993.

Flinders, D. J. "Teacher isolation and the new reform." *Journal of Curriculum and Supervision* 4 (1988): 17–29.

Fowler, D. "Democracy's next generation." *Educational Leadership* (1990, November): 10–15.

Friere, P. *The pedagogy of the oppressed.* New York: Continuum Publishing Corp., 1970.

Friesem, J. "Intergenerational service learning unit: How can we help our elders?—Nespelem School." *The Clearinghouse database*, New York: National Helpers Network, Inc., 1994.

Fullan, M.G. *The new meaning of educational change*. New York: Teachers College Press, 1991.

Furco, A. "A conceptual framework for the institutionalization of youth service programs in primary and secondary education." *Journal of Adolescence* 17 (1994, August): 395–409.

Gardner, J. W. *Self-renewal: The individual and innovative society*. New York: Harper and Row, 1965.

George, N., S. Hunt, D. Nixon, R. Ortiz, and J. Anderson. *Beginning teachers' perceptions and use of community service-learning as a teacher method*. Paper presented at the National Serivce-Learning Conference, March 8–12, Philadelphia, PA, 1995.

Giles, D., E. P. Honnet, and S. Migliore. *Research agenda for combining service and learning in the 1990's*. Raleigh, NC: National Society for Experiential Education, 1991.

Giles Jr., D. E. and J. Eyler. "The impact of a college community service laboratory on students' personal, social, and cognitive outcomes." *Journal of Adolescence* 17 (1994, August): 327–40.

Goldstein, M. B. "Legal issues in combining service and learning." Pp. 39–60 in *Combining service and learning: A resource book for community and public service*, volume II, ed. J. C. Kendall and Associates. Raleigh, NC: National Society for Experiential Education, 1990.

Gorham, E. B. *National Service, citizenship, and political education*. Albany, N.Y.: State University of New York Press, 1992.

Gray, B. *Collaborating*. San Francisco: Jossey-Boss, 1989.

Green, P. "A few kind words for liberalism." *The Nation* 255 (1992, September): 309, 324–29.

Guest, K. and J. Anderson. *Reaching out at Seattle University: Infusing service into teacher preparation*. The Generator 13 (1993, Fall): 11–12.

Halsted, A. and J. Schine. "Service learning: The promise and the risk." *New England Journal of Public Policy* (1994, Summer/Fall): 251–57.

Hamilton, S. F. and L. M. Fenzel. "The impact of volunteer experience on adolescent social development: Evidence of program effects." *Journal of Adolescent Research* 3 (1988): 65–80.

Hamilton, S. F. and R. S. Zeldin. "Learning civics in the community." *Curriculum Inquiry* 17 (1987): 407–20.

Hanh, T. N. *The miracle of mindfulness*. Boston: Beacon Press, 1975.

Hechinger, F. M. *Fateful choices: Healthy youth for the twenty-first century.* New York: Oxford University Press, 1992.

Hedin, D. "Students as teachers: A tool for improving school climate." *Social Policy* 17 (1987): 42–47.

Henderson, A. T. *The evidence continues to grow: Parent involvement improves student achievement.* Columbia, MD: National Committee for Citizens in Education, 1989.

Hill, D. "Death of a dream: Service Learning 1994–2010." Unpublished paper, 1994.

Hillman, S. B., P. C. Wood, M. J. Becker, and D. T. Alter. "Young adolescent risk-taking behavior: Theory, research and implications for middle schools." *Research in middle level education: Selected studies* (1990): 39–50.

Himmelman, A. "Community-based collaboration: Working together for a change." *Northwest Report* (1990, Nov.): 26.

Hodgkinson, V. A. and M. S. Weitzman. *Giving and volunteering in the United States.* Washington, D.C.: Independent Sector, 1992a.

Hodgkinson, V. A. and M. S. Weitzman. *Volunteering and giving among American teenagers 12 to 17 years of age.* Washington, D.C.: Independent Sector, 1992b.

Hondagneu-Sotelo, P. and S. Raskoff. "Community service-learning: Promises and problems." *Teaching Sociology* 22 (1994): 248–54.

Honnet, E. and S. Paulsen, eds. *Wingspread special report: Principles of good practice for combining service and learning.* Racine, WI: The Johnson Foundation, 1989, May.

Illich, I. *Deschooling society.* New York: Harper & Row, 1972.

Jackson, J. "Service and a new world order." Pp. 225–32 in *Service-learning reader: Reflections and perspectives on service,* ed. G. Albert. Raleigh, NC: National Society for Experiential Education, 1984.

Jarolimek, J. and W. C. Parker. *Social studies in elementary education.* New York: Macmillan, 1993.

Johnson, D. and R. Johnson. *Learning together and alone: Cooperation, competition, and individualization.* Englewood Cliffs, NJ: Prentice Hall, 1975.

Johnson, S. M. "The primacy and potential of high school departments." P. 167 in *The contexts of teaching in secondary schools: Teachers' realities,* eds. M. McLaughlin, J. Talbert, and N. Bascia. New York: Teachers College Press, 1990a.

Johnson, S. M. *Teachers at work: Achieving success in our schools.* New York: Basic Books, 1990b.

Joseph, J. A. "Cultivating compassion." *Foundation News* 31 (1990): 28–31.

Joyce, B. and B. Showers. *Student achievement through staff development*. New York: Longman, 1988.

Joyce, B., M. Weil, and B. Showers. *Models of teaching*. Needham Heights, MA: Allyn and Bacon, 1992.

Kemmis, D. *Community and the politics of place*. Norman, OK: University of Oklahoma Press, 1990.

Kendall, J. C. and Associates. *Combining service and learning: A resource book for community and public service. Volumes I and II*. Raleigh, N.C.: National Society for Experiential Education, 1990.

Khan, P. V. "Service." *Keeping in touch No. 18*. Lebanon Springs, NY: The Sufi Order, 1985.

Kielsmeier, J. "Reflections: Doing, knowing, and being." *The Generator* 12 (1992): 5.

King, M. L., Jr. "On being a good neighbour." Pp. 197–202 in *Service-learning reader: Reflections and perspectives on service*, ed. G. Albert. Raleigh, NC: National Society for Experiential Education, 1994.

Kinsley, C., ed. *Community service learning sourcebook*. Springfield, MA: Springfield Public Schools, 1988, September.

Kinsley, C., ed. *Whole learning through service: A guide for integrating service into the curriculum K–8*. Springfield, MA: Community Service Learning Center, 1991.

Kinsley, C. W. *Developing an elementary service-learning curriculum: The unit method*. Springfield, M: Community Service Learning Center, 1989.

Kinsley, C. W. "Creating New Structures-Community Service Learning." *Community Education Journal* 18 (1990, Fall): 2–4.

Knapp, C. *Lasting lessons: A teachers' guide to reflecting on experience*. Charleston, WV: ERIC Clearinghouse on Rural Education and Small Schools, 1993.

Kolb, D. *Experiential learning: Experience as the source of learning and development*. Englewood Cliffs, NJ: Prentice-Hall, 1984.

Kriedler, W. J. *Creative conflict resolution: More than 200 activities for keeping peace in the classroom*. Glenview, IL: Scott, Foresman and Co., 1984.

Landrum, R. *National service: Roots and flowers*. Washington: Youth Service America, 1992.

Langseth, M. "Service-learning: Core elements." *The Generator* 10 (1990, Spring): 6.

Laplante, L. and C. W. Kinsley. *Things that work in community service-learning*. Springfield, MA: Community Service Learning Center, 1995.

Laplante, L. J. and C. W. Kinsley. *Service-learning as an integrated experience in K–5 education: An introduction to resources and information.* Springfield, MA: Community Service Learning Center, 1994.

Lappe, R. M. and P. M. DuBois. *The quickening of America: Rebuilding our nation, remaking our lives.* San Francisco: Jossey-Bass, 1994.

Lawson, H. "Toward healthy learners, schools, and communities." *Journal of Teacher Education* 45 (1994): 62–70.

Lawton, E. J. *A journey through time: A chronology of middle level education resources.* Columbus, OH: National Middle School Association and National Association of Secondary School Principals, 1989.

Leeds, J. "National service: The challenge. *National Society for Experiential Education Quarterly* 20 (1994, Fall): 16–17.

Lewis, B. *The kid's guide to social action.* Minneapolis: Free Spirit Publishing, 1991.

Lickona, T. "An integrated approach to character development in the elementary classroom." Pp. 67–83 in *Moral, character, and civic education*, ed. J. S. Beninga. New York: Teachers College Press, 1991.

Lortie, D.C. *Schoolteacher: A sociological study.* Chicago: University of Chicago Press, 1975.

Louis, K. S. and S. D. Kruse. *Professionalism and community: Perspectives on reforming urban schools.* Thousand Oaks, CA: Corwin Press, 1995.

Louis, K. S. and M. Miles. *Improving the urban high school: What works and why.* New York: Teacher's College Press, 1990.

Luchs, K .P. "Selected changes in urban high school students after participation in community-based learning and service activities." Ph.D. Dissertation, University of Maryland, 1981.

MacNichol, R. "Service learning: A challenge to do the right thing." *Equity and Excellence in Education* 26 (1993, September): 9–11.

Mansbridge, J. Review of the book "Strong democracy: Participatory politics for a new age." *American Political Science Review* 81 (1987, Dec.): 1341–42.

Maryland Student Service Alliance. *Maryland's best practices: An improvement guide for school-based service-learning.* Baltimore, MD: Maryland Department of Education, 1995.

Mattessich, P. W. and B. R. Monsey. *Collaboration: What makes it work. A review of research literature on factors influencing successful collaboration.* St. Paul, MN: Amherst H. Wilder Foundation, 1992.

McLaughlin, M., M. Irby, and J. Langman. *Urban sanctuaries.* San Francisco: Jossey-Bass, 1994.

McPherson, K. *Enriching learning through service*. Seattle: Project Service Leadership, 1989a.

McPherson, K. *Learning through service*. Seattle: Safeco Insurance Company, 1989b.

McPherson, K. *Service-learning concept paper*. (Unpublished paper), 1989c.

McPherson, K. "Outcomes of reflection." P. 77 in *Growing Hope*, eds. R. W. Cairn and J. C. Kielsmeier. St. Paul, MN: National Youth Leadership Council, 1991a.

McPherson, K. "Putting service-learning into action: Educational leadership for service-learning." Pp. 81–107 in *Growing hope: A sourcebook for integrating youth service into the school curriculum*, eds. R. W. Cairn and J. Kielsmeier. Roseville, MN: National Youth Leadership Council, 1991b.

Mellon Bank Corporation. *Discover total resources: A guide for nonprofits*. Pittsburgh: Author, 1985.

Merelman, R. "Democratic politics and the culture of American education." *American Political Science Review* 74 (1980): 319–32.

Minnesota Office on Volunteer Services. *The power and potential of youth in service to communities*. St. Paul, MN: Department of Administration, 1993.

Mitchell, J. J. *The nature of adolescence*. Calgary, Alberta: Detselig Enterprises, Ltd., 1986.

Nathan, J. and J. Kielsmeier. "The sleeping giant of school reform." *Phi Delta Kappan* 72 (1991): 739–42.

National Center for Education Statistics. *Youth indicators, 1993: Trends in the well-being of American youth*. Washington, DC: U.S. Department of Education, 1993.

National Education Goals Panel. *Data volume for the national education goals report*. Washington, DC, 1994.

National Helpers Network. *Critical components of a quality program*. New York: Author, 1995.

Neal, P. "Liberalism and the communitarian critique: A guide for the perplexed." *Canadian Journal of Political Science* 23 (1990, September): 419–39.

Neusner, J. "Righteousness, not charity: Judaism's view of philanthropy." *Liberal Education* 74 (1988): 16–18.

Newmann, F. M. and R. A. Rutter. "A profile of high school community service programs." *Educational Leadership* 43 (1986): 65–71.

Newmann, F. M. and R. A. Rutter. *The effects of high school community service programs on students' social development*. Madison, WI: Wisconsin Center for Education Research, University of Wisconsin, 1983.

Newmann, F. M., G Wehlage G., and S. Lamborn. "The significance and sources of student engagement." In *Student engagement and achievement in American secondary schools*, ed. F. Newmann. New York: Teachers College Press, 1992.

Nikol. R. G. "Community service as a teaching tool." *NJEA Review* (1993, March): 14–16.

Noddings, N. *The challenge to care in schools*. New York: Teachers College Press, 1992.

Oakeshott, M. "Learning and teaching." In *The concept of education*, ed. R. S. Peters. New York: Humanities Press, 1967.

Olasky, M. *The tragedy of American compassion*. Washington, D.C.: Regency Gateway, 1992.

Paris, C. L. *Teacher agency and curriculum making in classrooms*. New York: Teachers College Press, 1993.

Parsons, C. *Removing barriers: Service learning in rural areas*. Washington, DC: Council of Chief State School Officers, Resource Center on Educational Equity, 1993.

Parsons, C. *Serving to learn, learning to serve*. Corwin Press, 1995.

Patton, M. Q. *Qualitative evaluation methods*. Newbury Park, CA: Sage, 1989.

Pennekamp, M. "Toward school-linked and school-based human services for children and families." *Social Work in Education* 14 (1992): 125–30.

Peter D. Hart Research Associates. *Democracy's next generation*. Washington, DC: People For the American Way, 1989.

Phelan, P., A. Davidson, and H. Cao. "Speaking up: Students' perspectives on school." *Phi Delta Kappan* 73 (1992, May): 699.

Phelan, P., H. Yu, and A. Davidson. "Navigating the psychosocial pressures of adolescence: The voices and experiences of high school youth." *American Educational Research Journal* 31 (1994, Summer): 416–17.

Phillips, G. "Ideas for high impact educational techniques." P. 84 in *Growing hope*, eds. R. W. Cairn and J. C. Kielsmeier. St. Paul, MN: National Youth Leadership Council, 1991.

Points of Light Foundation. *Communities as places of learning*. Washington, D.C.: Author, 1995.

Poulsen, S. J. "Learning is the thing." In *National Conference on Service-Learning, School Reform, and Higher Education in Alexandria, VA*, 1994.

Pratte, R. *The civic imperative: Examining the need for civic education*. New York: Teachers College Press, 1988.

Prawat, R. S. "From individual differences to learning communities—our changing focus." *Education Leadership* 49 (1992, April): 9–13.

Purpel, D. *The moral and spiritual crisis in education.* Granby, MA: Bergin and Garvey, 1989.

Purpel, D. and H. Giroux. *The hidden curriculum and moral education.* Berkeley: McCutchan, 1987.

Putnam, R. "Bowling alone: America's declining social capital." *Journal of Democracy* 6 (1995, January): 65–78.

Resnick, L. B. and L. Klopfer, eds. *Toward a thinking curriculum: Current cognitive research.* Alexandria, VA: Association for supervision and curriculum development, 1989.

Rolzinski, C. A. *The adventure of adolescence: Middle school students and community service.* Washington, D.C.: Youth Service America, 1990.

Root, S. "Service-learning in teacher education: A third rationale." *Michigan Journal of Community Service-Learning* 1 (1994): 94–97.

Root, S., A. Moon, and T. Kromer. "Service-learning in teacher education: A constructivist model." Pp. 31–40 in *Integrating Service Learning into Teacher Education: Why and How?*, ed. B. Bomez. Washington, D.C.: Council of Chief State School Officers, 1995.

Rosenholtz, S. J. *Teacher's workplace: The social organization of schools.* New York: Teacher's College Press, 1991.

Ruenzel, D. "Looking for John Dewey." *Teacher Magazine* (1995, February): 36.

Rutter, R. A. and F. M. Newmann. "The potential of community service to enhance civic responsibility." *Social Education* (1989, October): 371–74.

Sager, W. G. "A study of changes in attitudes, values, and self-concepts of senior high youth while working as full-time volunteers with institutionalized mentally retarded people." Ph.D. dissertation, University of South Dakota, 1973.

Salz, A. and J. Trubowitz. "You can see the sky from here: The Queens College Big Buddy program." *Phi Delta Kappan* 73 (1992): 551–56.

Sandel, M. J. "The procedural republic and the unencumbered self." *Political Theory* 12 (1984): 81–96.

Sarason, S. B. *The predictable failure of educational reform.* San Francisco: Jossey-Bass, 1990.

Schervish, P. G., Hodgkinson, V. A., Gates, M., and Associates. *Care and community in modern society: Passing on the tradition of service to future generations.* San Francisco: Jossey-Bass, 1995.

Schine, J. *Young adolescents and community service*. Washington, DC: The Carnegie Council on Adolescent Development, 1989.

Seidman, A. and C. Tremper. *Legal issues for service-learning programs*. Washington, DC: Nonprofit Risk Management Center, 1994.

Seigel, S. *Community service learning as empowering pedagogy: Implications for middle school teachers*. Unpublished doctoral dissertation. University of Massachusetts at Amherst, 1995.

Sergiovanni, T. J. *Building community in schools*. San Francisco: Jossey-Bass, 1994.

Serow, R. C. "Volunteering and values: An analysis of students' participation in community service." *Journal of Research and Development in Education* 23 (1990): 198–203.

Serow, R. C. "Community service enhances undergraduate experience: North Carolina research results." *Experiential Education* 16 (1991a): 1, 12.

Serow, R. C. "Students and voluntarism: Looking into the motives of community service participants." *American Educational Research Journal* 28 (1991b): 543–56.

Service Learning 2000. *Learning through service: Ideas from the field*. Palo Alto, CA: Author, 1994.

Sharrad, J. *Meeting of community service-learning task force*. Springfield, MA: Springfield Public Schools, 1992.

Shields, K. *In the tiger's mouth: An empowerment guide for social action*. Philadelphia: New Society Publishers, 1994.

Shumer, R. "A report from the field: Teachers talk about service-learning." Paper presented at the Annual Meeting of the American Educational Research Association, April 15–20, 1994a, San Francisco, CA.

Shumer, R. "Community-based learning: Humanizing education." *Journal of Adolescence* 17 (1994b, August): 357–68.

Shumer, R. and T. H. Berkas. *Doing self-directed study for service-learning*. Minneapolis, MN: University of Minnesota Department of Vocational and Technical Education, 1992.

Sigmon, R. "Sit down. Be quiet. Pay attention." *National Society for Experiential Education Quarterly* 20 (1995, Spring): 31.

Silberman, C. *Crisis in the classroom*. New York: Random House, 1970.

Silcox, H. C. *A how to guide to reflection: Adding cognitive learning to community service programs*. Philadelphia: Brighton Press, 1993.

Sizer, T. *Horace's compromise*. Boston: Houghton Mifflin, 1984.

Slavin, R. *Cooperative learning: Student teams,* 2nd ed. Washington, DC: National Education Association, 1987.

Sleeter, C. and C. Grant. "An analysis of multi-cultural education in the United States." *Harvard Educational Review* 57 (1987): 421–44.

Smith, R. M. "'One united people': Second-class female citizenship and the American quest for community." *Yale Journal of Law and Humanities* 1 (1989): 229–93.

Sparks, D. "A paradigm shift in staff development." *The ERIC Review* 3 (1995, Winter): 2–4.

Sprinthall, N. A. and R. L Mosher, eds. *Value development as the aim of education.* Schenectady, NY: Character Research Press, 1978.

Stephens, L. S. *The complete guide to learning through community service. Grades K–9.* Boston: Allyn and Bacon, 1995.

Sullivan, R. "The role of service-learning in restructuring teacher education." In paper presented at the annual meeting of the Association of Teacher Educators, New Orleans, LA in 1991.

Sunstein, B. "The personal portfolio: Redefining literacy, rethinking assessment, reexamining evaluation." *The Writing Notebook* 9 (1992): 36–39.

Tellez, K. and P. S. Hlebowitsh. "Being there: Social service and teacher education at the University of Houston." *Innovative Higher Education* 18 (1993): 87–95.

Thomas, G.R. "Commitment and action: New directions in citizenship education research." *The History and Social Science Teacher* 19 (1984): 238–39.

Thoreau, H. D. *Walden and Civil Disobedience.* ed. N. H. Pearson. New York: Holt, Rinehart & Winston, 1948.

Tocqueville, A. de. *Democracy in America.* Vol. II. Translated by G. Lawrence, ed. J. P. Mayer. New York: Doubleday, Anchor Books, 1969/1945.

Toole, J. and P. Toole. "Reflection as a tool for turning service experiences into learning experiences." Pp. 99–114 in *Enriching the curriculum through service-learning,* ed. C. Kinsley and K. MacPherson. Alexandria, VA: Association for Supervision and Curriculum Development, 1995.

Toole, J., Toole, P., Gomez, B., and C. Allam. *Possible links between community service and teacher preparation.* Washington, D.C.: Council of Chief State School Officers, 1992.

United States Department of Education Office of Education Research and Improvement. *Digest of Education Statistics 1993.* Washington, DC: National Center for Education Statistics, 1993.

University of Pittsburgh. *Evaluation Report for Senior Semester Program 1974–75.* Morgantown, WV: Author, 1975.

Urie, R. *Student aides for handicapped college students: Final report and manual.* Laurinburg: St. Andrews Presbyterian College, 1971.

Urke, B. and M. Wenger. *Profiles in service: A handbook of service-learning program design models.* National Youth Leadership Council, 1993.

Usher, B. R. *Etiobicke community involvement program evaluation.* Ontario: Canada's Ministry of Education, 1977.

Viadero, D. "Changes in attitude." *Education Week* (1995, January 25): 28.

Wade, R. "The social participation project." *Democracy and Education* 6 (1991, Fall): 17–19.

Wade, R. "Social action: Expanding the role of citizenship in the social studies curriculum." *Inquiry in Social Studies: Curriculum Research, and Instruction* 29 (1993, Spring): 2–18.

Wade, R. C. "A Century of Service-Learning." *National Society for Experiential Education Quarterly* 20 (1994, Fall): 6–7, 26.

Wade, R. C. *Teachers of service-learning.* Paper presented at the National Service Learning Conference, Philadelphia, 1995a, March 4–8.

Wade, R. C. "Community service-learning in the University of Iowa's elementary teacher education program." Pp. 41–54 in *Integrating service-learning into teacher education: Why and how?*, ed. B. Gomez. Washington, DC: Council of Chief State School Officers, 1995b.

Wade, R. C. "Developing active citizens: Community service-learning in social studies teacher education." *The Social Studies* (1995c): 122–28.

Wade, R. C. *Contextual Influences on teachers' experiences with community service-learning.* Paper presented at the Annual Meeting of the American Educational Research Association, April 15–20, 1995d, San Francisco, CA.

Wade, R. C. and J. Anderson. Community service-learning: A strategy for preparing human service-oriented teachers. *Teacher Education Quarterly*, in press.

Wade, R. C. and D. W. Saxe. "A case for community service-learning in the social studies: Historical and empirical evidence." Paper presented at the National Council for the Social Studies Annual Conference in Chicago, 1995, November 9.

Wade, R. C. and D Yarbrough. "Portfolios: A tool for reflection in teacher education?" *Teaching and Teacher Education: An International Journal Of Research And Studies* 12 (1996): 63–79.

Walzer, M. "The communitarian critique of liberalism." *Political Theory* 18 (1990, February): 6–23.

Walzer, M. "Liberalism and the art of separation." *Political Theory* 12 (1984, August): 315–30.

Whelage, G., R. Rutter, G. Smith, N. Lasko, and R. Fernandez. *Reducing the risk: Schools as communities of support.* London: Falmer Press, 1989.

Wigginton, E. "Foxfire Grows Up." *Harvard Educational Review* 59 (1989): 24–31.

William T. Grant Foundation. *The forgotten half: Pathways to success for America's youth and young families.* Washington, DC: Author, 1988.

Williams, R. "The impact of field education on student development: Research findings." *Journal of Cooperative Education* 27 (1991): 29–45.

Willis, S. "Learning Through Service." *Association for Supervision and Curriculum Development Update* (1993, August): 1–8.

Willison, S. "When Students Volunteer to Feed the Hungry: Some Considerations for Educators." *Social Studies* 85 (1994, March–April): 88–90.

Wilson, T. C. *An alternative community based secondary school education program and student political development.* Ph.D. dissertation, University of Southern California, 1974).

Winer, M. and K. Ray. *Collaboration handbook: Creating, sustaining, and enjoying the journey.* St. Paul, MN: Amherst H. Wilder Foundation, 1994.

Winokur, V. *Service-learning program: A. McArthur Barr Middle School.* The Clearinghouse database, New York: National Helpers Network, 1995.

Wirthlin Group. *The prudential spirit of community youth survey: A survey of high school students on community involvement.* The Prudential Spirit of Community Initiative, 1995.

Witmer, J. T. and C. S. Anderson. *How to establish a high school service-learning program.* Alexandria, VA: Association for Supervision and Curriculum Development, 1994.

Wolfe, A. "Review of 'Strong democracy: Participatory politics for a new age.'" *Society* 23 (1986, January/February): 91–2.

Worthen, B. R. and J. R. Sanders. *Educational evaluation: Alternative approaches and practical guidelines.* New York and London: Longman, 1987.

About the Contributors

Carolyn S. Anderson is the Assistant Superintendent in the Niles Township High School District in Skokie, Illinois.

Richard Battistoni is the Director of the Feinstein Institute for Public Service at Providence College in Providence, Rhode Island.

Donna Boynton is a former elementary school teacher at Sky City Community School on the Acoma Pueblo Reservation in Grants, New Mexico.

Denise Clark Pope is a graduate student at Stanford University working with Service-Learning 2000 Center in Palo Alto, California.

Felicia George is Vice President of the National Helpers Network in New York City.

Don Hill is Director of Service-Learning 2000 Center at Stanford University Graduate School of Education in Palo Alto, California.

David Kelly-Hedrick is a Field Organizer for the West with the Youth Volunteers Corps of America in Seattle, Washington.

Carol Kinsley is the Executive Director of the Community Service-Learning Center in Springfield, Massachusetts.

Jean McMenimen is Program Assistant with the Iowa Service-Learning Partnership, Iowa City, Iowa.

Winifred Pardo is a former Community Service Director in the Shoreham-Wading River Middle School in Shoreham, New York.

Cynthia Parsons is SerVermont's Coordinator in Chester, Vermont.

Susan Seigel is an educational consultant in the field of Community Service-Learning. She is currently Program Director for the Middle School Community Service Learning Network in Springfield, Massachusetts.

John Shepard is Parent Teacher Organization President at St. Anthony Park Elementary School in St. Paul, Minnesota.

Tracy Thomas is a senior at Marion High School in Marion, Iowa.

James and Pamela Toole are Co-Directors of Compass Institute and lecturers in the College of Education and Youth Studies/Social Work at the University of Minnesota. Pamela is also Director of Professional Development for the National Youth Leadership Council in St. Paul, Minnesota.

Judith T. Witmer is a former central office administrator in the Lower Dauphin School District in Hummelstown, Pennsylvania.

Subject Index

A

Academic achievement, 22, 31, 80, 155, 241, 315

Administrators, 38, 183–84, 238–49, 255, 261; recommendations for, 247–49; role in service-learning, 168, 170, 176, 198, 199, 209–10; principal, 50, 143, 168, 174, 175, 209–10, 281–82, 284; superintendent, 50, 266

Adolescence, 162–66, 180–88, 217–19. *See also* middle schools and high schools

Advocacy, 301–4, projects and reflection, 101; service, 69

Assessment, 23, 156, 171, 222; alternative assessment, 295. *See also* evaluation

Animals, 45–46, 72–73, 143

B

Businesses, 52–53, 155, 208–9, 226

C

Careers, 82, 92

Caring, 8, 12, 15, 67–68, 156, 173, 210

Celebration, 22–23, 116–17 154–55; types of, 117–19

Challenges, 211, 301–13; for elementary programs, 156–57; for high school programs, 126, 194–95; for middle school programs, 112, 176–77

Citizenship, 4, 5, 14, 101–2, 135, 138, 145, 154–55, 229

Civic attitudes, 11, 12, 14, 136–37

Civic education, 3, 4–6, 7, 11–15, 140–41, 188–89

Collaboration, 21, 59–62, 207–8, 302, 316; characteristics of successful, 53, 58–59; definition of, 47–48; ownership of, 58; rationale for, 48; stages of, 54–56

Collaborators in service-learning programs, 49–51, 170, 262–63; scheduling with, 40; teachers as, 28

Common good, 10, 11, 306

Communication, 58–59, 135, 256–57

Community, 132, 133, 144, 229–30

Community agencies, 29, 39, 47–62, 51–54, 109, 175–76, 208–9, 251–52, 273–80; clients of, 52; issues for, 277–78; recommendations for, 279–80

Community service, 186–87, 202–3, 217, 239, 259; history of, 23–25

Name Index

Printed in the United States
771700002B